ghSchool

Host Club

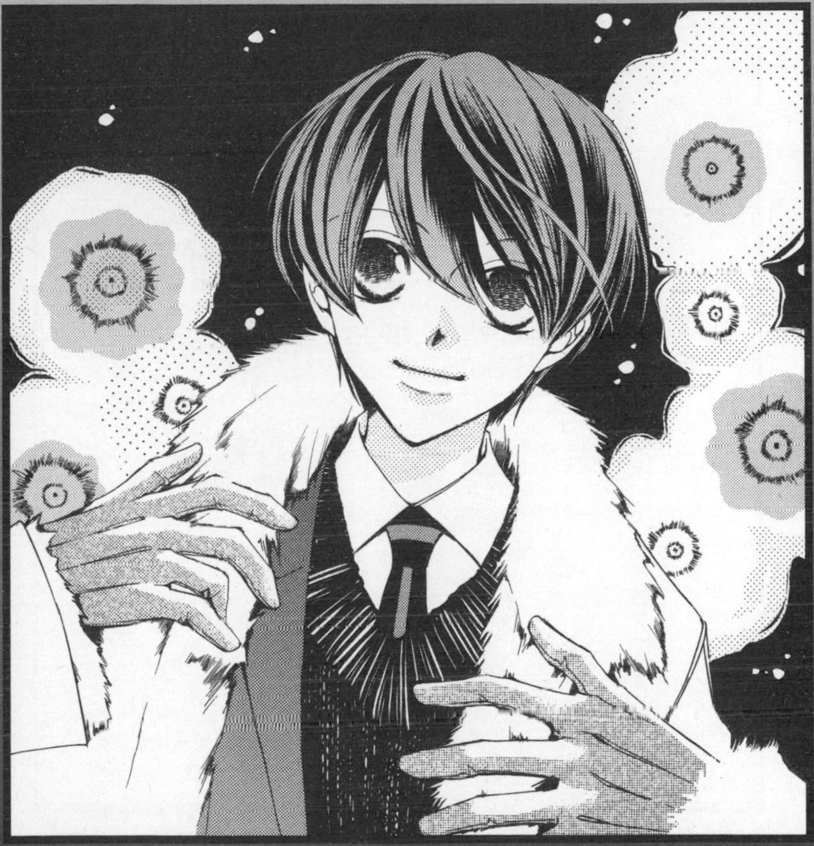

Vol. 5

Bisco Hatori

Ouran High School

Host Club

Vol. 5

CONTENTS

Ouran High School Host Club........3
Extra Episode: Mori's Secret...165
Egoistic Club........173
Editor's Notes.....175

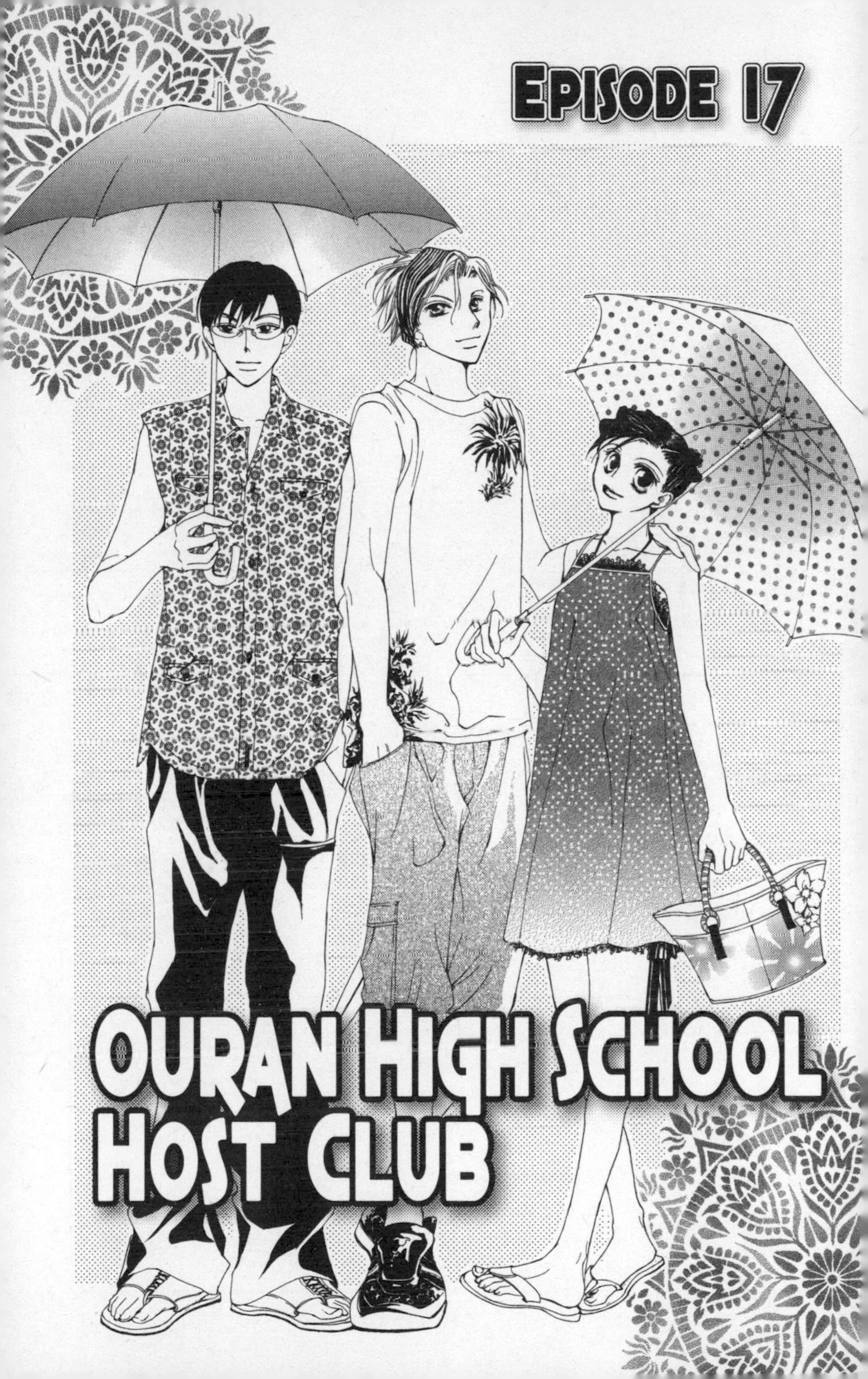
Episode 17
Ouran High School Host Club

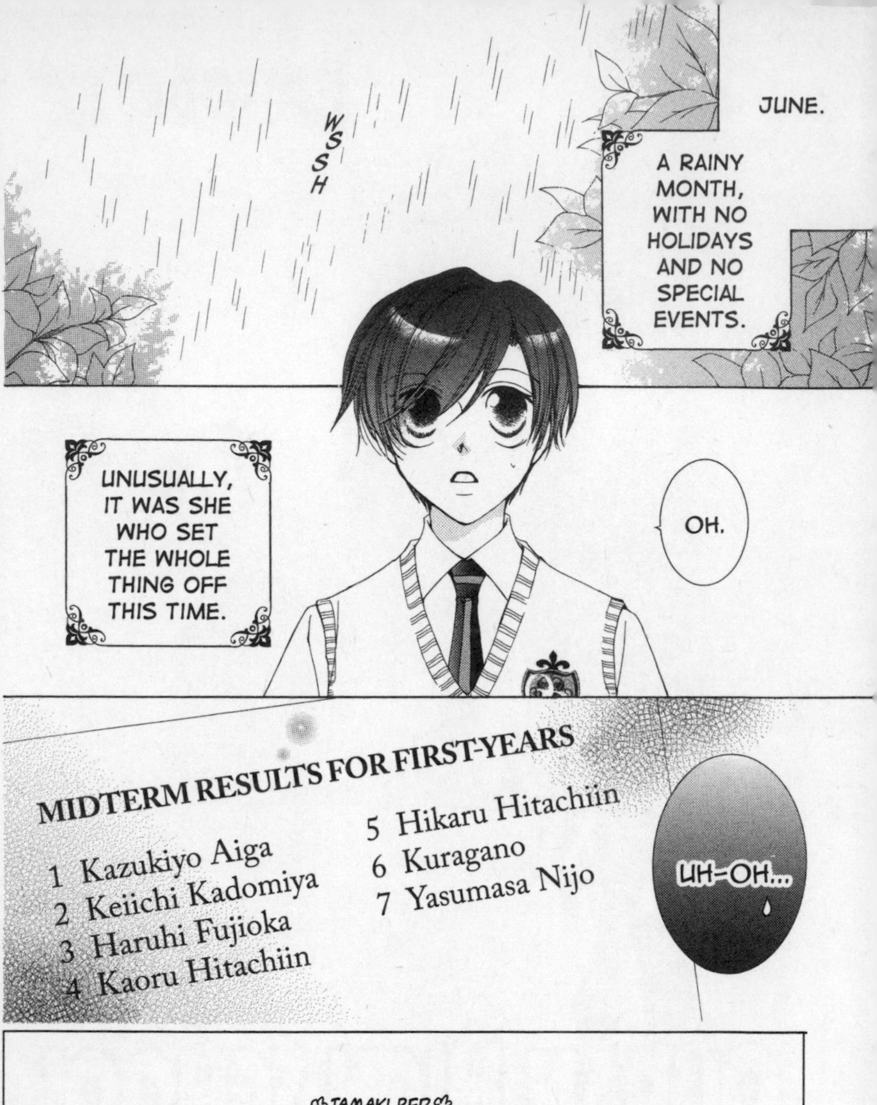
JUNE.
A RAINY MONTH, WITH NO HOLIDAYS AND NO SPECIAL EVENTS.
WSSH
OH.
UNUSUALLY, IT WAS SHE WHO SET THE WHOLE THING OFF THIS TIME.
UH-OH...
MIDTERM RESULTS FOR FIRST-YEARS
1 Kazukiyo Aiga
2 Keiichi Kadomiya
3 Haruhi Fujioka
4 Kaoru Hitachiin
5 Hikaru Hitachiin
6 Kuragano
7 Yasumasa Nijo

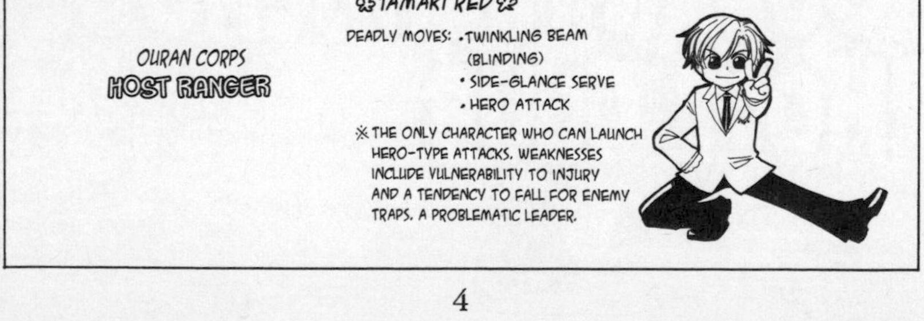
OURAN CORPS
HOST RANGER
TAMAKI RED
DEADLY MOVES: •TWINKLING BEAM (BLINDING)
• SIDE-GLANCE SERVE
• HERO ATTACK
※ THE ONLY CHARACTER WHO CAN LAUNCH HERO-TYPE ATTACKS. WEAKNESSES INCLUDE VULNERABILITY TO INJURY AND A TENDENCY TO FALL FOR ENEMY TRAPS. A PROBLEMATIC LEADER.

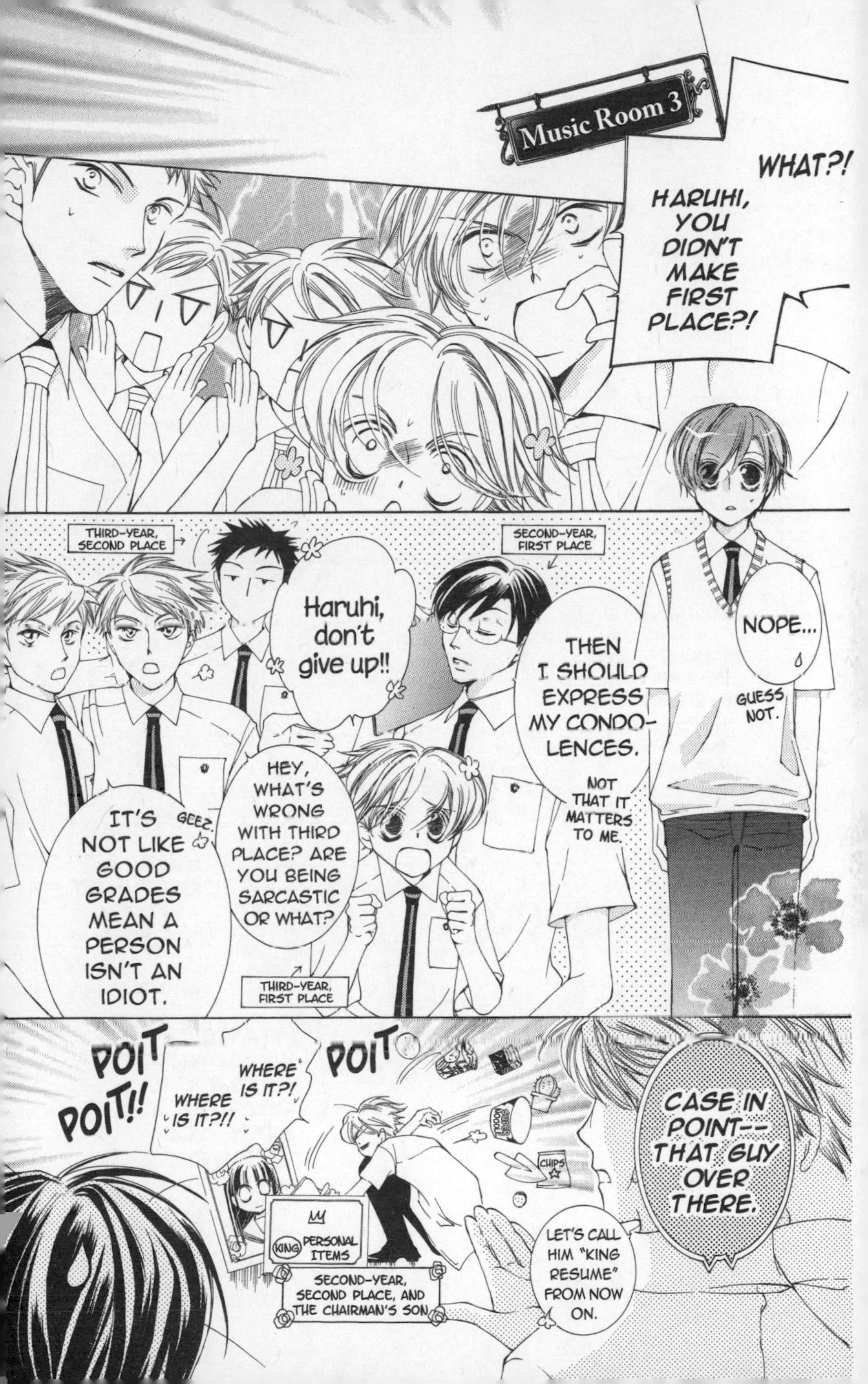
Music Room 3
WHAT?!
HARUHI, YOU DIDN'T MAKE FIRST PLACE?!
NOPE...
GUESS NOT.
SECOND-YEAR, FIRST PLACE
THEN I SHOULD EXPRESS MY CONDOLENCES.
NOT THAT IT MATTERS TO ME.
THIRD-YEAR, FIRST PLACE
HEY, WHAT'S WRONG WITH THIRD PLACE? ARE YOU BEING SARCASTIC OR WHAT?
Haruhi, don't give up!!
THIRD-YEAR, SECOND PLACE
GEEZ.
IT'S NOT LIKE GOOD GRADES MEAN A PERSON ISN'T AN IDIOT.
CASE IN POINT--THAT GUY OVER THERE.
LET'S CALL HIM "KING RESUME" FROM NOW ON.
CHIPS
KING PERSONAL ITEMS
SECOND-YEAR, SECOND PLACE, AND THE CHAIRMAN'S SON
POIT
WHERE IS IT?!
WHERE IS IT?!!
POIT POIT!!

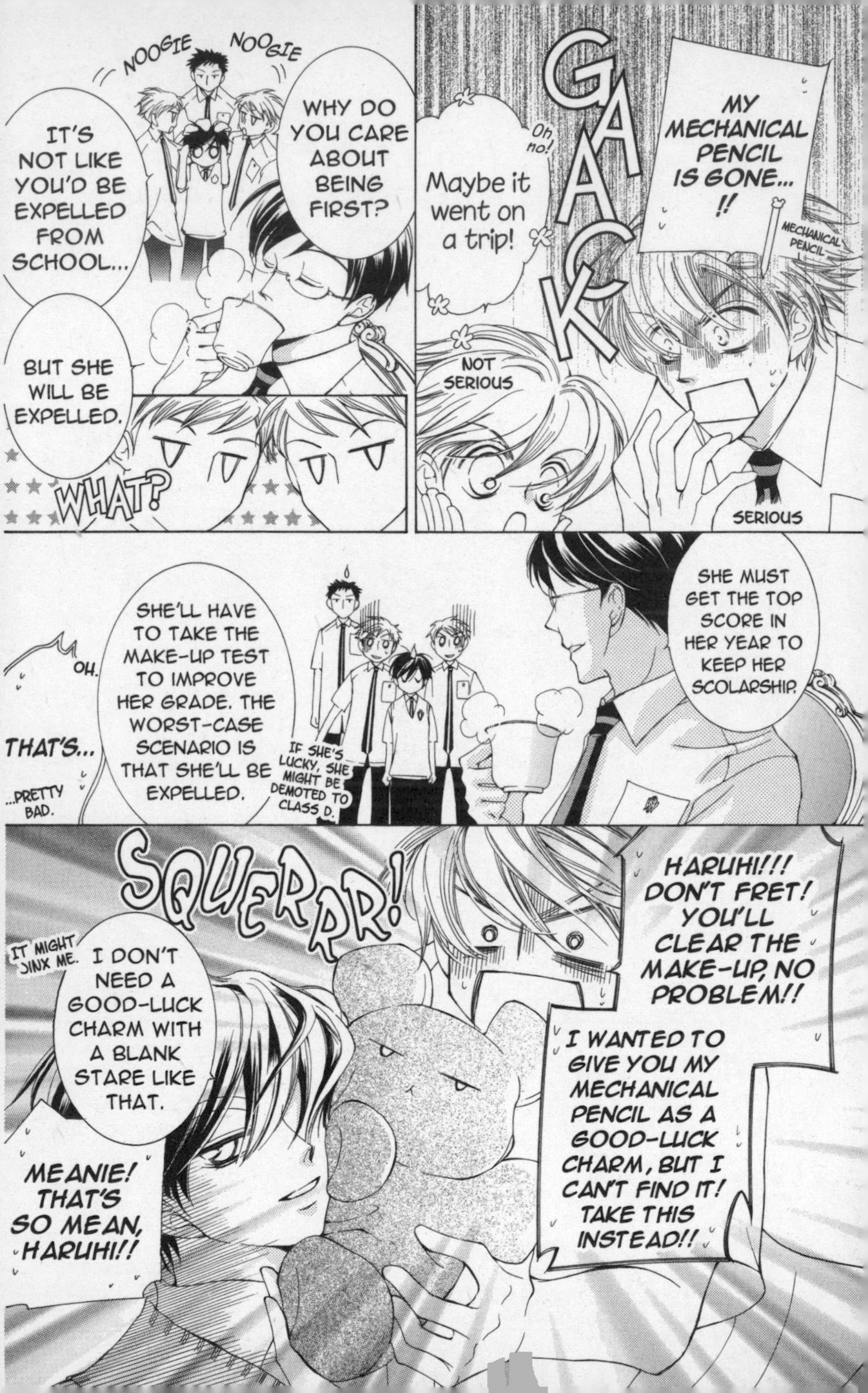
GACK
MY MECHANICAL PENCIL IS GONE... !!
MECHANICAL PENCIL
Oh no!
Maybe it went on a trip!
NOT SERIOUS
SERIOUS
NOOGIE NOOGIE
WHY DO YOU CARE ABOUT BEING FIRST?
IT'S NOT LIKE YOU'D BE EXPELLED FROM SCHOOL...
BUT SHE WILL BE EXPELLED.
WHAT?
SHE MUST GET THE TOP SCORE IN HER YEAR TO KEEP HER SCOLARSHIP.
IF SHE'S LUCKY, SHE MIGHT BE DEMOTED TO CLASS D.
SHE'LL HAVE TO TAKE THE MAKE-UP TEST TO IMPROVE HER GRADE. THE WORST-CASE SCENARIO IS THAT SHE'LL BE EXPELLED.
OH.
THAT'S...
...PRETTY BAD.
HARUHI!!! DON'T FRET! YOU'LL CLEAR THE MAKE-UP, NO PROBLEM!!
I WANTED TO GIVE YOU MY MECHANICAL PENCIL AS A GOOD-LUCK CHARM, BUT I CAN'T FIND IT! TAKE THIS INSTEAD!!
SQUERRR!
IT MIGHT JINX ME.
I DON'T NEED A GOOD-LUCK CHARM WITH A BLANK STARE LIKE THAT.
MEANIE! THAT'S SO MEAN, HARUHI!!

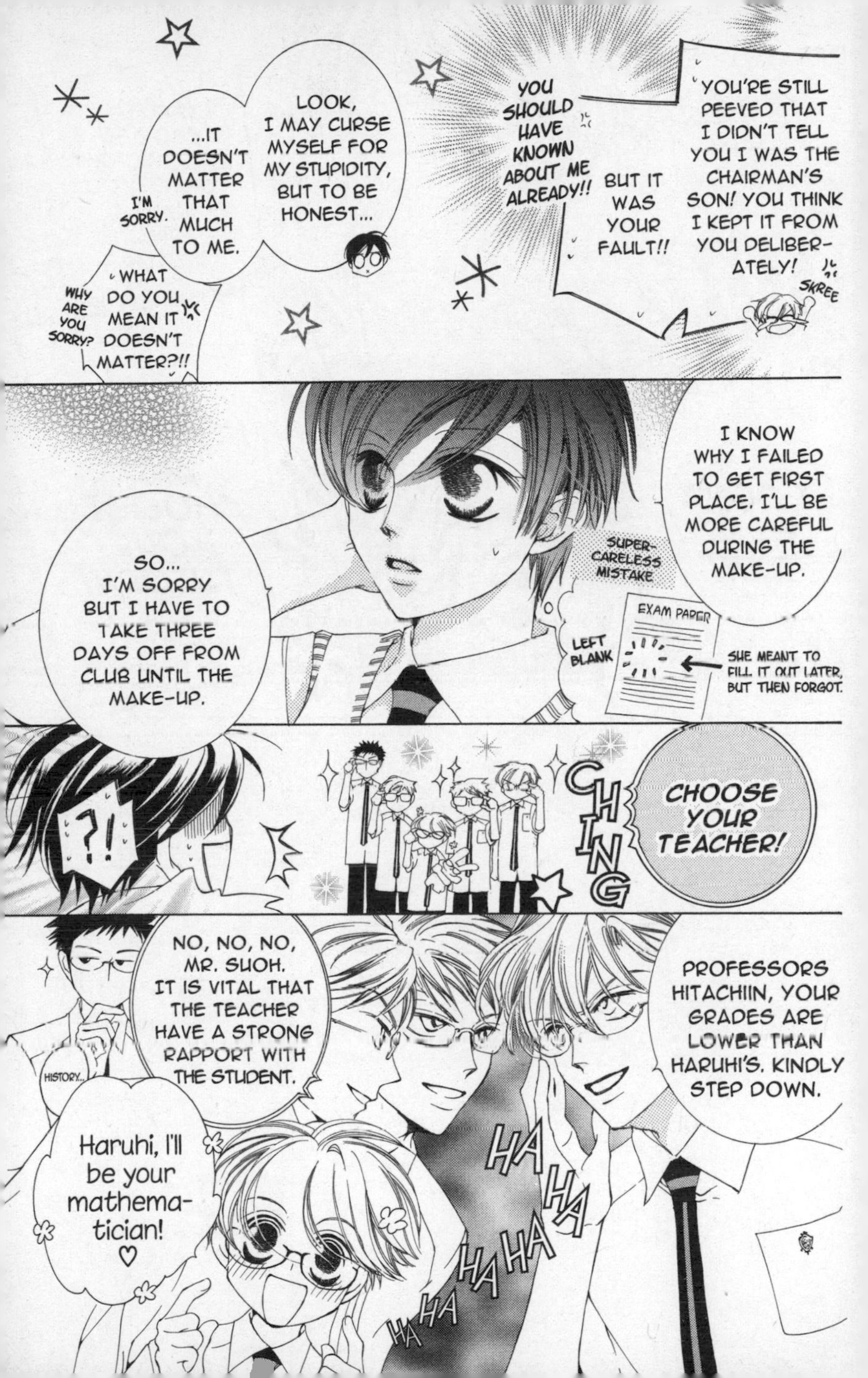
YOU'RE STILL PEEVED THAT I DIDN'T TELL YOU I WAS THE CHAIRMAN'S SON! YOU THINK I KEPT IT FROM YOU DELIBERATELY!
SKREE
BUT IT WAS YOUR FAULT!!
YOU SHOULD HAVE KNOWN ABOUT ME ALREADY!!
LOOK, I MAY CURSE MYSELF FOR MY STUPIDITY, BUT TO BE HONEST...
...IT DOESN'T MATTER THAT MUCH TO ME.
I'M SORRY.
WHAT DO YOU MEAN IT DOESN'T MATTER?!!
WHY ARE YOU SORRY?
I KNOW WHY I FAILED TO GET FIRST PLACE. I'LL BE MORE CAREFUL DURING THE MAKE-UP.
SUPER-CARELESS MISTAKE
EXAM PAPER
LEFT BLANK
SHE MEANT TO FILL IT OUT LATER, BUT THEN FORGOT.
SO... I'M SORRY BUT I HAVE TO TAKE THREE DAYS OFF FROM CLUB UNTIL THE MAKE-UP.
CHOOSE YOUR TEACHER!
CHING
?!
PROFESSORS HITACHIIN, YOUR GRADES ARE LOWER THAN HARUHI'S. KINDLY STEP DOWN.
HAHA HAHA HAHAHAHAHAHA
NO, NO, NO, MR. SUOH. IT IS VITAL THAT THE TEACHER HAVE A STRONG RAPPORT WITH THE STUDENT.
HISTORY...
Haruhi, I'll be your mathematician! ♡

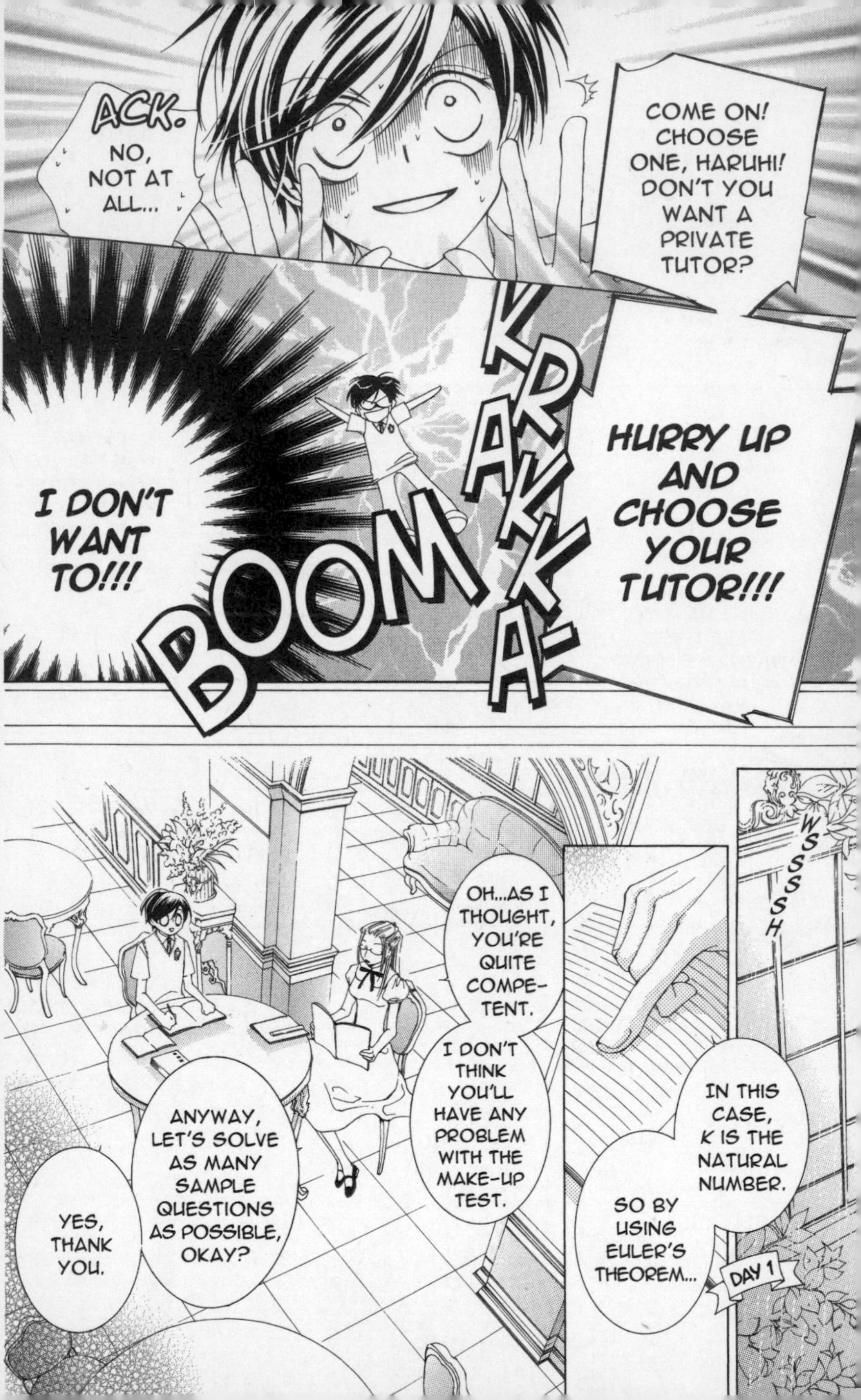
COME ON! CHOOSE ONE, HARUHI! DON'T YOU WANT A PRIVATE TUTOR?
ACK.
NO, NOT AT ALL...
HURRY UP AND CHOOSE YOUR TUTOR!!!
KRAKKA-
BOOM
I DON'T WANT TO!!!
DAY 1
WSSSSH
IN THIS CASE, K IS THE NATURAL NUMBER.
SO BY USING EULER'S THEOREM...
OH...AS I THOUGHT, YOU'RE QUITE COMPETENT.
I DON'T THINK YOU'LL HAVE ANY PROBLEM WITH THE MAKE-UP TEST.
ANYWAY, LET'S SOLVE AS MANY SAMPLE QUESTIONS AS POSSIBLE, OKAY?
YES, THANK YOU.

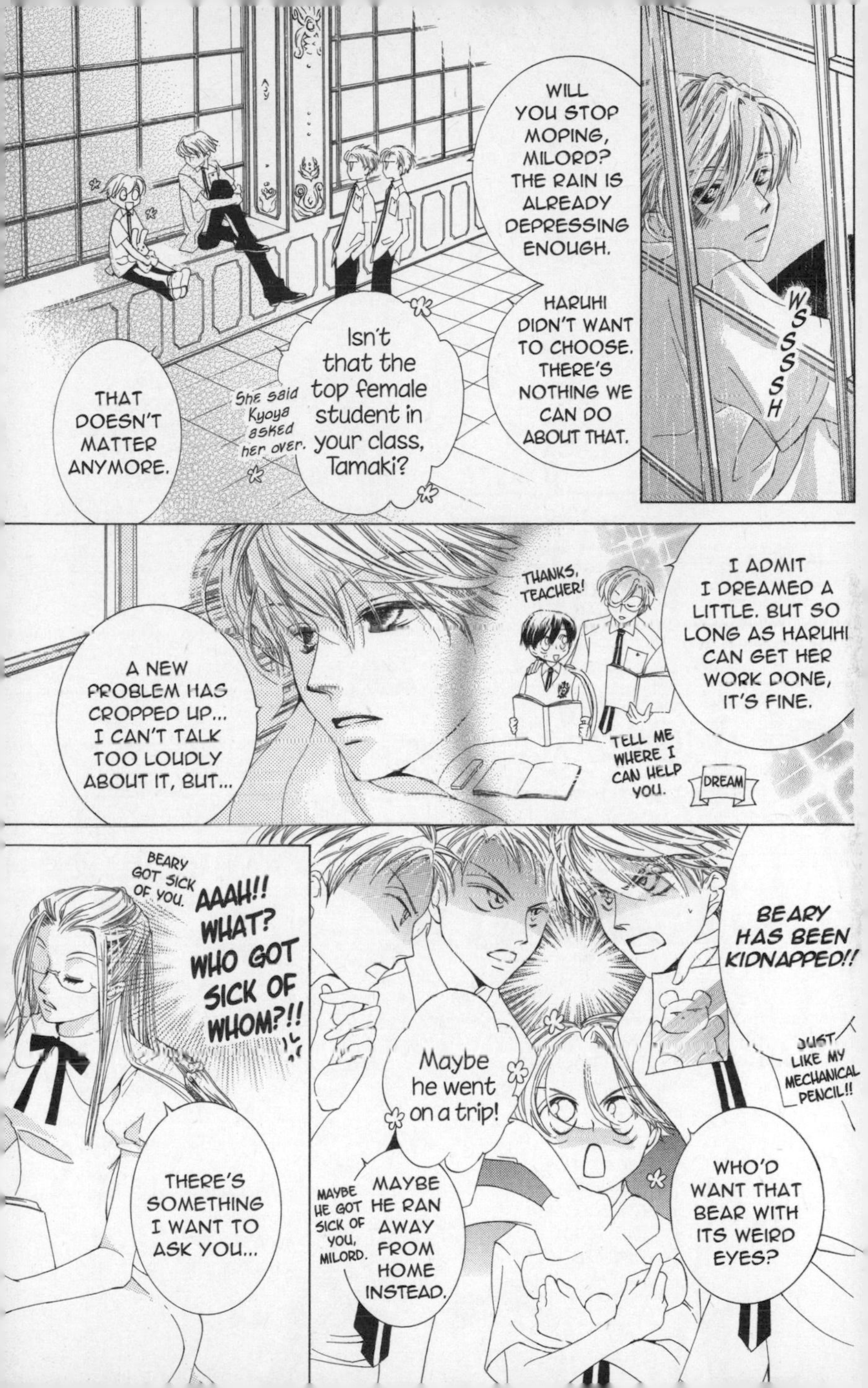
WSSSSH
WILL YOU STOP MOPING, MILORD? THE RAIN IS ALREADY DEPRESSING ENOUGH.
HARUHI DIDN'T WANT TO CHOOSE. THERE'S NOTHING WE CAN DO ABOUT THAT.
Isn't that the top female student in your class, Tamaki?
She said Kyoya asked her over.
THAT DOESN'T MATTER ANYMORE.
I ADMIT I DREAMED A LITTLE. BUT SO LONG AS HARUHI CAN GET HER WORK DONE, IT'S FINE.
THANKS, TEACHER!
TELL ME WHERE I CAN HELP YOU.
DREAM
A NEW PROBLEM HAS CROPPED UP... I CAN'T TALK TOO LOUDLY ABOUT IT, BUT...
BEARY HAS BEEN KIDNAPPED!!
JUST LIKE MY MECHANICAL PENCIL!!
WHO'D WANT THAT BEAR WITH ITS WEIRD EYES?
Maybe he went on a trip!
MAYBE HE RAN AWAY FROM HOME INSTEAD.
MAYBE HE GOT SICK OF YOU, MILORD.
BEARY GOT SICK OF YOU.
AAAH!! WHAT? WHO GOT SICK OF WHOM?!!
THERE'S SOMETHING I WANT TO ASK YOU...

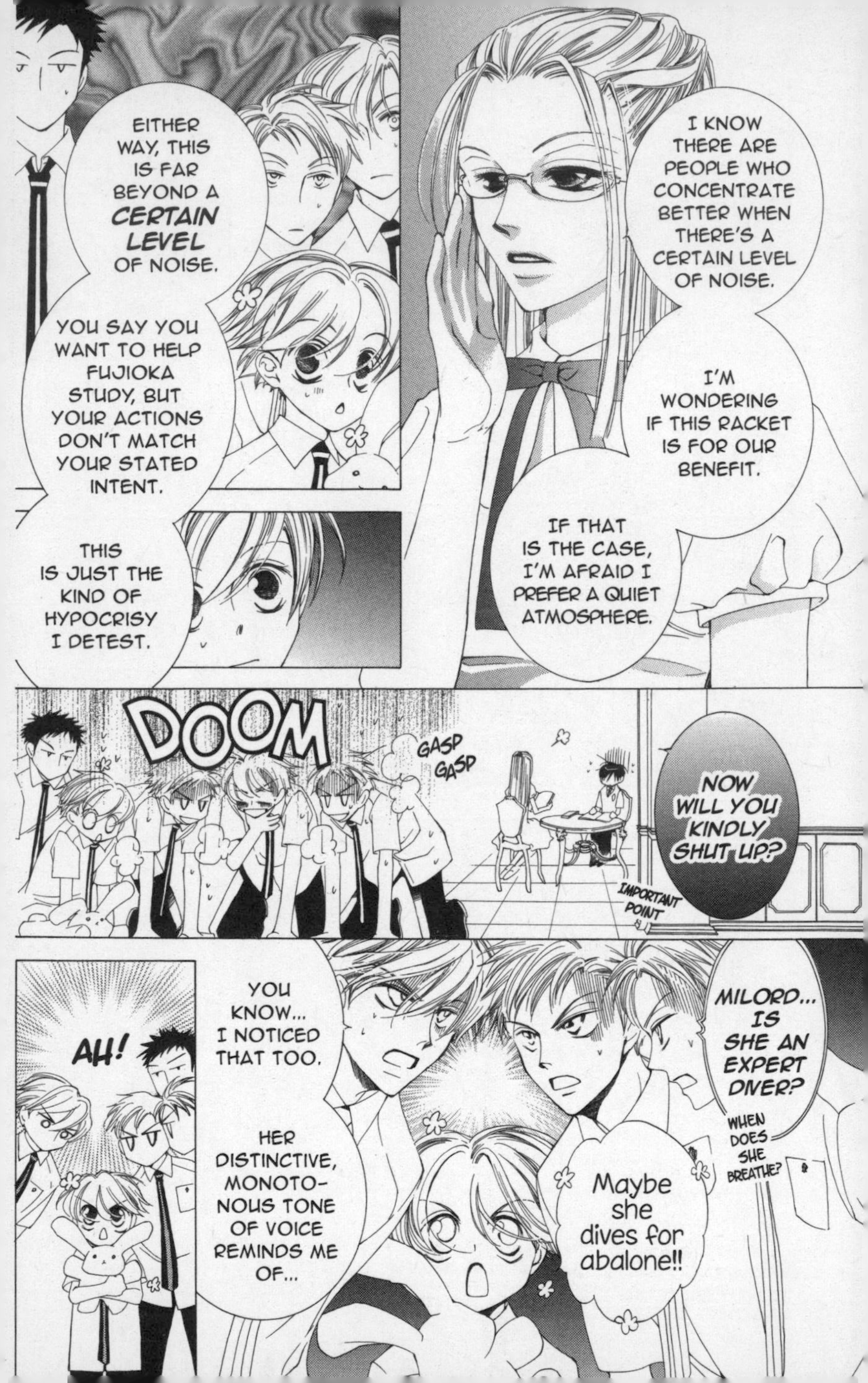
I KNOW THERE ARE PEOPLE WHO CONCENTRATE BETTER WHEN THERE'S A CERTAIN LEVEL OF NOISE.
I'M WONDERING IF THIS RACKET IS FOR OUR BENEFIT.
IF THAT IS THE CASE, I'M AFRAID I PREFER A QUIET ATMOSPHERE.
EITHER WAY, THIS IS FAR BEYOND A CERTAIN LEVEL OF NOISE.
YOU SAY YOU WANT TO HELP FUJIOKA STUDY, BUT YOUR ACTIONS DON'T MATCH YOUR STATED INTENT.
THIS IS JUST THE KIND OF HYPOCRISY I DETEST.
NOW WILL YOU KINDLY SHUT UP?
IMPORTANT POINT
GASP GASP
DOOM
MILORD... IS SHE AN EXPERT DIVER?
WHEN DOES SHE BREATHE?
YOU KNOW... I NOTICED THAT TOO.
HER DISTINCTIVE, MONOTONOUS TONE OF VOICE REMINDS ME OF...
Maybe she dives for abalone!!
AH!

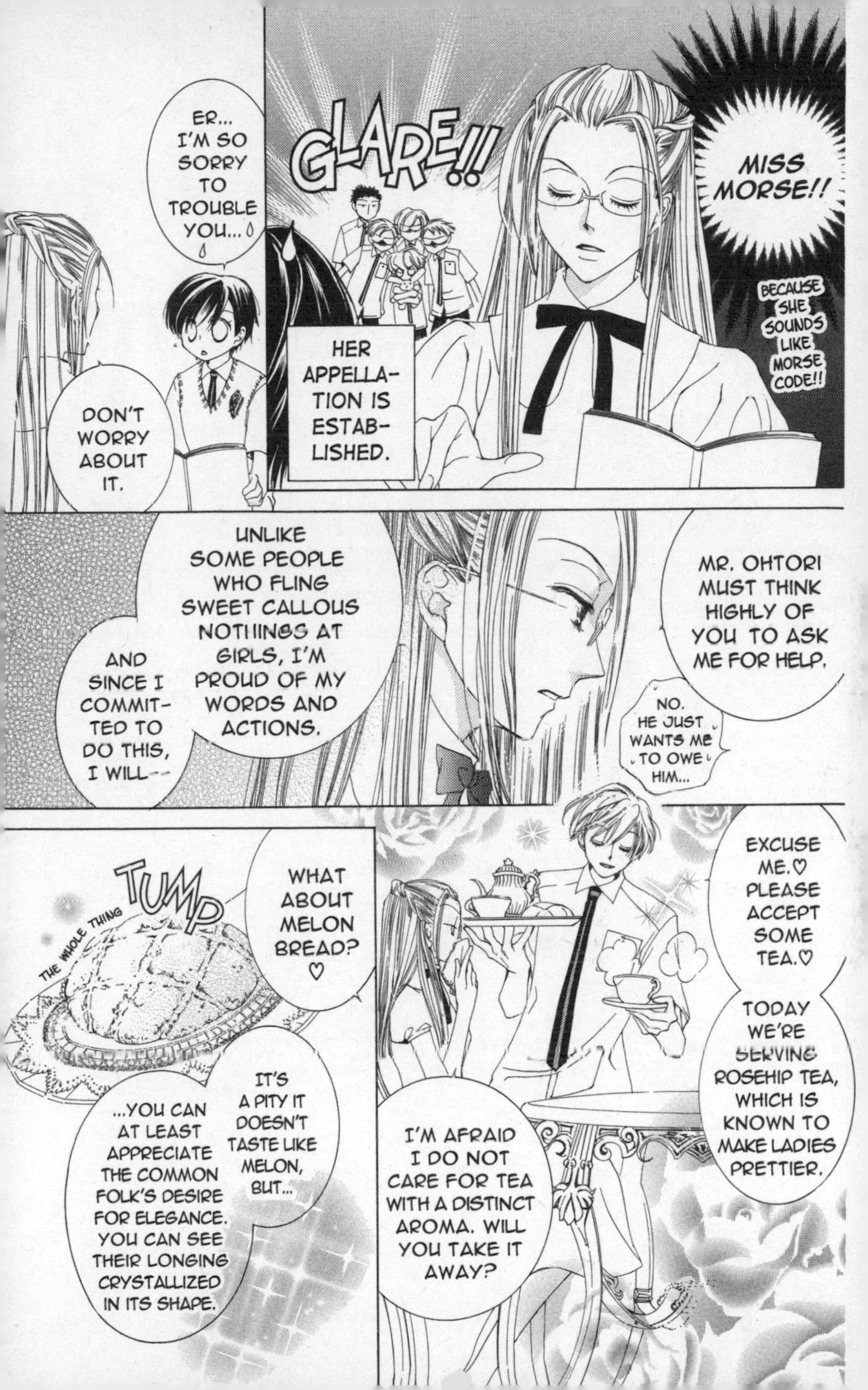

MISS MORSE!!
GLARE!!
BECAUSE SHE SOUNDS LIKE MORSE CODE!!
HER APPELLATION IS ESTABLISHED.
ER... I'M SO SORRY TO TROUBLE YOU...
DON'T WORRY ABOUT IT.
MR. OHTORI MUST THINK HIGHLY OF YOU TO ASK ME FOR HELP.
NO. HE JUST WANTS ME TO OWE HIM...
UNLIKE SOME PEOPLE WHO FLING SWEET CALLOUS NOTHINGS AT GIRLS, I'M PROUD OF MY WORDS AND ACTIONS.
AND SINCE I COMMITTED TO DO THIS, I WILL--
EXCUSE ME.♡ PLEASE ACCEPT SOME TEA.♡
TODAY WE'RE SERVING ROSEHIP TEA, WHICH IS KNOWN TO MAKE LADIES PRETTIER.
I'M AFRAID I DO NOT CARE FOR TEA WITH A DISTINCT AROMA. WILL YOU TAKE IT AWAY?
WHAT ABOUT MELON BREAD? ♡
TUMP
THE WHOLE THING
IT'S A PITY IT DOESN'T TASTE LIKE MELON, BUT...
...YOU CAN AT LEAST APPRECIATE THE COMMON FOLK'S DESIRE FOR ELEGANCE. YOU CAN SEE THEIR LONGING CRYSTALLIZED IN ITS SHAPE.

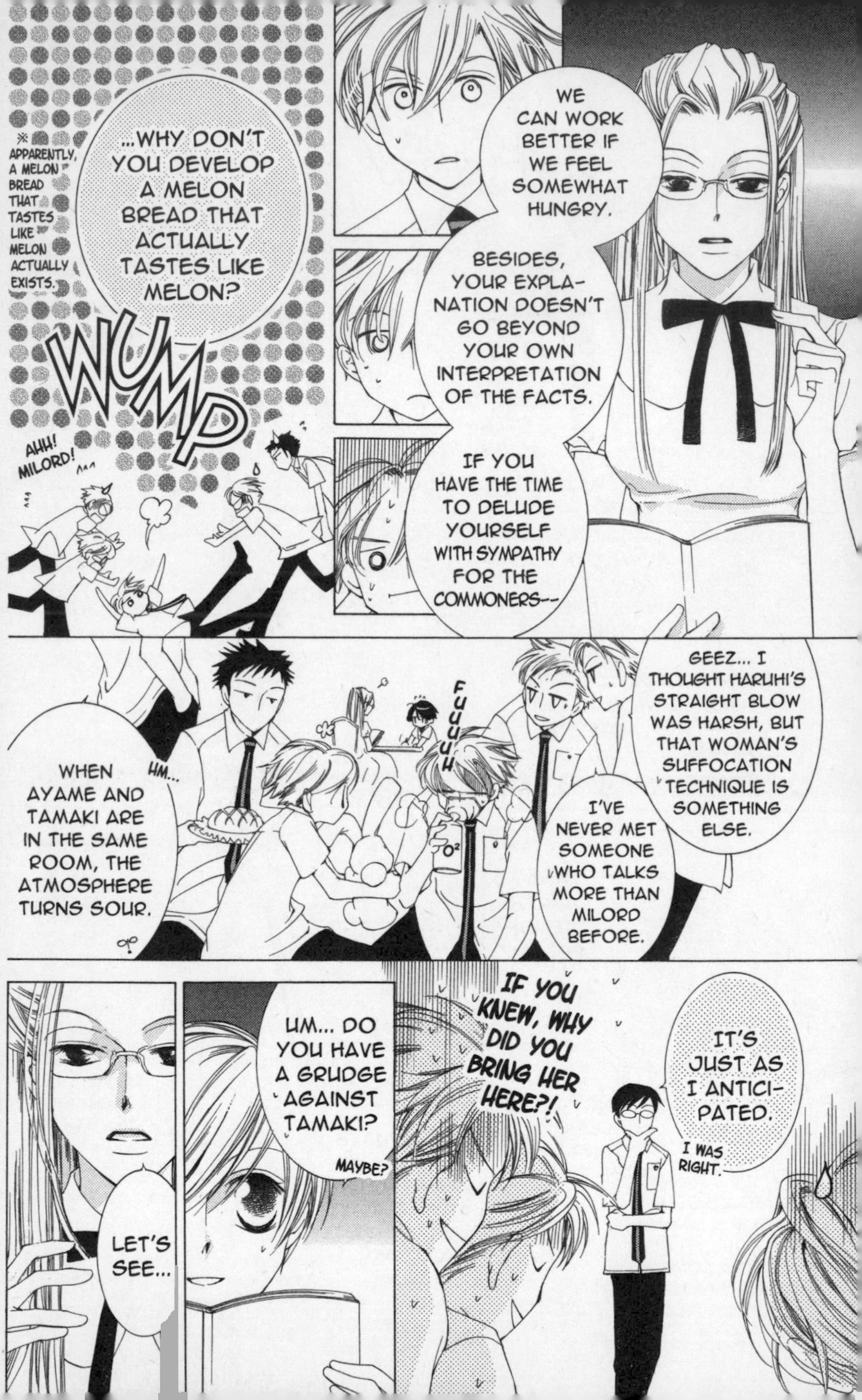

WE CAN WORK BETTER IF WE FEEL SOMEWHAT HUNGRY.
BESIDES, YOUR EXPLANATION DOESN'T GO BEYOND YOUR OWN INTERPRETATION OF THE FACTS.
IF YOU HAVE THE TIME TO DELUDE YOURSELF WITH SYMPATHY FOR THE COMMONERS--
...WHY DON'T YOU DEVELOP A MELON BREAD THAT ACTUALLY TASTES LIKE MELON?
※ APPARENTLY, A MELON BREAD THAT TASTES LIKE MELON ACTUALLY EXISTS.
WUMP
AHH! MILORD!
GEEZ... I THOUGHT HARUHI'S STRAIGHT BLOW WAS HARSH, BUT THAT WOMAN'S SUFFOCATION TECHNIQUE IS SOMETHING ELSE.
I'VE NEVER MET SOMEONE WHO TALKS MORE THAN MILORD BEFORE.
FUUUUH
O²
HM...
WHEN AYAME AND TAMAKI ARE IN THE SAME ROOM, THE ATMOSPHERE TURNS SOUR.
IT'S JUST AS I ANTICIPATED.
I WAS RIGHT.
IF YOU KNEW, WHY DID YOU BRING HER HERE?!
UM... DO YOU HAVE A GRUDGE AGAINST TAMAKI?
MAYBE?
LET'S SEE...

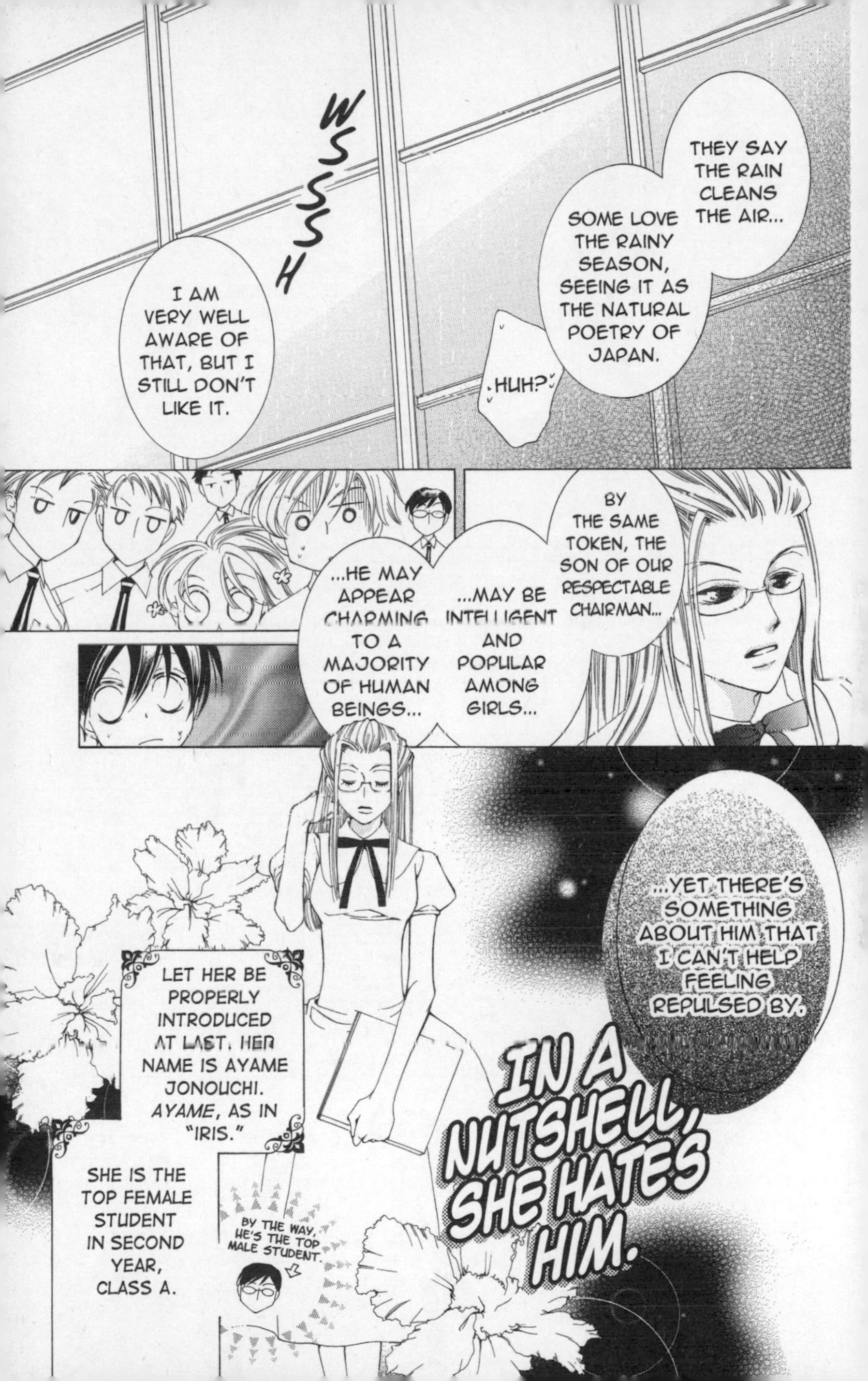
THEY SAY THE RAIN CLEANS THE AIR...
SOME LOVE THE RAINY SEASON, SEEING IT AS THE NATURAL POETRY OF JAPAN.
HUH?
WSSSH
I AM VERY WELL AWARE OF THAT, BUT I STILL DON'T LIKE IT.
BY THE SAME TOKEN, THE SON OF OUR RESPECTABLE CHAIRMAN...
...MAY BE INTELLIGENT AND POPULAR AMONG GIRLS...
...HE MAY APPEAR CHARMING TO A MAJORITY OF HUMAN BEINGS...
...YET THERE'S SOMETHING ABOUT HIM THAT I CAN'T HELP FEELING REPULSED BY.
IN A NUTSHELL, SHE HATES HIM.
LET HER BE PROPERLY INTRODUCED AT LAST. HER NAME IS AYAME JONOUCHI. *AYAME*, AS IN "IRIS."
SHE IS THE TOP FEMALE STUDENT IN SECOND YEAR, CLASS A.
BY THE WAY, HE'S THE TOP MALE STUDENT.

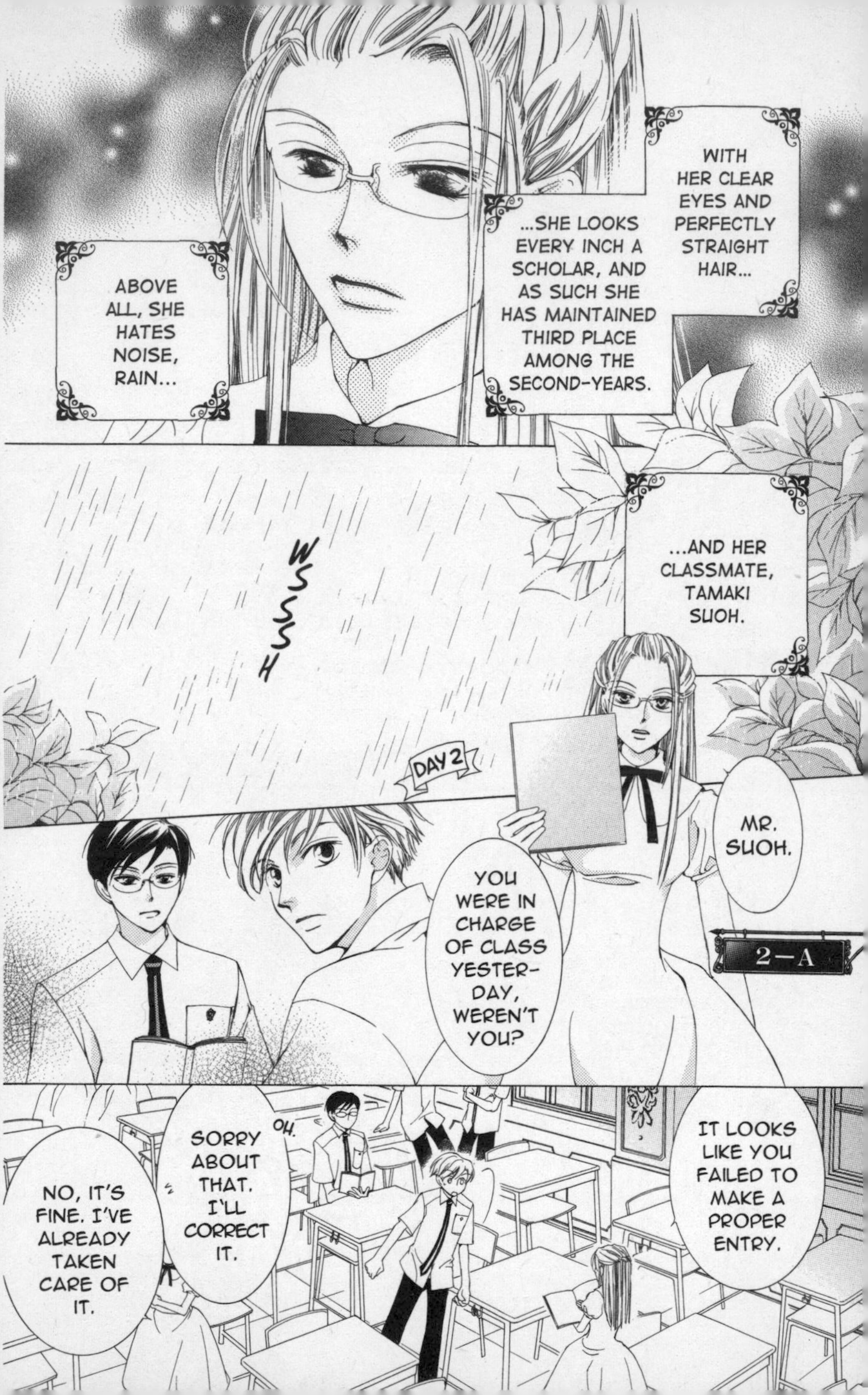
WITH HER CLEAR EYES AND PERFECTLY STRAIGHT HAIR...
...SHE LOOKS EVERY INCH A SCHOLAR, AND AS SUCH SHE HAS MAINTAINED THIRD PLACE AMONG THE SECOND-YEARS.
ABOVE ALL, SHE HATES NOISE, RAIN...
...AND HER CLASSMATE, TAMAKI SUOH.
WSSSH
DAY 2
MR. SUOH.
2-A
YOU WERE IN CHARGE OF CLASS YESTER-DAY, WEREN'T YOU?
IT LOOKS LIKE YOU FAILED TO MAKE A PROPER ENTRY.
OH.
SORRY ABOUT THAT. I'LL CORRECT IT.
NO, IT'S FINE. I'VE ALREADY TAKEN CARE OF IT.

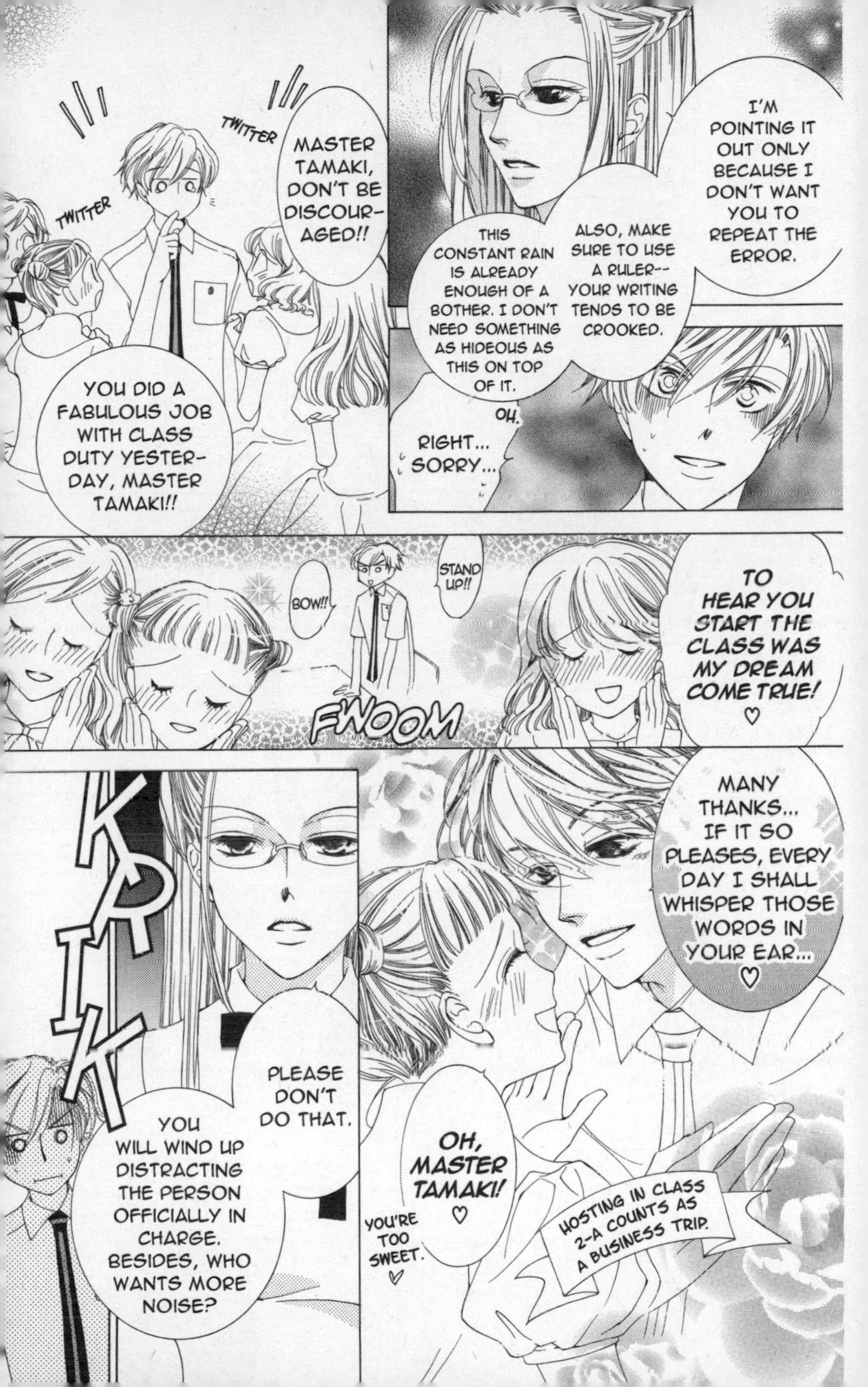
I'M POINTING IT OUT ONLY BECAUSE I DON'T WANT YOU TO REPEAT THE ERROR.
ALSO, MAKE SURE TO USE A RULER-- YOUR WRITING TENDS TO BE CROOKED.
THIS CONSTANT RAIN IS ALREADY ENOUGH OF A BOTHER. I DON'T NEED SOMETHING AS HIDEOUS AS THIS ON TOP OF IT.
OH.
RIGHT... SORRY...
MASTER TAMAKI, DON'T BE DISCOURAGED!!
TWITTER
TWITTER
YOU DID A FABULOUS JOB WITH CLASS DUTY YESTERDAY, MASTER TAMAKI!!
TO HEAR YOU START THE CLASS WAS MY DREAM COME TRUE! ♡
STAND UP!!
BOW!!
FWOOM
MANY THANKS... IF IT SO PLEASES, EVERY DAY I SHALL WHISPER THOSE WORDS IN YOUR EAR... ♡
OH, MASTER TAMAKI! ♡
YOU'RE TOO SWEET. ♡
HOSTING IN CLASS 2-A COUNTS AS A BUSINESS TRIP.
KRIK
PLEASE DON'T DO THAT.
YOU WILL WIND UP DISTRACTING THE PERSON OFFICIALLY IN CHARGE. BESIDES, WHO WANTS MORE NOISE?

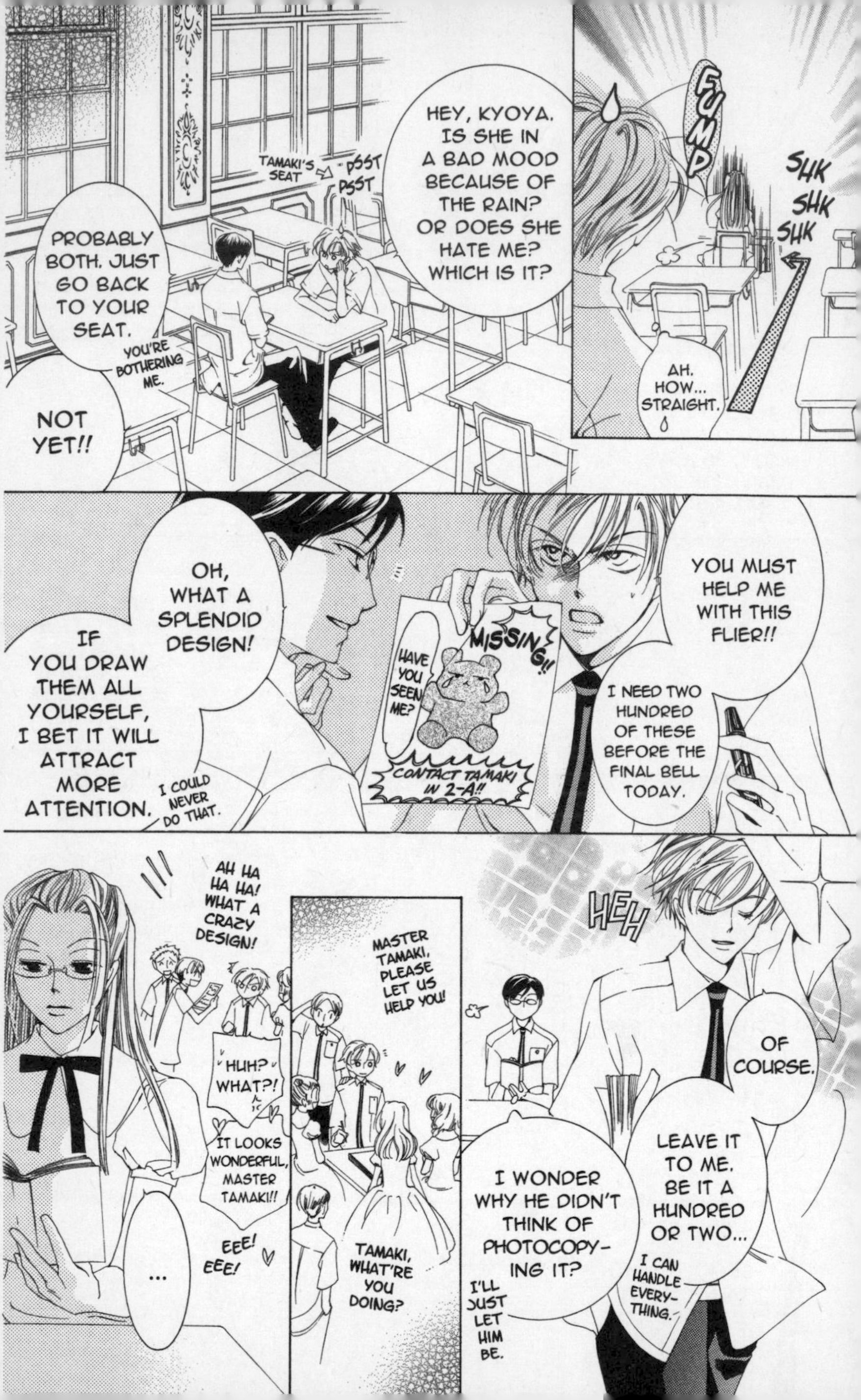
FUMP
SHK SHK SHK
AH. HOW... STRAIGHT.
HEY, KYOYA. IS SHE IN A BAD MOOD BECAUSE OF THE RAIN? OR DOES SHE HATE ME? WHICH IS IT?
TAMAKI'S SEAT
PSST PSST
PROBABLY BOTH. JUST GO BACK TO YOUR SEAT.
YOU'RE BOTHERING ME.
NOT YET!!
YOU MUST HELP ME WITH THIS FLIER!!
I NEED TWO HUNDRED OF THESE BEFORE THE FINAL BELL TODAY.
MISSING!!
HAVE YOU SEEN ME?
CONTACT TAMAKI IN 2-A!!
OH, WHAT A SPLENDID DESIGN!
IF YOU DRAW THEM ALL YOURSELF, I BET IT WILL ATTRACT MORE ATTENTION.
I COULD NEVER DO THAT.
HEH
OF COURSE.
LEAVE IT TO ME. BE IT A HUNDRED OR TWO...
I CAN HANDLE EVERYTHING.
I WONDER WHY HE DIDN'T THINK OF PHOTOCOPYING IT?
I'LL JUST LET HIM BE.
MASTER TAMAKI, PLEASE LET US HELP YOU!
TAMAKI, WHAT'RE YOU DOING?
AH HA HA HA! WHAT A CRAZY DESIGN!
HUH? WHAT?!
IT LOOKS WONDERFUL, MASTER TAMAKI!!
EEE! EEE!
...

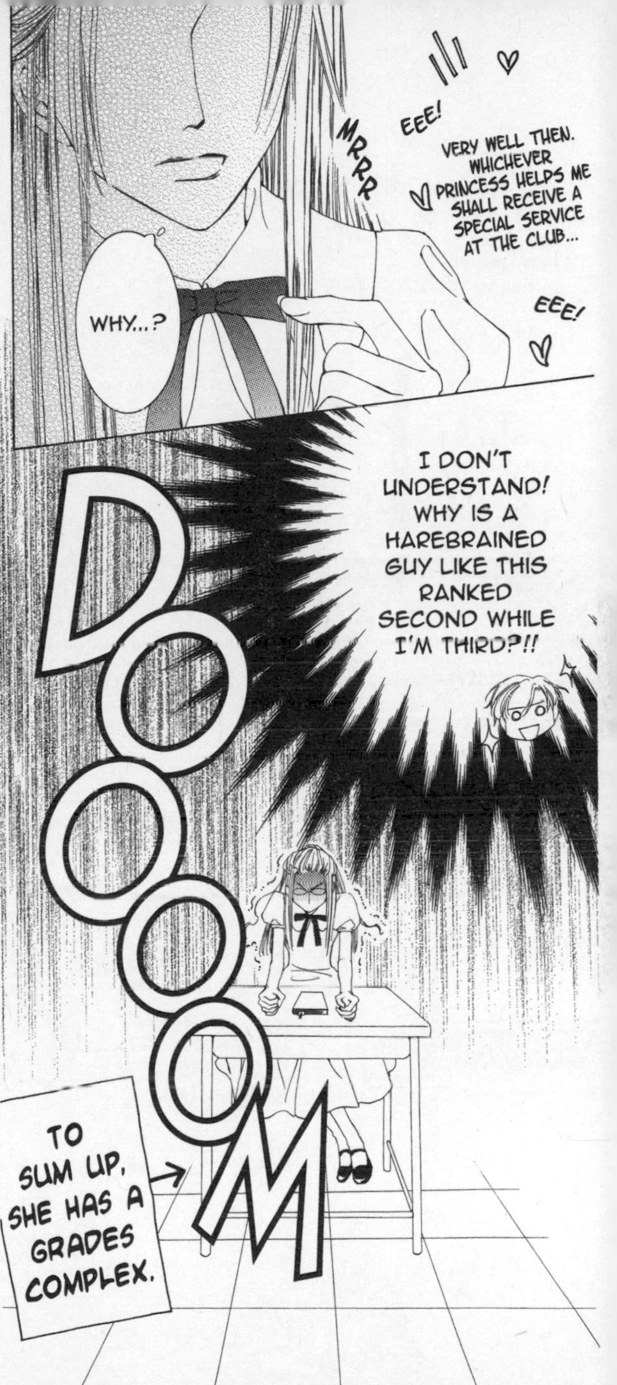
EEE!
VERY WELL THEN. WHICHEVER PRINCESS HELPS ME SHALL RECEIVE A SPECIAL SERVICE AT THE CLUB...
EEE!
MRRR
WHY...?
I DON'T UNDERSTAND! WHY IS A HAREBRAINED GUY LIKE THIS RANKED SECOND WHILE I'M THIRD?!!
DOOOOOM
TO SUM UP, SHE HAS A GRADES COMPLEX.

1

HELLO EVERYONE!! HATORI HERE. I'M TOTALLY HOOKED ON FENG SHUI OF LATE...JUST KIDDING. I'M NOT EXACTLY ADDICTED, BUT I DO THINK ABOUT IT. I CAN'T HELP PUTTING COVERS OVER THE TV AND PC. (IT SEEMS TO HELP ME CONCENTRATE.) I USE SCENIC IMAGES FOR WALLPAPER ON MY PC. I'VE PLACED GREEN POTTED PLANTS AROUND, AND SO ON. MY BED IS FACING NORTH (BUT I OFTEN END UP SLEEPING AT MY DESK OR ON THE FLOOR, SO I HARDLY EVER USE MY BED).

MAYBE IT'S BECAUSE OF MY JOB OR MY AGE, BUT I CAN'T HELP NOTICING THINGS THAT NEVER BOTHERED ME BEFORE, LIKE MY HEALTH. THUS, THERE'S FENG SHUI AND HEALING PRODUCTS!!

THE THING IS, MOST OF MY FRIENDS AT WORK ARE THIS WAY TOO. QUESTIONS KEEP POPPING UP IN OUR CASUAL CONVERSATIONS, LIKE WHETHER ONE'S DESK SHOULD FACE NORTH OR WEST. (MY DESK FACES WEST AT THE MOMENT, BUT I'M CONSIDERING SWITCHING IT TO FACE NORTH.) WHEN I START TO THINK ABOUT FENG SHUI, I CAN'T STOP. BUT I NEVER EVER WANT TO GET HOOKED. AND SO GO MY DAYS.

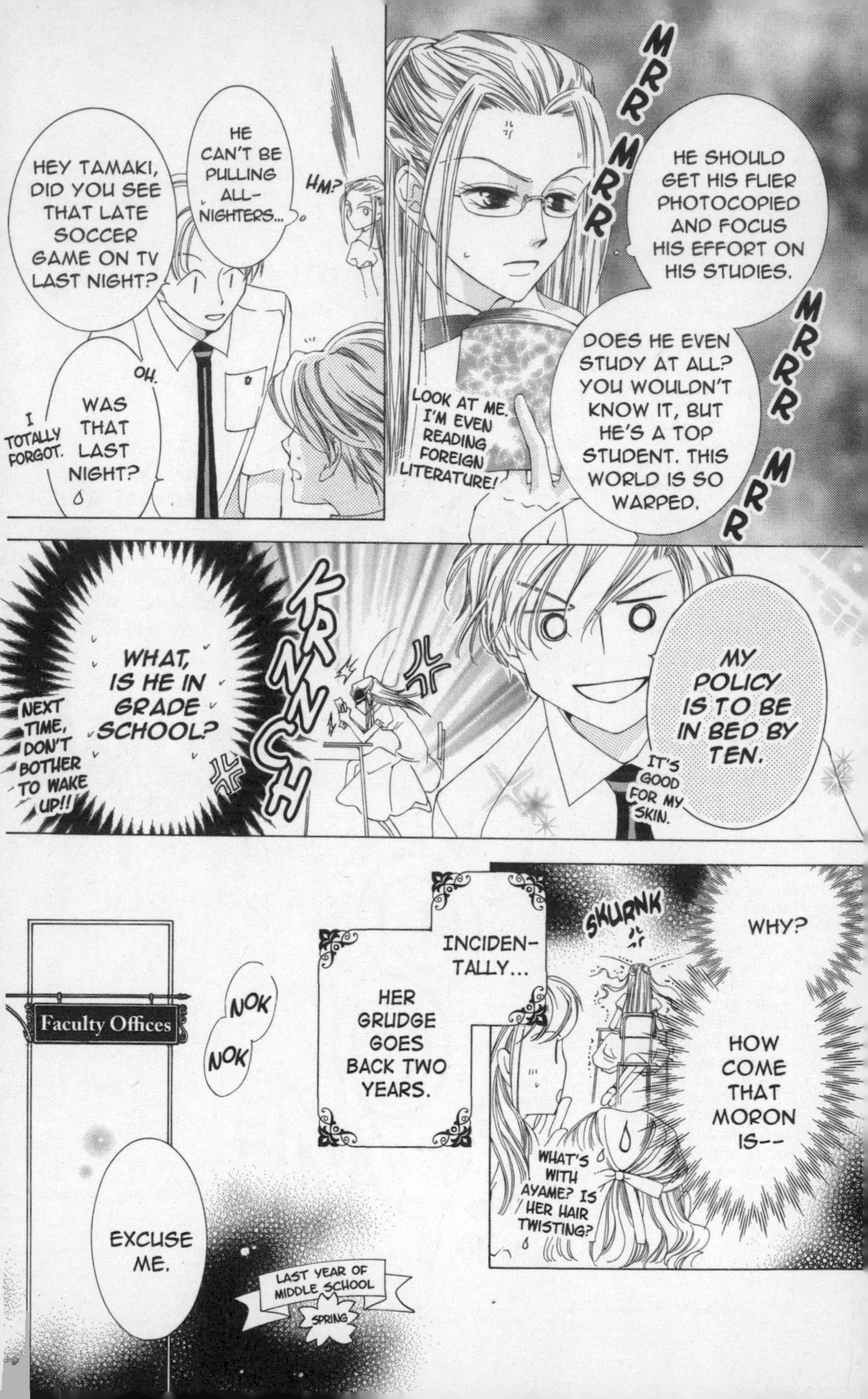
MRR MRR
HE SHOULD GET HIS FLIER PHOTOCOPIED AND FOCUS HIS EFFORT ON HIS STUDIES.
MRRR MRR
DOES HE EVEN STUDY AT ALL? YOU WOULDN'T KNOW IT, BUT HE'S A TOP STUDENT. THIS WORLD IS SO WARPED.
LOOK AT ME. I'M EVEN READING FOREIGN LITERATURE!
HE CAN'T BE PULLING ALL-NIGHTERS...
HM?
HEY TAMAKI, DID YOU SEE THAT LATE SOCCER GAME ON TV LAST NIGHT?
OH.
WAS THAT LAST NIGHT?
I TOTALLY FORGOT.
MY POLICY IS TO BE IN BED BY TEN.
IT'S GOOD FOR MY SKIN.
KRNCH
WHAT, IS HE IN GRADE SCHOOL?
NEXT TIME, DON'T BOTHER TO WAKE UP!!
SKURNK
WHY?
HOW COME THAT MORON IS--
WHAT'S WITH AYAME? IS HER HAIR TWISTING?
INCIDENTALLY...
HER GRUDGE GOES BACK TWO YEARS.
Faculty Offices
NOK NOK
LAST YEAR OF MIDDLE SCHOOL
SPRING
EXCUSE ME.

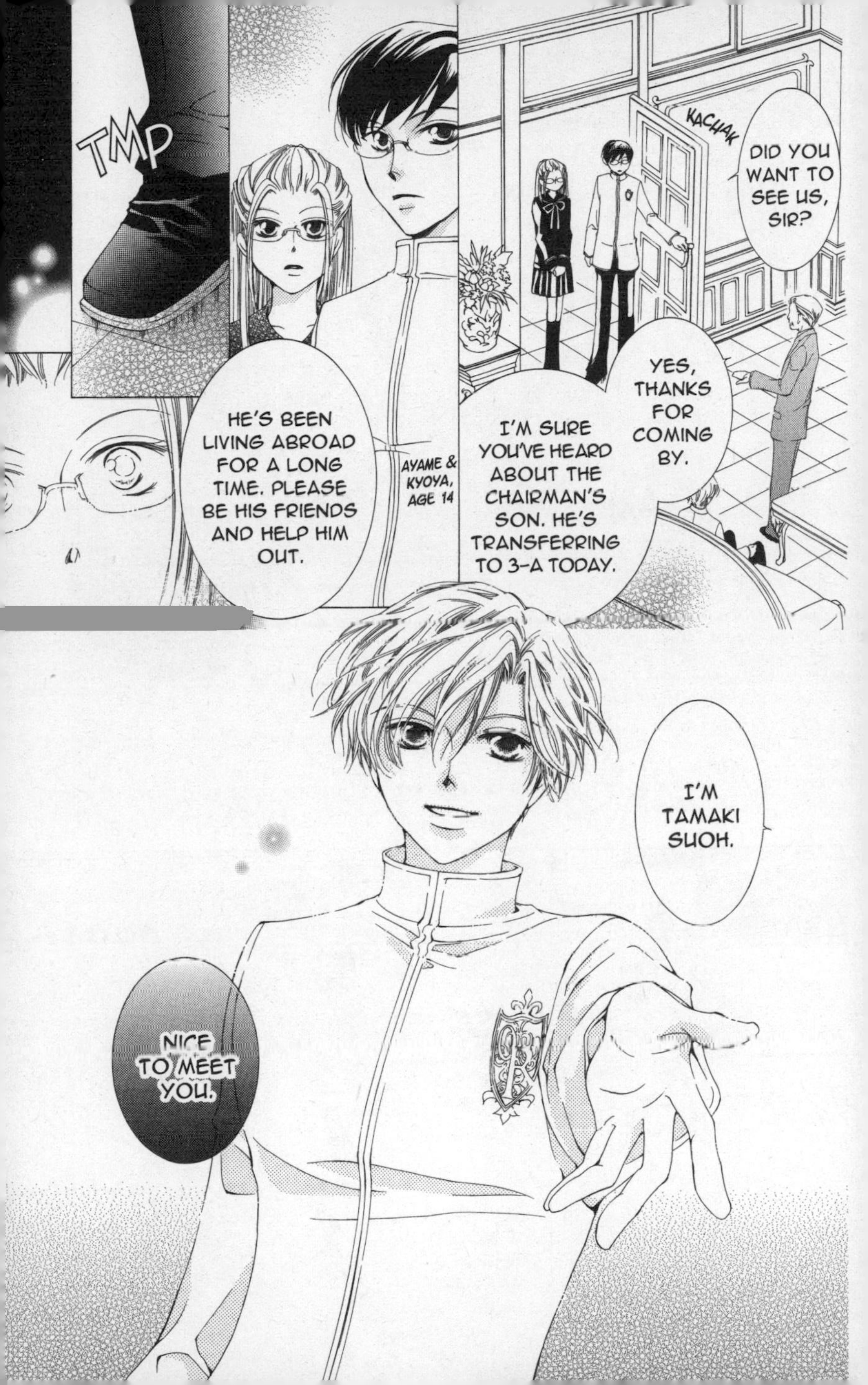
KACHAK
DID YOU WANT TO SEE US, SIR?
YES, THANKS FOR COMING BY.
I'M SURE YOU'VE HEARD ABOUT THE CHAIRMAN'S SON. HE'S TRANSFERRING TO 3-A TODAY.
AYAME & KYOYA, AGE 14
HE'S BEEN LIVING ABROAD FOR A LONG TIME. PLEASE BE HIS FRIENDS AND HELP HIM OUT.
TMP
I'M TAMAKI SUOH.
NICE TO MEET YOU.

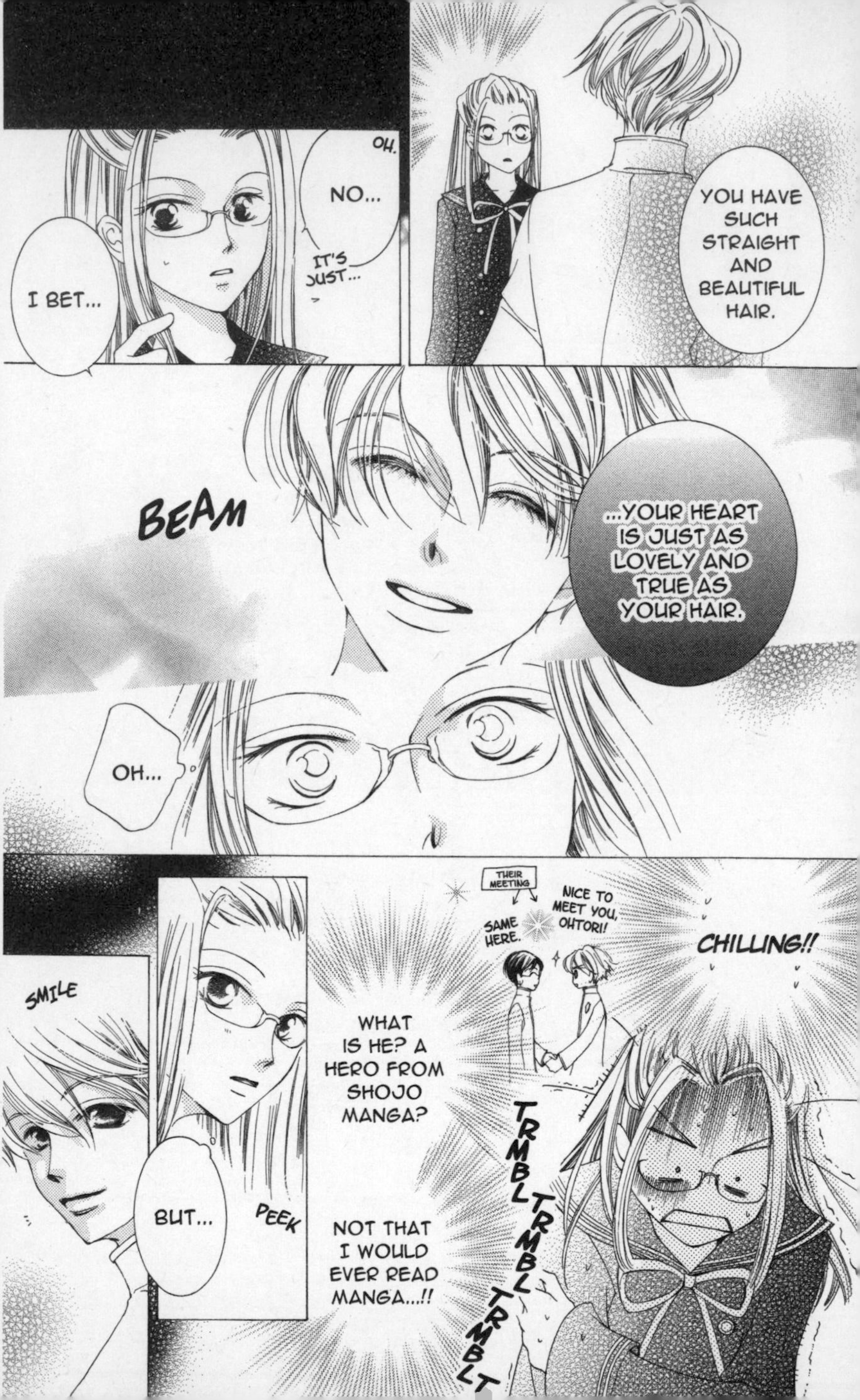
YOU HAVE SUCH STRAIGHT AND BEAUTIFUL HAIR.
OH.
NO...
IT'S JUST...
I BET...
...YOUR HEART IS JUST AS LOVELY AND TRUE AS YOUR HAIR.
BEAM
OH...
CHILLING!!
THEIR MEETING
NICE TO MEET YOU, OHTORI!
SAME HERE.
TRMBL TRMBL TRMBL TRMBLT
WHAT IS HE? A HERO FROM SHOJO MANGA?
NOT THAT I WOULD EVER READ MANGA...!!
PEEK
BUT...
SMILE

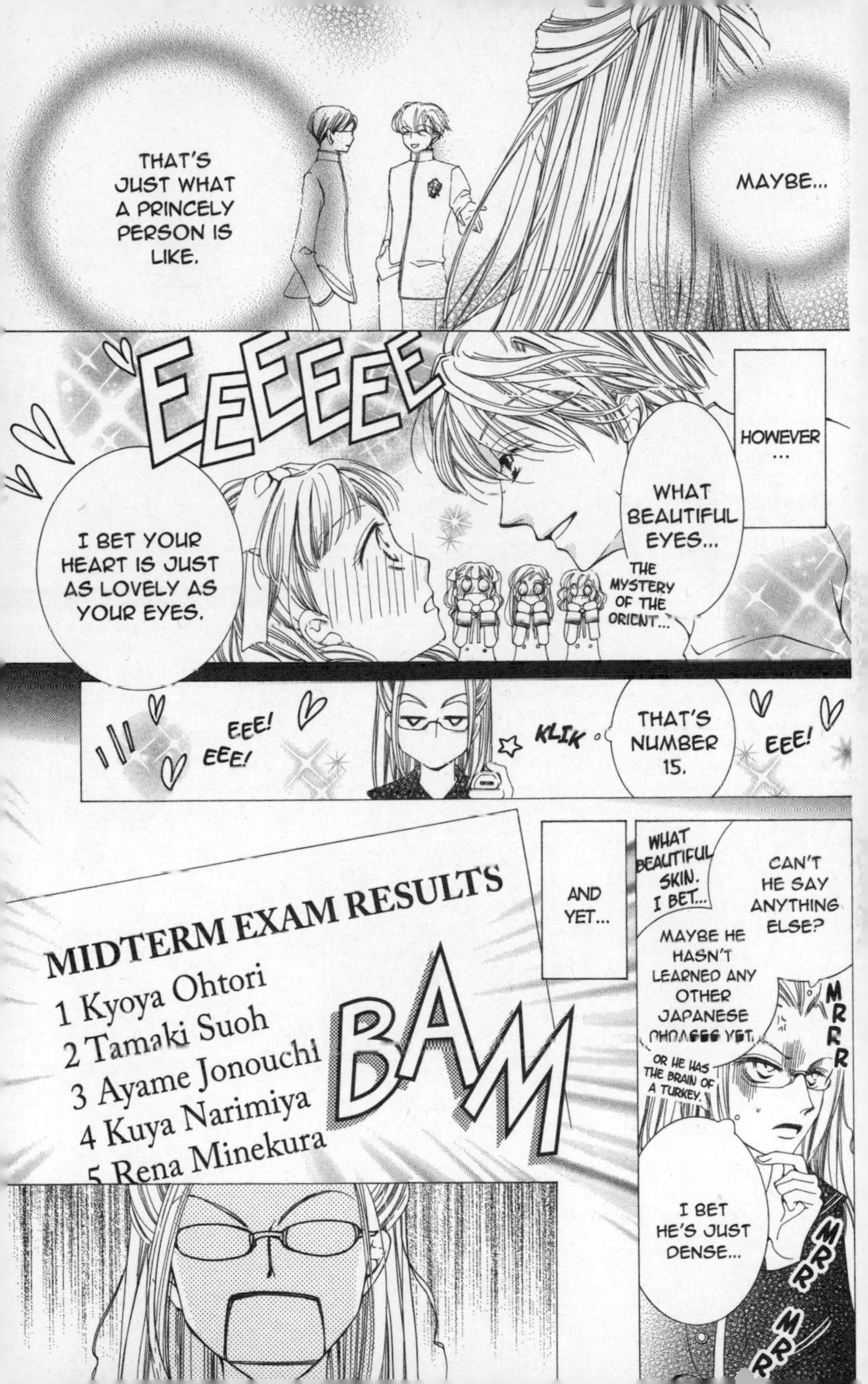
MAYBE...
THAT'S JUST WHAT A PRINCELY PERSON IS LIKE.
HOWEVER...
WHAT BEAUTIFUL EYES...
THE MYSTERY OF THE ORIENT...
EEEEEE
I BET YOUR HEART IS JUST AS LOVELY AS YOUR EYES.
EEE!
THAT'S NUMBER 15.
KLIK
EEE! EEE!
WHAT BEAUTIFUL SKIN. I BET...
CAN'T HE SAY ANYTHING ELSE?
MAYBE HE HASN'T LEARNED ANY OTHER JAPANESE PHRASES YET.
OR HE HAS THE BRAIN OF A TURKEY.
MRRR
I BET HE'S JUST DENSE...
MRR MRR
AND YET...
MIDTERM EXAM RESULTS
1 Kyoya Ohtori
2 Tamaki Suoh
3 Ayame Jonouchi
4 Kuya Narimiya
5 Rena Minekura
BAM

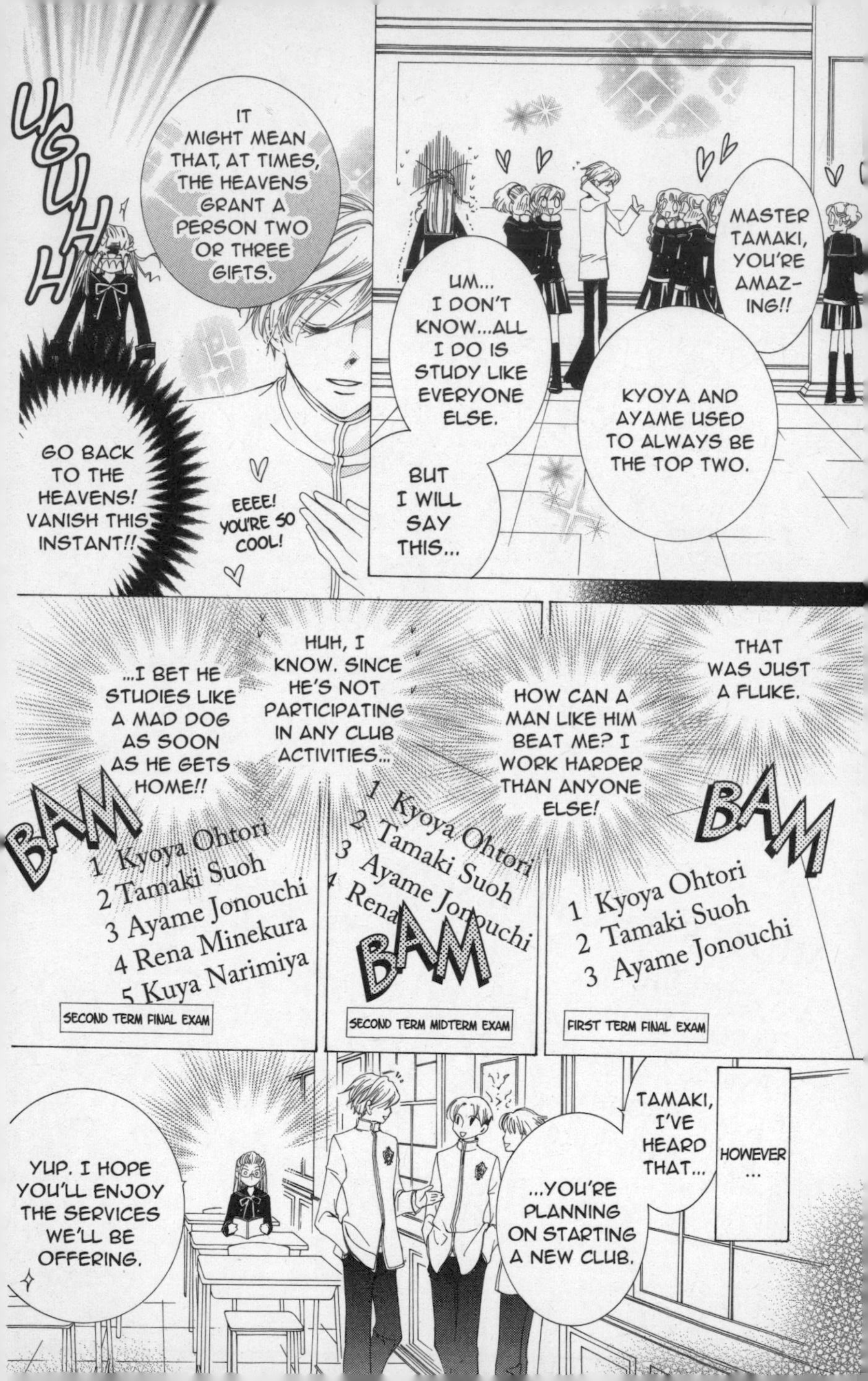
MASTER TAMAKI, YOU'RE AMAZ-ING!!
KYOYA AND AYAME USED TO ALWAYS BE THE TOP TWO.
UM... I DON'T KNOW...ALL I DO IS STUDY LIKE EVERYONE ELSE.
BUT I WILL SAY THIS...
IT MIGHT MEAN THAT, AT TIMES, THE HEAVENS GRANT A PERSON TWO OR THREE GIFTS.
UGUHH
EEEE! YOU'RE SO COOL!
GO BACK TO THE HEAVENS! VANISH THIS INSTANT!!
THAT WAS JUST A FLUKE.
BAM
1 Kyoya Ohtori
2 Tamaki Suoh
3 Ayame Jonouchi
FIRST TERM FINAL EXAM
HOW CAN A MAN LIKE HIM BEAT ME? I WORK HARDER THAN ANYONE ELSE!
HUH, I KNOW. SINCE HE'S NOT PARTICIPATING IN ANY CLUB ACTIVITIES...
1 Kyoya Ohtori
2 Tamaki Suoh
3 Ayame Jonouchi
4 Rena
BAM
SECOND TERM MIDTERM EXAM
...I BET HE STUDIES LIKE A MAD DOG AS SOON AS HE GETS HOME!!
BAM
1 Kyoya Ohtori
2 Tamaki Suoh
3 Ayame Jonouchi
4 Rena Minekura
5 Kuya Narimiya
SECOND TERM FINAL EXAM
HOWEVER ...
TAMAKI, I'VE HEARD THAT...
...YOU'RE PLANNING ON STARTING A NEW CLUB.
YUP. I HOPE YOU'LL ENJOY THE SERVICES WE'LL BE OFFERING.

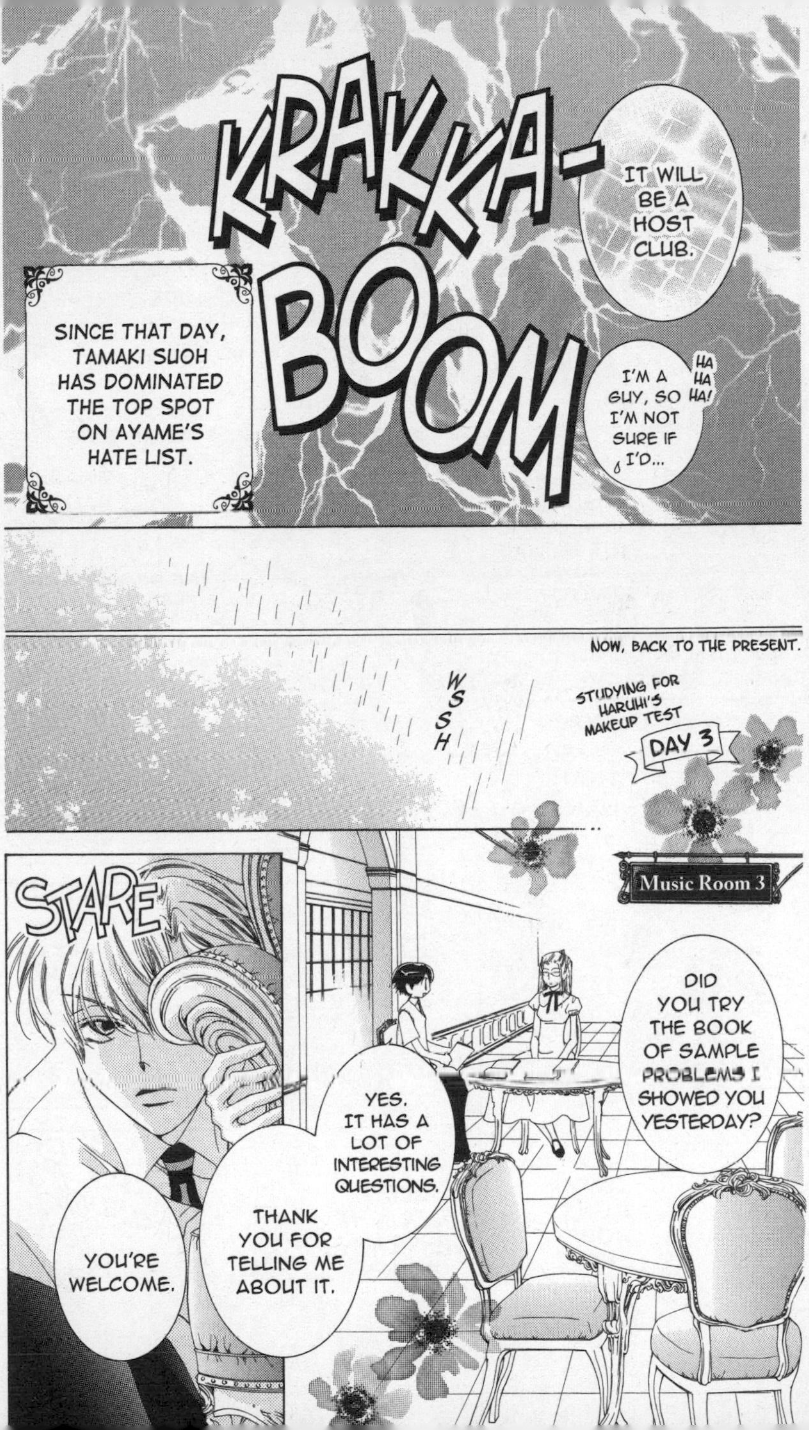
IT WILL BE A HOST CLUB.
I'M A GUY, SO I'M NOT SURE IF I'D...
HA HA HA!
KRAKKA-BOOM
SINCE THAT DAY, TAMAKI SUOH HAS DOMINATED THE TOP SPOT ON AYAME'S HATE LIST.
NOW, BACK TO THE PRESENT.
STUDYING FOR HARUHI'S MAKEUP TEST
DAY 3
WSSH
Music Room 3
DID YOU TRY THE BOOK OF SAMPLE PROBLEMS I SHOWED YOU YESTERDAY?
YES. IT HAS A LOT OF INTERESTING QUESTIONS.
THANK YOU FOR TELLING ME ABOUT IT.
STARE
YOU'RE WELCOME.

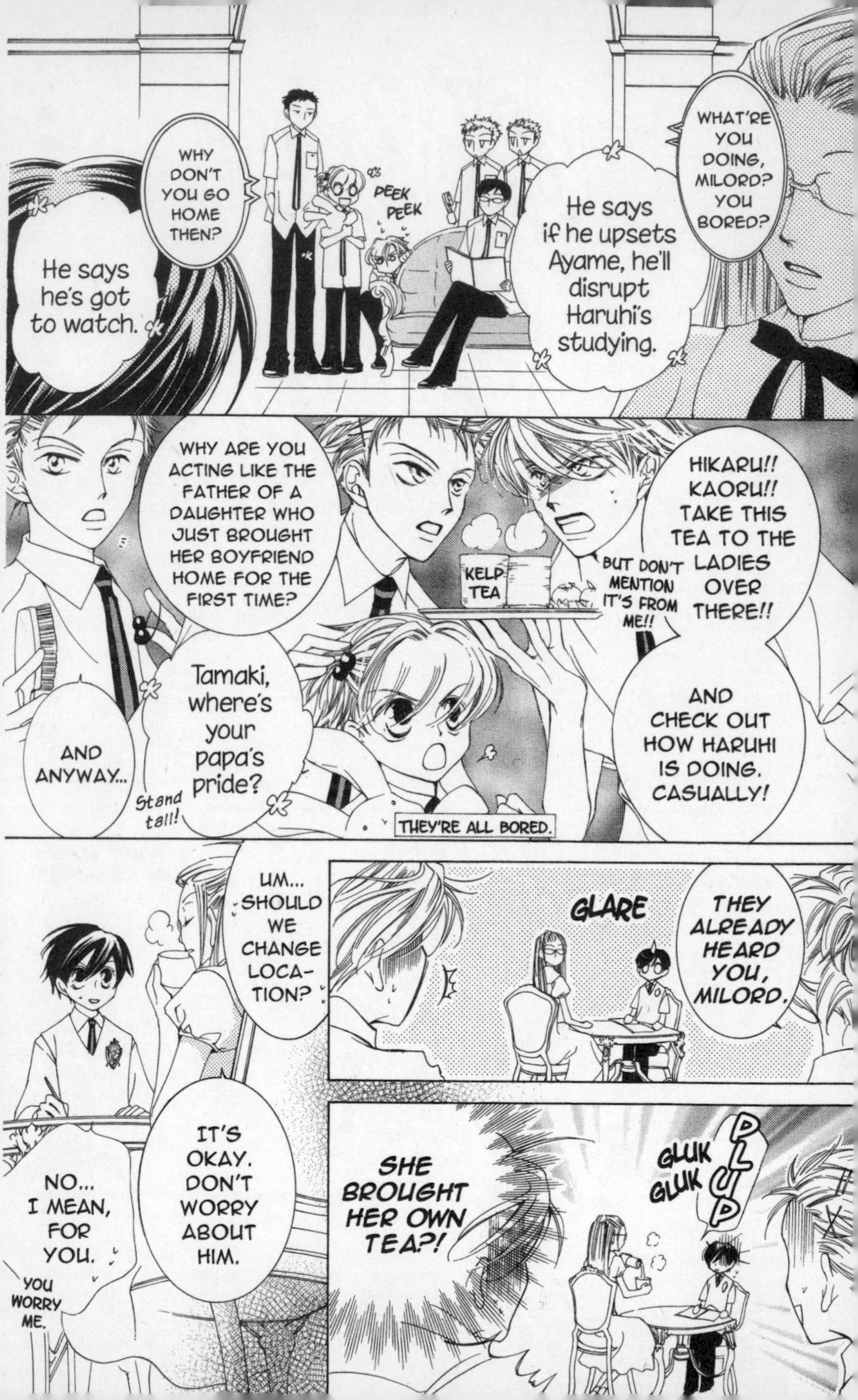
WHAT'RE YOU DOING, MILORD? YOU BORED?
He says if he upsets Ayame, he'll disrupt Haruhi's studying.
PEEK PEEK
WHY DON'T YOU GO HOME THEN?
He says he's got to watch.
HIKARU!! KAORU!! TAKE THIS TEA TO THE LADIES OVER THERE!!
BUT DON'T MENTION IT'S FROM ME!!
KELP TEA
AND CHECK OUT HOW HARUHI IS DOING. CASUALLY!
WHY ARE YOU ACTING LIKE THE FATHER OF A DAUGHTER WHO JUST BROUGHT HER BOYFRIEND HOME FOR THE FIRST TIME?
THEY'RE ALL BORED.
Tamaki, where's your papa's pride?
Stand tall!
AND ANYWAY...
THEY ALREADY HEARD YOU, MILORD.
GLARE
PLUP
GLUK GLUK
SHE BROUGHT HER OWN TEA?!
UM... SHOULD WE CHANGE LOCATION?
IT'S OKAY. DON'T WORRY ABOUT HIM.
NO... I MEAN, FOR YOU.
YOU WORRY ME.

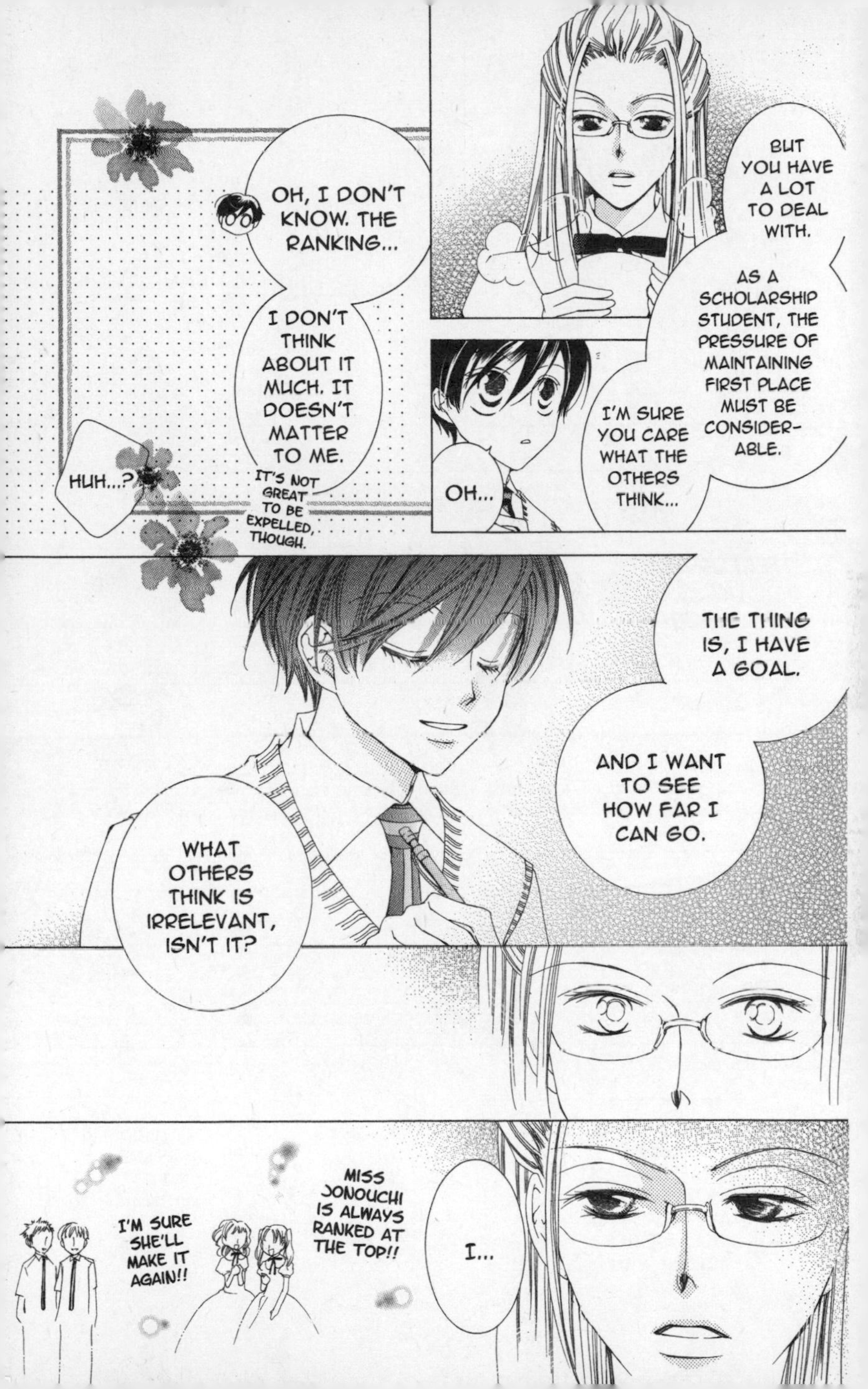
BUT YOU HAVE A LOT TO DEAL WITH.
AS A SCHOLARSHIP STUDENT, THE PRESSURE OF MAINTAINING FIRST PLACE MUST BE CONSIDERABLE.
I'M SURE YOU CARE WHAT THE OTHERS THINK...
OH...
OH, I DON'T KNOW. THE RANKING...
I DON'T THINK ABOUT IT MUCH. IT DOESN'T MATTER TO ME.
IT'S NOT GREAT TO BE EXPELLED, THOUGH.
HUH...?
THE THING IS, I HAVE A GOAL.
AND I WANT TO SEE HOW FAR I CAN GO.
WHAT OTHERS THINK IS IRRELEVANT, ISN'T IT?
I...
MISS JONOUCHI IS ALWAYS RANKED AT THE TOP!!
I'M SURE SHE'LL MAKE IT AGAIN!!

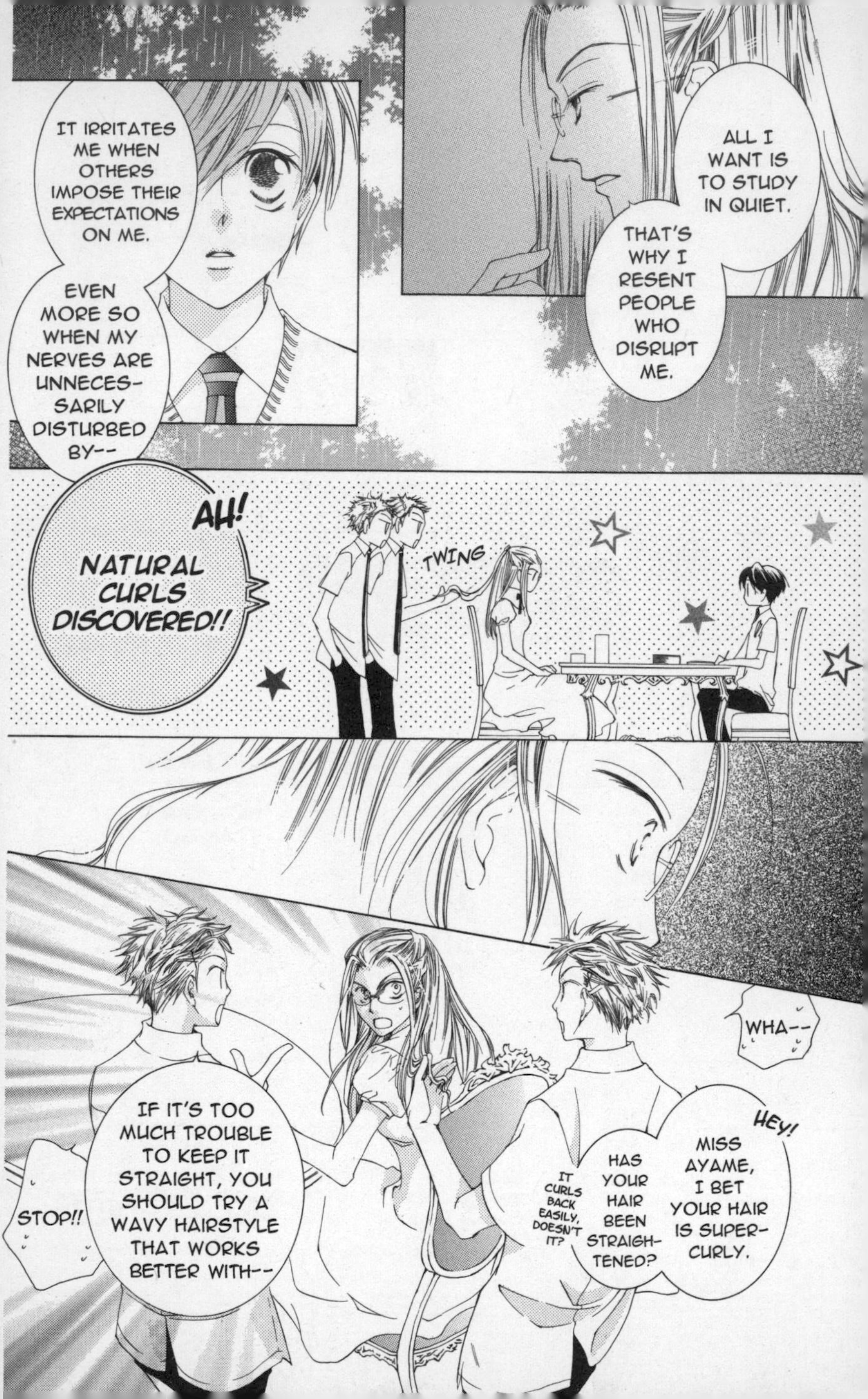
ALL I WANT IS TO STUDY IN QUIET.
THAT'S WHY I RESENT PEOPLE WHO DISRUPT ME.
IT IRRITATES ME WHEN OTHERS IMPOSE THEIR EXPECTATIONS ON ME.
EVEN MORE SO WHEN MY NERVES ARE UNNECES-SARILY DISTURBED BY--
AH!
NATURAL CURLS DISCOVERED!!
TWING
WHA--
HEY!
MISS AYAME, I BET YOUR HAIR IS SUPER-CURLY.
HAS YOUR HAIR BEEN STRAIGH-TENED?
IT CURLS BACK EASILY, DOESN'T IT?
IF IT'S TOO MUCH TROUBLE TO KEEP IT STRAIGHT, YOU SHOULD TRY A WAVY HAIRSTYLE THAT WORKS BETTER WITH--
STOP!!

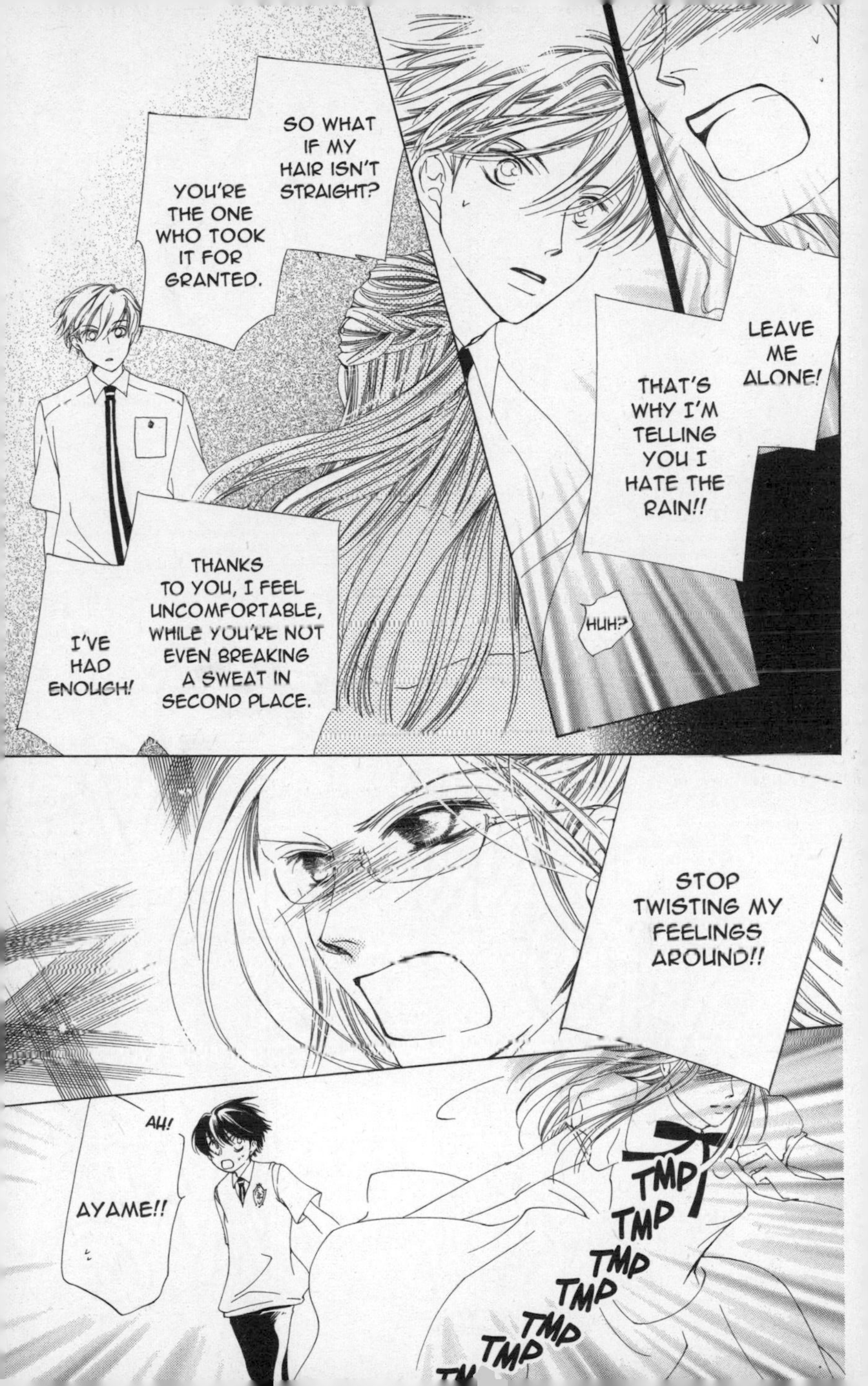
LEAVE ME ALONE!
THAT'S WHY I'M TELLING YOU I HATE THE RAIN!!
HUH?
SO WHAT IF MY HAIR ISN'T STRAIGHT?
YOU'RE THE ONE WHO TOOK IT FOR GRANTED.
THANKS TO YOU, I FEEL UNCOMFORTABLE, WHILE YOU'RE NOT EVEN BREAKING A SWEAT IN SECOND PLACE.
I'VE HAD ENOUGH!
STOP TWISTING MY FEELINGS AROUND!!
TMP TMP TMP TMP TMP TMP
AH!
AYAME!!

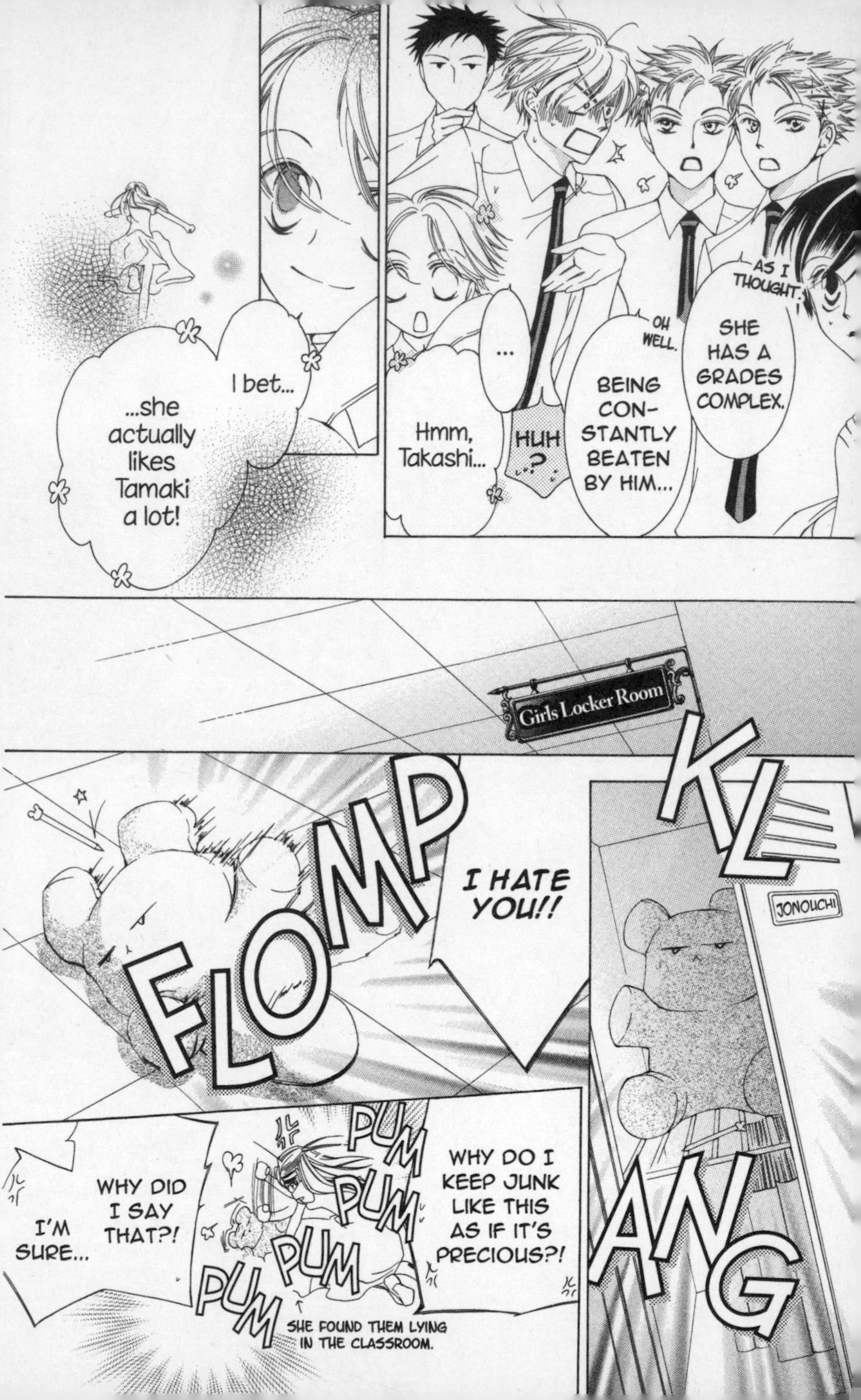

AS I THOUGHT.
SHE HAS A GRADES COMPLEX.
OH WELL.
BEING CON-STANTLY BEATEN BY HIM...
HUH ...?
...
Hmm, Takashi...
I bet...
...she actually likes Tamaki a lot!
Girls Locker Room
KLANG
JONOUCHI
I HATE YOU!!
FLOMP
WHY DO I KEEP JUNK LIKE THIS AS IF IT'S PRECIOUS?!
PUM PUM PUM PUM PUM
SHE FOUND THEM LYING IN THE CLASSROOM.
WHY DID I SAY THAT?!
I'M SURE...

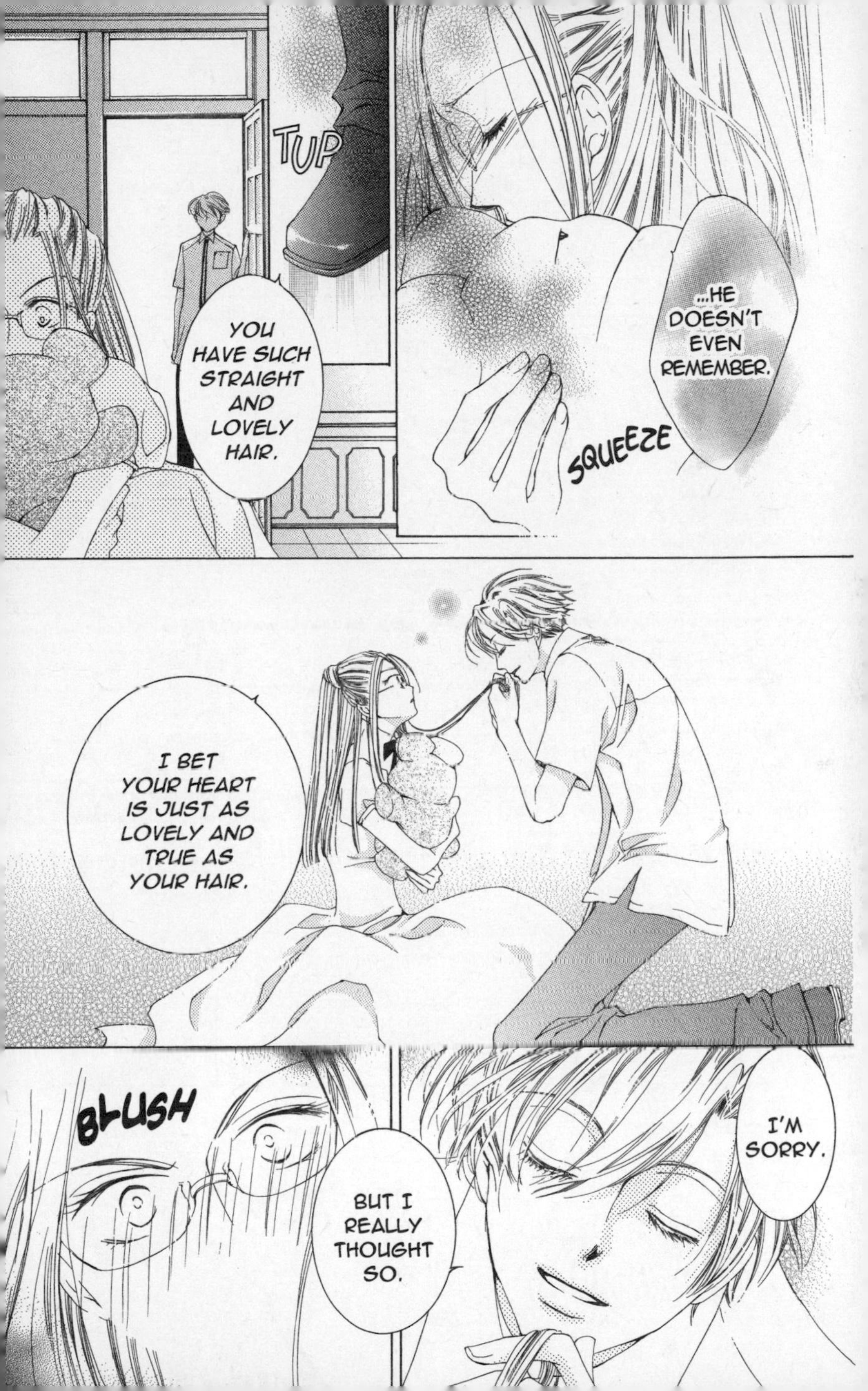
...HE DOESN'T EVEN REMEMBER.
SQUEEZE
TUP
YOU HAVE SUCH STRAIGHT AND LOVELY HAIR.
I BET YOUR HEART IS JUST AS LOVELY AND TRUE AS YOUR HAIR.
I'M SORRY.
BUT I REALLY THOUGHT SO.
BLUSH

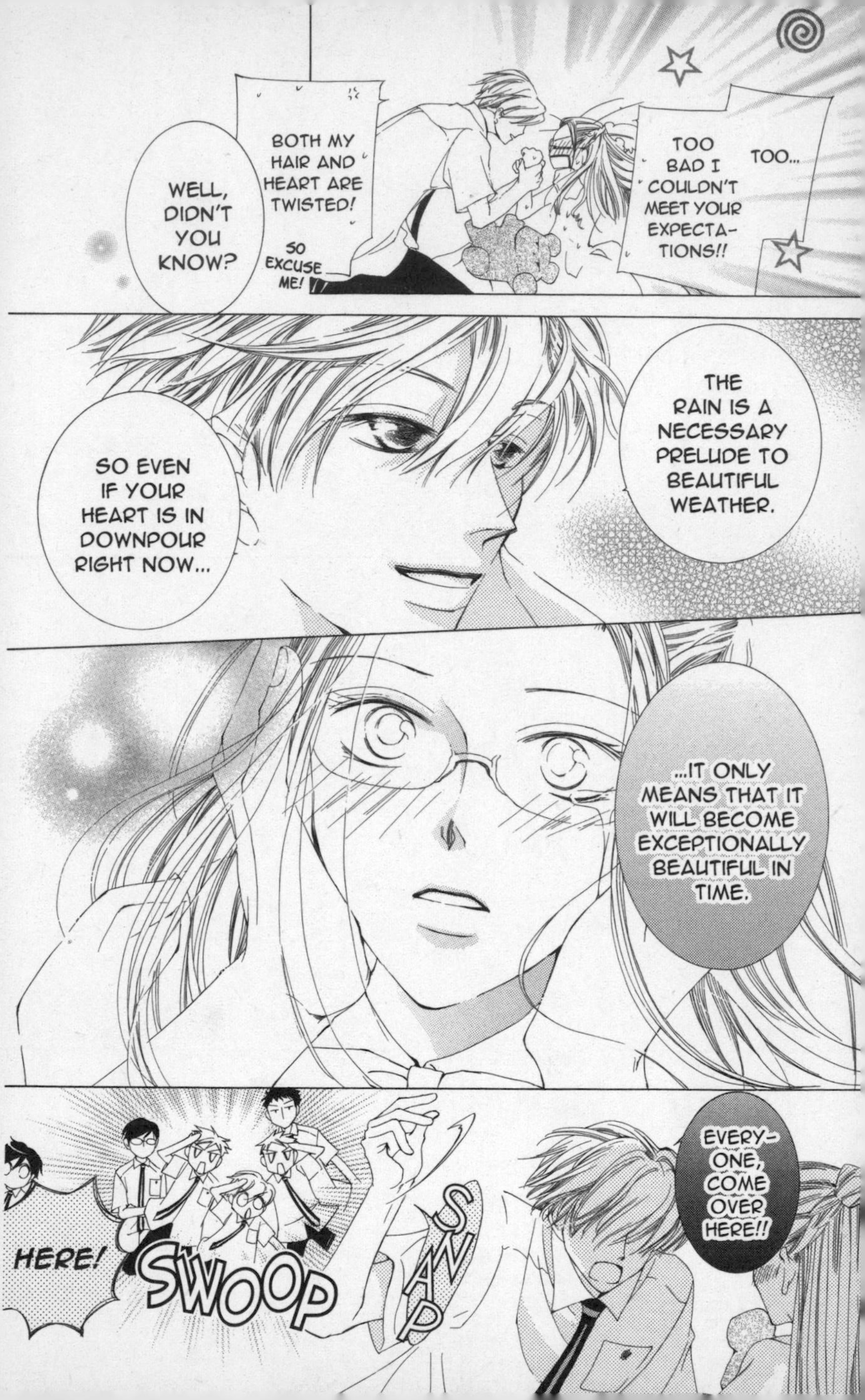
TOO BAD I COULDN'T MEET YOUR EXPECTA-TIONS!!
TOO...
BOTH MY HAIR AND HEART ARE TWISTED!
SO EXCUSE ME!
WELL, DIDN'T YOU KNOW?
THE RAIN IS A NECESSARY PRELUDE TO BEAUTIFUL WEATHER.
SO EVEN IF YOUR HEART IS IN DOWNPOUR RIGHT NOW...
...IT ONLY MEANS THAT IT WILL BECOME EXCEPTIONALLY BEAUTIFUL IN TIME.
EVERY-ONE, COME OVER HERE!!
SNAP
SWOOP
HERE!

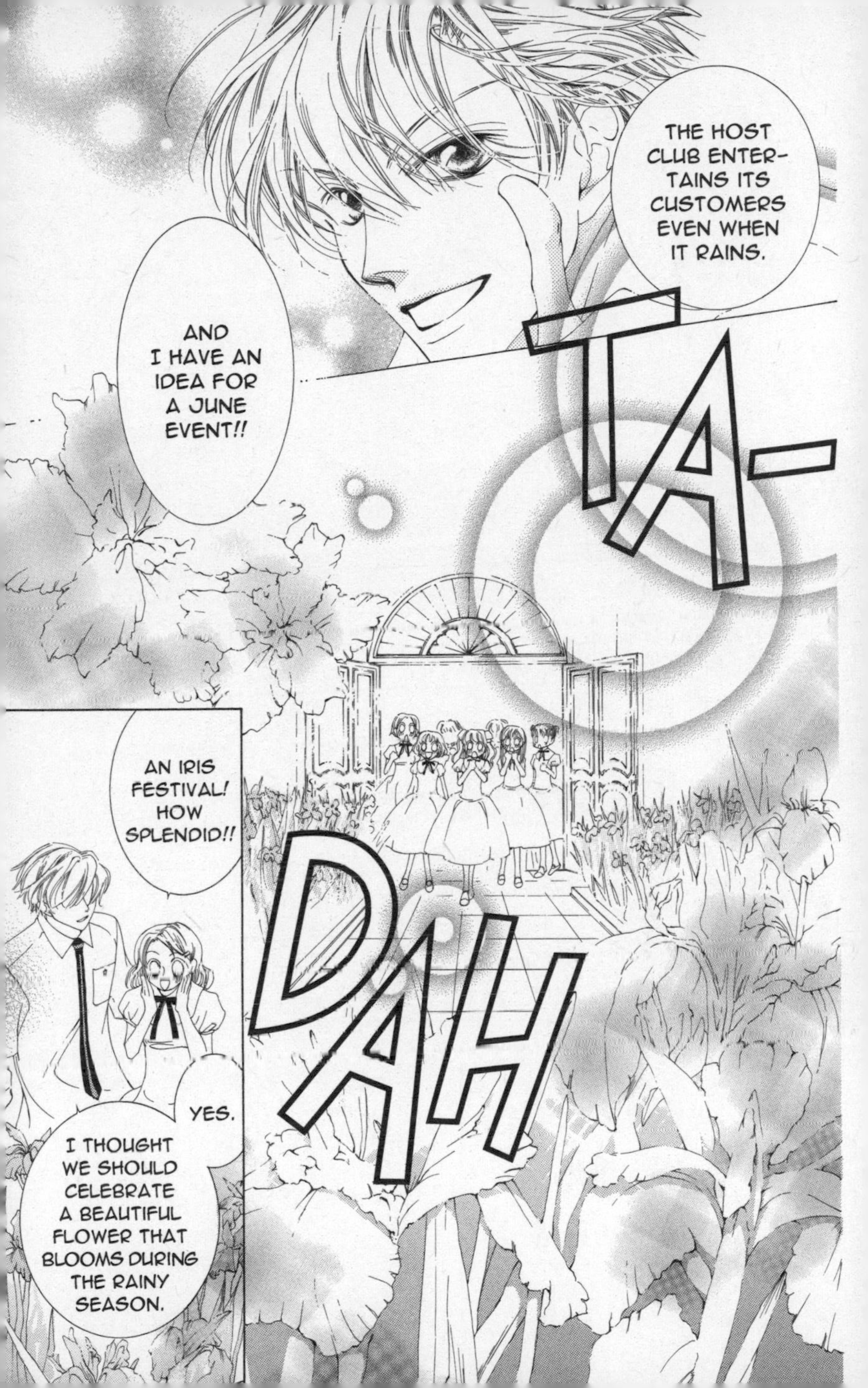
THE HOST CLUB ENTER-TAINS ITS CUSTOMERS EVEN WHEN IT RAINS.
AND I HAVE AN IDEA FOR A JUNE EVENT!!
TA-DAH
AN IRIS FESTIVAL! HOW SPLENDID!!
YES.
I THOUGHT WE SHOULD CELEBRATE A BEAUTIFUL FLOWER THAT BLOOMS DURING THE RAINY SEASON.

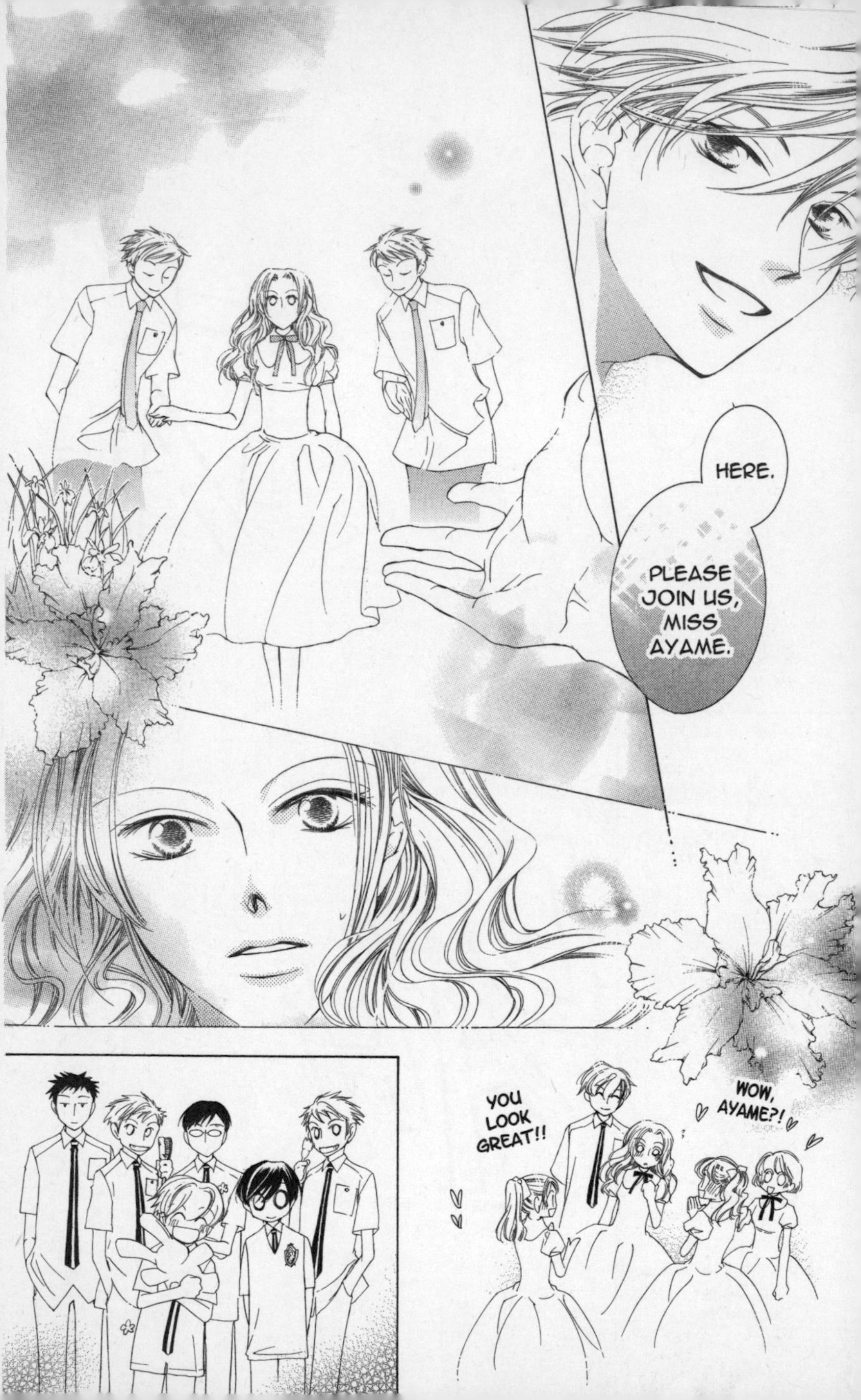
HERE.
PLEASE JOIN US, MISS AYAME.
WOW, AYAME?!
YOU LOOK GREAT!!

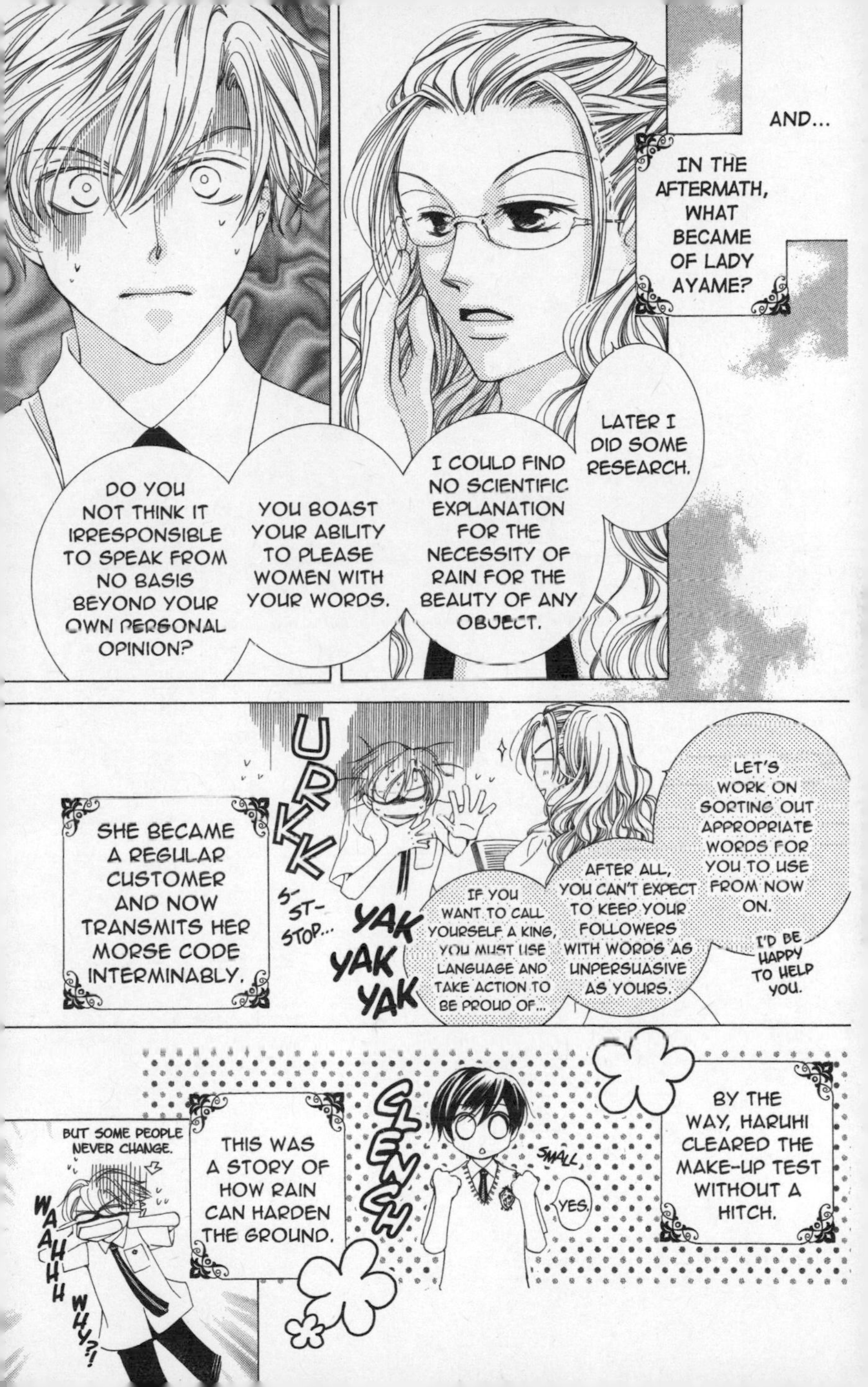
AND...
IN THE AFTERMATH, WHAT BECAME OF LADY AYAME?
LATER I DID SOME RESEARCH.
I COULD FIND NO SCIENTIFIC EXPLANATION FOR THE NECESSITY OF RAIN FOR THE BEAUTY OF ANY OBJECT.
YOU BOAST YOUR ABILITY TO PLEASE WOMEN WITH YOUR WORDS.
DO YOU NOT THINK IT IRRESPONSIBLE TO SPEAK FROM NO BASIS BEYOND YOUR OWN PERSONAL OPINION?
LET'S WORK ON SORTING OUT APPROPRIATE WORDS FOR YOU TO USE FROM NOW ON.
I'D BE HAPPY TO HELP YOU.
AFTER ALL, YOU CAN'T EXPECT TO KEEP YOUR FOLLOWERS WITH WORDS AS UNPERSUASIVE AS YOURS.
IF YOU WANT TO CALL YOURSELF A KING, YOU MUST USE LANGUAGE AND TAKE ACTION TO BE PROUD OF...
YAK YAK YAK
S-ST-STOP...
URKK
SHE BECAME A REGULAR CUSTOMER AND NOW TRANSMITS HER MORSE CODE INTERMINABLY.
BY THE WAY, HARUHI CLEARED THE MAKE-UP TEST WITHOUT A HITCH.
SMALL
YES.
CLENCH
THIS WAS A STORY OF HOW RAIN CAN HARDEN THE GROUND.
BUT SOME PEOPLE NEVER CHANGE.
WAAHHH
WHY?!

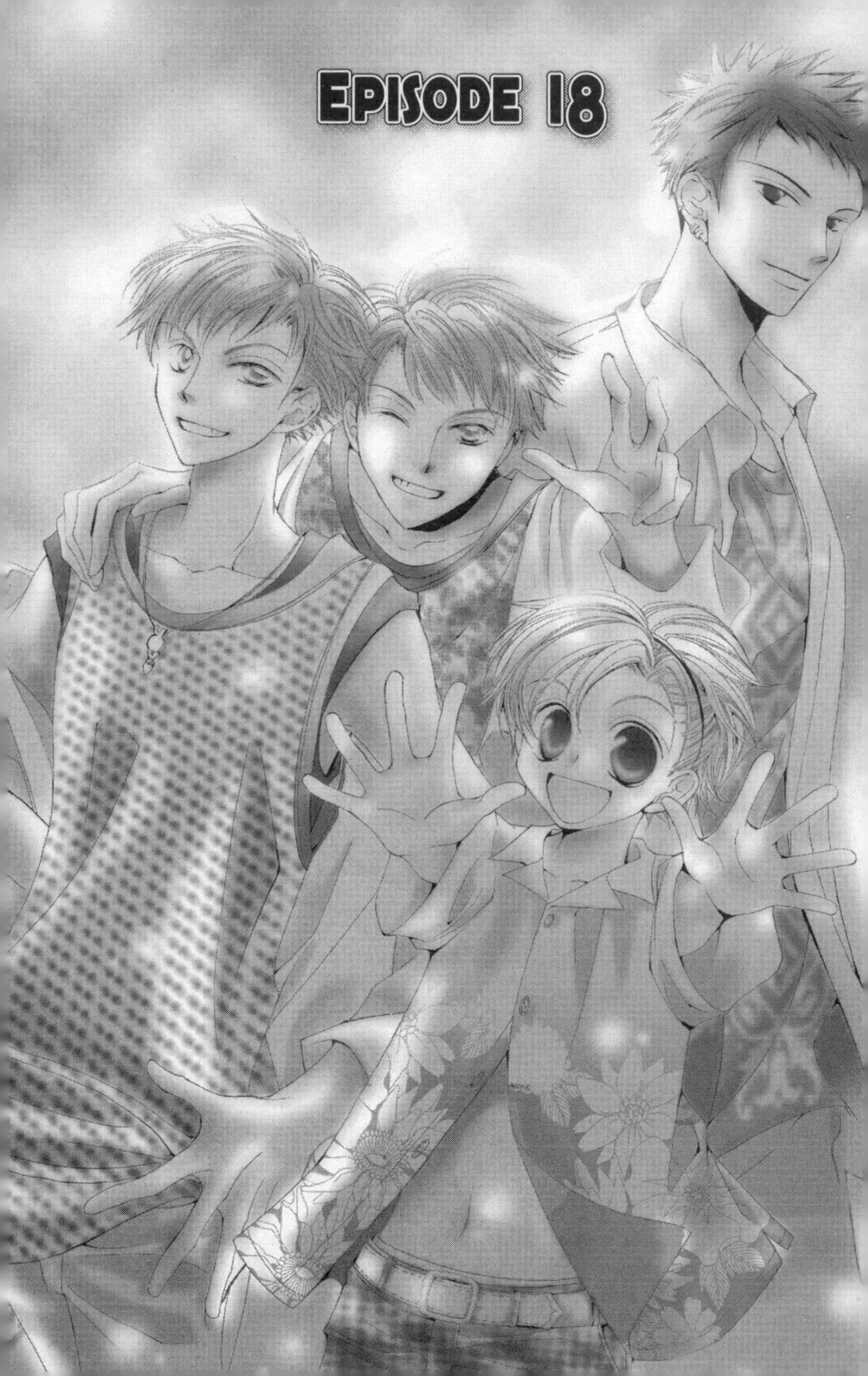
Episode 18

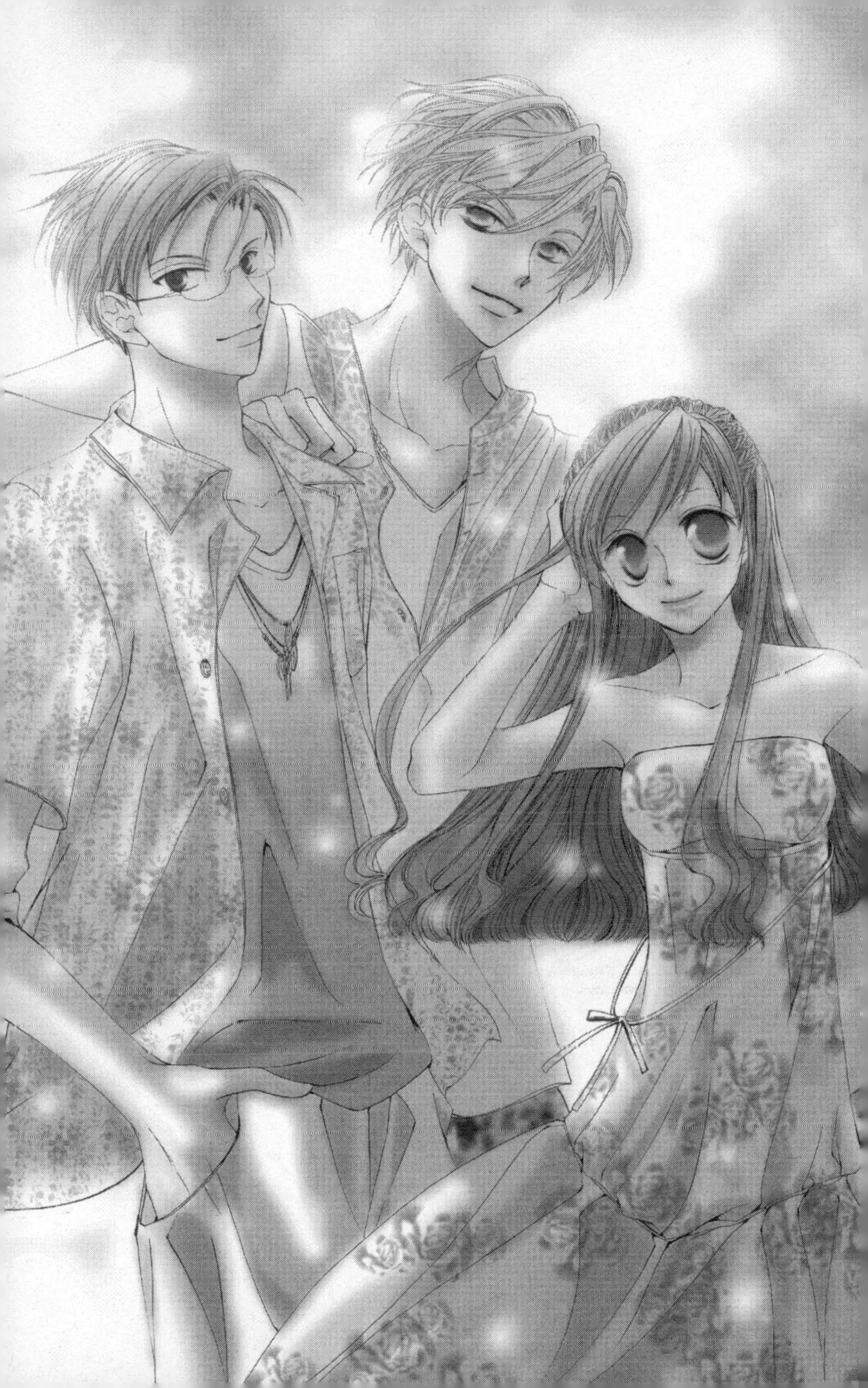

EXTRA

BESPECTACLED WITCH

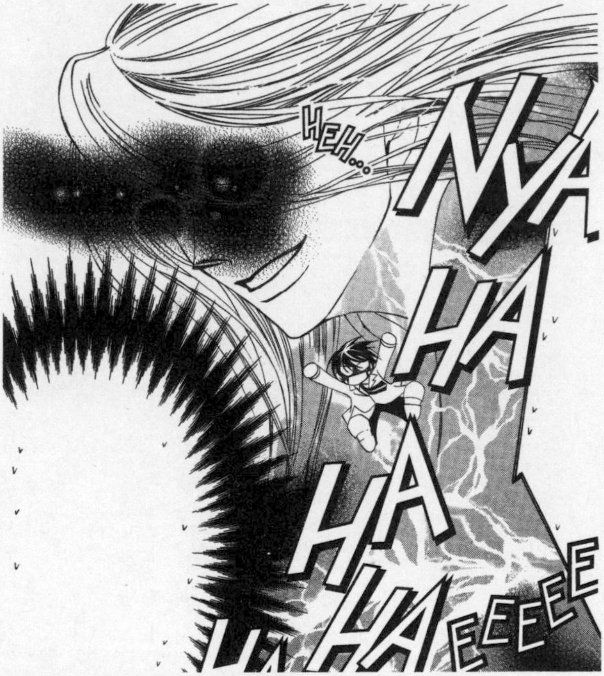
HEH...
NYA HA HA HA HA EEEEE

THIS IS WHAT HAPPENED WHEN I WAS TESTING FOR PLACEMENT OF SOME SCREENTONES. I MADE A COPY OF IT, AND JUST NOW I FOUND IT AGAIN, SO HERE IT IS. I HOPE IT'LL PRINT OKAY.

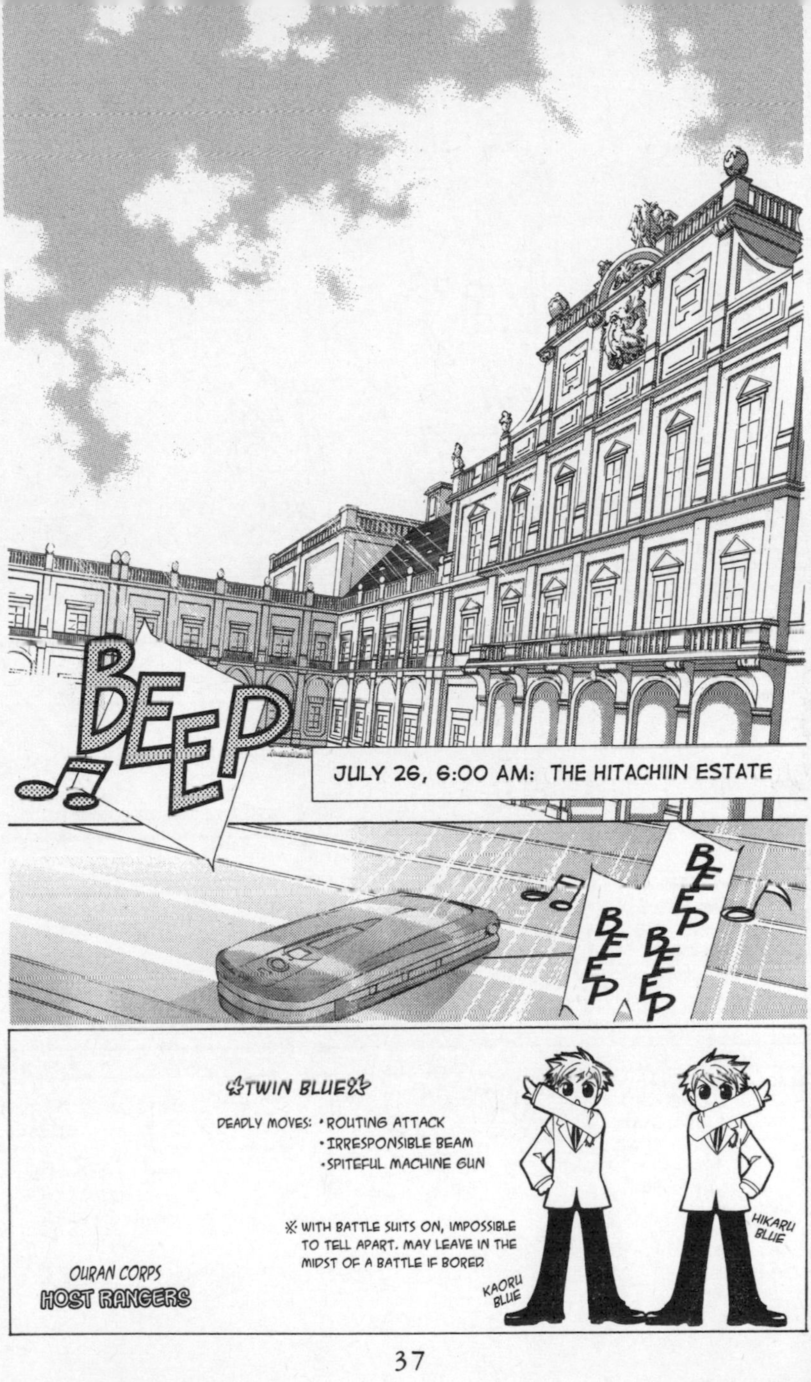
JULY 26, 6:00 AM: THE HITACHIIN ESTATE
BEEP
BEEP
BEEP
BEEP
BEEP
TWIN BLUE
DEADLY MOVES: • ROUTING ATTACK
• IRRESPONSIBLE BEAM
• SPITEFUL MACHINE GUN
HIKARU BLUE
KAORU BLUE
※ WITH BATTLE SUITS ON, IMPOSSIBLE TO TELL APART. MAY LEAVE IN THE MIDST OF A BATTLE IF BORED.
OURAN CORPS
HOST RANGERS

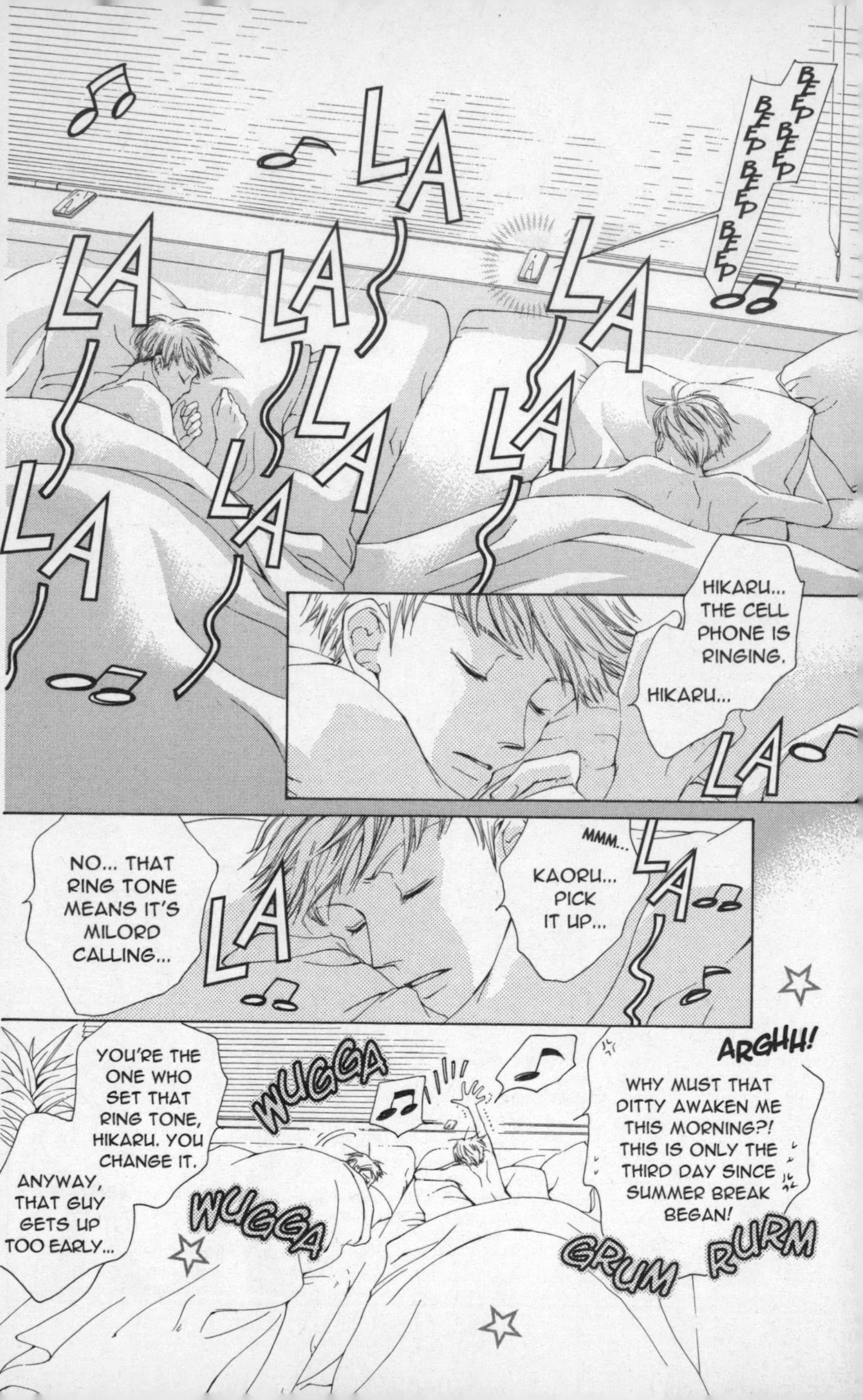
BEEP BEEP BEEP BEEP BEEP BEEP
LA LA LA LA LA LA LA LA LA
HIKARU... THE CELL PHONE IS RINGING.
HIKARU...
LA
MMM...
KAORU... PICK IT UP...
LA
NO... THAT RING TONE MEANS IT'S MILORD CALLING...
LA
ARGHH!
WHY MUST THAT DITTY AWAKEN ME THIS MORNING?! THIS IS ONLY THE THIRD DAY SINCE SUMMER BREAK BEGAN!
GRUM RURM
YOU'RE THE ONE WHO SET THAT RING TONE, HIKARU. YOU CHANGE IT.
ANYWAY, THAT GUY GETS UP TOO EARLY...
WUGGA
WUGGA

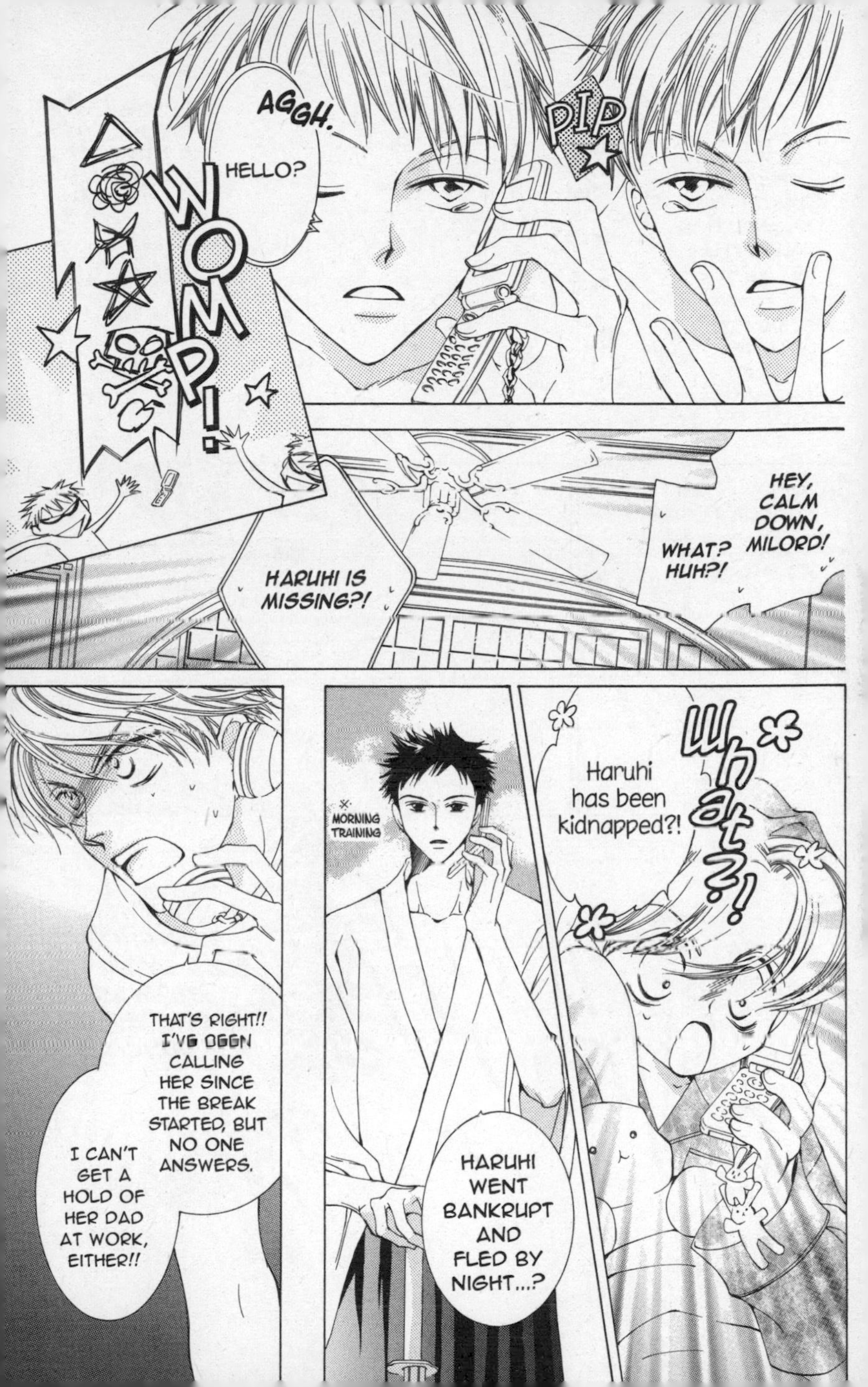
PIP
AGGH.
HELLO?
WOMP!
HEY, CALM DOWN, MILORD!
WHAT? HUH?!
HARUHI IS MISSING?!
What?!
Haruhi has been kidnapped?!
※ MORNING TRAINING
HARUHI WENT BANKRUPT AND FLED BY NIGHT...?
THAT'S RIGHT!! I'VE BEEN CALLING HER SINCE THE BREAK STARTED, BUT NO ONE ANSWERS.
I CAN'T GET A HOLD OF HER DAD AT WORK, EITHER!!

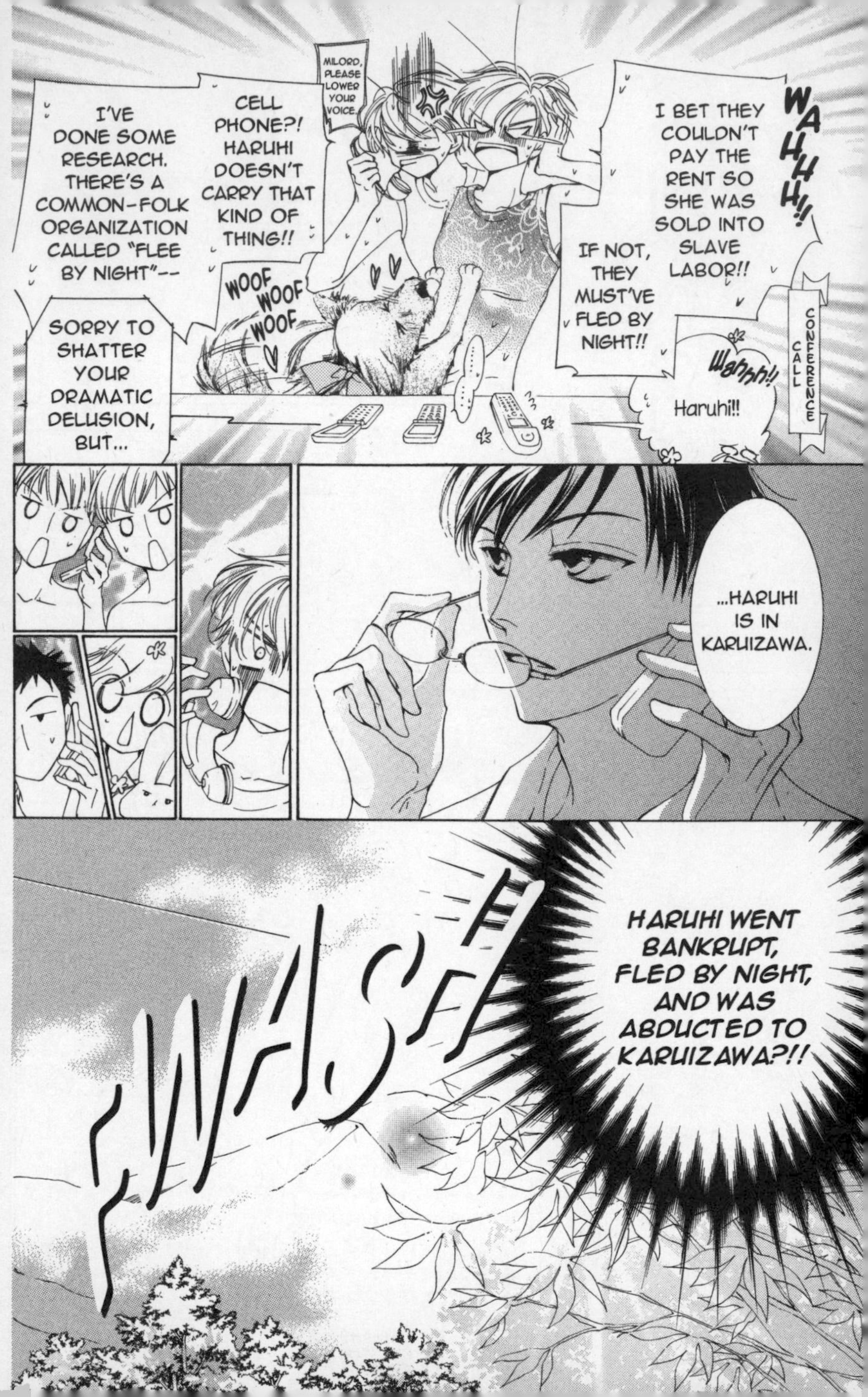
WAHHHH!!
I BET THEY COULDN'T PAY THE RENT SO SHE WAS SOLD INTO SLAVE LABOR!!
IF NOT, THEY MUST'VE FLED BY NIGHT!!
CONFERENCE CALL
Haruhi!!
MILORD, PLEASE LOWER YOUR VOICE.
CELL PHONE?! HARUHI DOESN'T CARRY THAT KIND OF THING!!
WOOF WOOF WOOF
I'VE DONE SOME RESEARCH. THERE'S A COMMON-FOLK ORGANIZATION CALLED "FLEE BY NIGHT"--
SORRY TO SHATTER YOUR DRAMATIC DELUSION, BUT...
...HARUHI IS IN KARUIZAWA.
HARUHI WENT BANKRUPT, FLED BY NIGHT, AND WAS ABDUCTED TO KARUIZAWA?!!

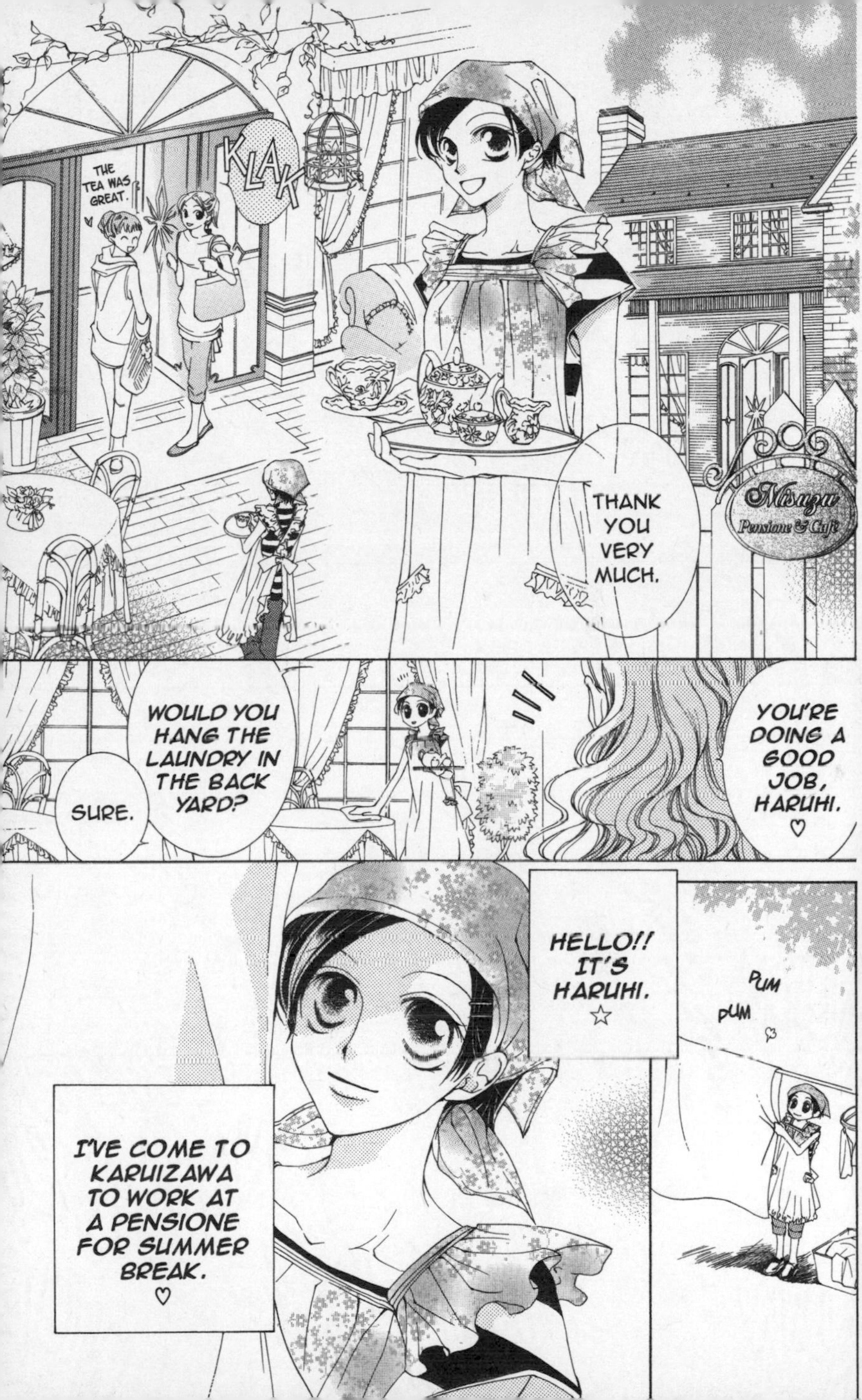
KLAK
THE TEA WAS GREAT.
Misuzu Pensione & Café
THANK YOU VERY MUCH.
YOU'RE DOING A GOOD JOB, HARUHI. ♡
WOULD YOU HANG THE LAUNDRY IN THE BACK YARD?
SURE.
PUM PUM
HELLO!! IT'S HARUHI. ☆
I'VE COME TO KARUIZAWA TO WORK AT A PENSIONE FOR SUMMER BREAK. ♡

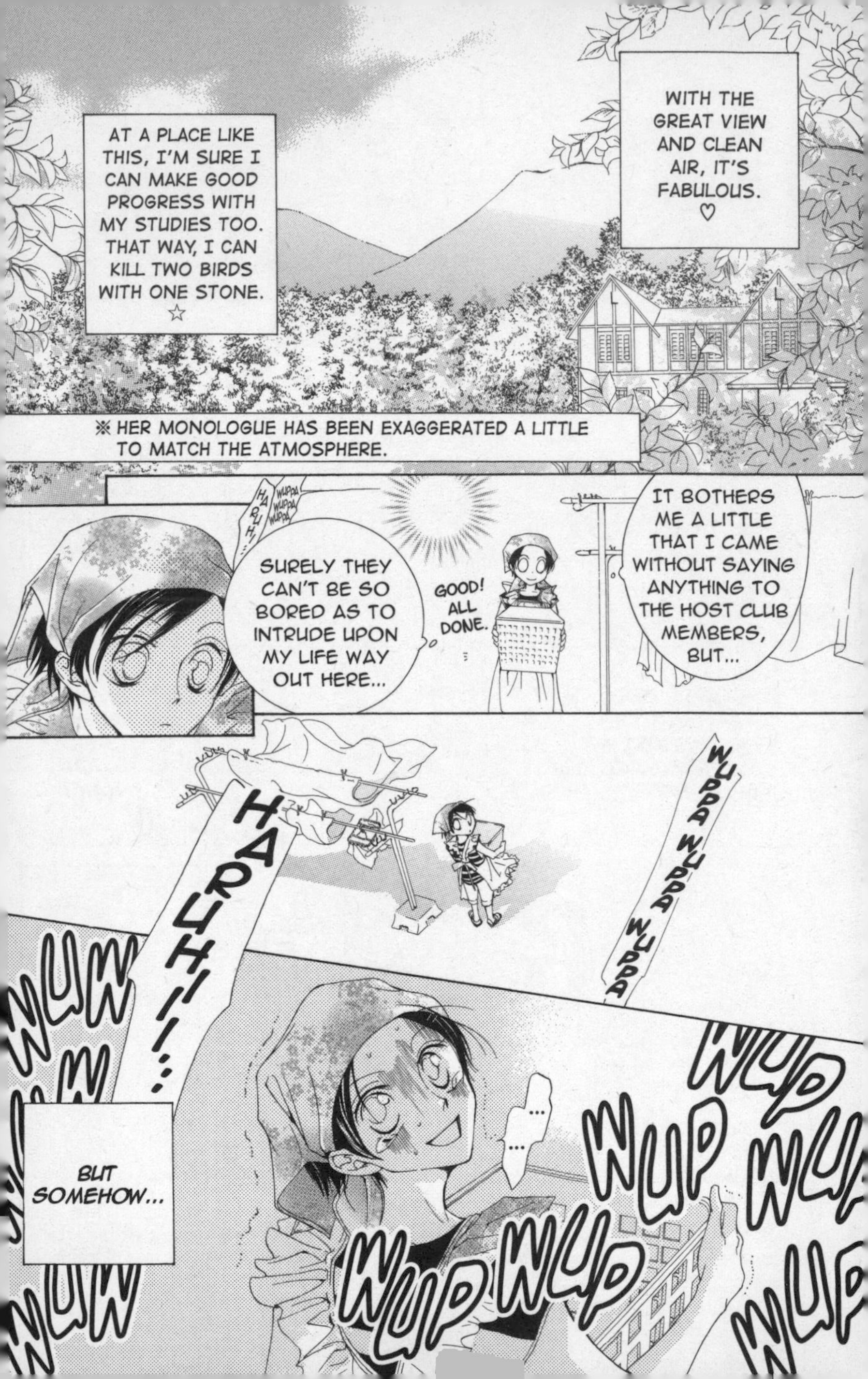

WITH THE GREAT VIEW AND CLEAN AIR, IT'S FABULOUS. ♡
AT A PLACE LIKE THIS, I'M SURE I CAN MAKE GOOD PROGRESS WITH MY STUDIES TOO. THAT WAY, I CAN KILL TWO BIRDS WITH ONE STONE. ☆
※ HER MONOLOGUE HAS BEEN EXAGGERATED A LITTLE TO MATCH THE ATMOSPHERE.
IT BOTHERS ME A LITTLE THAT I CAME WITHOUT SAYING ANYTHING TO THE HOST CLUB MEMBERS, BUT...
GOOD! ALL DONE.
SURELY THEY CAN'T BE SO BORED AS TO INTRUDE UPON MY LIFE WAY OUT HERE...
WUPPA WUPPA WUPPA
HARUHI...
WUPPA WUPPA WUPPA WUPPA
HARUHI...!
WUP WUP WUP WUP
...
...
WUP WUP WUP WUP
BUT SOMEHOW...
WUW WUW WUW

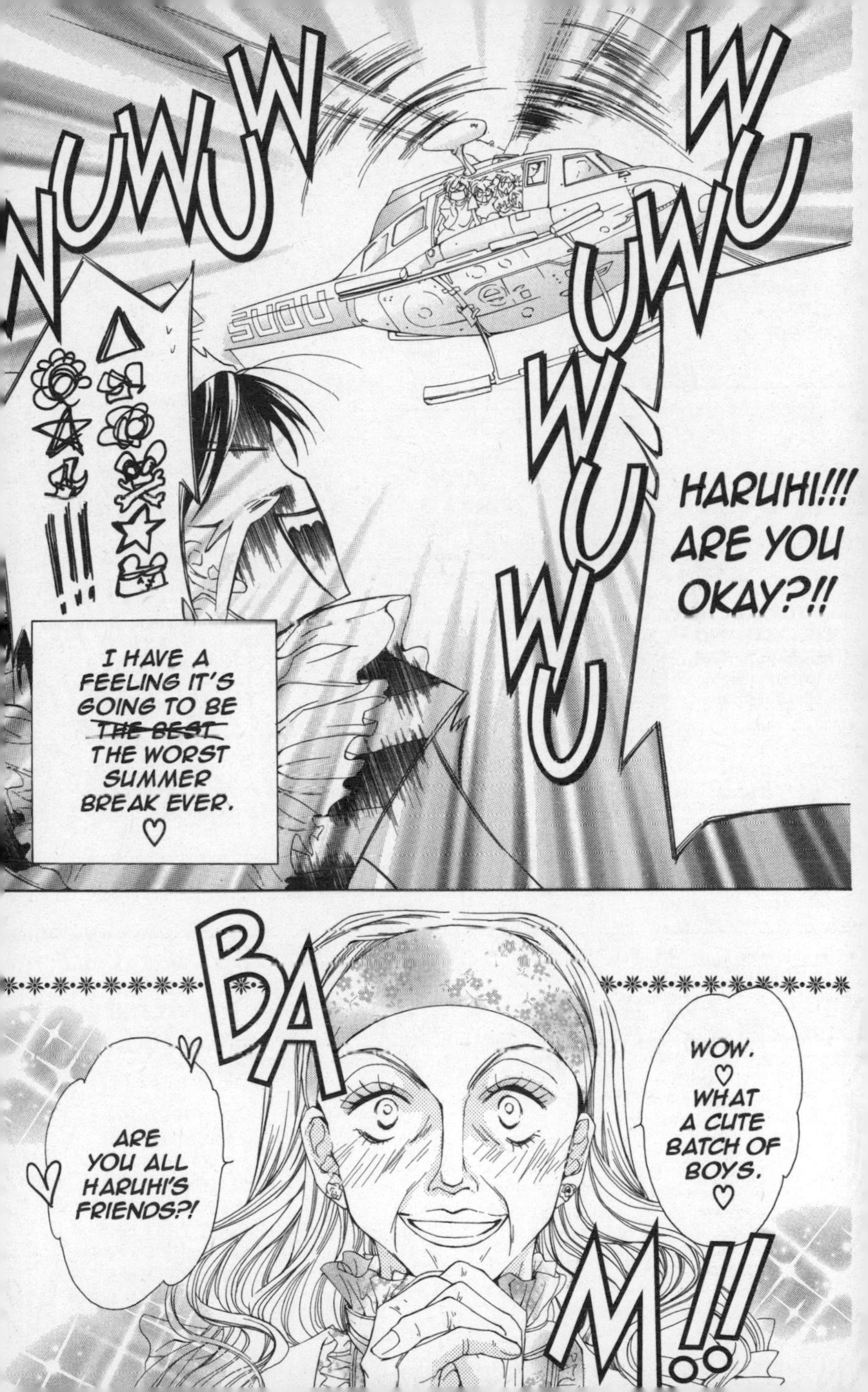
WUWUWUWU
HARUHI!!! ARE YOU OKAY?!!
WUWUW
!!!
I HAVE A FEELING IT'S GOING TO BE ~~THE BEST~~ THE WORST SUMMER BREAK EVER. ♡
BAM!!
WOW. ♡ WHAT A CUTE BATCH OF BOYS. ♡
ARE YOU ALL HARUHI'S FRIENDS?!

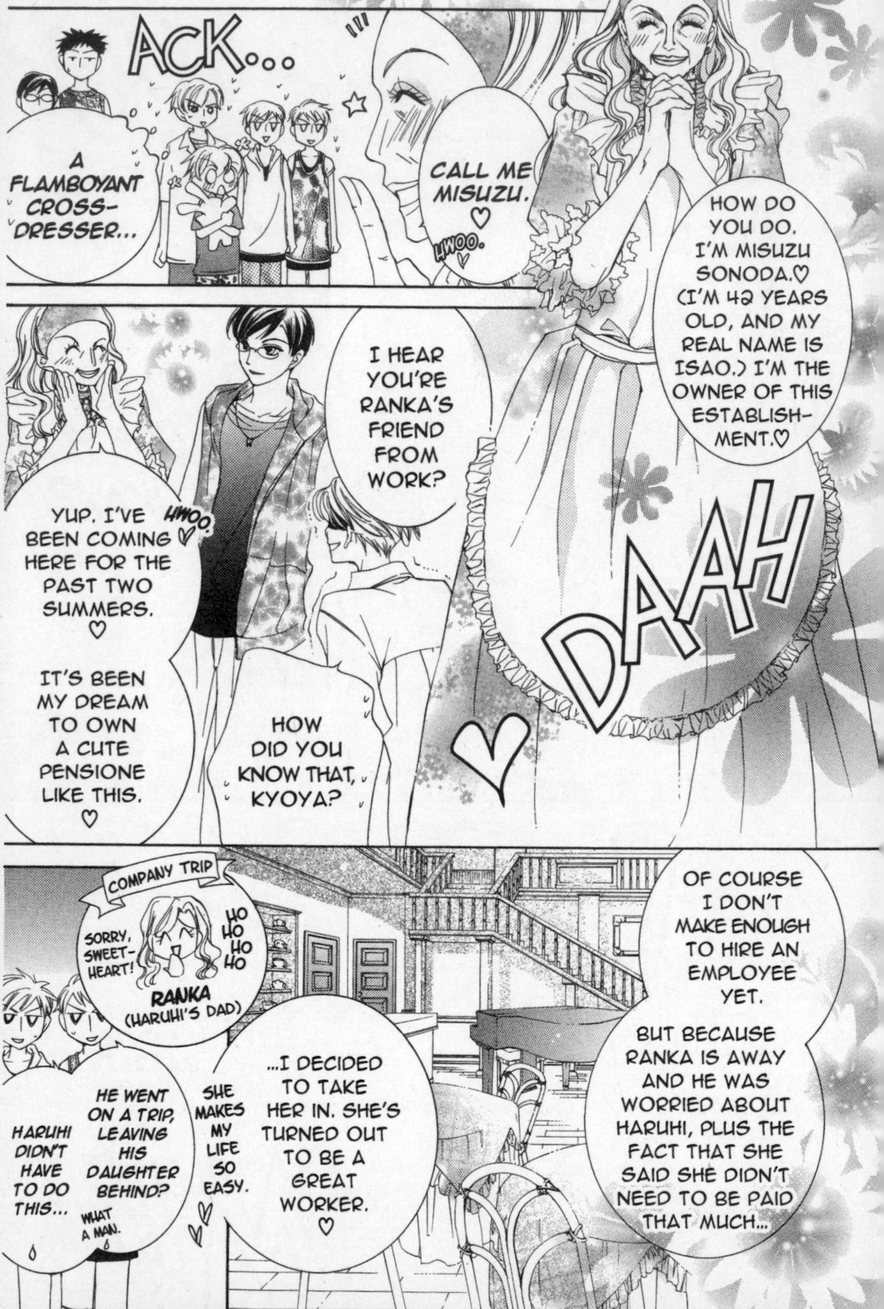

HOW DO YOU DO. I'M MISUZU SONODA.♡ (I'M 42 YEARS OLD, AND MY REAL NAME IS ISAO.) I'M THE OWNER OF THIS ESTABLISHMENT.♡
DAAH
♡
CALL ME MISUZU. ♡
HWOO. ♡
ACK...
A FLAMBOYANT CROSS-DRESSER...
I HEAR YOU'RE RANKA'S FRIEND FROM WORK?
YUP. I'VE BEEN COMING HERE FOR THE PAST TWO SUMMERS. ♡
HWOO. ♡
HOW DID YOU KNOW THAT, KYOYA?
IT'S BEEN MY DREAM TO OWN A CUTE PENSIONE LIKE THIS. ♡
OF COURSE I DON'T MAKE ENOUGH TO HIRE AN EMPLOYEE YET.
BUT BECAUSE RANKA IS AWAY AND HE WAS WORRIED ABOUT HARUHI, PLUS THE FACT THAT SHE SAID SHE DIDN'T NEED TO BE PAID THAT MUCH...
...I DECIDED TO TAKE HER IN. SHE'S TURNED OUT TO BE A GREAT WORKER. ♡
SHE MAKES MY LIFE SO EASY.
COMPANY TRIP
HO HO HO HO
SORRY, SWEET-HEART!
RANKA (HARUHI'S DAD)
HE WENT ON A TRIP, LEAVING HIS DAUGHTER BEHIND?
WHAT A MAN.
HARUHI DIDN'T HAVE TO DO THIS...

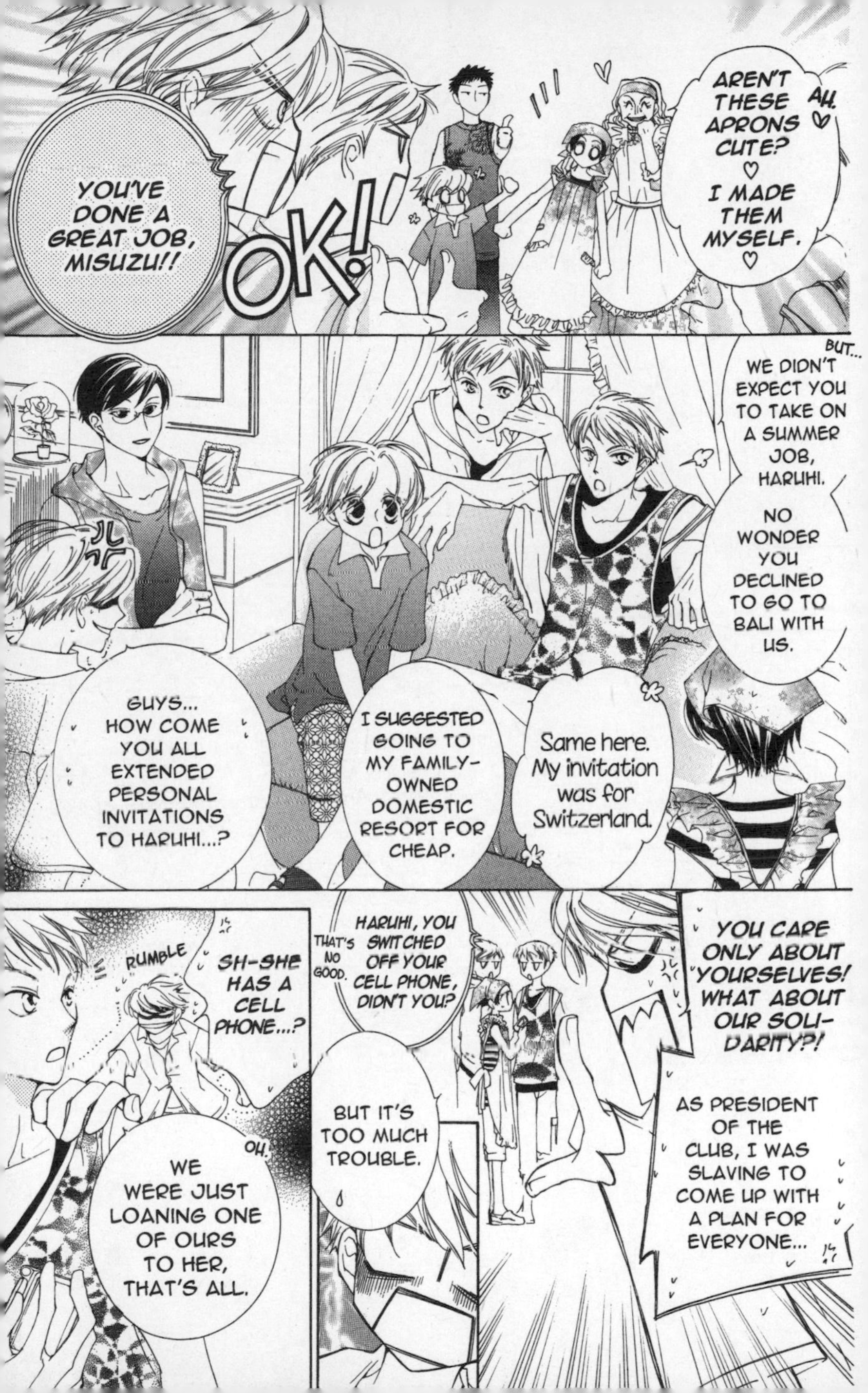

AREN'T THESE APRONS CUTE? ♡ I MADE THEM MYSELF. ♡
AH. ♡
OK!
YOU'VE DONE A GREAT JOB, MISUZU!!
BUT...
WE DIDN'T EXPECT YOU TO TAKE ON A SUMMER JOB, HARUHI.
NO WONDER YOU DECLINED TO GO TO BALI WITH US.
Same here. My invitation was for Switzerland.
I SUGGESTED GOING TO MY FAMILY-OWNED DOMESTIC RESORT FOR CHEAP.
GUYS... HOW COME YOU ALL EXTENDED PERSONAL INVITATIONS TO HARUHI...?
YOU CARE ONLY ABOUT YOURSELVES! WHAT ABOUT OUR SOLI-DARITY?!
AS PRESIDENT OF THE CLUB, I WAS SLAVING TO COME UP WITH A PLAN FOR EVERYONE...
HARUHI, YOU SWITCHED OFF YOUR CELL PHONE, DIDN'T YOU?
THAT'S NO GOOD.
BUT IT'S TOO MUCH TROUBLE.
SH-SHE HAS A CELL PHONE...?
RUMBLE
OH.
WE WERE JUST LOANING ONE OF OURS TO HER, THAT'S ALL.

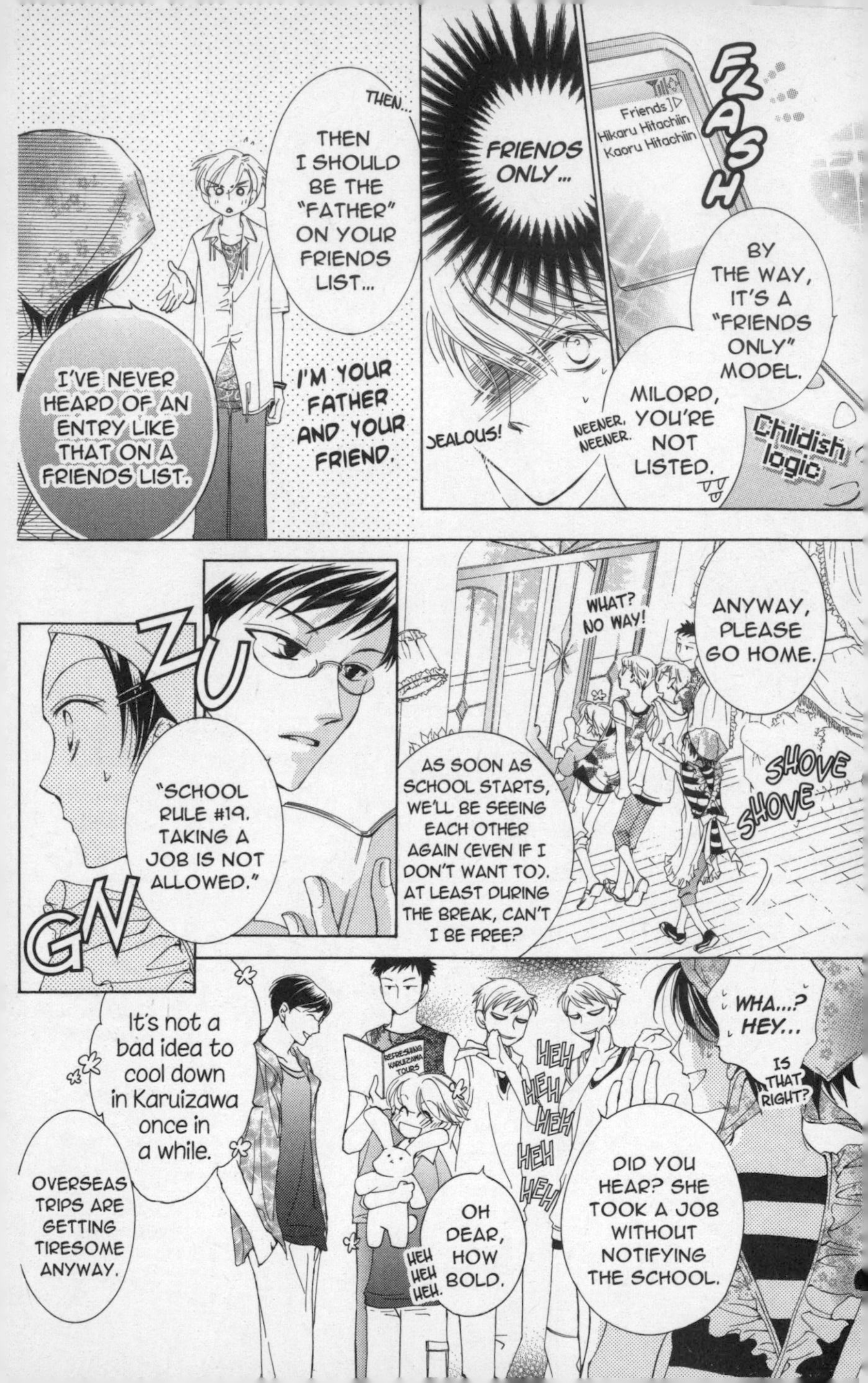
FLASH
Friends
Hikaru Hitachiin
Kaoru Hitachiin
FRIENDS ONLY...
BY THE WAY, IT'S A "FRIENDS ONLY" MODEL.
Childish logic
MILORD, YOU'RE NOT LISTED.
NEENER, NEENER.
JEALOUS!
THEN...
THEN I SHOULD BE THE "FATHER" ON YOUR FRIENDS LIST...
I'M YOUR FATHER AND YOUR FRIEND.
I'VE NEVER HEARD OF AN ENTRY LIKE THAT ON A FRIENDS LIST.
ANYWAY, PLEASE GO HOME.
WHAT? NO WAY!
SHOVE SHOVE
AS SOON AS SCHOOL STARTS, WE'LL BE SEEING EACH OTHER AGAIN (EVEN IF I DON'T WANT TO). AT LEAST DURING THE BREAK, CAN'T I BE FREE?
ZU
"SCHOOL RULE #19. TAKING A JOB IS NOT ALLOWED."
GN
WHA...? HEY...
IS THAT RIGHT?
DID YOU HEAR? SHE TOOK A JOB WITHOUT NOTIFYING THE SCHOOL.
HEH HEH HEH HEH HEH
OH DEAR, HOW BOLD.
HEH HEH HEH.
REFRESHING KARUIZAWA TOURS
It's not a bad idea to cool down in Karuizawa once in a while.
OVERSEAS TRIPS ARE GETTING TIRESOME ANYWAY.

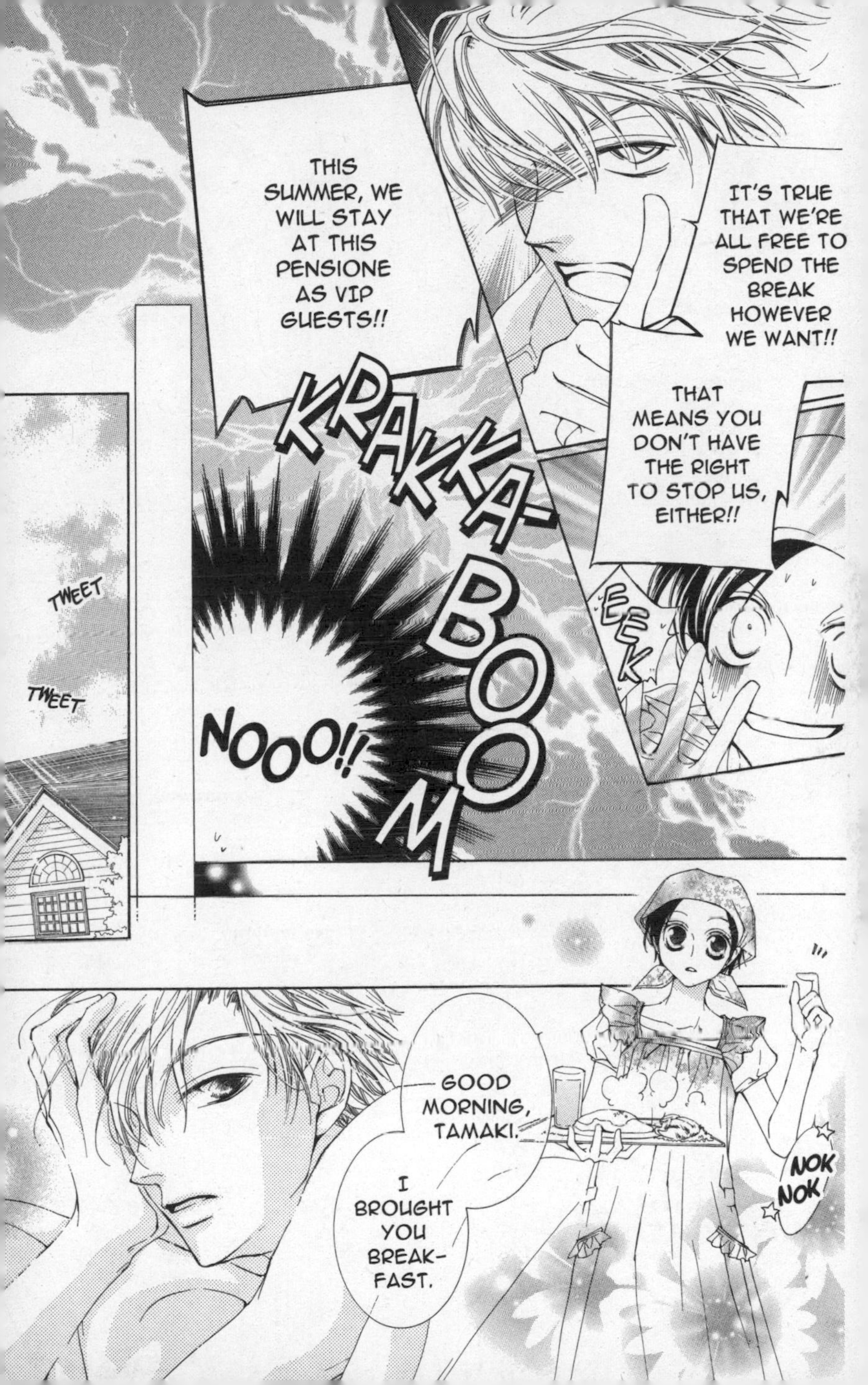
IT'S TRUE THAT WE'RE ALL FREE TO SPEND THE BREAK HOWEVER WE WANT!!
THAT MEANS YOU DON'T HAVE THE RIGHT TO STOP US, EITHER!!
EEK
THIS SUMMER, WE WILL STAY AT THIS PENSIONE AS VIP GUESTS!!
KRAKKA-BOOM
NOOO!!
TWEET
TWEET
NOK NOK
GOOD MORNING, TAMAKI.
I BROUGHT YOU BREAK-FAST.

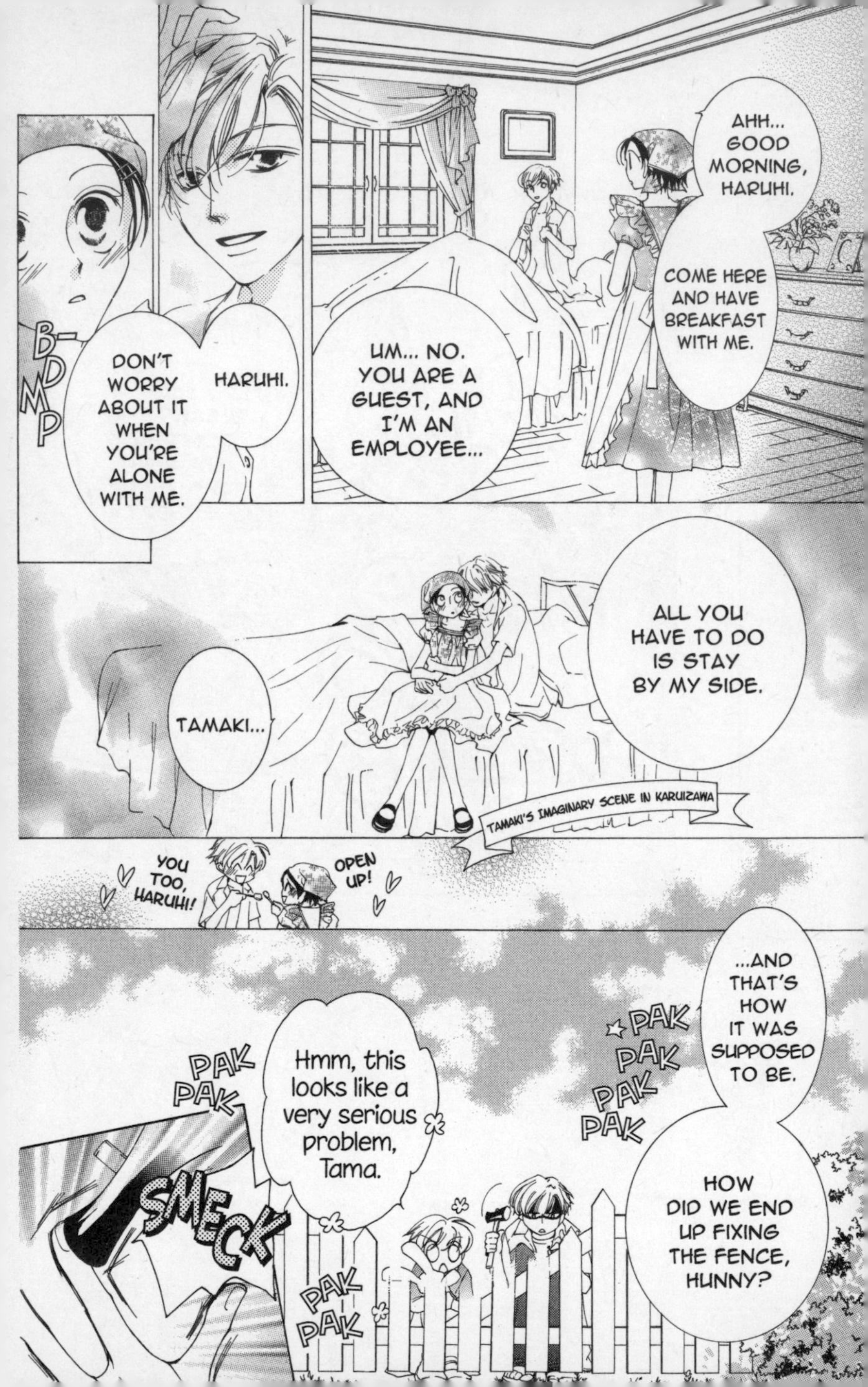
AHH... GOOD MORNING, HARUHI.
COME HERE AND HAVE BREAKFAST WITH ME.
UM... NO. YOU ARE A GUEST, AND I'M AN EMPLOYEE...
HARUHI.
DON'T WORRY ABOUT IT WHEN YOU'RE ALONE WITH ME.
B-DMP
ALL YOU HAVE TO DO IS STAY BY MY SIDE.
TAMAKI...
TAMAKI'S IMAGINARY SCENE IN KARUIZAWA
OPEN UP!
YOU TOO, HARUHI!
...AND THAT'S HOW IT WAS SUPPOSED TO BE.
HOW DID WE END UP FIXING THE FENCE, HUNNY?
PAK PAK PAK PAK
Hmm, this looks like a very serious problem, Tama.
PAK PAK
SMECK
PAK PAK

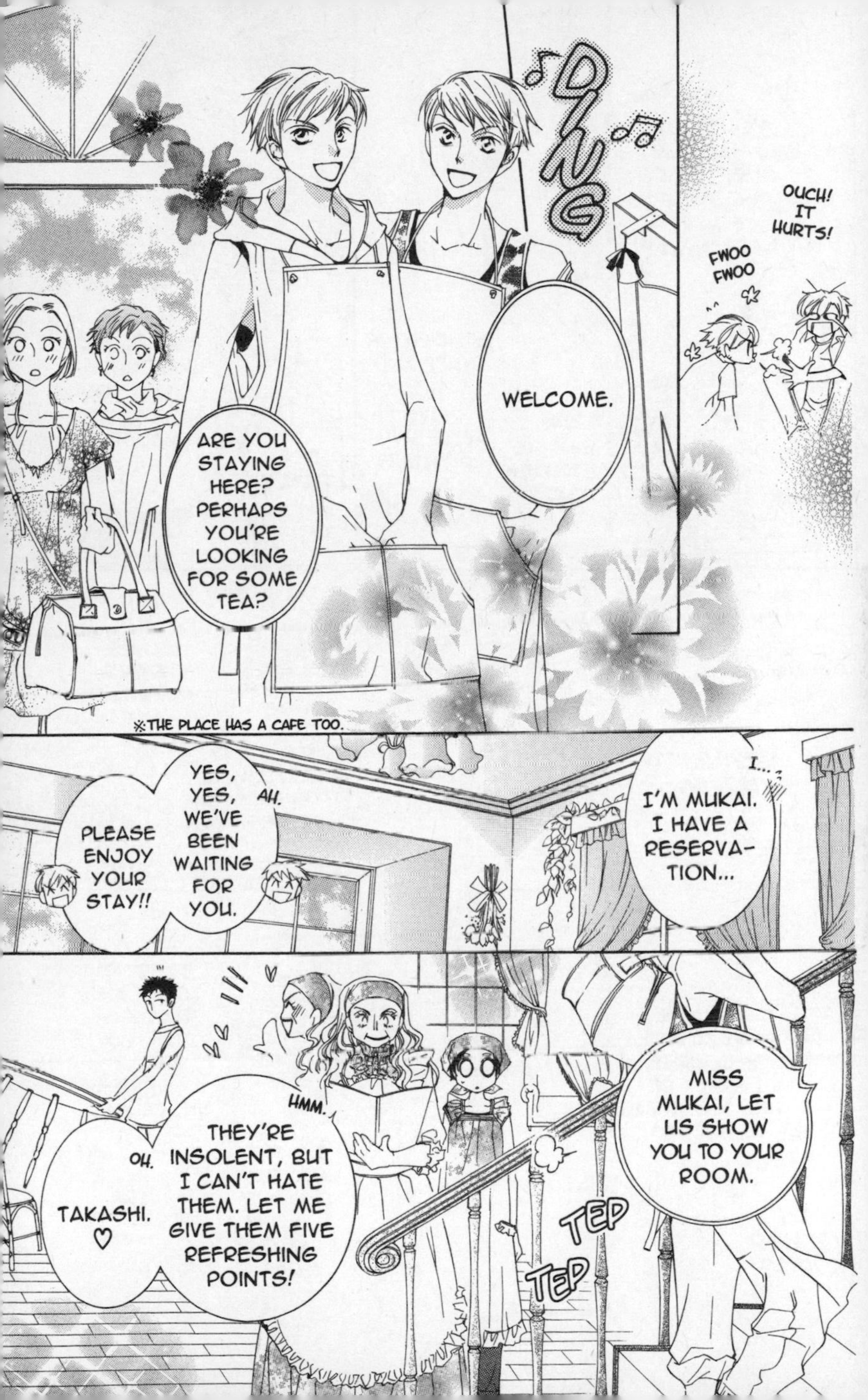
OUCH! IT HURTS!
FWOO FWOO
DING
WELCOME.
ARE YOU STAYING HERE? PERHAPS YOU'RE LOOKING FOR SOME TEA?
※THE PLACE HAS A CAFE TOO.
I...
I'M MUKAI. I HAVE A RESERVATION...
AH.
YES, YES, WE'VE BEEN WAITING FOR YOU.
PLEASE ENJOY YOUR STAY!!
MISS MUKAI, LET US SHOW YOU TO YOUR ROOM.
TEP
TEP
HMM.
THEY'RE INSOLENT, BUT I CAN'T HATE THEM. LET ME GIVE THEM FIVE REFRESHING POINTS!
OH.
TAKASHI. ♡

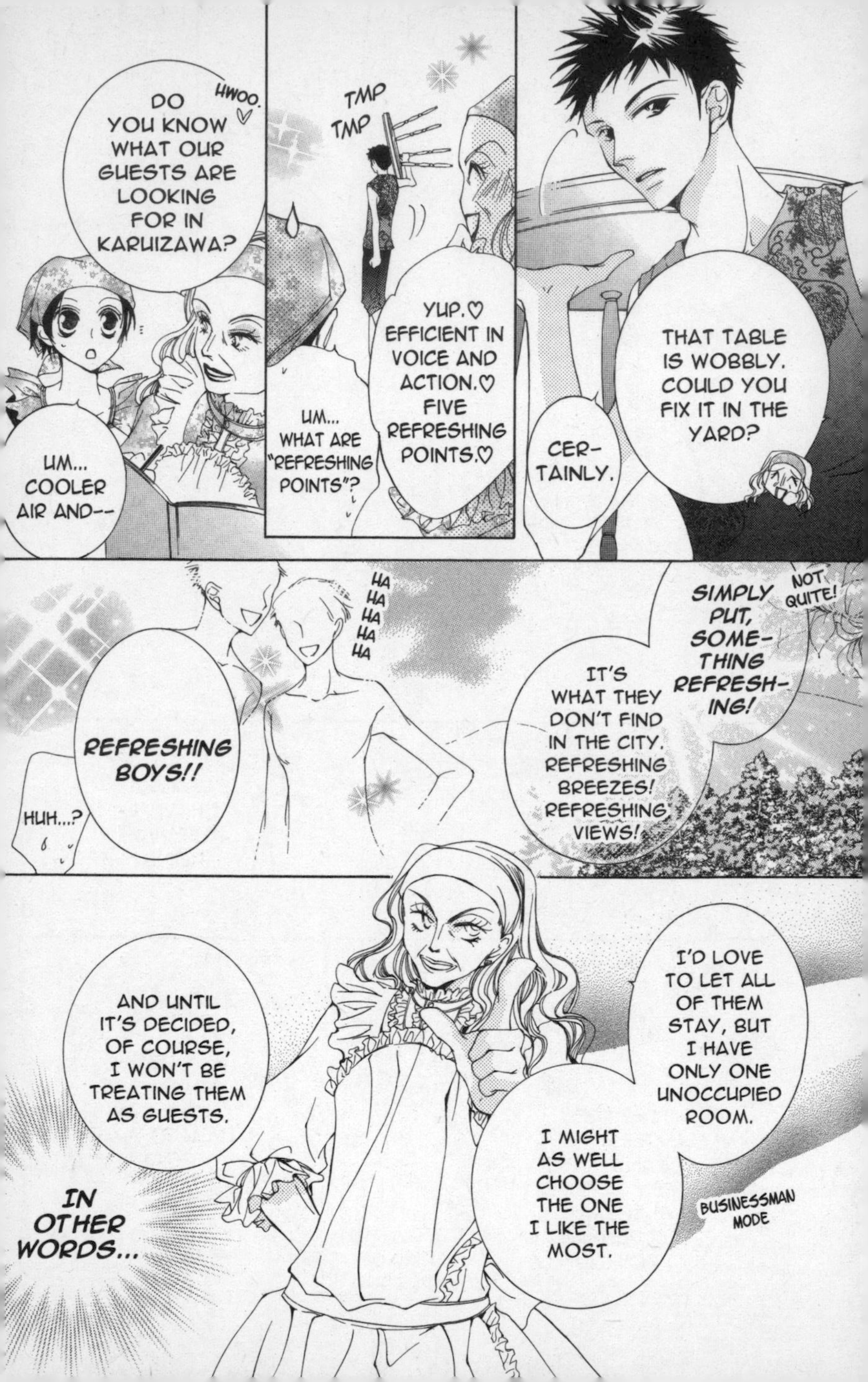

THAT TABLE IS WOBBLY. COULD YOU FIX IT IN THE YARD?
CER-TAINLY.
TMP TMP
YUP.♡ EFFICIENT IN VOICE AND ACTION.♡ FIVE REFRESHING POINTS.♡
UM... WHAT ARE "REFRESHING POINTS"?
HWOO.♡
DO YOU KNOW WHAT OUR GUESTS ARE LOOKING FOR IN KARUIZAWA?
UM... COOLER AIR AND--
NOT QUITE!
SIMPLY PUT, SOME-THING REFRESH-ING!
IT'S WHAT THEY DON'T FIND IN THE CITY. REFRESHING BREEZES! REFRESHING VIEWS!
HA HA HA HA HA
REFRESHING BOYS!!
HUH...?
I'D LOVE TO LET ALL OF THEM STAY, BUT I HAVE ONLY ONE UNOCCUPIED ROOM.
BUSINESSMAN MODE
I MIGHT AS WELL CHOOSE THE ONE I LIKE THE MOST.
AND UNTIL IT'S DECIDED, OF COURSE, I WON'T BE TREATING THEM AS GUESTS.
IN OTHER WORDS...

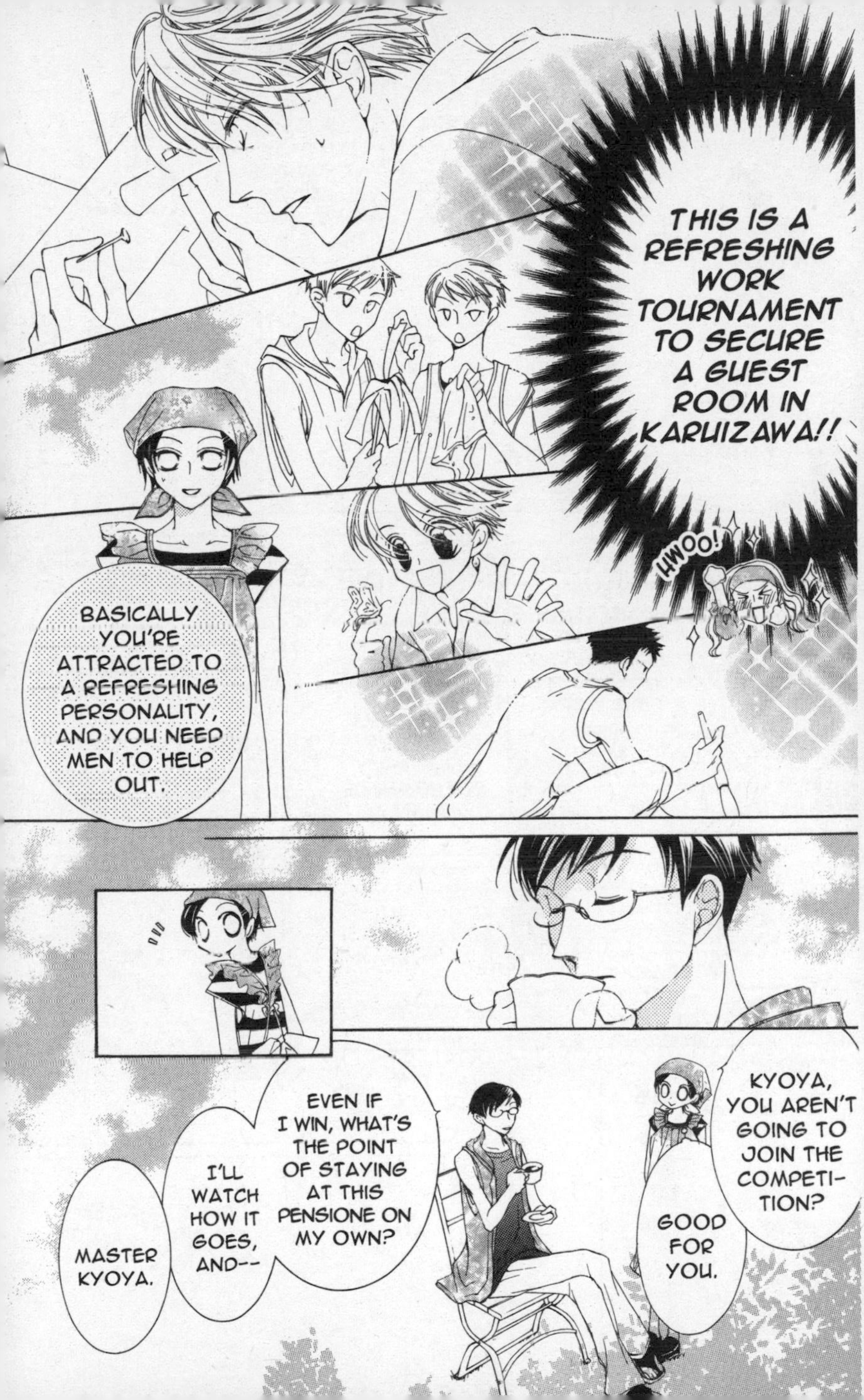
THIS IS A REFRESHING WORK TOURNAMENT TO SECURE A GUEST ROOM IN KARUIZAWA!!
HWOO!
BASICALLY YOU'RE ATTRACTED TO A REFRESHING PERSONALITY, AND YOU NEED MEN TO HELP OUT.
KYOYA, YOU AREN'T GOING TO JOIN THE COMPETITION?
GOOD FOR YOU.
EVEN IF I WIN, WHAT'S THE POINT OF STAYING AT THIS PENSIONE ON MY OWN?
I'LL WATCH HOW IT GOES, AND--
MASTER KYOYA.

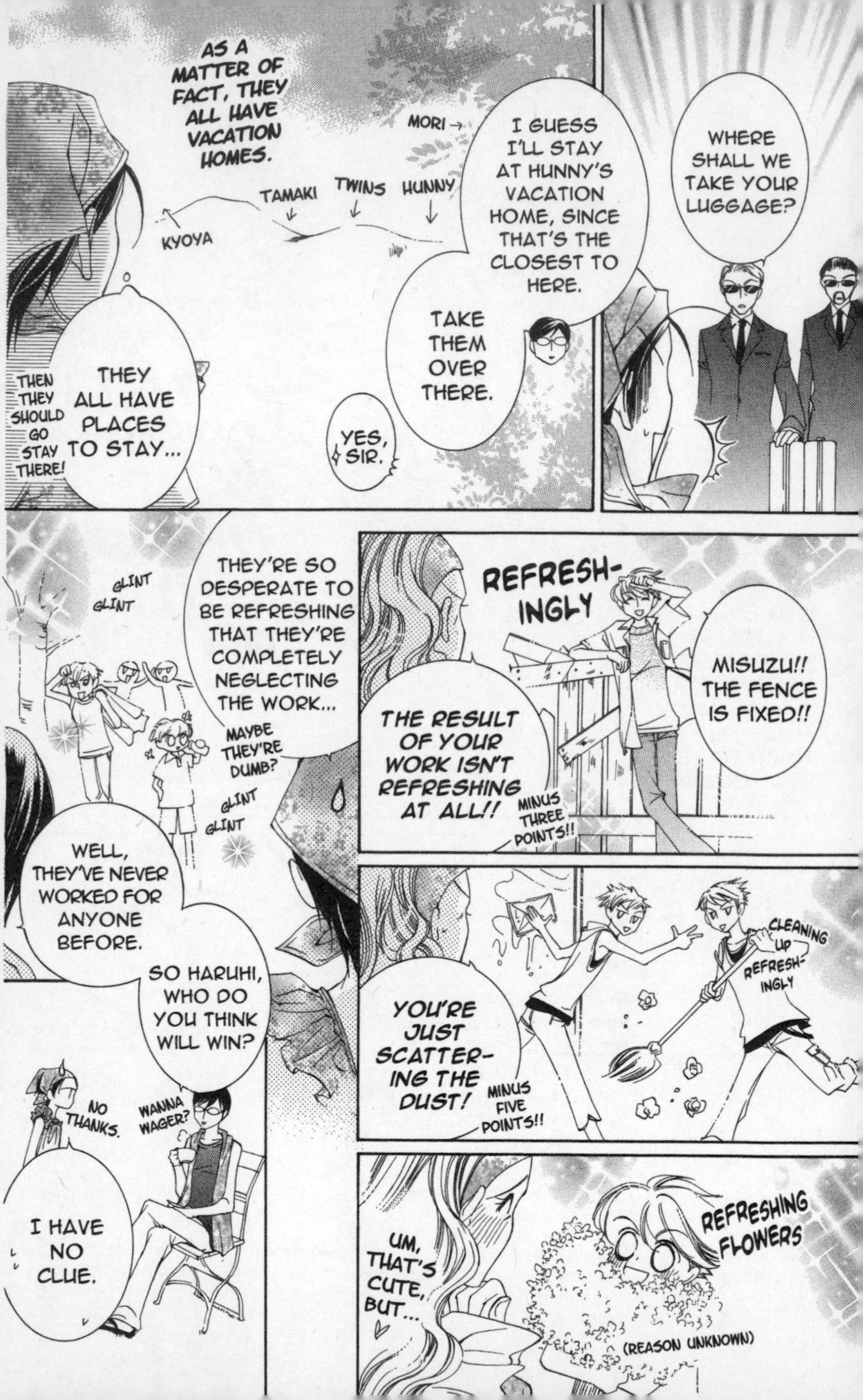
WHERE SHALL WE TAKE YOUR LUGGAGE?
AS A MATTER OF FACT, THEY ALL HAVE VACATION HOMES.
MORI →
HUNNY
TWINS
TAMAKI
KYOYA
I GUESS I'LL STAY AT HUNNY'S VACATION HOME, SINCE THAT'S THE CLOSEST TO HERE.
TAKE THEM OVER THERE.
YES, SIR.
THEY ALL HAVE PLACES TO STAY...
THEN THEY SHOULD GO STAY THERE!
REFRESH-INGLY
MISUZU!! THE FENCE IS FIXED!!
THE RESULT OF YOUR WORK ISN'T REFRESHING AT ALL!!
MINUS THREE POINTS!!
CLEANING UP REFRESH-INGLY
YOU'RE JUST SCATTER-ING THE DUST!
MINUS FIVE POINTS!!
REFRESHING FLOWERS
UM, THAT'S CUTE, BUT...
(REASON UNKNOWN)
THEY'RE SO DESPERATE TO BE REFRESHING THAT THEY'RE COMPLETELY NEGLECTING THE WORK...
GLINT GLINT
MAYBE THEY'RE DUMB?
GLINT GLINT
WELL, THEY'VE NEVER WORKED FOR ANYONE BEFORE.
SO HARUHI, WHO DO YOU THINK WILL WIN?
WANNA WAGER?
NO THANKS.
I HAVE NO CLUE.

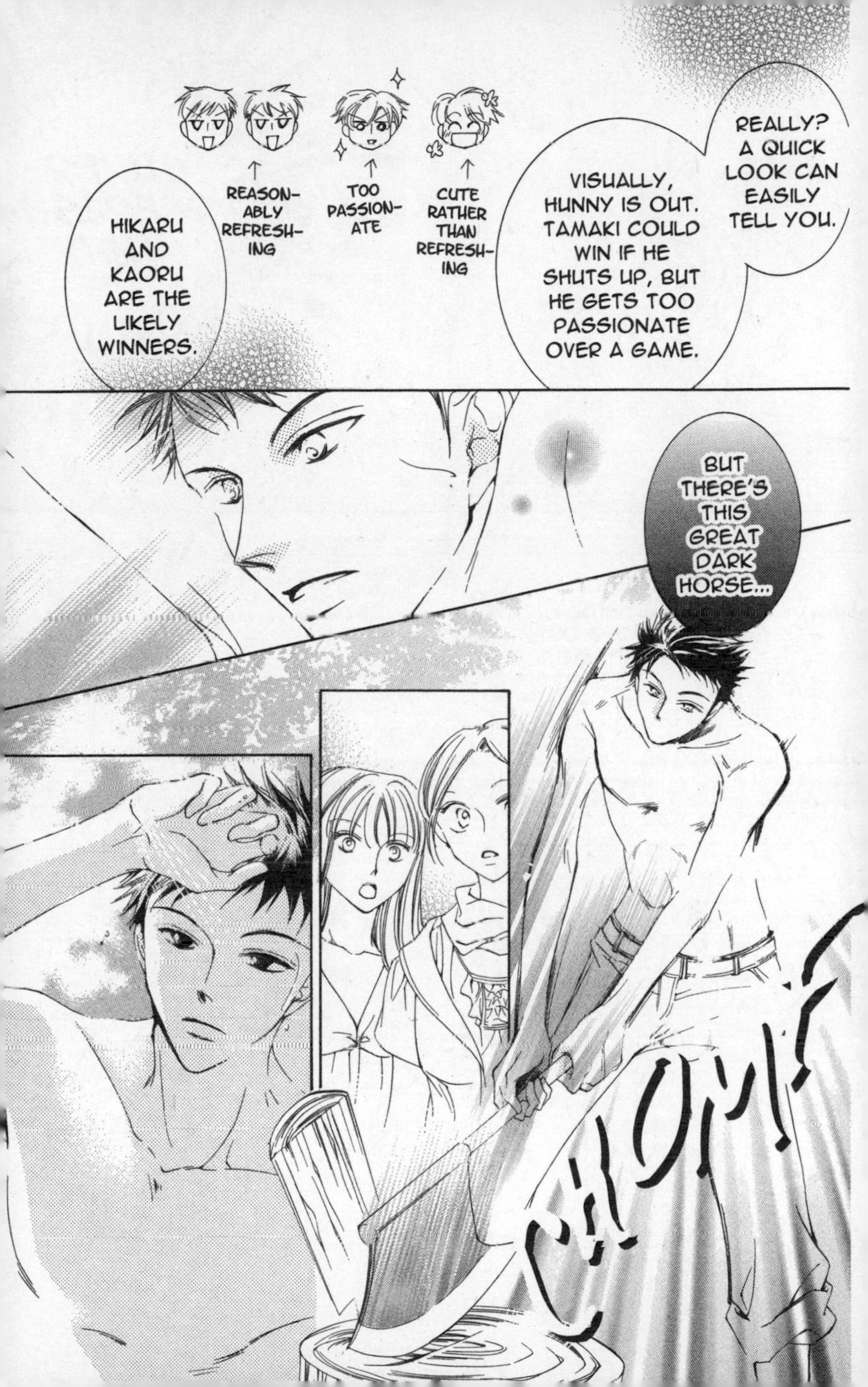
REALLY? A QUICK LOOK CAN EASILY TELL YOU.
VISUALLY, HUNNY IS OUT. TAMAKI COULD WIN IF HE SHUTS UP, BUT HE GETS TOO PASSIONATE OVER A GAME.
CUTE RATHER THAN REFRESH-ING
TOO PASSION-ATE
REASON-ABLY REFRESH-ING
HIKARU AND KAORU ARE THE LIKELY WINNERS.
BUT THERE'S THIS GREAT DARK HORSE...
CHOMP!

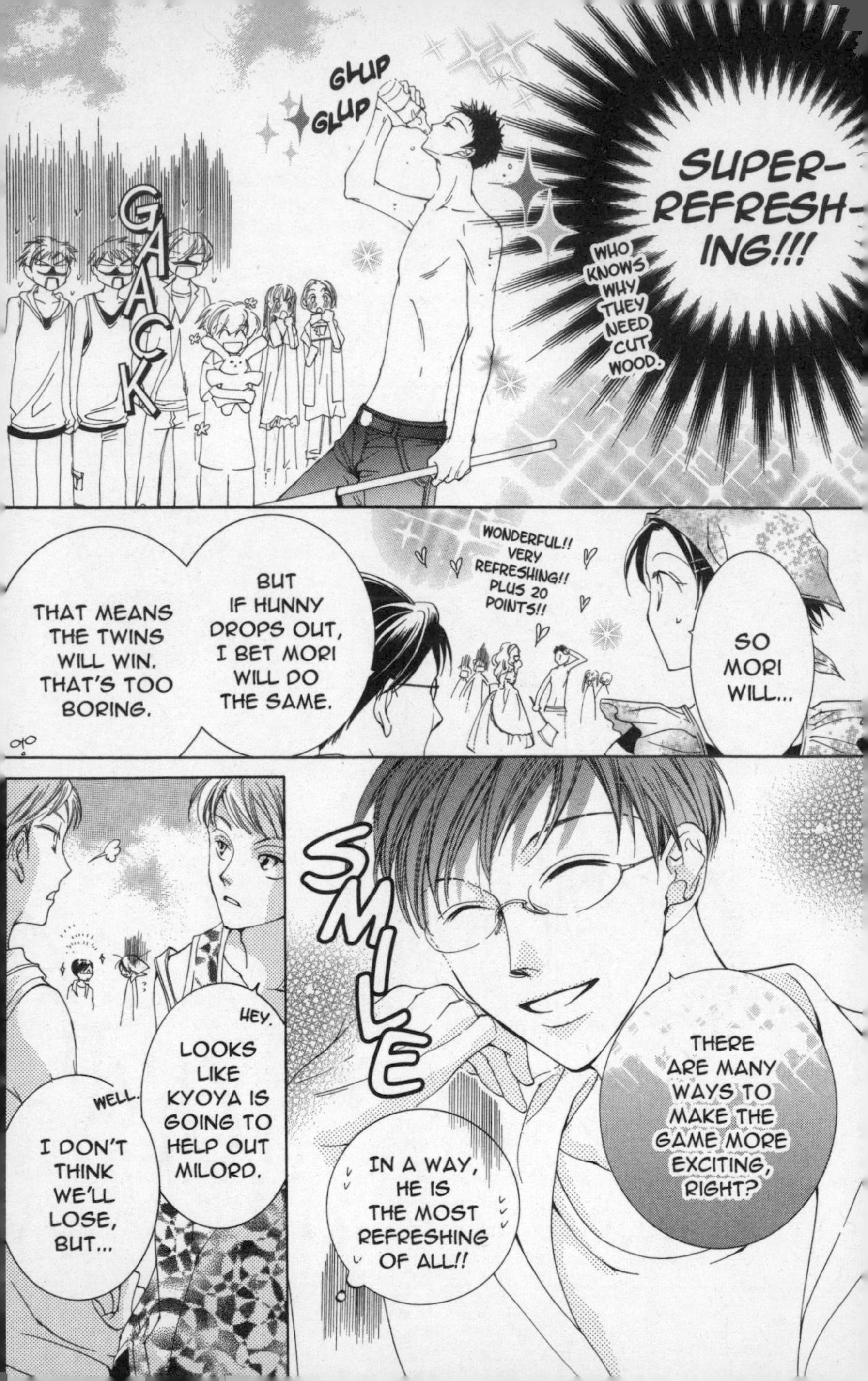
GLUP GLUP
SUPER-REFRESHING!!!
WHO KNOWS WHY THEY NEED CUT WOOD.
GACK
SO MORI WILL...
WONDERFUL!! VERY REFRESHING!! PLUS 20 POINTS!!
BUT IF HUNNY DROPS OUT, I BET MORI WILL DO THE SAME.
THAT MEANS THE TWINS WILL WIN. THAT'S TOO BORING.
SMILE
THERE ARE MANY WAYS TO MAKE THE GAME MORE EXCITING, RIGHT?
IN A WAY, HE IS THE MOST REFRESHING OF ALL!!
HEY.
LOOKS LIKE KYOYA IS GOING TO HELP OUT MILORD.
WELL.
I DON'T THINK WE'LL LOSE, BUT...

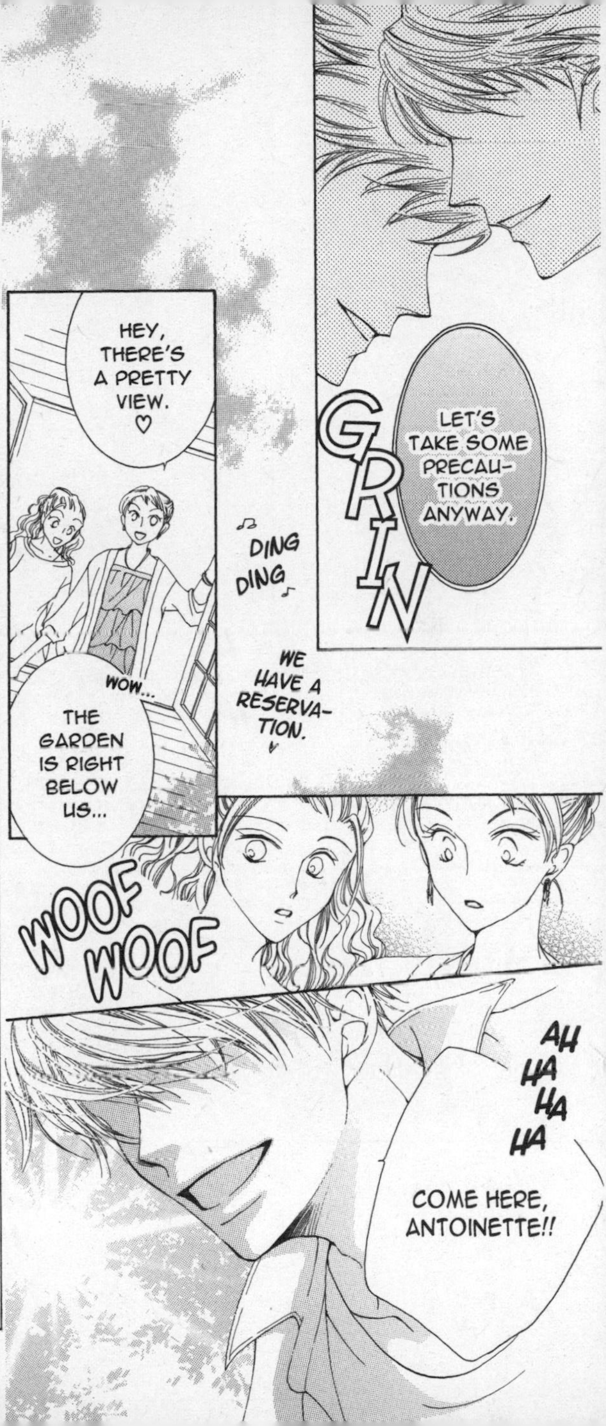
GRIN
LET'S TAKE SOME PRECAU-TIONS ANYWAY.
DING DING
WE HAVE A RESERVA-TION.
HEY, THERE'S A PRETTY VIEW. ♡
WOW...
THE GARDEN IS RIGHT BELOW US...
WOOF WOOF
AH HA HA HA
COME HERE, ANTOINETTE!!

2

✿I GET A LOT OF LETTERS WITH "AT FIRST THE TITLE SCARED ME OFF--SORRY!" BUT IT DOESN'T BOTHER ME. DON'T WORRY, IT'S NO PROBLEM!!

OCCASIONALLY, AT THE END OF THE SAME PARAGRAPH WITH THAT LINE, THERE'S "BECAUSE OF THE TITLE, I THOUGHT IT WAS A YAOI MANGA." WHAT?!

DOES "HOST CLUB"= "BOYS LOVE"? DOESN'T IT SOUND MORE LIKE A BUNCH OF BOYS FOR THE GIRLS' BENEFIT?

MAYBE "HOST CLUB"= "LOTS OF BOYS"= "BOYS LOVE." UM... SO ALL RIGHT! I THINK I GET IT NOW (LAUGH)! THAT'S WHAT THE TITLE MEANS!! (I'M KIDDING.)

✿ALSO THERE'S A CORRECTION I HAVE TO MAKE FOR "I LOVE THE WARM COLORS YOU USE. IT'S AMAZING YOU CAN HAND-PAINT LIKE THAT!" ...

I'M SORRY. IT'S DONE IN CG!!!

WAHH!!

← CONTINUES IN 3

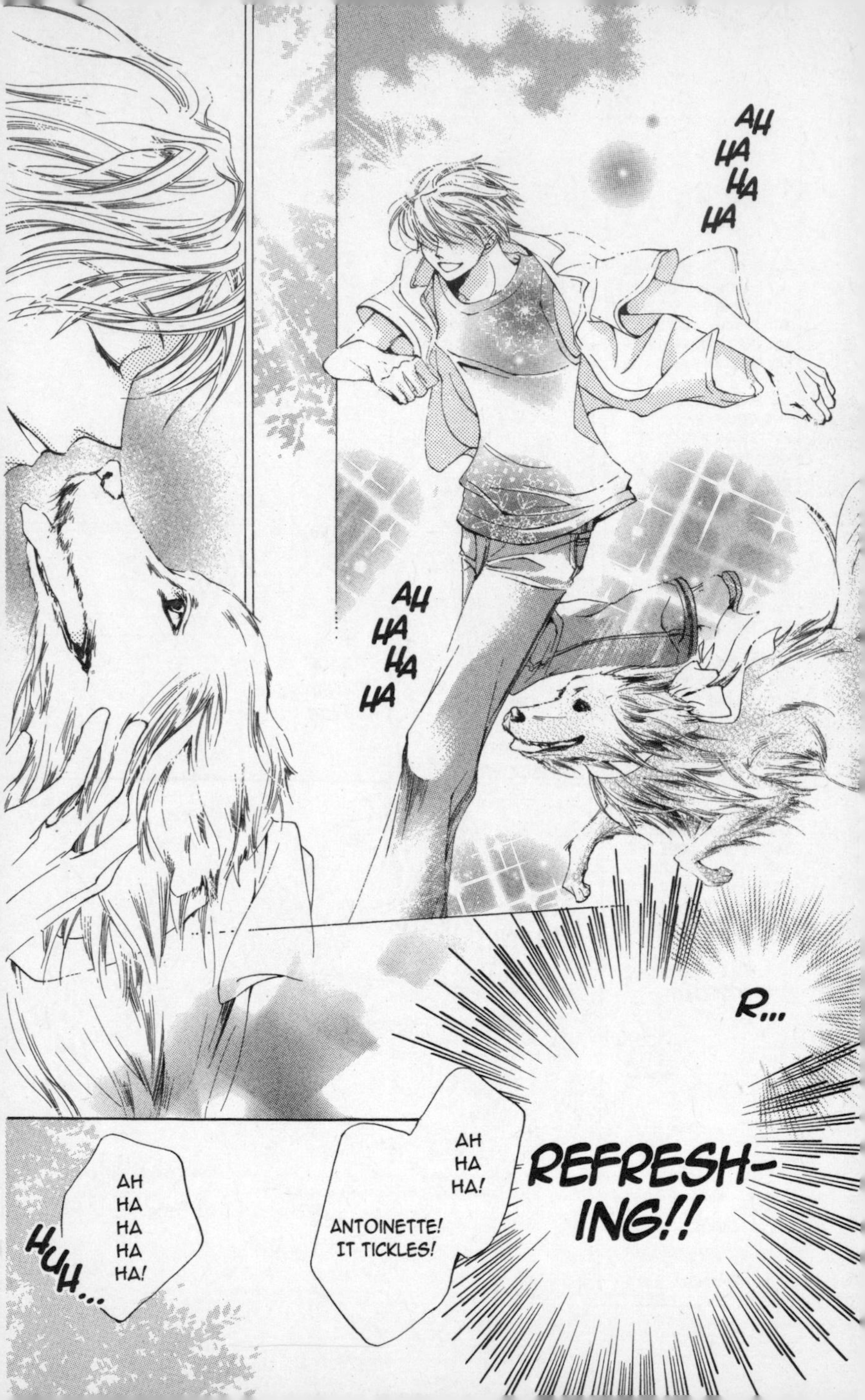
AH HA HA HA
AH HA HA HA
R...
REFRESH-ING!!
AH HA HA!
ANTOINETTE! IT TICKLES!
AH HA HA HA HA!
HUH...

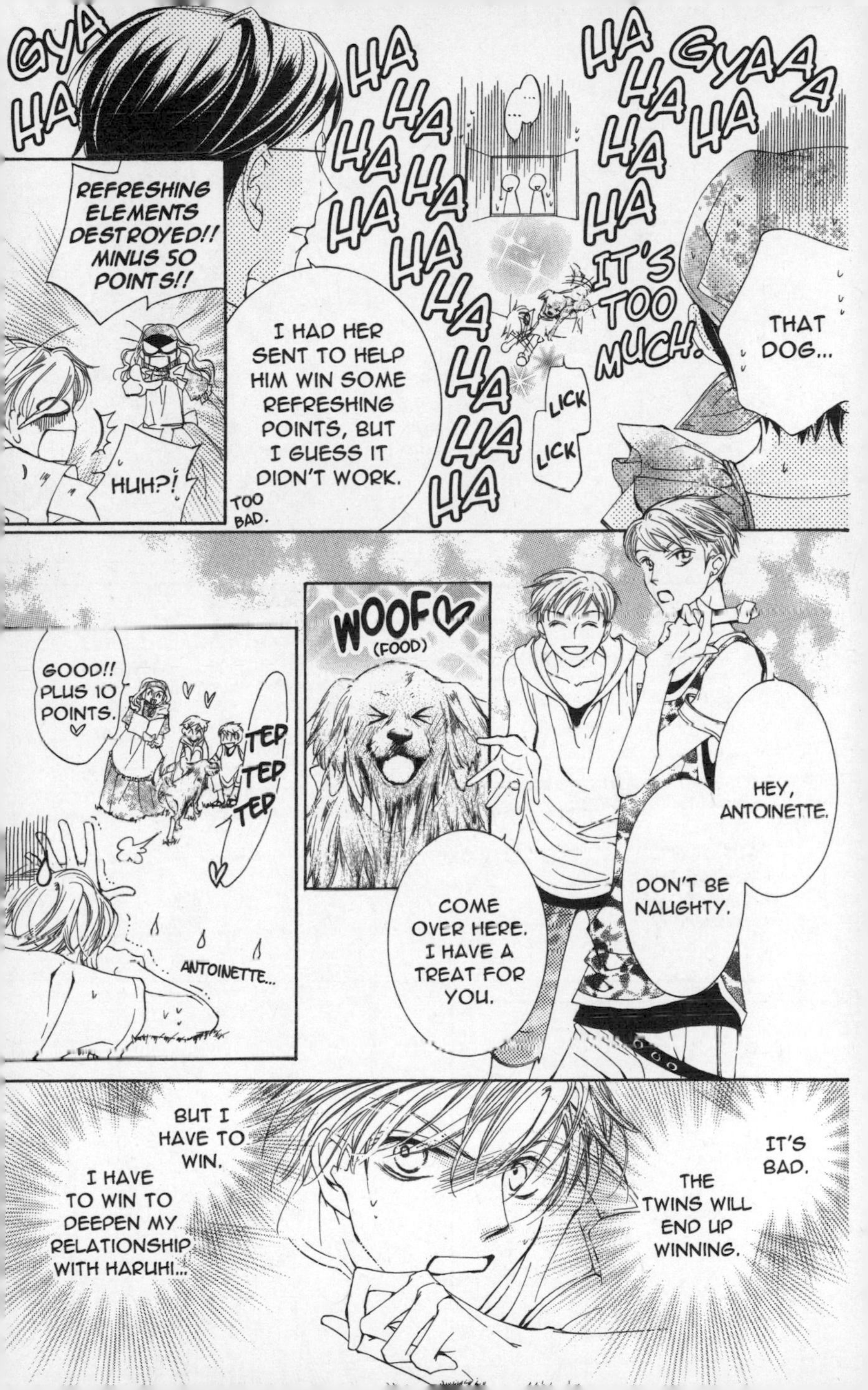
HA GYAAA HA HA HA HA HA
THAT DOG...
IT'S TOO MUCH.
HA HA HA HA HA HA HA HA HA HA HA
...
...
LICK
LICK
GYA HA
I HAD HER SENT TO HELP HIM WIN SOME REFRESHING POINTS, BUT I GUESS IT DIDN'T WORK.
TOO BAD.
REFRESHING ELEMENTS DESTROYED!! MINUS 50 POINTS!!
HUH?!
HEY, ANTOINETTE.
DON'T BE NAUGHTY.
COME OVER HERE. I HAVE A TREAT FOR YOU.
WOOF♡
(FOOD)
GOOD!! PLUS 10 POINTS. ♡
TEP TEP TEP
ANTOINETTE...
IT'S BAD.
THE TWINS WILL END UP WINNING.
BUT I HAVE TO WIN.
I HAVE TO WIN TO DEEPEN MY RELATIONSHIP WITH HARUHI...

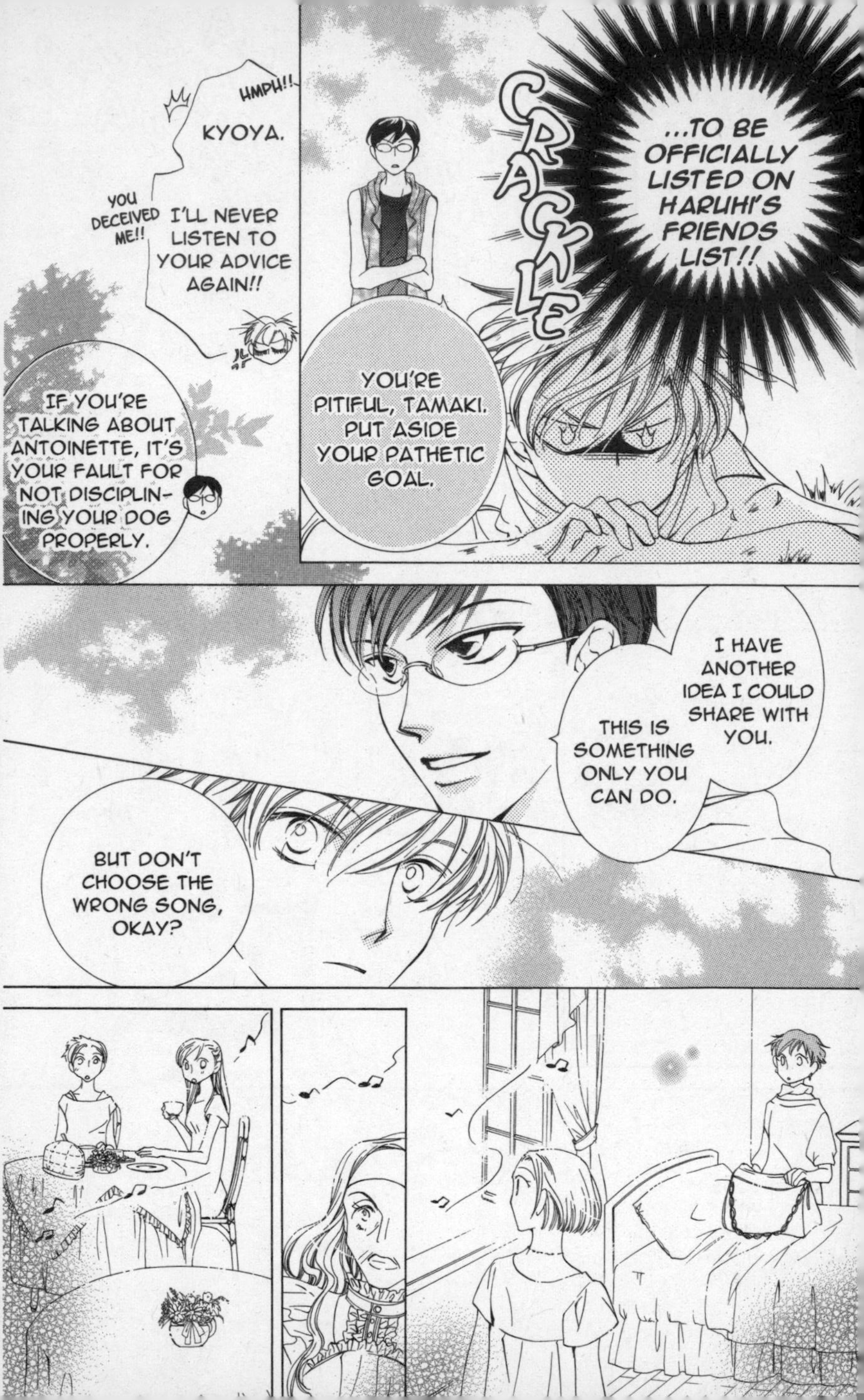
...TO BE OFFICIALLY LISTED ON HARUHI'S FRIENDS LIST!!
CRACKLE
YOU'RE PITIFUL, TAMAKI. PUT ASIDE YOUR PATHETIC GOAL.
HMPH!!
KYOYA.
I'LL NEVER LISTEN TO YOUR ADVICE AGAIN!!
YOU DECEIVED ME!!
IF YOU'RE TALKING ABOUT ANTOINETTE, IT'S YOUR FAULT FOR NOT DISCIPLINING YOUR DOG PROPERLY.
I HAVE ANOTHER IDEA I COULD SHARE WITH YOU.
THIS IS SOMETHING ONLY YOU CAN DO.
BUT DON'T CHOOSE THE WRONG SONG, OKAY?

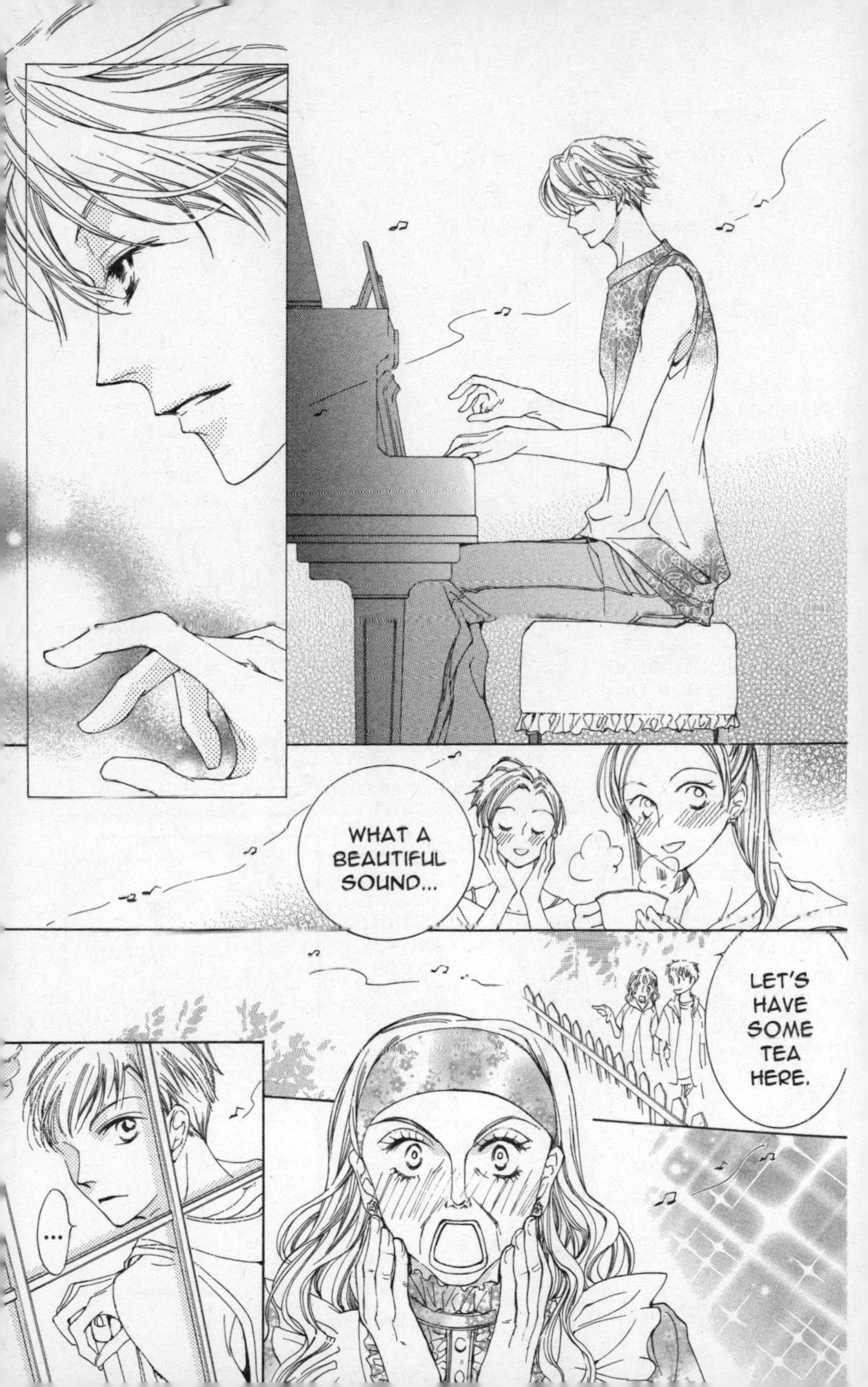
WHAT A BEAUTIFUL SOUND...
LET'S HAVE SOME TEA HERE.
...

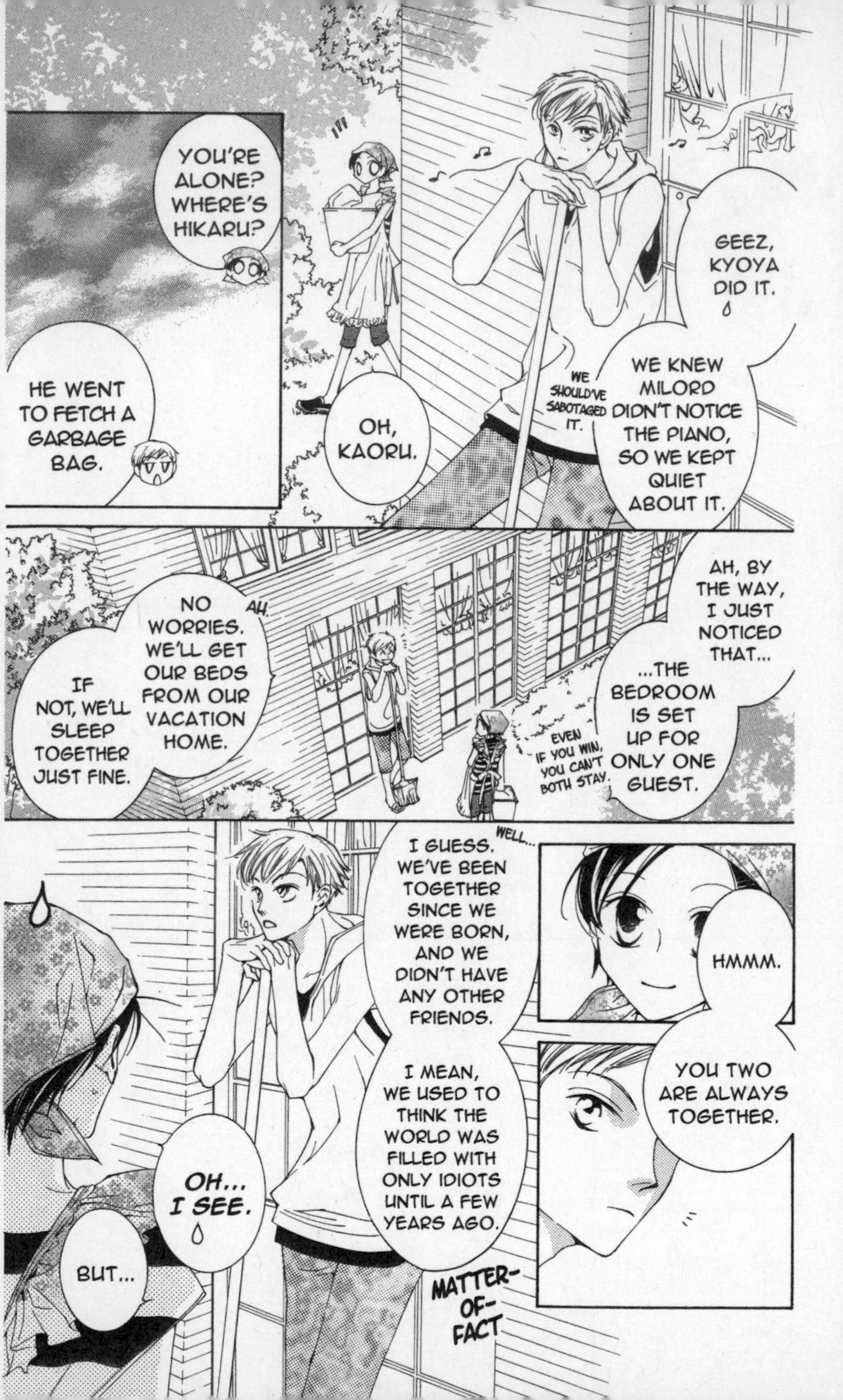
GEEZ, KYOYA DID IT.
WE KNEW MILORD DIDN'T NOTICE THE PIANO, SO WE KEPT QUIET ABOUT IT.
WE SHOULD'VE SABOTAGED IT.
OH, KAORU.
YOU'RE ALONE? WHERE'S HIKARU?
HE WENT TO FETCH A GARBAGE BAG.
AH, BY THE WAY, I JUST NOTICED THAT...
...THE BEDROOM IS SET UP FOR ONLY ONE GUEST.
EVEN IF YOU WIN, YOU CAN'T BOTH STAY.
AH.
NO WORRIES. WE'LL GET OUR BEDS FROM OUR VACATION HOME.
IF NOT, WE'LL SLEEP TOGETHER JUST FINE.
HMMM.
YOU TWO ARE ALWAYS TOGETHER.
WELL...
I GUESS. WE'VE BEEN TOGETHER SINCE WE WERE BORN, AND WE DIDN'T HAVE ANY OTHER FRIENDS.
I MEAN, WE USED TO THINK THE WORLD WAS FILLED WITH ONLY IDIOTS UNTIL A FEW YEARS AGO.
MATTER-OF-FACT
OH... I SEE.
BUT...

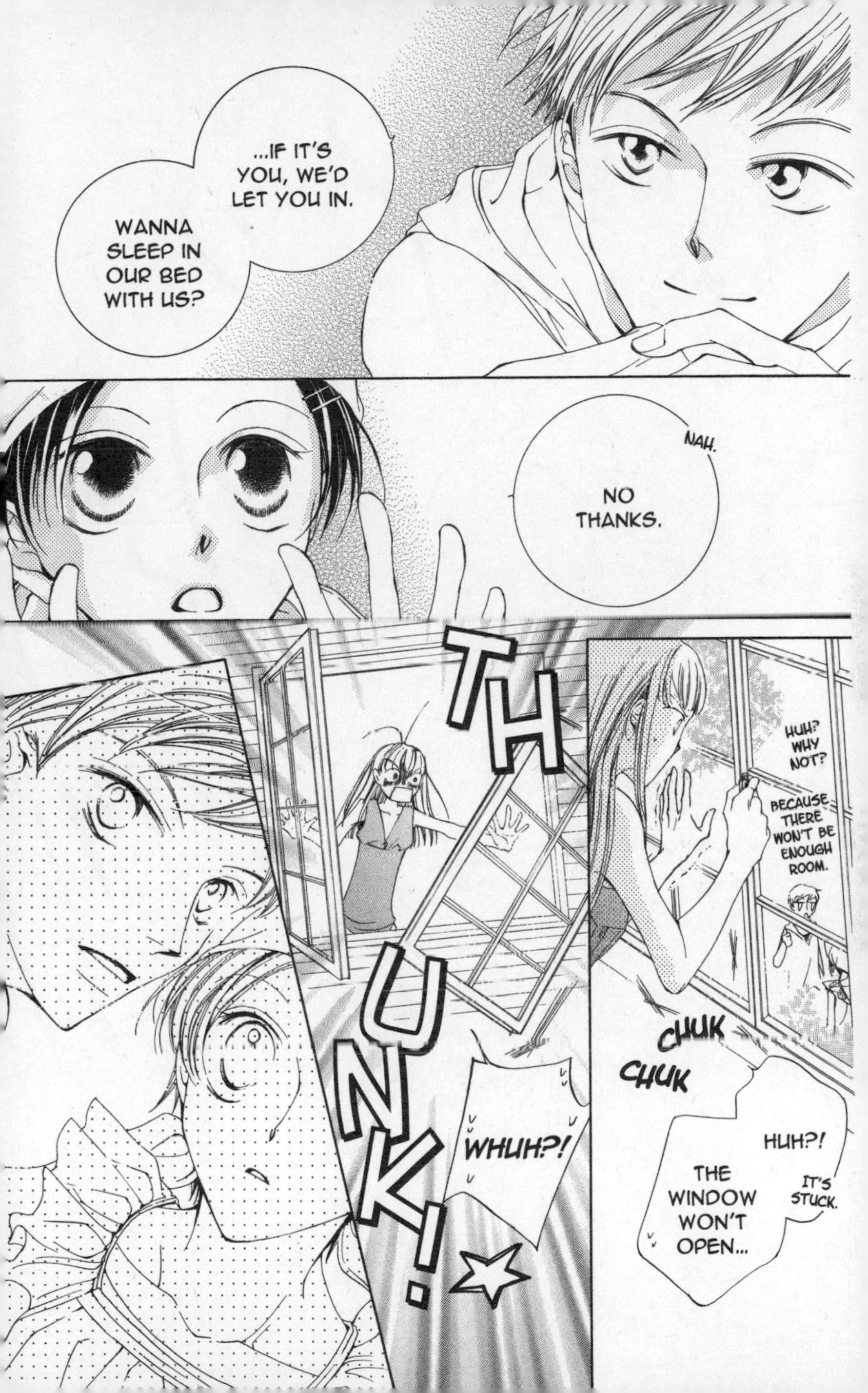
...IF IT'S YOU, WE'D LET YOU IN.
WANNA SLEEP IN OUR BED WITH US?
NAH.
NO THANKS.
HUH? WHY NOT?
BECAUSE THERE WON'T BE ENOUGH ROOM.
CHUK
CHUK
HUH?!
IT'S STUCK.
THE WINDOW WON'T OPEN...
THUNK!
WHUH?!

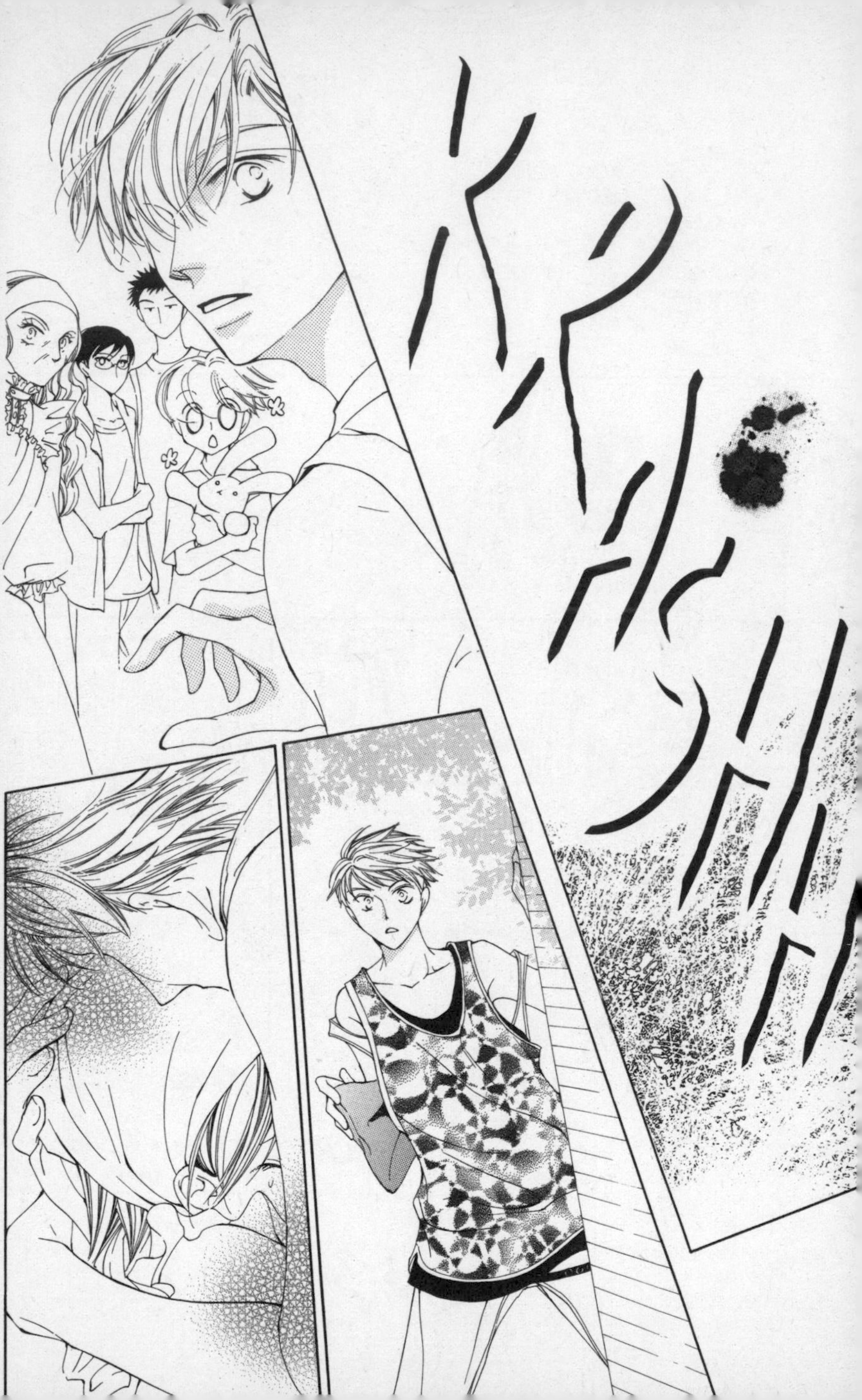

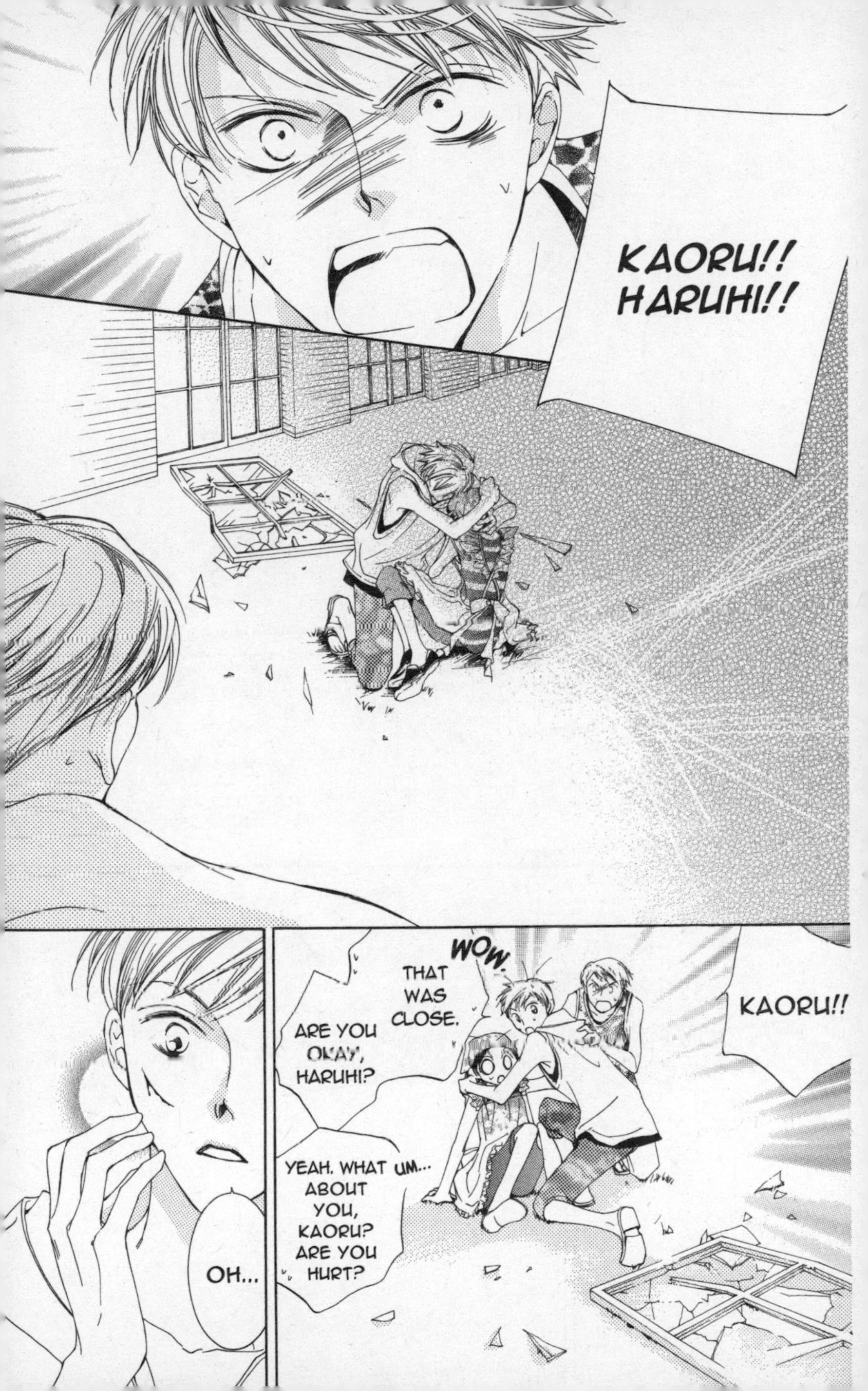
KAORU!! HARUHI!!
KAORU!!
WOW
THAT WAS CLOSE.
ARE YOU OKAY, HARUHI?
UM...
YEAH. WHAT ABOUT YOU, KAORU? ARE YOU HURT?
OH...

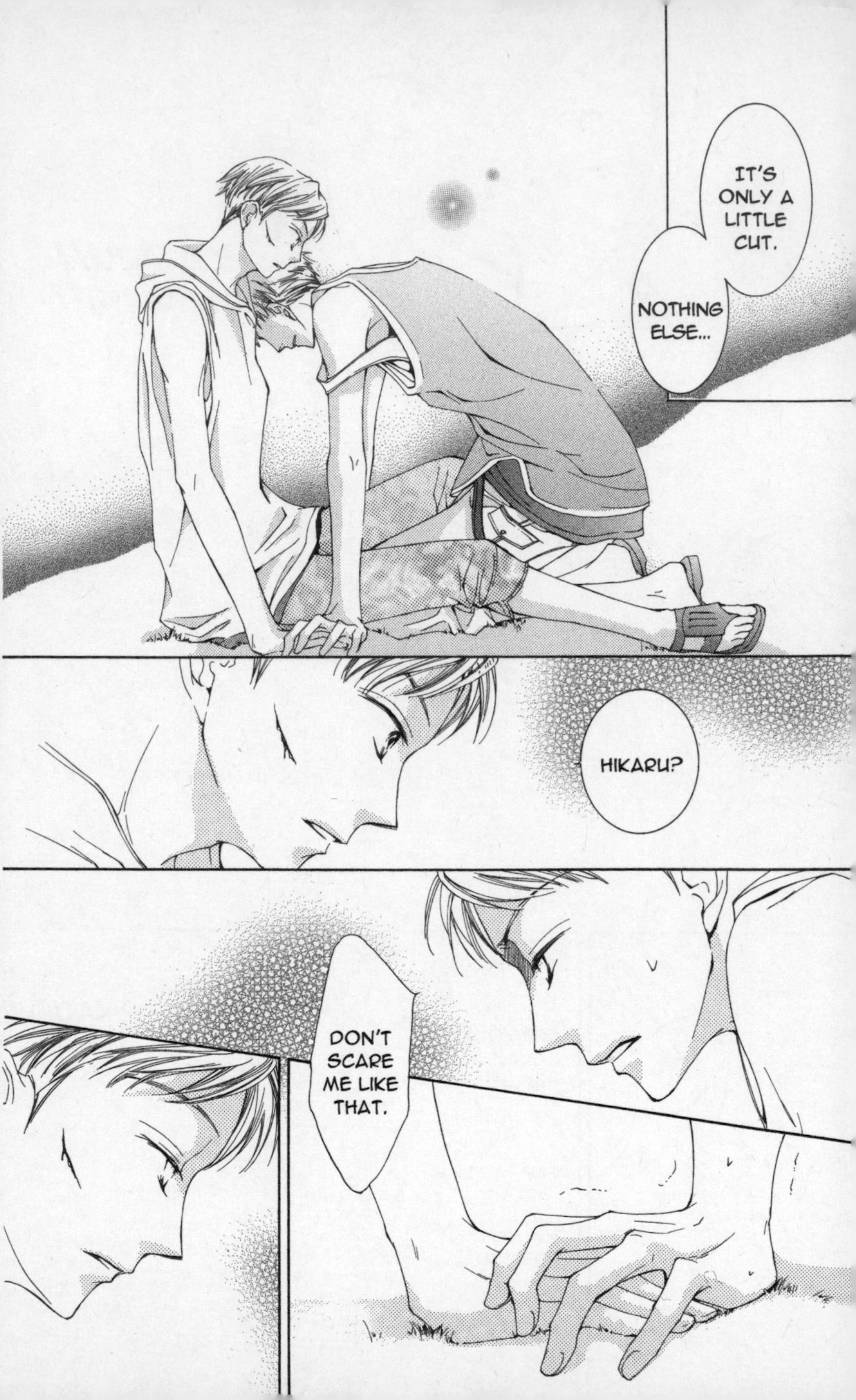
IT'S ONLY A LITTLE CUT.
NOTHING ELSE...
HIKARU?
DON'T SCARE ME LIKE THAT.

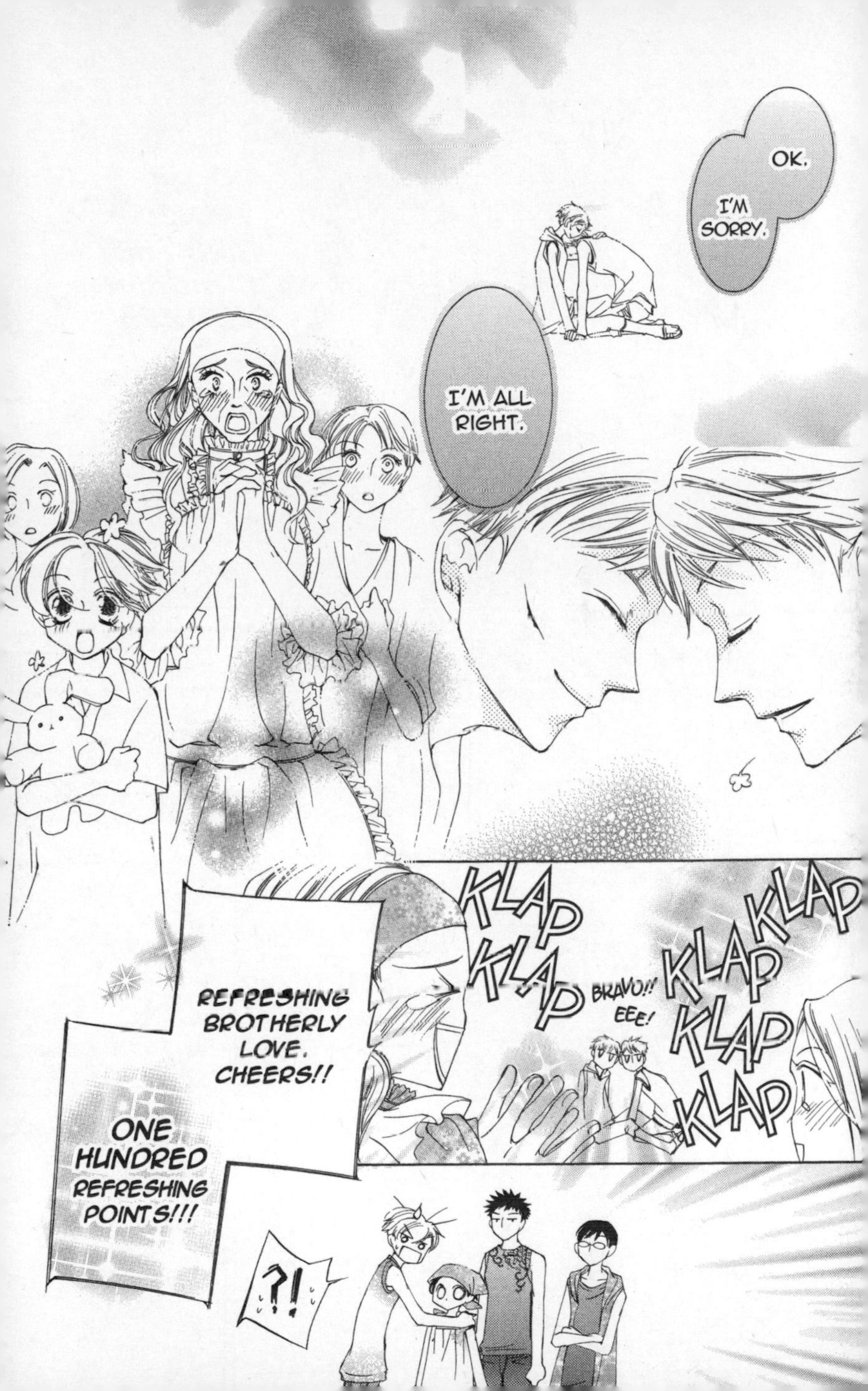

OK.
I'M SORRY.
I'M ALL RIGHT.
KLAP KLAP KLAP KLAP KLAP
BRAVO!! EEE!
KLAP KLAP
REFRESHING BROTHERLY LOVE. CHEERS!!
ONE HUNDRED REFRESHING POINTS!!!
?!

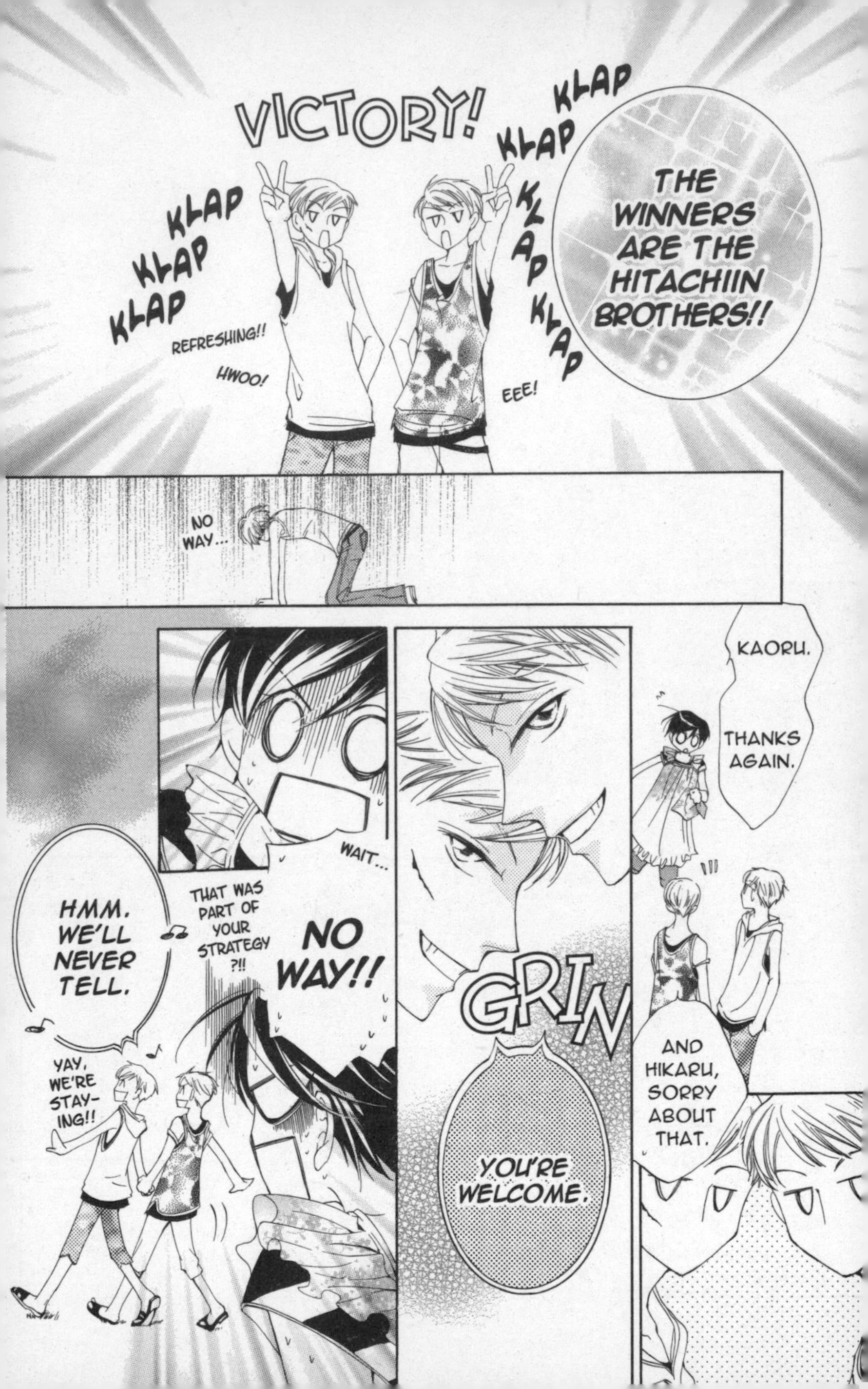
THE WINNERS ARE THE HITACHIIN BROTHERS!!
KLAP KLAP
KLAP KLAP
VICTORY!
KLAP KLAP KLAP
REFRESHING!!
HWOO!
EEE!
NO WAY...
KAORU.
THANKS AGAIN.
AND HIKARU, SORRY ABOUT THAT.
GRIN
YOU'RE WELCOME.
WAIT...
NO WAY!!
THAT WAS PART OF YOUR STRATEGY?!!
HMM. WE'LL NEVER TELL.
YAY, WE'RE STAYING!!

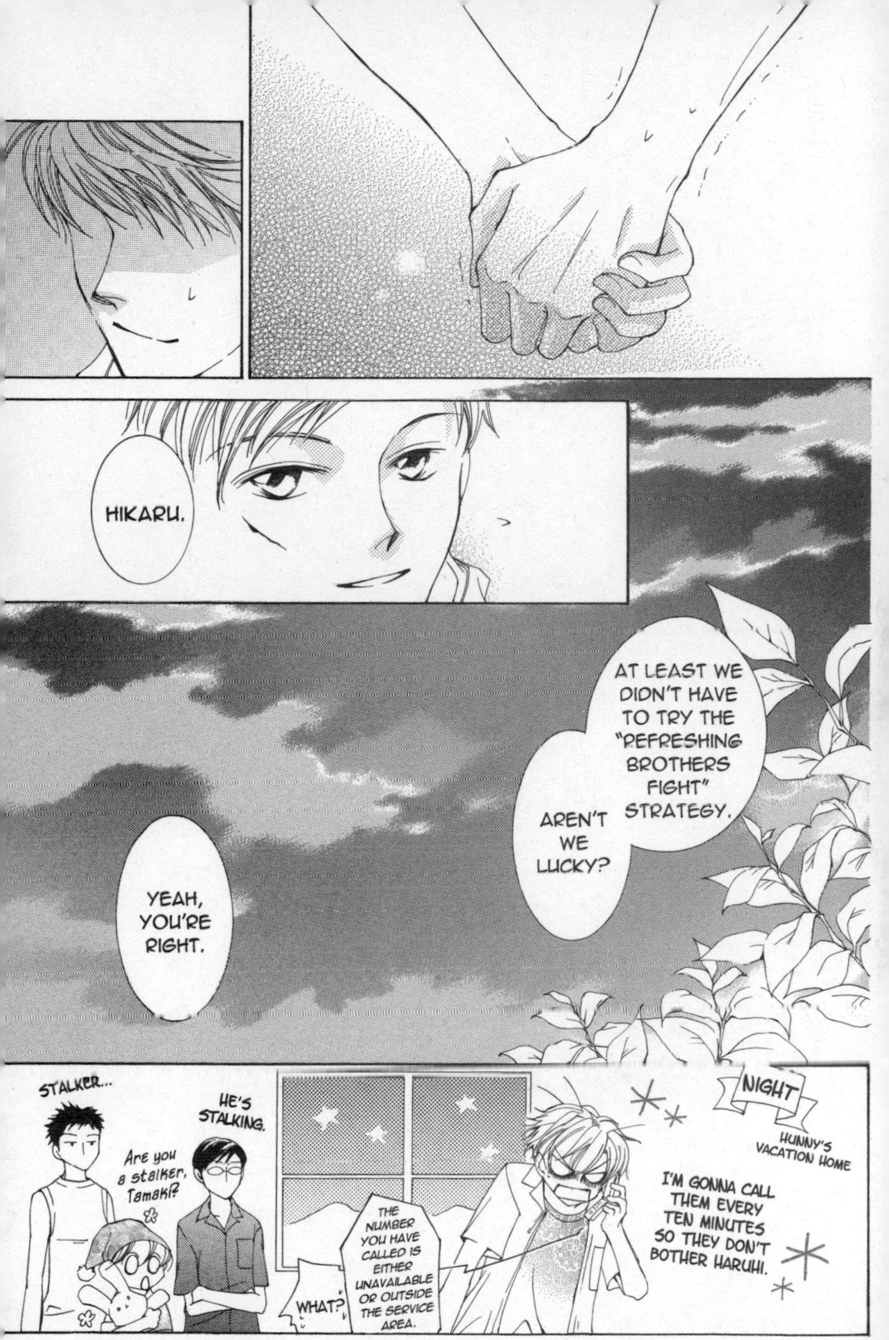
HIKARU.
AT LEAST WE DIDN'T HAVE TO TRY THE "REFRESHING BROTHERS FIGHT" STRATEGY.
AREN'T WE LUCKY?
YEAH, YOU'RE RIGHT.
NIGHT
HUNNY'S VACATION HOME
I'M GONNA CALL THEM EVERY TEN MINUTES SO THEY DON'T BOTHER HARUHI.
THE NUMBER YOU HAVE CALLED IS EITHER UNAVAILABLE OR OUTSIDE THE SERVICE AREA.
WHAT?
HE'S STALKING.
Are you a stalker, Tamaki?
STALKER...

ROUGH ILLUSTRATION FOR THE PRIZE WATCH

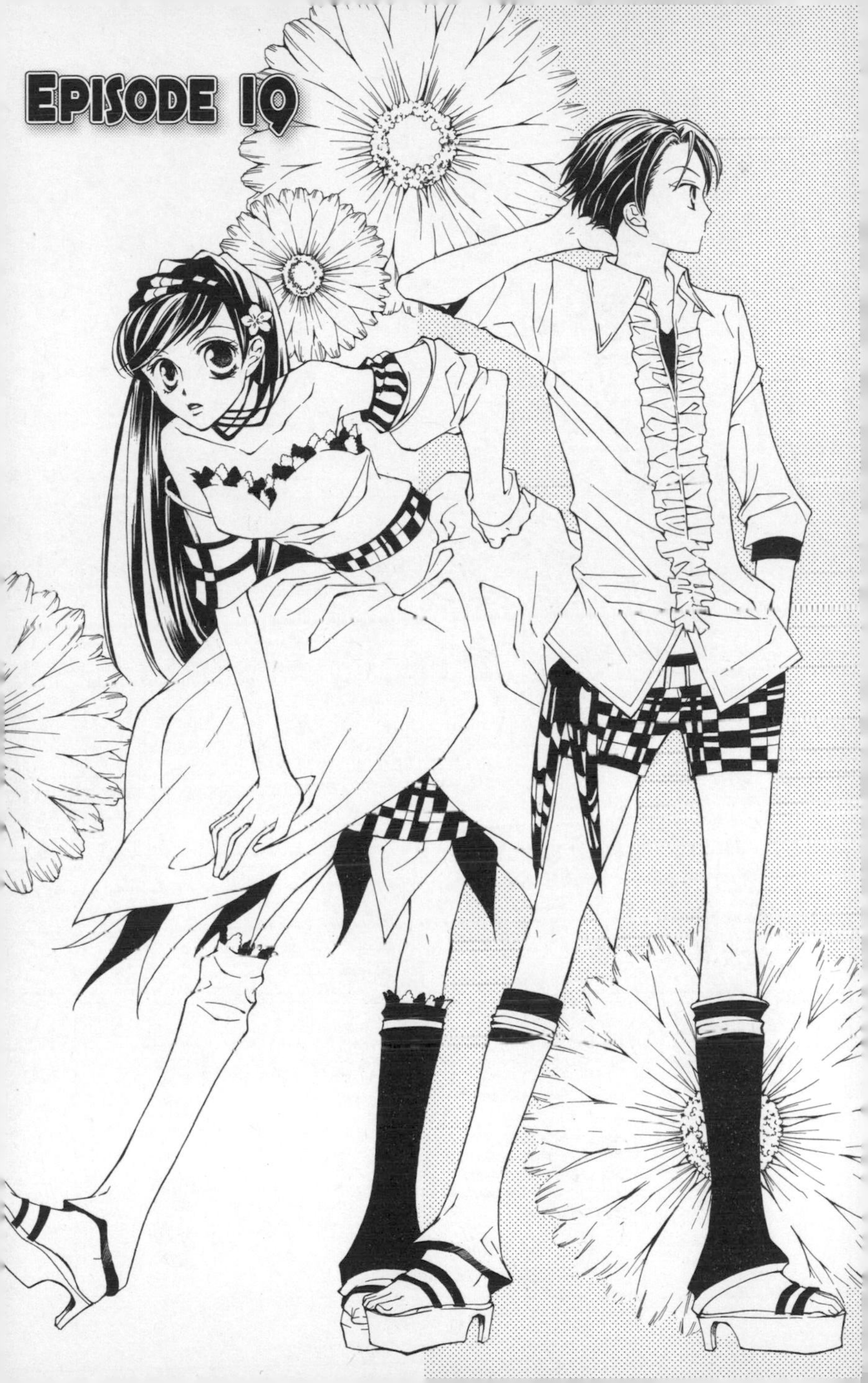
Episode 19

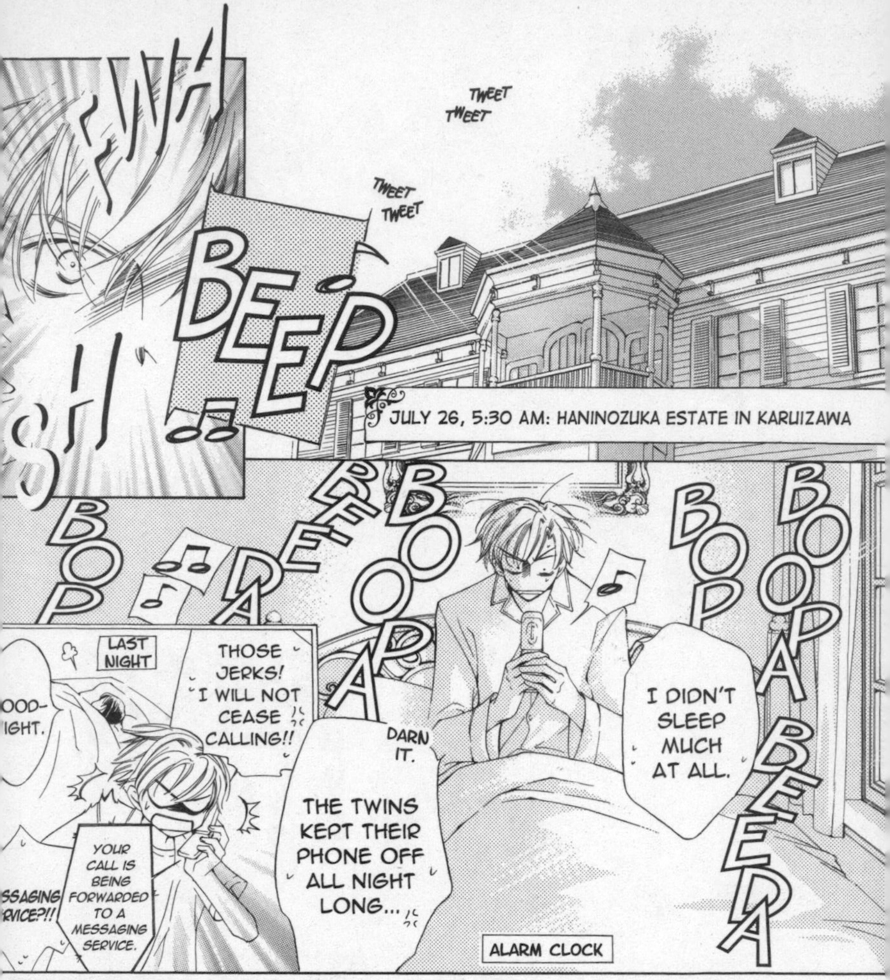
TWEET
TWEET
TWEET
TWEET
BEEP
JULY 26, 5:30 AM: HANINOZUKA ESTATE IN KARUIZAWA
FWA
SH
BOOP
BOOPA BEEDA
I DIDN'T SLEEP MUCH AT ALL.
BOOPA
BEEDA
BOOP
DARN IT.
THE TWINS KEPT THEIR PHONE OFF ALL NIGHT LONG...
ALARM CLOCK
LAST NIGHT
THOSE JERKS! I WILL NOT CEASE CALLING!!
OOD- IGHT.
YOUR CALL IS BEING FORWARDED TO A MESSAGING SERVICE.
SSAGING RVICE?!!

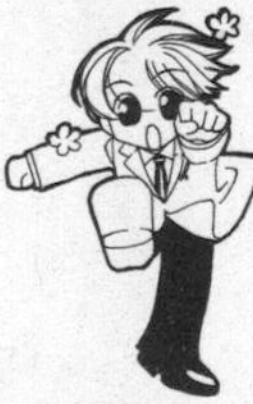

HUNNY PINK

DEADLY MOVES: · FLOWER BOMB
· BUNNY KICK + PUNCH

※LOWERS ENEMY'S GUARD WITH PRETENSE OF CUTENESS, THEN LAUNCHES A SUDDEN ATTACK. WHEN UPSET, TRANSFORMS INTO DARK HUNNY, WHO CAN DESTROY AN ENTIRE TOWN.

HARUHI WHITE

DEADLY MOVE: · NATURAL KNIFE

※ THOUGH APPARENTLY FRAGILE AND UNINTERESTED, HER UNEXPECTED WORDS CAN CARVE OUT AN ENEMY'S HEART.

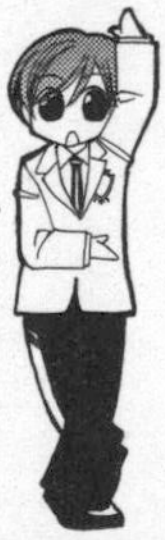

OURAN CORPS
HOST RANGERS

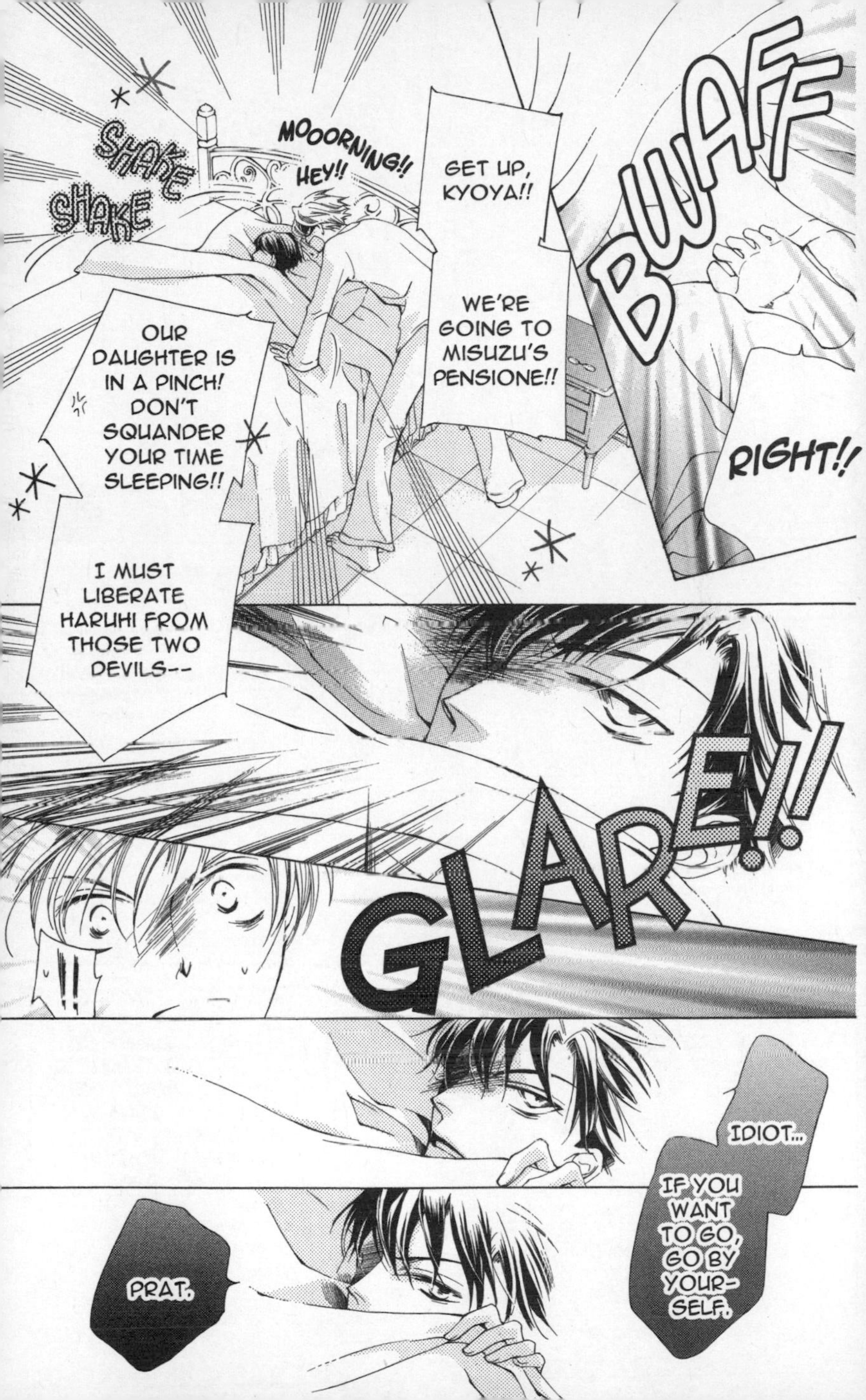
BWAFF
RIGHT!!
GET UP, KYOYA!!
MOOORNING!! HEY!!
SHAKE SHAKE
WE'RE GOING TO MISUZU'S PENSIONE!!
OUR DAUGHTER IS IN A PINCH! DON'T SQUANDER YOUR TIME SLEEPING!!
I MUST LIBERATE HARUHI FROM THOSE TWO DEVILS--
GLARE!!
!!
IDIOT...
IF YOU WANT TO GO, GO BY YOUR-SELF.
PRAT.

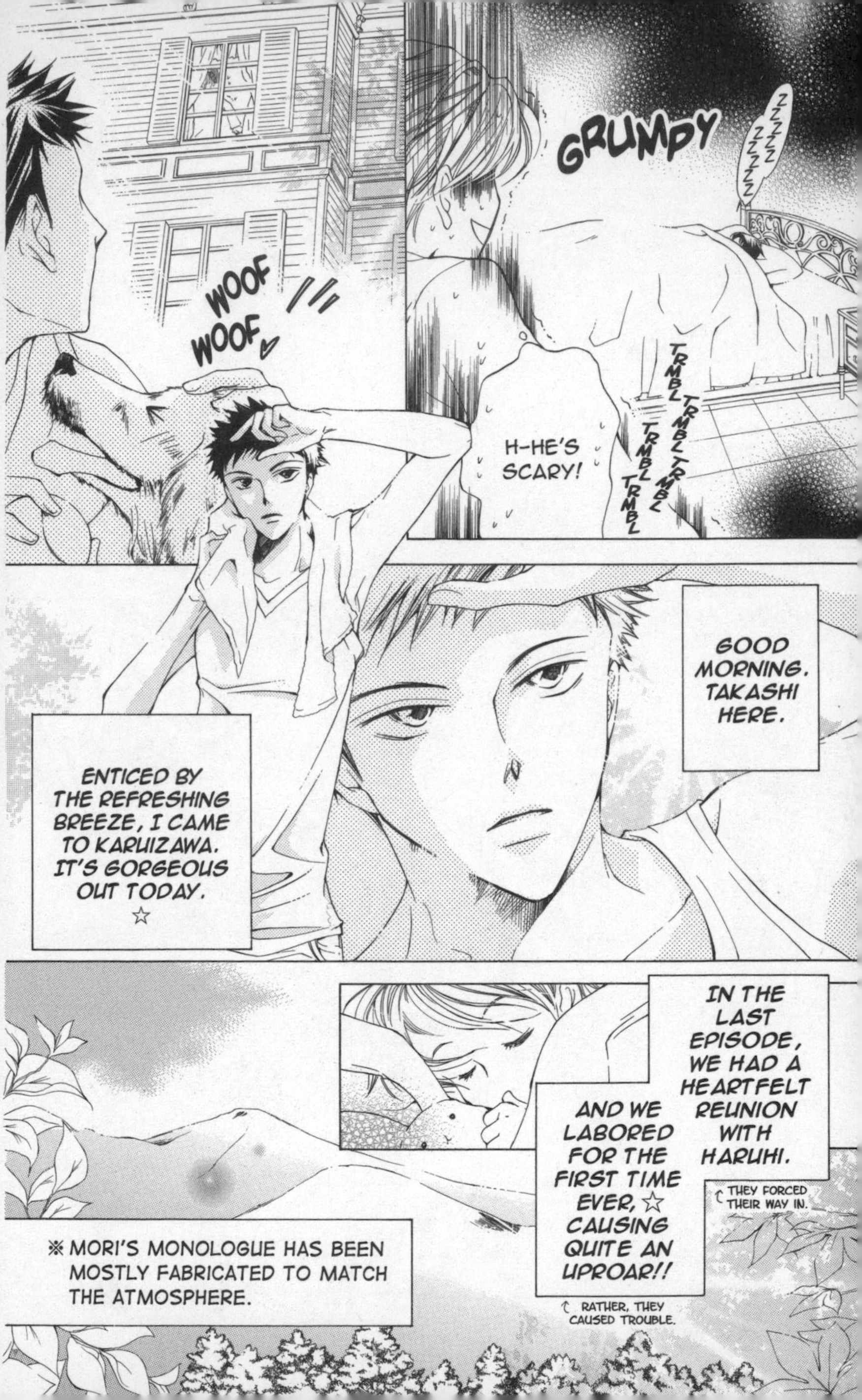
GRUMPY
ZZZZZZZ
H-HE'S SCARY!
TRMBL TRMBL TRMBL TRMBL TRMBL
WOOF WOOF
GOOD MORNING. TAKASHI HERE.
ENTICED BY THE REFRESHING BREEZE, I CAME TO KARUIZAWA. IT'S GORGEOUS OUT TODAY. ☆
IN THE LAST EPISODE, WE HAD A HEARTFELT REUNION WITH HARUHI.
THEY FORCED THEIR WAY IN.
AND WE LABORED FOR THE FIRST TIME EVER, ☆ CAUSING QUITE AN UPROAR!!
RATHER, THEY CAUSED TROUBLE.
※ MORI'S MONOLOGUE HAS BEEN MOSTLY FABRICATED TO MATCH THE ATMOSPHERE.

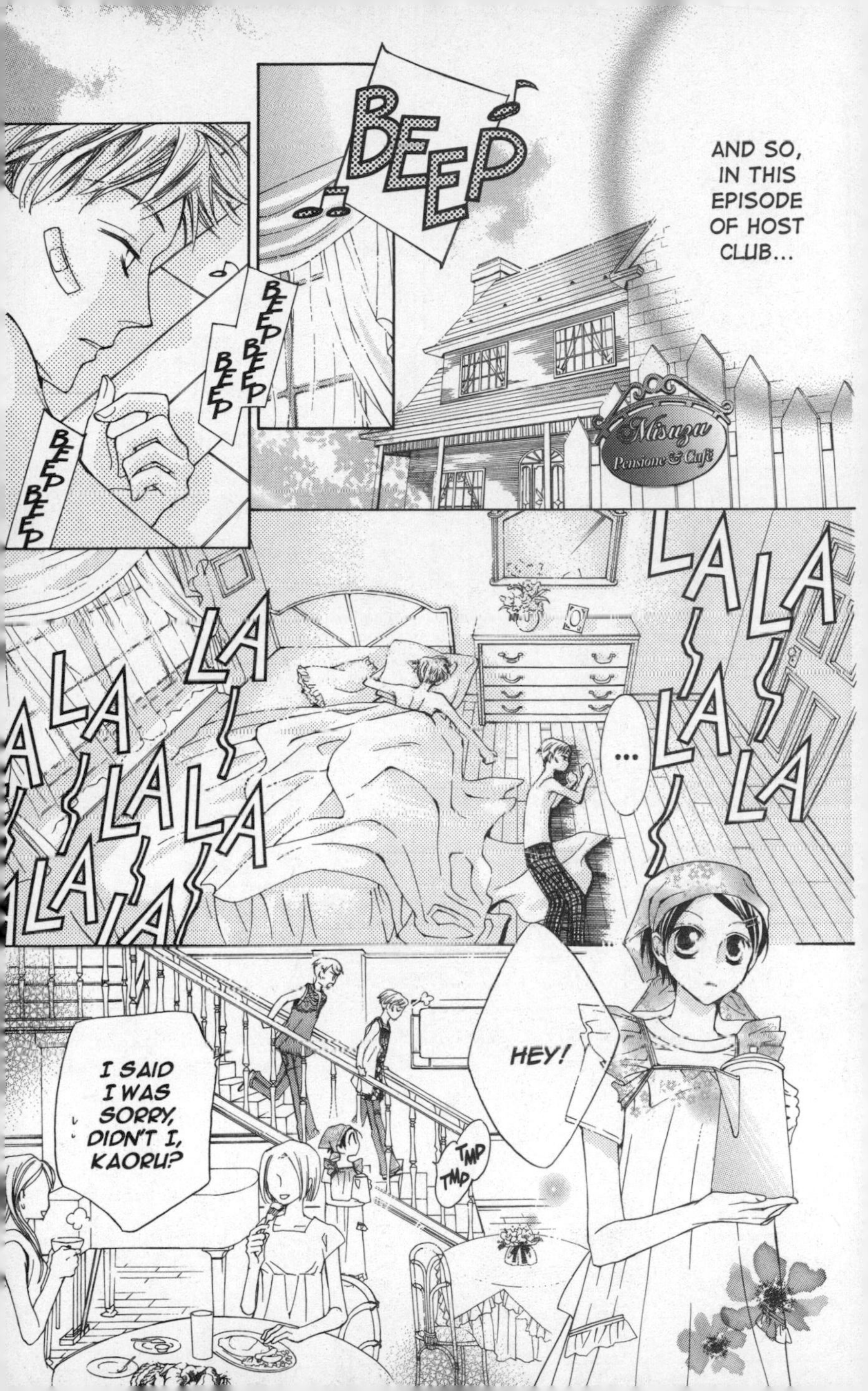
AND SO, IN THIS EPISODE OF HOST CLUB...
Misuzu Pensione & Café
BEEP
BEEP BEEP BEEP
BEEP BEEP
LA LA LA LA LA
...
LA LA LA LA LA LA LA LA
HEY!
TMP TMP
I SAID I WAS SORRY, DIDN'T I, KAORU?

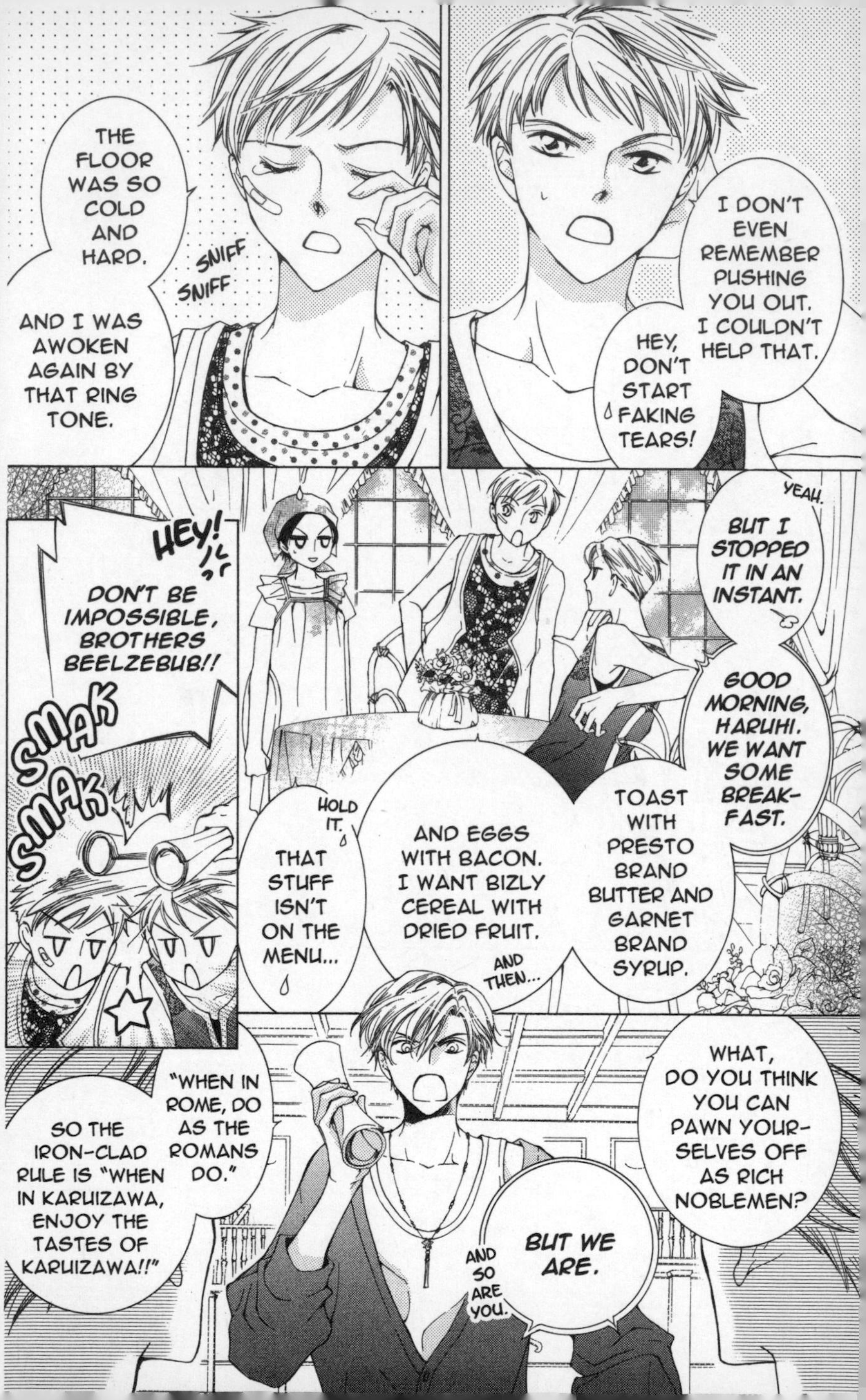
I DON'T EVEN REMEMBER PUSHING YOU OUT. I COULDN'T HELP THAT.
HEY, DON'T START FAKING TEARS!
THE FLOOR WAS SO COLD AND HARD.
SNIFF
SNIFF
AND I WAS AWOKEN AGAIN BY THAT RING TONE.
YEAH.
BUT I STOPPED IT IN AN INSTANT.
GOOD MORNING, HARUHI. WE WANT SOME BREAK-FAST.
TOAST WITH PRESTO BRAND BUTTER AND GARNET BRAND SYRUP.
AND THEN...
AND EGGS WITH BACON. I WANT BIZLY CEREAL WITH DRIED FRUIT.
HOLD IT.
THAT STUFF ISN'T ON THE MENU...
HEY!
DON'T BE IMPOSSIBLE, BROTHERS BEELZEBUB!!
SMAK
SMAK
WHAT, DO YOU THINK YOU CAN PAWN YOUR-SELVES OFF AS RICH NOBLEMEN?
BUT WE ARE.
AND SO ARE YOU.
"WHEN IN ROME, DO AS THE ROMANS DO."
SO THE IRON-CLAD RULE IS "WHEN IN KARUIZAWA, ENJOY THE TASTES OF KARUIZAWA!!"

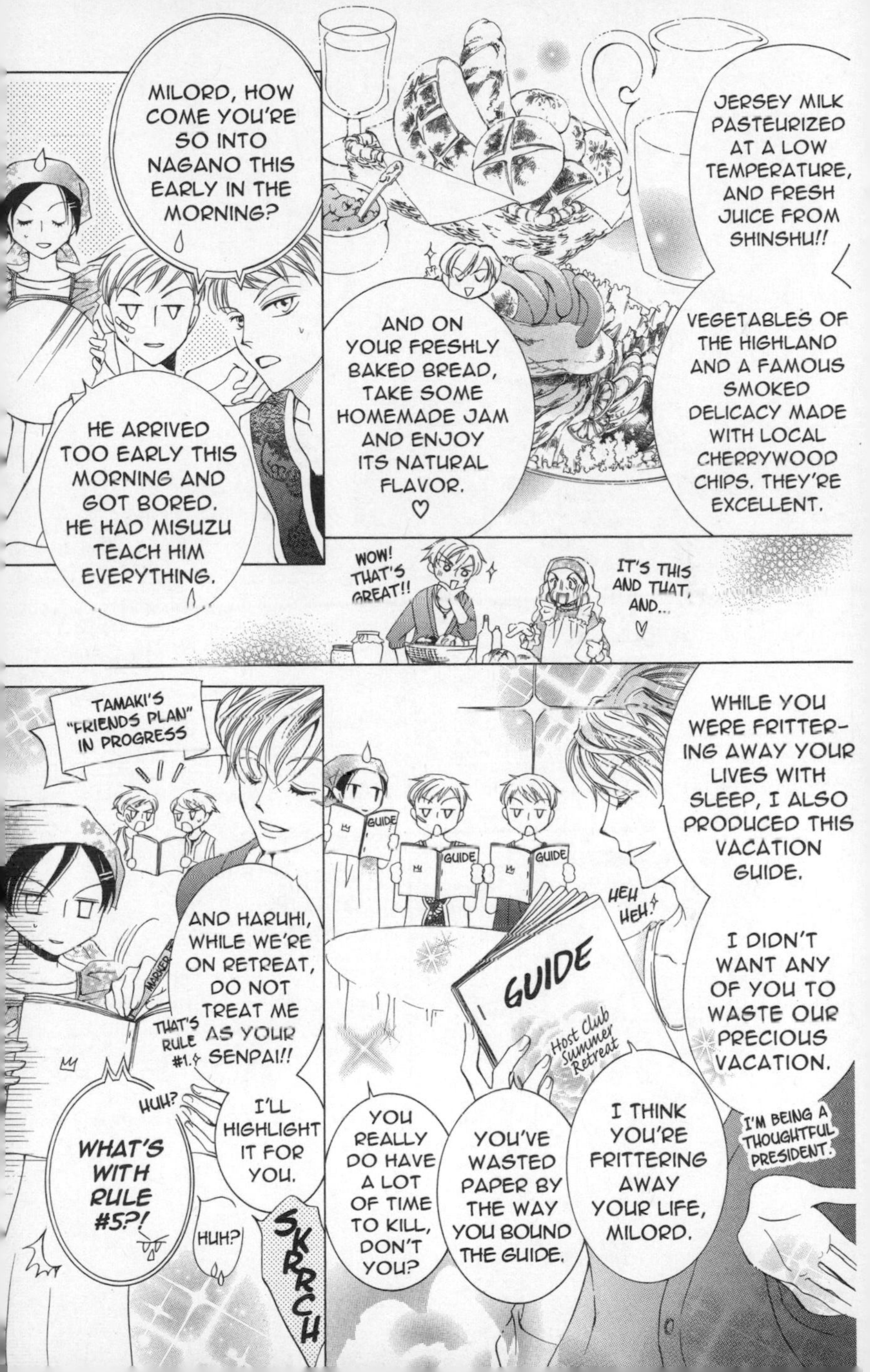
JERSEY MILK PASTEURIZED AT A LOW TEMPERATURE, AND FRESH JUICE FROM SHINSHU!!
VEGETABLES OF THE HIGHLAND AND A FAMOUS SMOKED DELICACY MADE WITH LOCAL CHERRYWOOD CHIPS. THEY'RE EXCELLENT.
AND ON YOUR FRESHLY BAKED BREAD, TAKE SOME HOMEMADE JAM AND ENJOY ITS NATURAL FLAVOR. ♡
IT'S THIS AND THAT, AND... ♡
WOW! THAT'S GREAT!!
MILORD, HOW COME YOU'RE SO INTO NAGANO THIS EARLY IN THE MORNING?
HE ARRIVED TOO EARLY THIS MORNING AND GOT BORED. HE HAD MISUZU TEACH HIM EVERYTHING.
WHILE YOU WERE FRITTERING AWAY YOUR LIVES WITH SLEEP, I ALSO PRODUCED THIS VACATION GUIDE.
HEH HEH♪
I DIDN'T WANT ANY OF YOU TO WASTE OUR PRECIOUS VACATION.
GUIDE
GUIDE
GUIDE
GUIDE
Host Club Summer Retreat
I'M BEING A THOUGHTFUL PRESIDENT.
I THINK YOU'RE FRITTERING AWAY YOUR LIFE, MILORD.
YOU'VE WASTED PAPER BY THE WAY YOU BOUND THE GUIDE.
YOU REALLY DO HAVE A LOT OF TIME TO KILL, DON'T YOU?
TAMAKI'S "FRIENDS PLAN" IN PROGRESS
AND HARUHI, WHILE WE'RE ON RETREAT, DO NOT TREAT ME AS YOUR SENPAI!!
THAT'S RULE #1.♪
I'LL HIGHLIGHT IT FOR YOU.
SKRRCH
HUH?
WHAT'S WITH RULE #5?!
HUH?

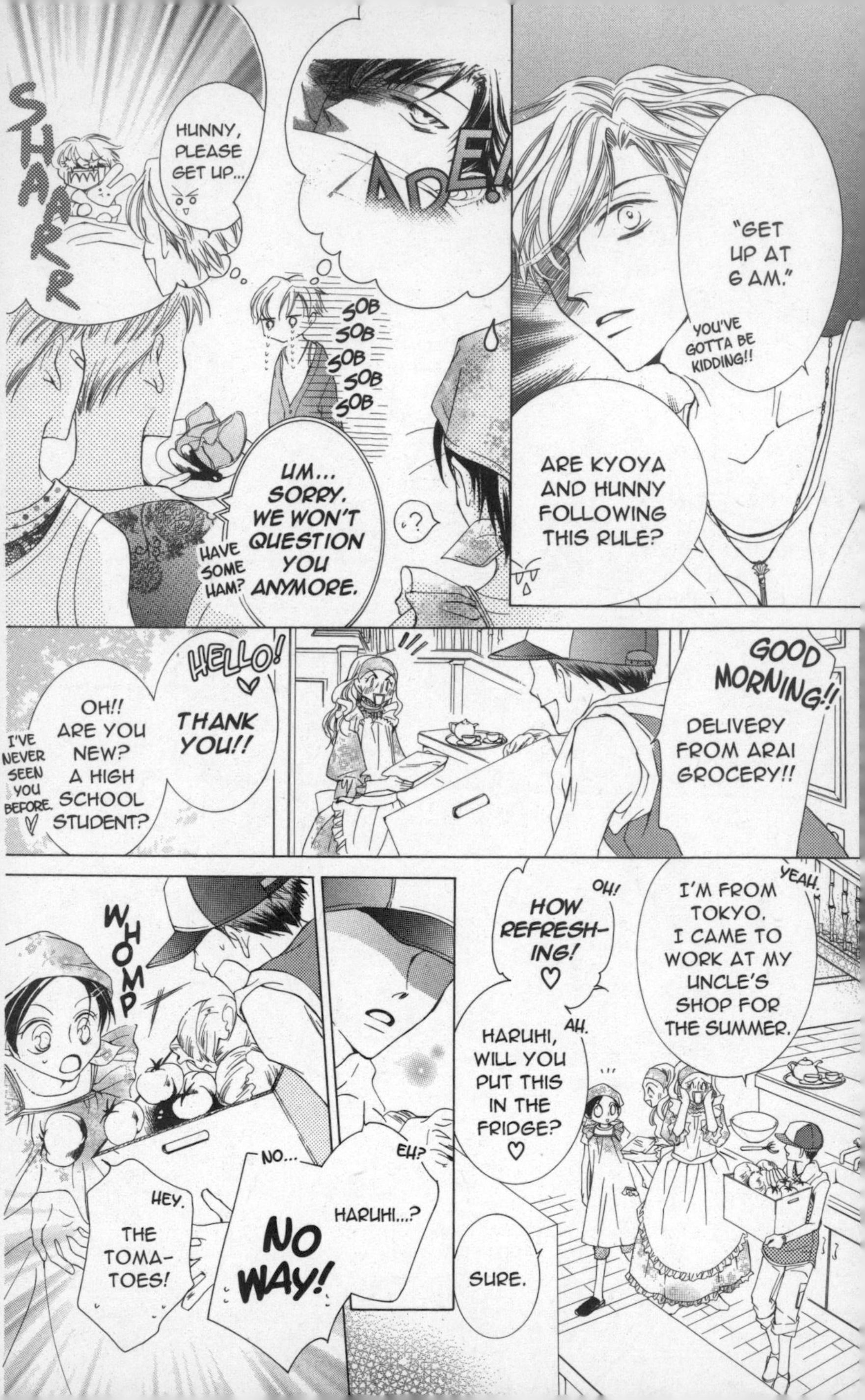
"GET UP AT 6 AM."
YOU'VE GOTTA BE KIDDING!!
ARE KYOYA AND HUNNY FOLLOWING THIS RULE?
HUNNY, PLEASE GET UP...
SHARRR
ADE!
SOB SOB SOB SOB SOB
UM... SORRY. WE WON'T QUESTION YOU ANYMORE.
HAVE SOME HAM?
?
GOOD MORNING!!
DELIVERY FROM ARAI GROCERY!!
HELLO!
THANK YOU!!
OH!! ARE YOU NEW? A HIGH SCHOOL STUDENT?
I'VE NEVER SEEN YOU BEFORE.
YEAH.
I'M FROM TOKYO. I CAME TO WORK AT MY UNCLE'S SHOP FOR THE SUMMER.
OH!
HOW REFRESHING!
AH.
HARUHI, WILL YOU PUT THIS IN THE FRIDGE?
SURE.
EH?
NO...
HARUHI...?
NO WAY!
WHOMP
HEY.
THE TOMATOES!

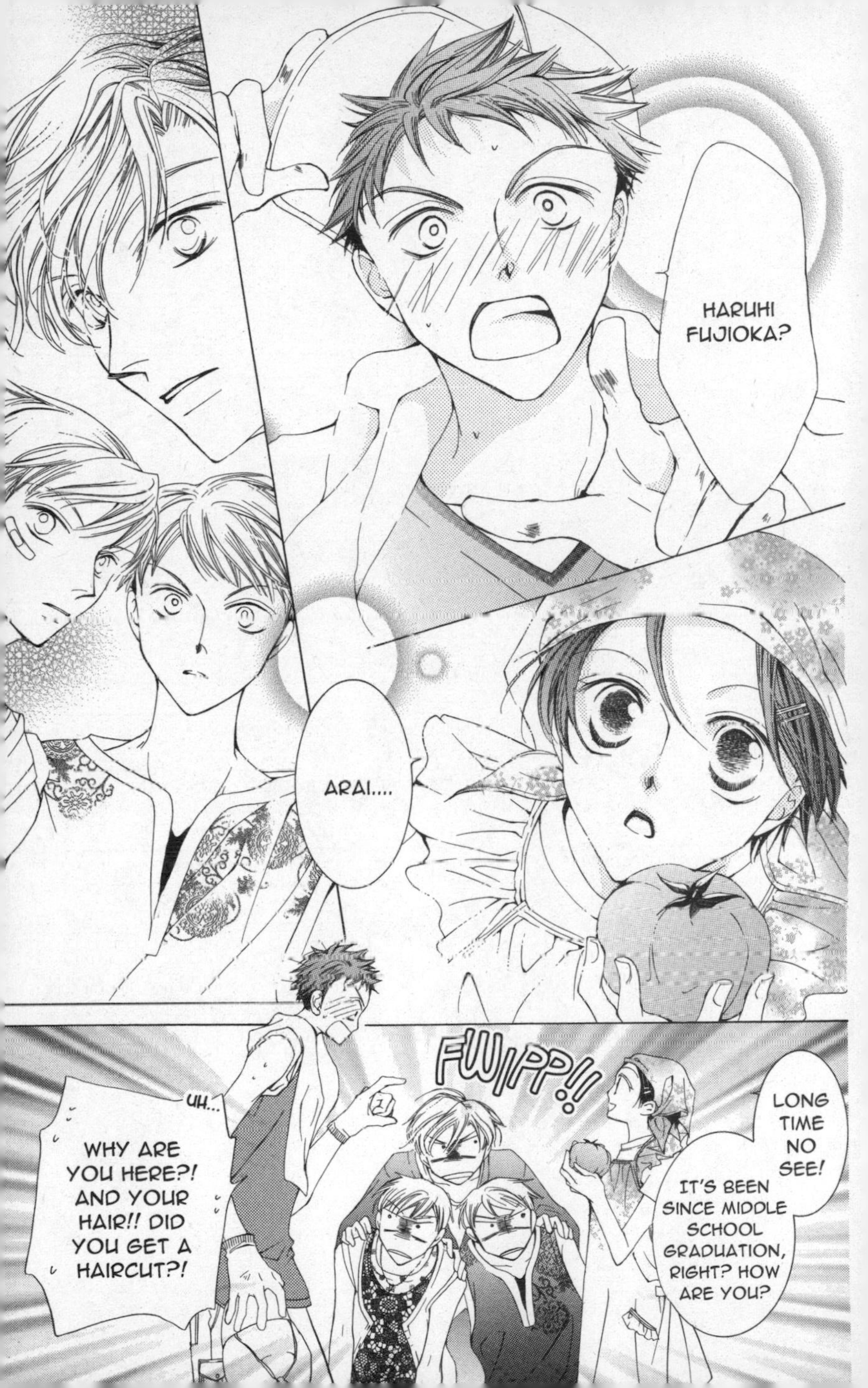
HARUHI FUJIOKA?
ARAI....
LONG TIME NO SEE!
IT'S BEEN SINCE MIDDLE SCHOOL GRADUATION, RIGHT? HOW ARE YOU?
FWIPP!!
UH...
WHY ARE YOU HERE?! AND YOUR HAIR!! DID YOU GET A HAIRCUT?!

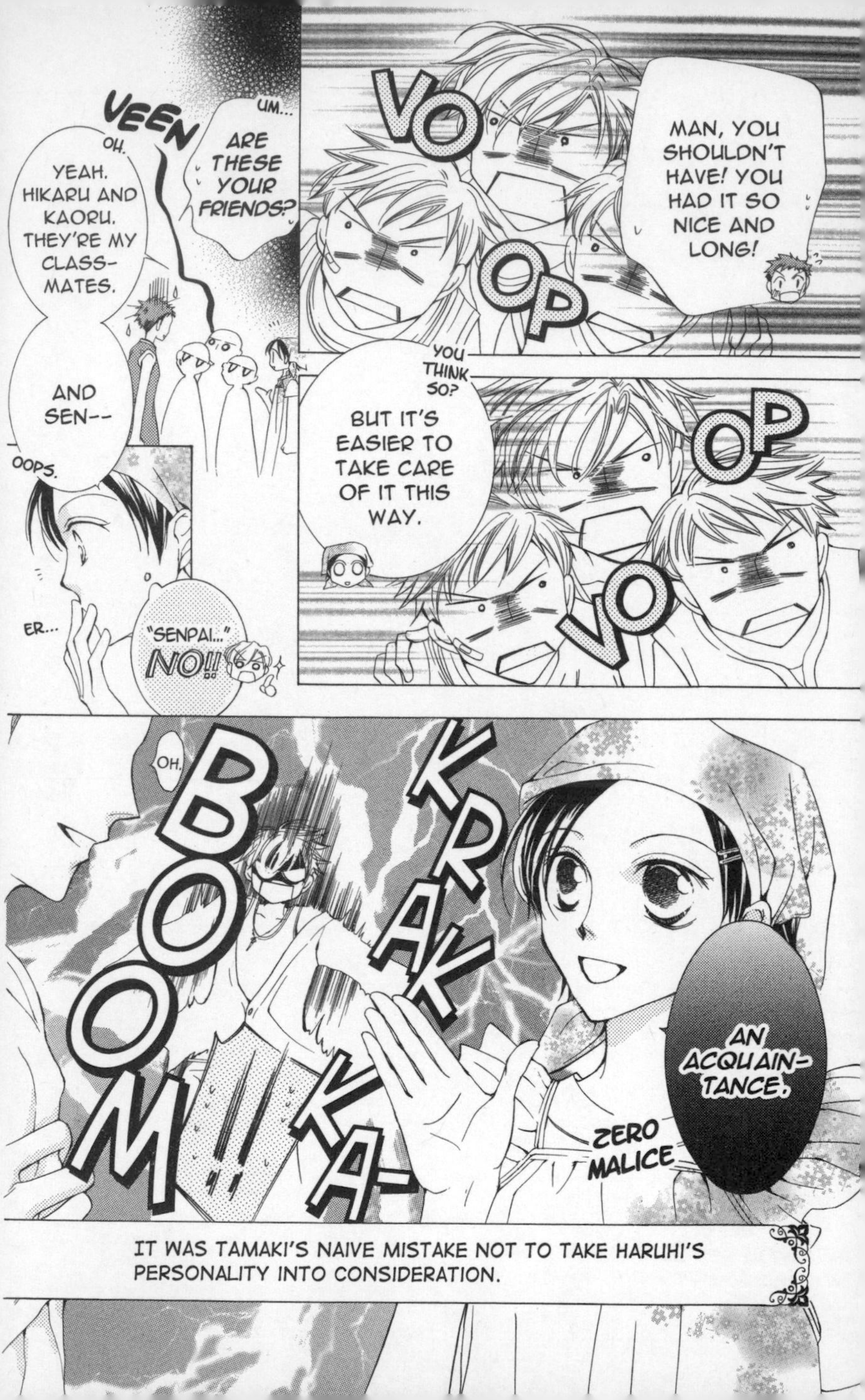
VO
OP
MAN, YOU SHOULDN'T HAVE! YOU HAD IT SO NICE AND LONG!
YOU THINK SO?
BUT IT'S EASIER TO TAKE CARE OF IT THIS WAY.
OP
VO
UM...
ARE THESE YOUR FRIENDS?
VEEN
OH.
YEAH. HIKARU AND KAORU. THEY'RE MY CLASS-MATES.
AND SEN--
OOPS.
ER...
"SENPAI..." NO!!
OH.
KRAKA-
BOOM!!
AN ACQUAIN-TANCE.
ZERO MALICE
IT WAS TAMAKI'S NAIVE MISTAKE NOT TO TAKE HARUHI'S PERSONALITY INTO CONSIDERATION.

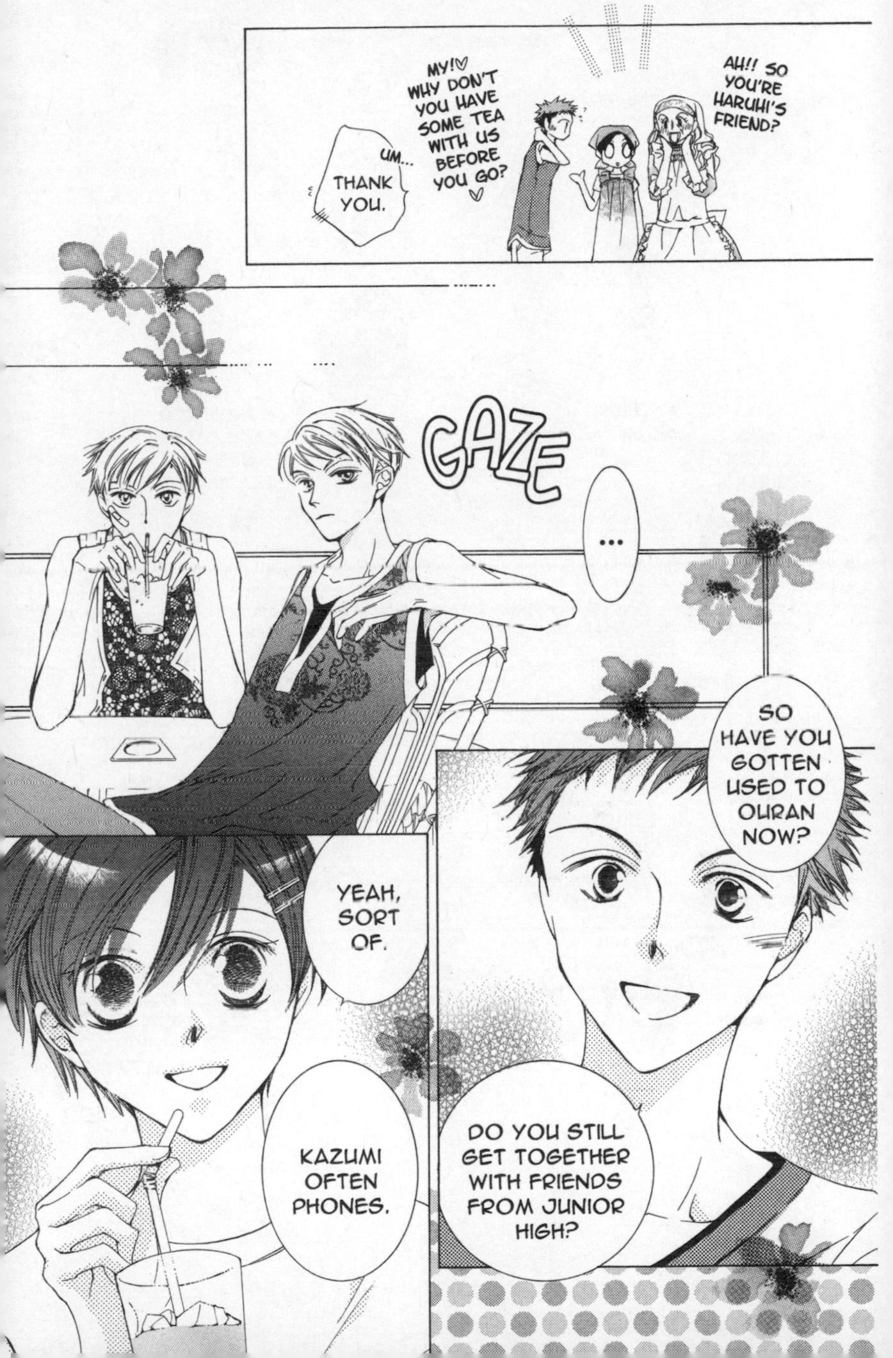
AH!! SO YOU'RE HARUHI'S FRIEND?
MY!♡ WHY DON'T YOU HAVE SOME TEA WITH US BEFORE YOU GO?♡
UM... THANK YOU.
......
... ...
GAZE
...
SO HAVE YOU GOTTEN USED TO OURAN NOW?
YEAH, SORT OF.
DO YOU STILL GET TOGETHER WITH FRIENDS FROM JUNIOR HIGH?
KAZUMI OFTEN PHONES.

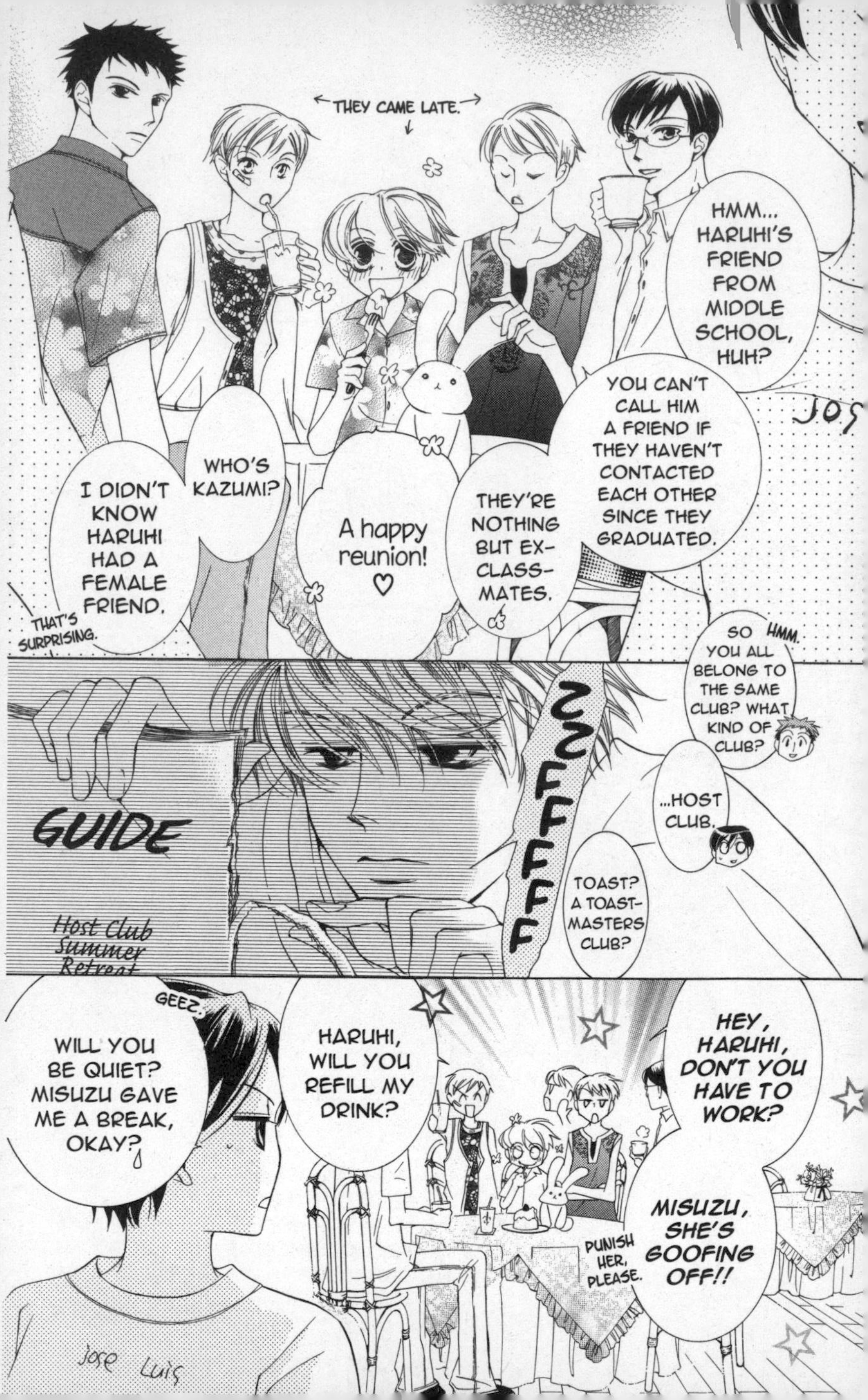
THEY CAME LATE.
HMM... HARUHI'S FRIEND FROM MIDDLE SCHOOL, HUH?
YOU CAN'T CALL HIM A FRIEND IF THEY HAVEN'T CONTACTED EACH OTHER SINCE THEY GRADUATED.
THEY'RE NOTHING BUT EX-CLASSMATES.
A happy reunion! ♡
WHO'S KAZUMI?
I DIDN'T KNOW HARUHI HAD A FEMALE FRIEND.
THAT'S SURPRISING.
SO YOU ALL BELONG TO THE SAME CLUB? WHAT KIND OF CLUB?
HMM.
...HOST CLUB.
TOAST? A TOASTMASTERS CLUB?
GUIDE
Host Club Summer Retreat
HEY, HARUHI, DON'T YOU HAVE TO WORK?
MISUZU, SHE'S GOOFING OFF!!
PUNISH HER, PLEASE.
HARUHI, WILL YOU REFILL MY DRINK?
GEEZ.
WILL YOU BE QUIET? MISUZU GAVE ME A BREAK, OKAY?

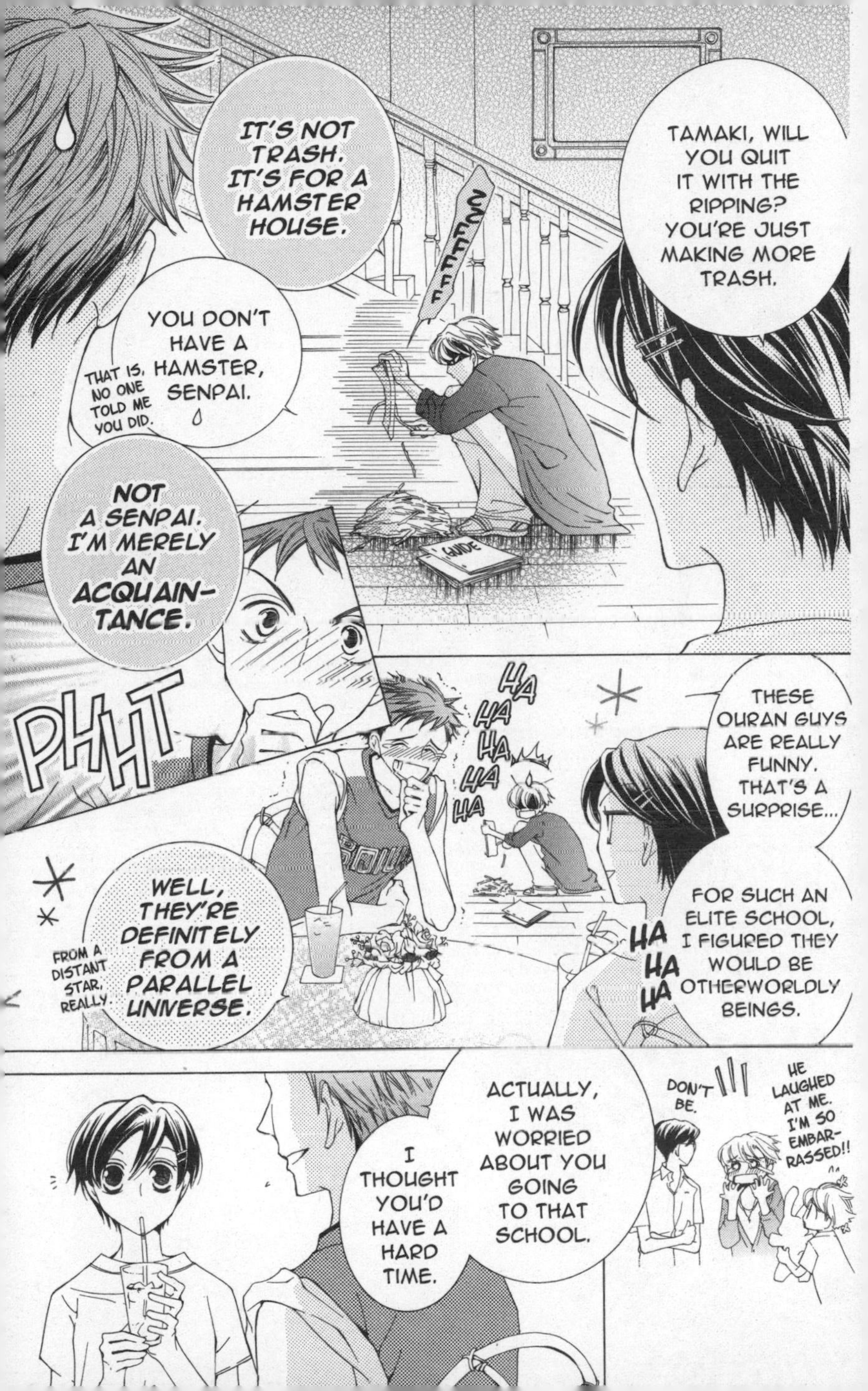
TAMAKI, WILL YOU QUIT IT WITH THE RIPPING? YOU'RE JUST MAKING MORE TRASH.
IT'S NOT TRASH. IT'S FOR A HAMSTER HOUSE.
YOU DON'T HAVE A HAMSTER, SENPAI.
THAT IS, NO ONE TOLD ME YOU DID.
GUIDE
NOT A SENPAI. I'M MERELY AN ACQUAINTANCE.
THESE OURAN GUYS ARE REALLY FUNNY. THAT'S A SURPRISE...
HA HA HA, HA HA
PHHT
FOR SUCH AN ELITE SCHOOL, I FIGURED THEY WOULD BE OTHERWORLDLY BEINGS.
HA HA HA
WELL, THEY'RE DEFINITELY FROM A PARALLEL UNIVERSE.
FROM A DISTANT STAR, REALLY.
HE LAUGHED AT ME. I'M SO EMBARRASSED!!
DON'T BE.
ACTUALLY, I WAS WORRIED ABOUT YOU GOING TO THAT SCHOOL.
I THOUGHT YOU'D HAVE A HARD TIME.

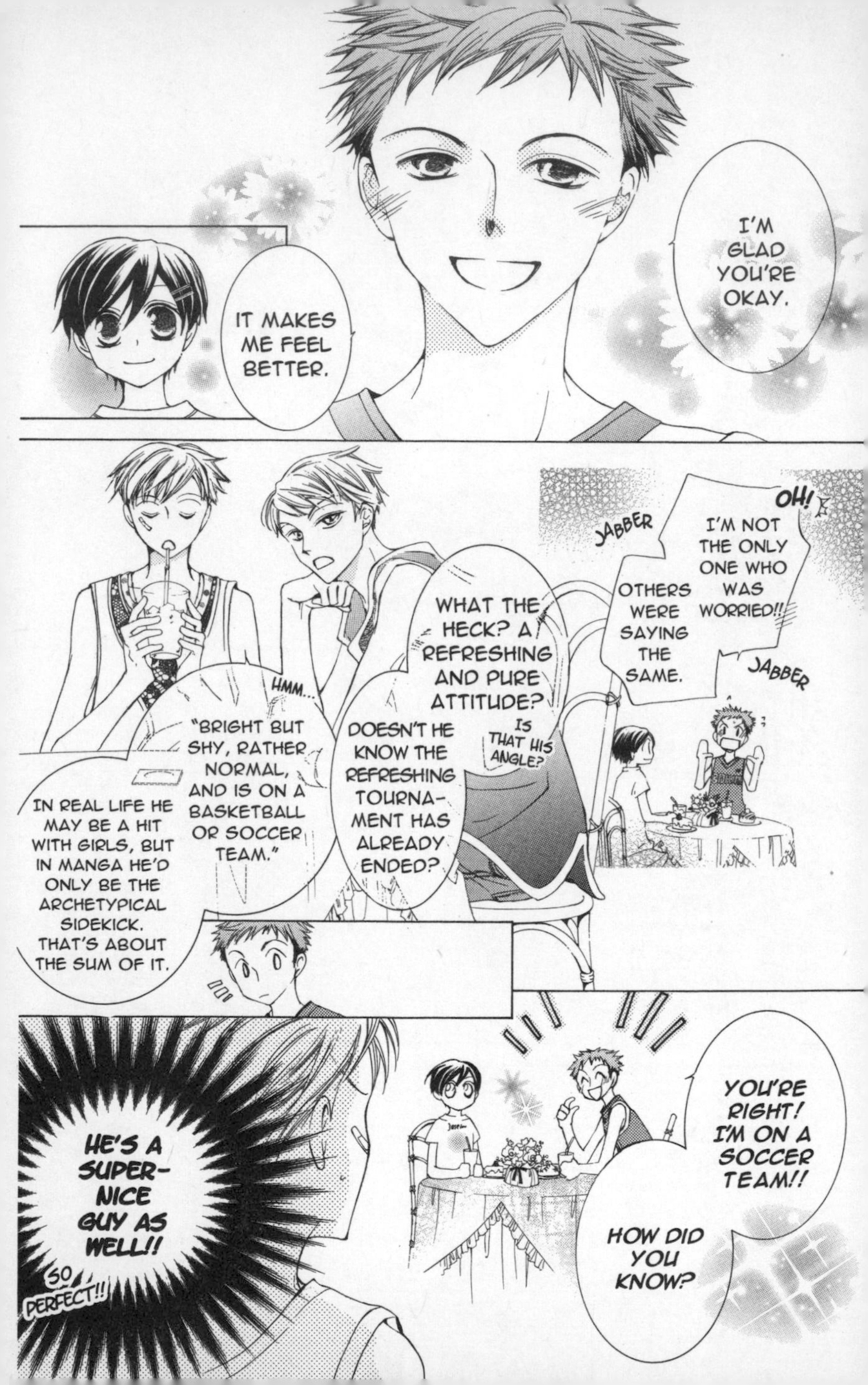
I'M GLAD YOU'RE OKAY.
IT MAKES ME FEEL BETTER.
OH!
I'M NOT THE ONLY ONE WHO WAS WORRIED!!
JABBER
OTHERS WERE SAYING THE SAME.
JABBER
WHAT THE HECK? A REFRESHING AND PURE ATTITUDE?
IS THAT HIS ANGLE?
DOESN'T HE KNOW THE REFRESHING TOURNAMENT HAS ALREADY ENDED?
HMM...
"BRIGHT BUT SHY, RATHER NORMAL, AND IS ON A BASKETBALL OR SOCCER TEAM."
IN REAL LIFE HE MAY BE A HIT WITH GIRLS, BUT IN MANGA HE'D ONLY BE THE ARCHETYPICAL SIDEKICK. THAT'S ABOUT THE SUM OF IT.
YOU'RE RIGHT! I'M ON A SOCCER TEAM!!
HOW DID YOU KNOW?
HE'S A SUPER-NICE GUY AS WELL!!
SO PERFECT!!

3

✿ IT MIGHT BE HARD TO TELL IN THE MANGA, BUT HATORI USES BOTH HAND-PAINTING AND CG TECHNIQUES. FOR EXAMPLE:

HAND-PAINTING

- THE MANGA COVERS (EXCEPT FOR *SENNIN NO YUKI*, VOL. 1)
- THE *LALA* COVERS
- THE "KID VERSION" TWINS, TAMAKI, AND HARUHI FOUND ON THE BACK COVER OF THIS VOLUME (DESIGNED FOR A PHONE CARD), AND SO ON.

CG

- OTHER VARIOUS IMAGES (I.E., MOST OF THEM)

RECENTLY, HATORI HAS COME TO A CONCLUSION THAT WHAT A MANGA-KA NEEDS THE MOST IS DECISIVENESS AND A CERTAIN LEVEL OF COURAGE--BE IT SETTLING ON A CONCEPT OR DRAWING IMAGES. AS FOR ME, I TOTALLY LACK SUCH ATTRIBUTES. (I'M THE TYPE WHO GOES TO BARGAIN SALES, ONLY TO RETURN EMPTY-HANDED.) IT MAKES ME WONDER. I MEAN, I'M SO SCARED TO MAKE A MISTAKE THAT I JUST DON'T WANT TO PAINT BY HAND. INSTEAD, I HIDE BEHIND THE SAFETY OF CG. YOU KNOW, I THINK THAT'S WHY I NEVER GET GOOD AT HAND PAINTING. (IT'S REALLY TOO BAD...)

BUT... I'LL TRY MY BEST! I MEAN IT!!

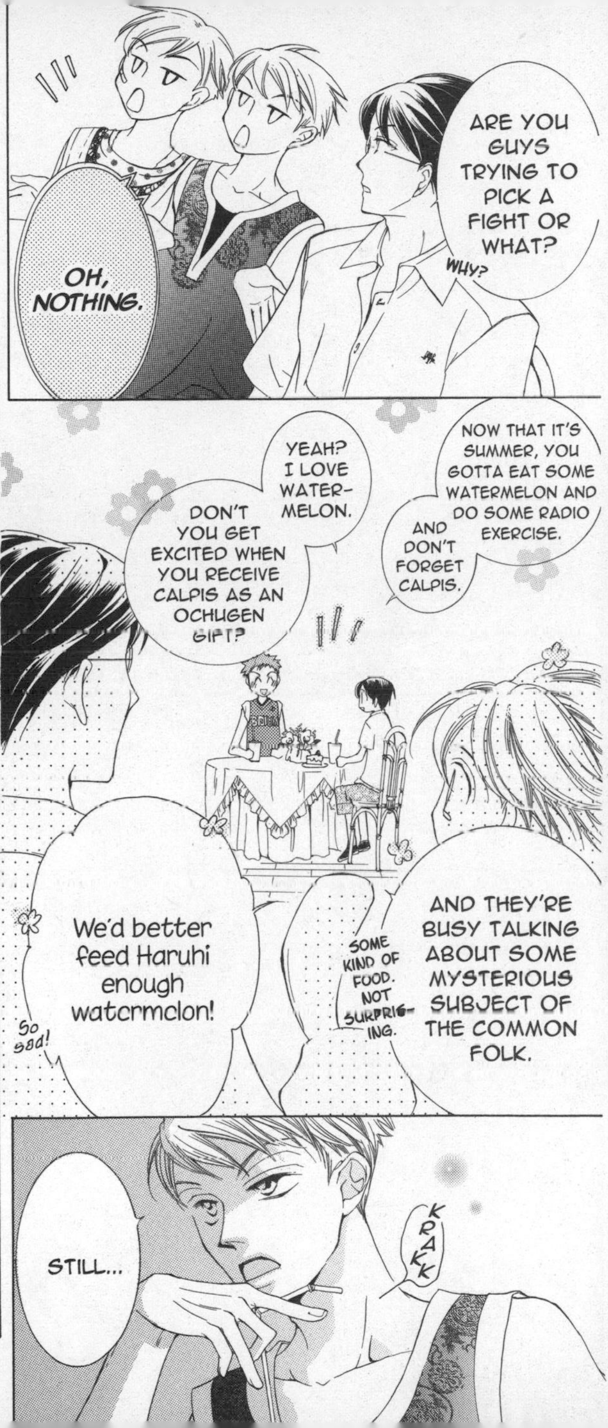
ARE YOU GUYS TRYING TO PICK A FIGHT OR WHAT?
WHY?
OH, NOTHING.
NOW THAT IT'S SUMMER, YOU GOTTA EAT SOME WATERMELON AND DO SOME RADIO EXERCISE.
AND DON'T FORGET CALPIS.
YEAH? I LOVE WATER-MELON.
DON'T YOU GET EXCITED WHEN YOU RECEIVE CALPIS AS AN OCHUGEN GIFT?
AND THEY'RE BUSY TALKING ABOUT SOME MYSTERIOUS SUBJECT OF THE COMMON FOLK.
SOME KIND OF FOOD. NOT SURPRIS-ING.
We'd better feed Haruhi enough watermelon!
So sad!
KRAKK
STILL...

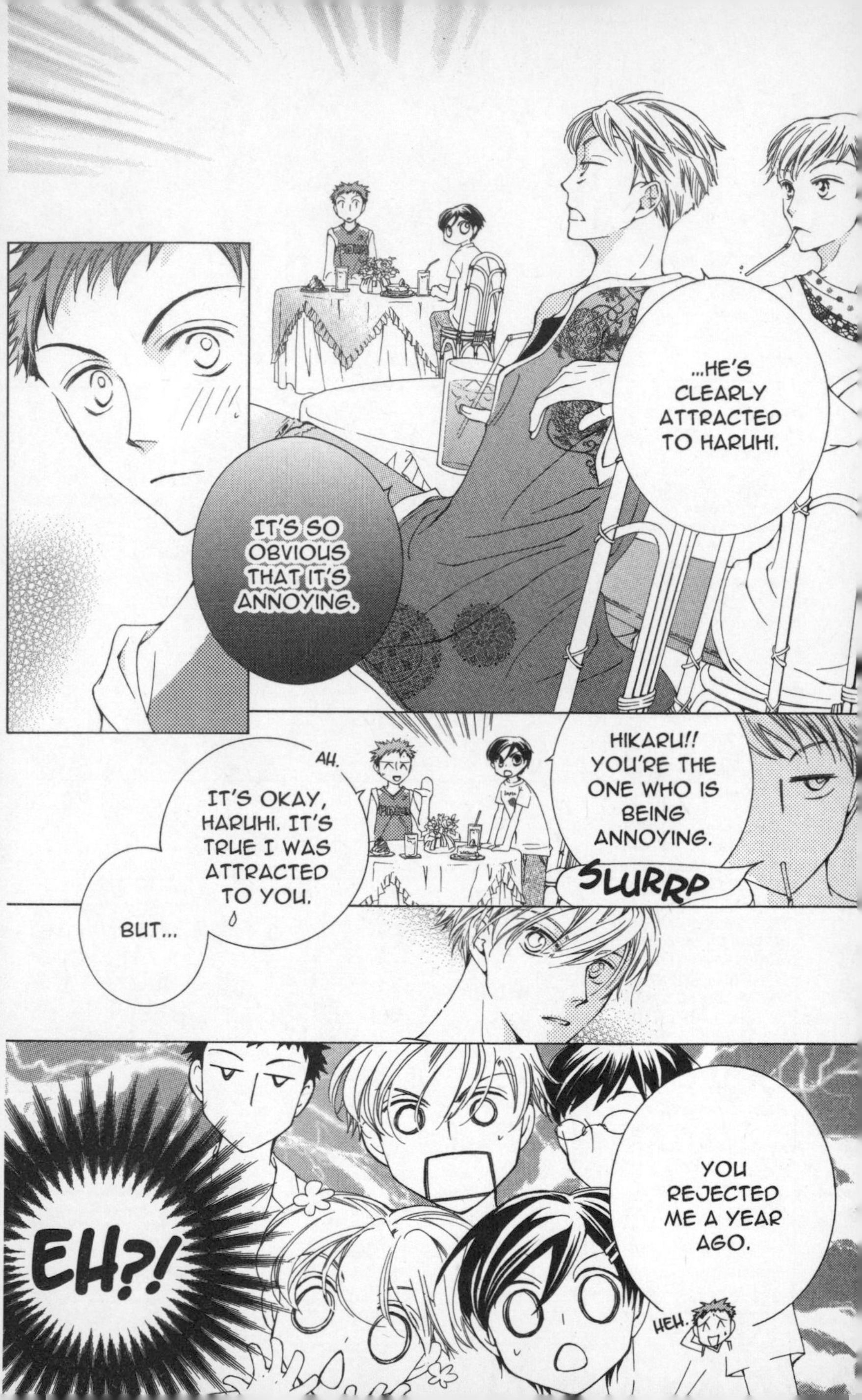
...HE'S CLEARLY ATTRACTED TO HARUHI.
IT'S SO OBVIOUS THAT IT'S ANNOYING.
HIKARU!! YOU'RE THE ONE WHO IS BEING ANNOYING.
SLURRP
AH.
IT'S OKAY, HARUHI. IT'S TRUE I WAS ATTRACTED TO YOU.
BUT...
YOU REJECTED ME A YEAR AGO.
HEH.
EH?!

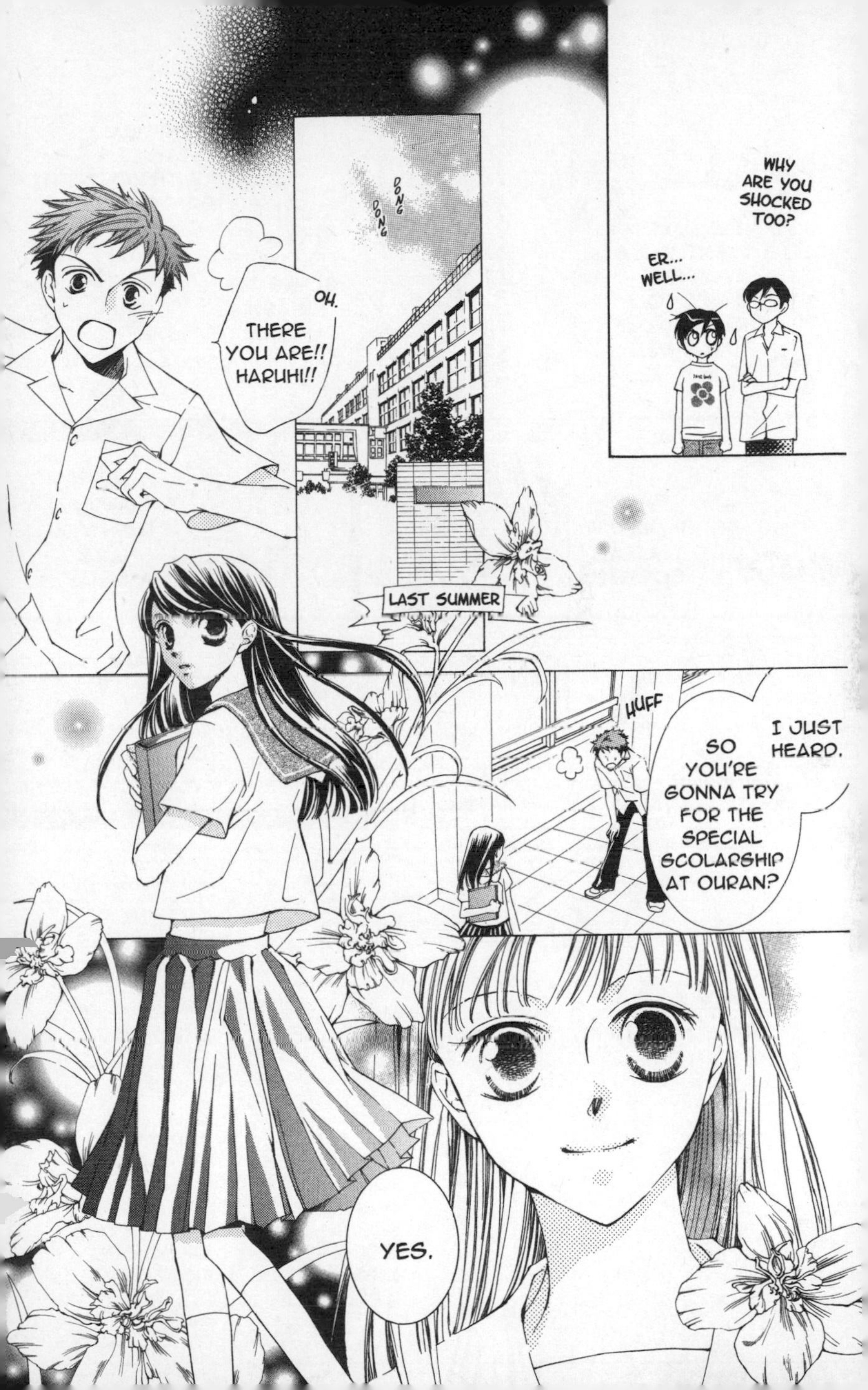
WHY ARE YOU SHOCKED TOO?
ER... WELL...
DONG DONG
LAST SUMMER
OH.
THERE YOU ARE!! HARUHI!!
HUFF
I JUST HEARD.
SO YOU'RE GONNA TRY FOR THE SPECIAL SCOLARSHIP AT OURAN?
YES.

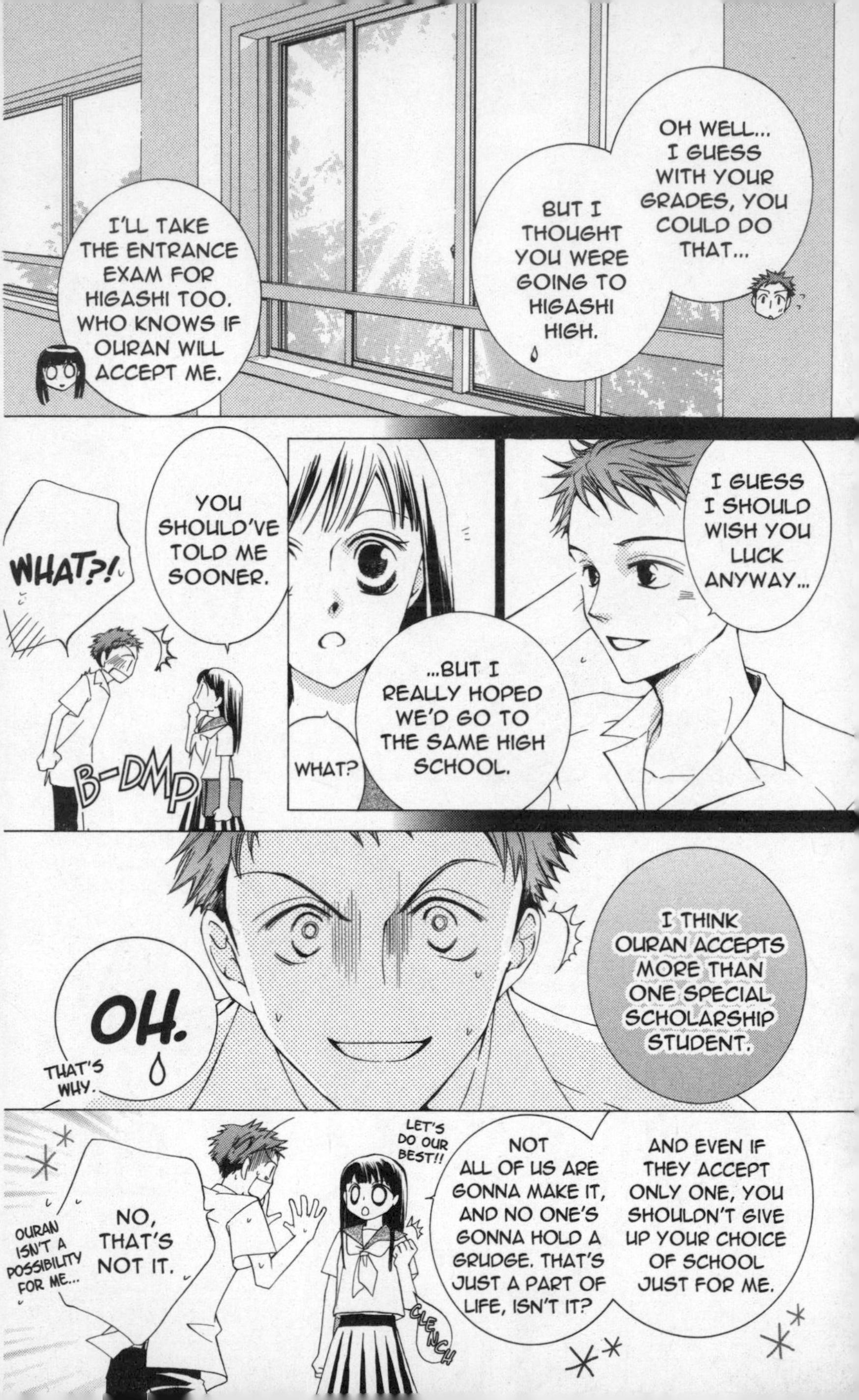
OH WELL... I GUESS WITH YOUR GRADES, YOU COULD DO THAT...
BUT I THOUGHT YOU WERE GOING TO HIGASHI HIGH.
I'LL TAKE THE ENTRANCE EXAM FOR HIGASHI TOO. WHO KNOWS IF OURAN WILL ACCEPT ME.
I GUESS I SHOULD WISH YOU LUCK ANYWAY...
...BUT I REALLY HOPED WE'D GO TO THE SAME HIGH SCHOOL.
WHAT?
YOU SHOULD'VE TOLD ME SOONER.
WHAT?!
B-DMP
I THINK OURAN ACCEPTS MORE THAN ONE SPECIAL SCHOLARSHIP STUDENT.
OH.
THAT'S WHY.
AND EVEN IF THEY ACCEPT ONLY ONE, YOU SHOULDN'T GIVE UP YOUR CHOICE OF SCHOOL JUST FOR ME.
NOT ALL OF US ARE GONNA MAKE IT, AND NO ONE'S GONNA HOLD A GRUDGE. THAT'S JUST A PART OF LIFE, ISN'T IT?
LET'S DO OUR BEST!!
CLENCH
NO, THAT'S NOT IT.
OURAN ISN'T A POSSIBILITY FOR ME...

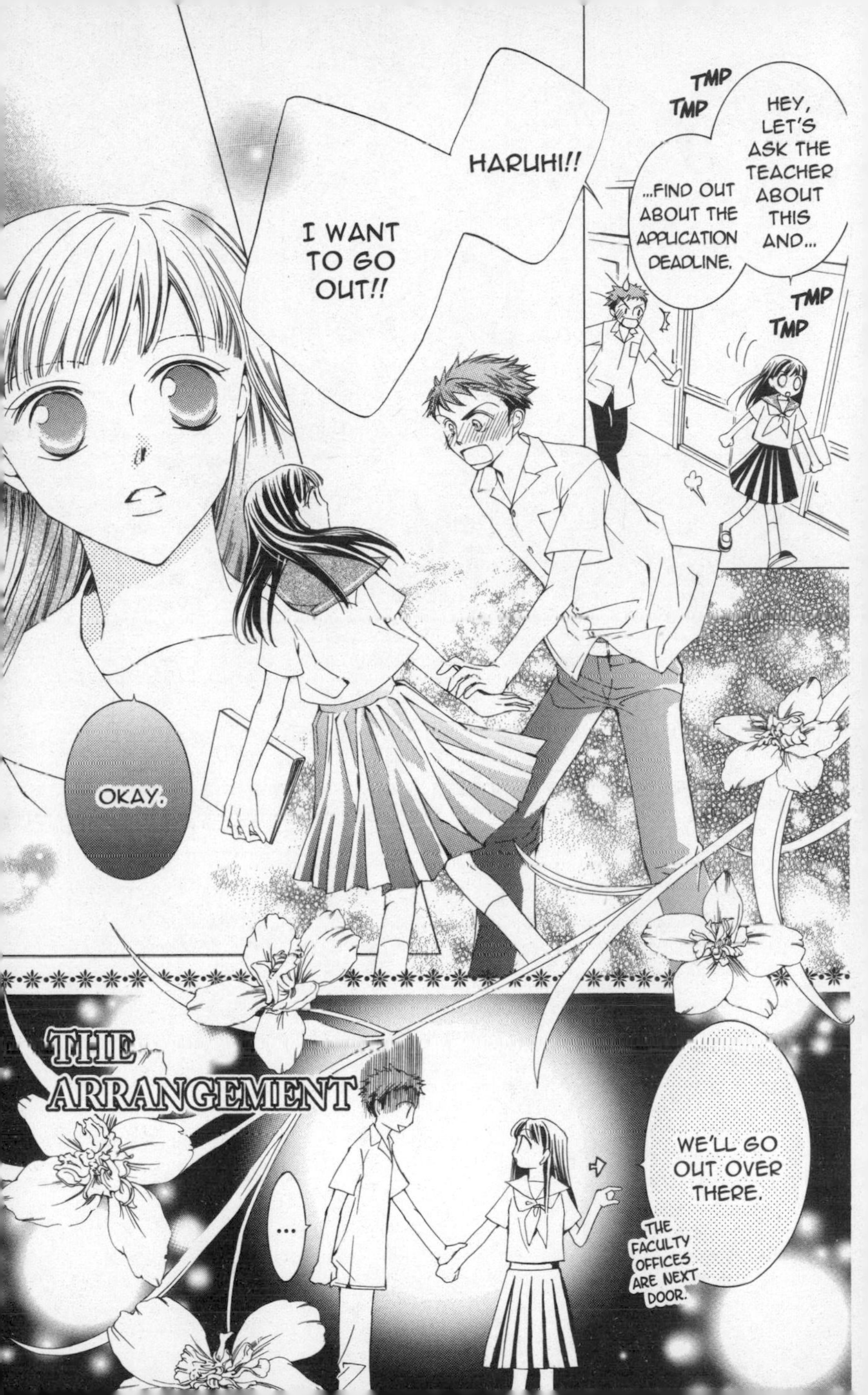
TMP TMP
HEY, LET'S ASK THE TEACHER ABOUT THIS AND...
...FIND OUT ABOUT THE APPLICATION DEADLINE.
TMP TMP
HARUHI!!
I WANT TO GO OUT!!
OKAY.
THE ARRANGEMENT
WE'LL GO OUT OVER THERE.
THE FACULTY OFFICES ARE NEXT DOOR.
...

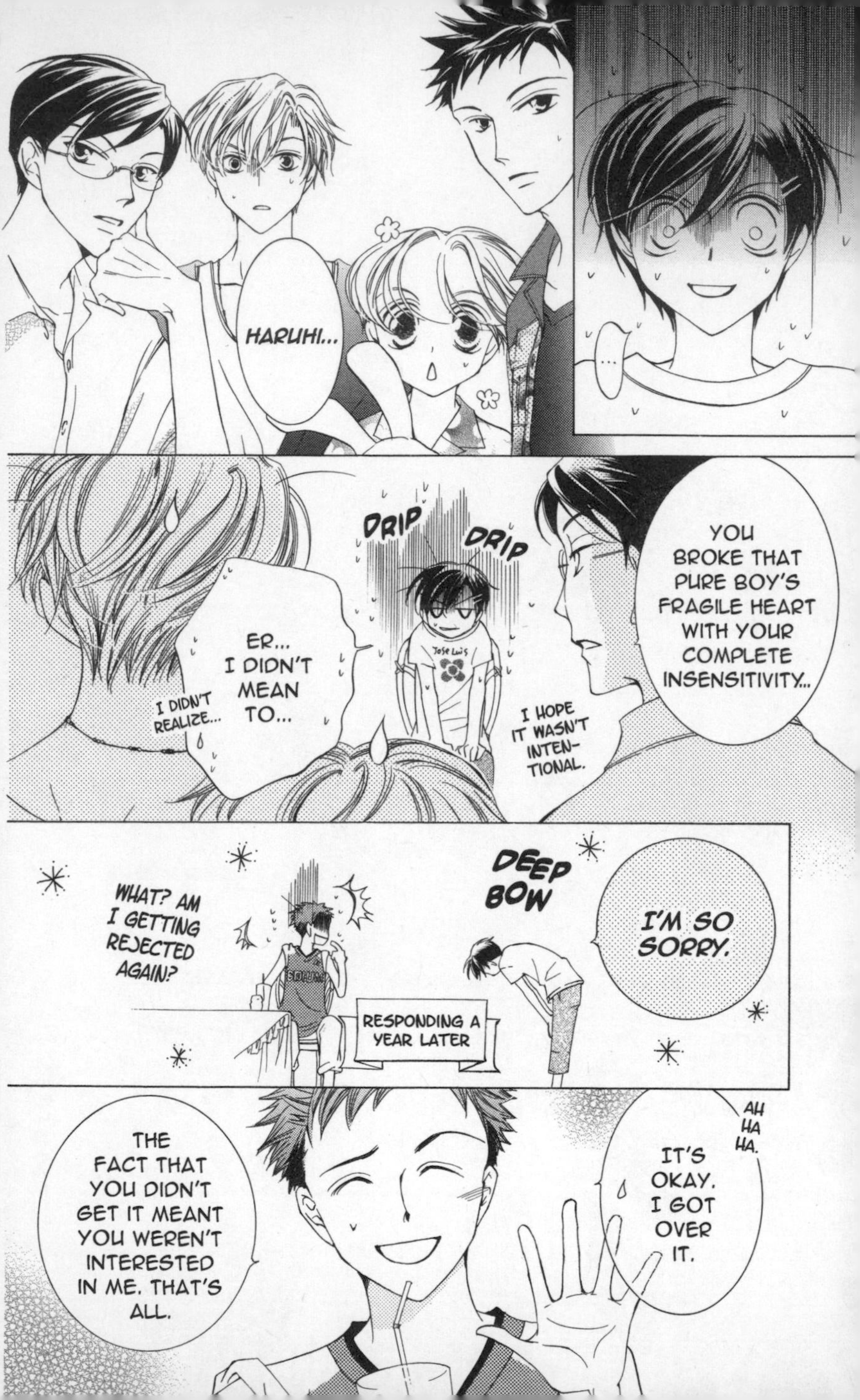
...
HARUHI...
YOU BROKE THAT PURE BOY'S FRAGILE HEART WITH YOUR COMPLETE INSENSITIVITY...
I HOPE IT WASN'T INTEN-TIONAL.
DRIP DRIP
ER... I DIDN'T MEAN TO...
I DIDN'T REALIZE...
I'M SO SORRY.
DEEP BOW
RESPONDING A YEAR LATER
WHAT? AM I GETTING REJECTED AGAIN?
AH HA HA.
IT'S OKAY. I GOT OVER IT.
THE FACT THAT YOU DIDN'T GET IT MEANT YOU WEREN'T INTERESTED IN ME. THAT'S ALL.

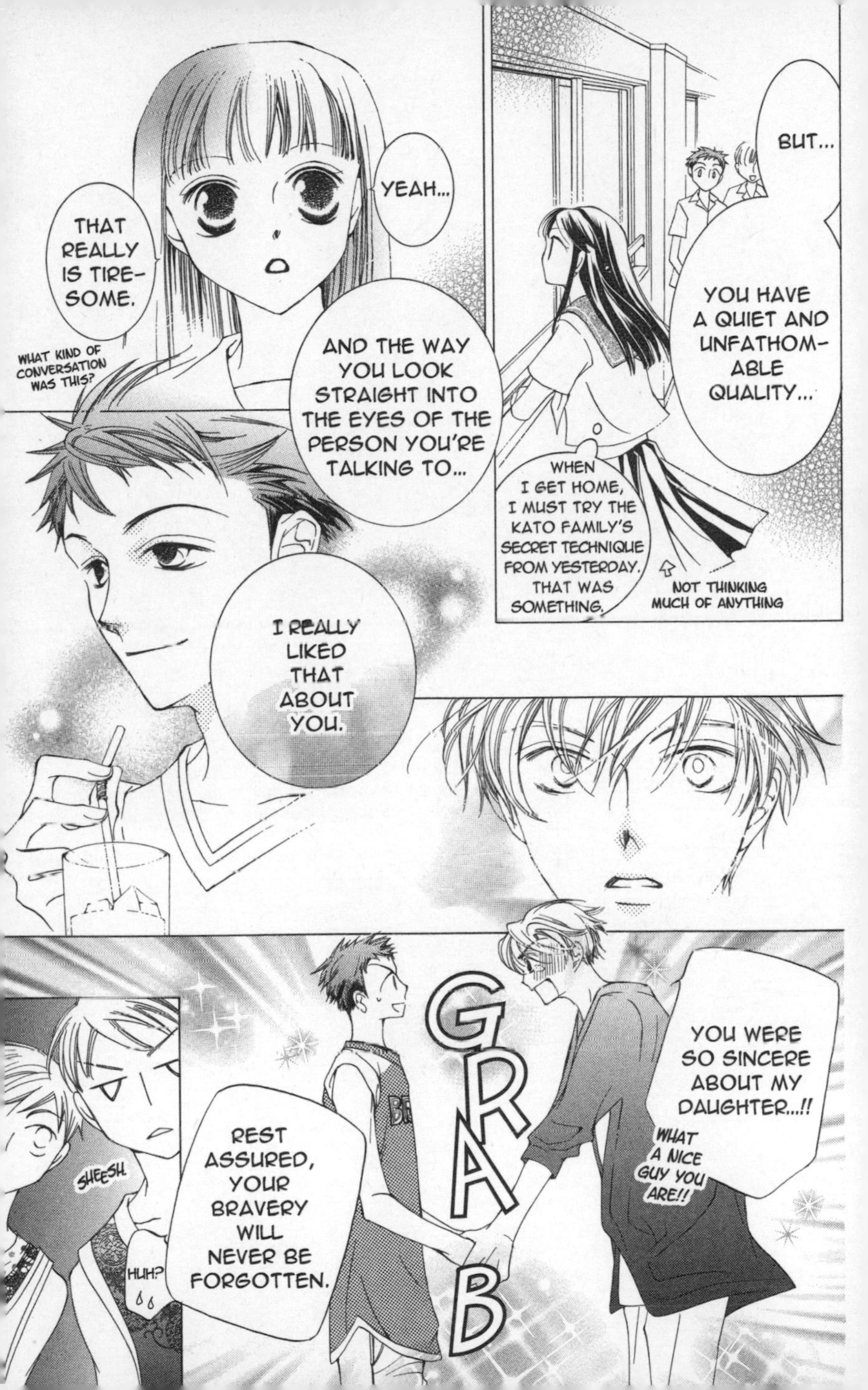
BUT...
YOU HAVE A QUIET AND UNFATHOMABLE QUALITY...
WHEN I GET HOME, I MUST TRY THE KATO FAMILY'S SECRET TECHNIQUE FROM YESTERDAY. THAT WAS SOMETHING.
NOT THINKING MUCH OF ANYTHING
YEAH...
THAT REALLY IS TIRESOME.
WHAT KIND OF CONVERSATION WAS THIS?
AND THE WAY YOU LOOK STRAIGHT INTO THE EYES OF THE PERSON YOU'RE TALKING TO...
I REALLY LIKED THAT ABOUT YOU.
YOU WERE SO SINCERE ABOUT MY DAUGHTER...!!
WHAT A NICE GUY YOU ARE!!
GRAB
REST ASSURED, YOUR BRAVERY WILL NEVER BE FORGOTTEN.
SHEESH.
HUH?

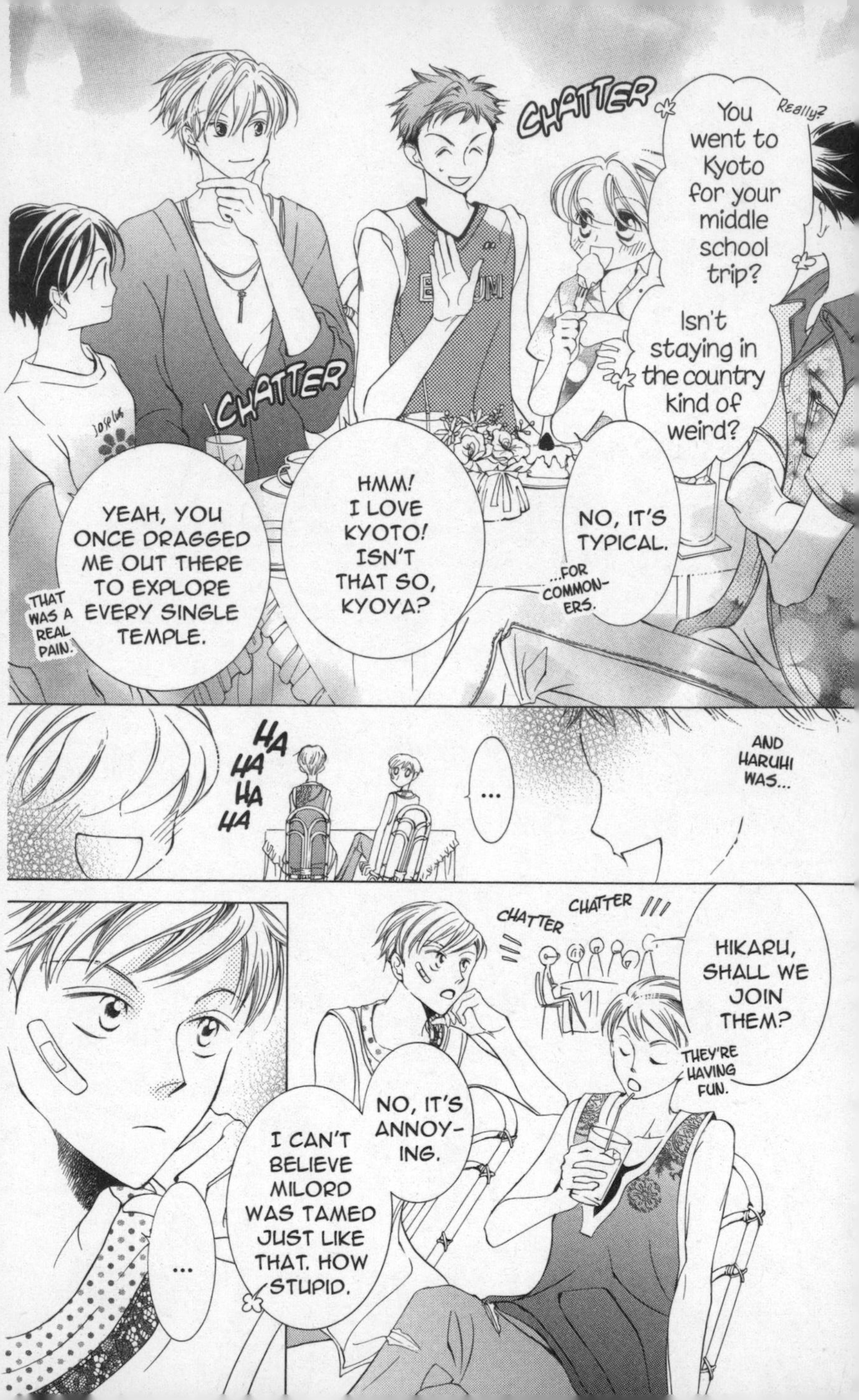
Really?
You went to Kyoto for your middle school trip?
Isn't staying in the country kind of weird?
CHATTER
NO, IT'S TYPICAL.
...FOR COMMONERS.
HMM! I LOVE KYOTO! ISN'T THAT SO, KYOYA?
CHATTER
YEAH, YOU ONCE DRAGGED ME OUT THERE TO EXPLORE EVERY SINGLE TEMPLE.
THAT WAS A REAL PAIN.
AND HARUHI WAS...
...
HA HA HA HA
HIKARU, SHALL WE JOIN THEM?
THEY'RE HAVING FUN.
CHATTER
CHATTER
NO, IT'S ANNOYING.
I CAN'T BELIEVE MILORD WAS TAMED JUST LIKE THAT. HOW STUPID.
...

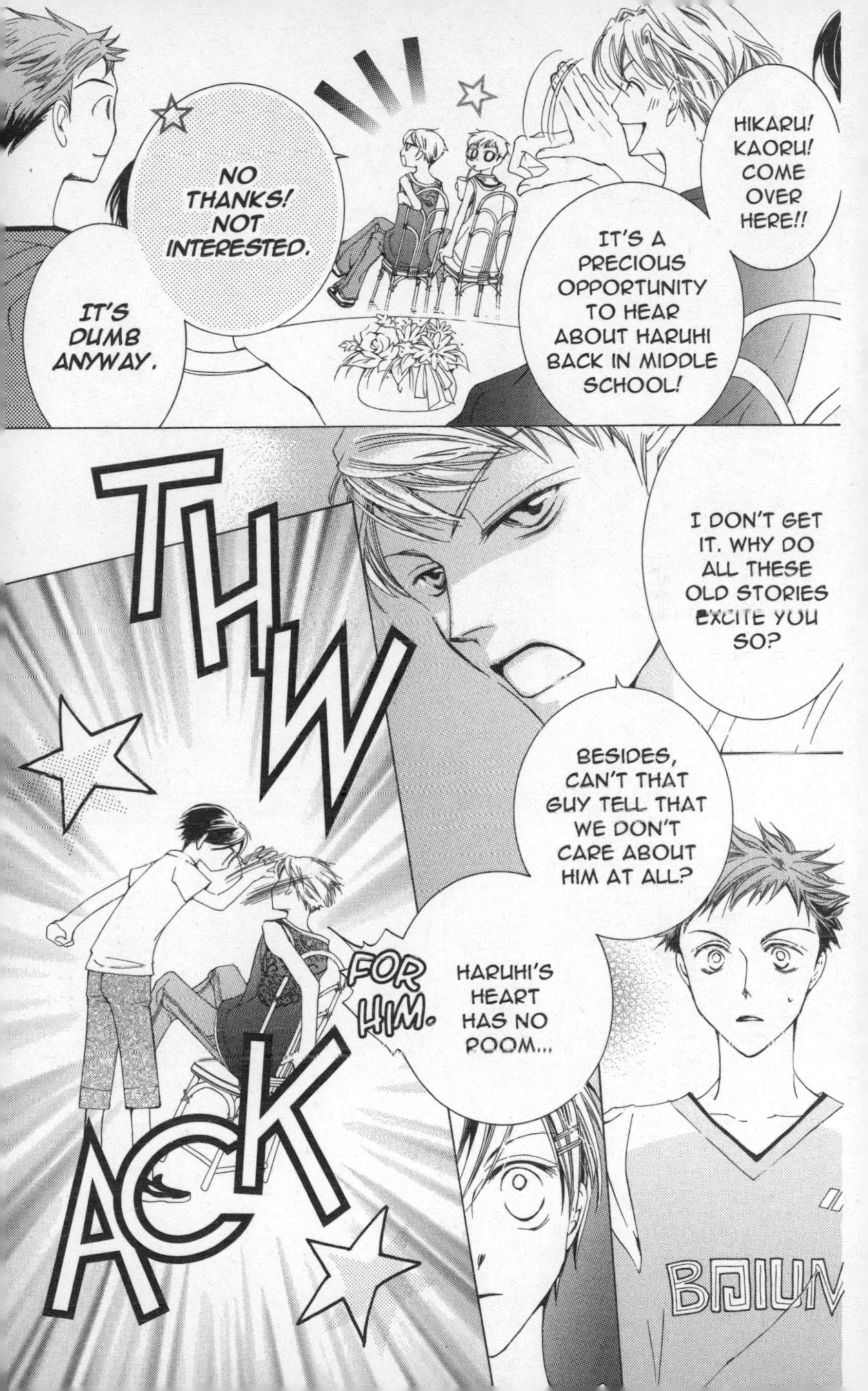
HIKARU! KAORU! COME OVER HERE!!
IT'S A PRECIOUS OPPORTUNITY TO HEAR ABOUT HARUHI BACK IN MIDDLE SCHOOL!
NO THANKS! NOT INTERESTED.
IT'S DUMB ANYWAY.
I DON'T GET IT. WHY DO ALL THESE OLD STORIES EXCITE YOU SO?
BESIDES, CAN'T THAT GUY TELL THAT WE DON'T CARE ABOUT HIM AT ALL?
HARUHI'S HEART HAS NO ROOM...
FOR HIM.
THWACK

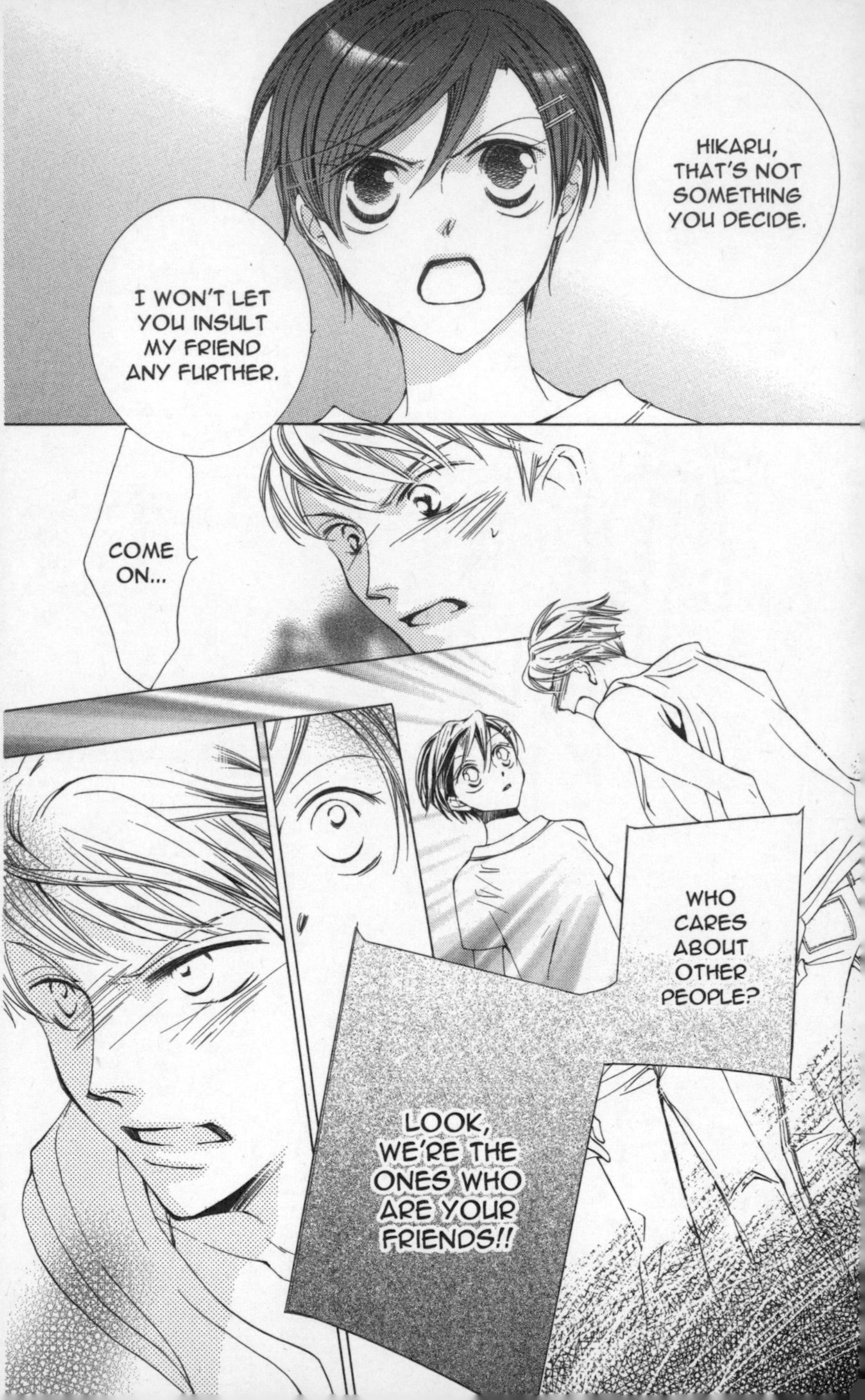
HIKARU, THAT'S NOT SOMETHING YOU DECIDE.
I WON'T LET YOU INSULT MY FRIEND ANY FURTHER.
COME ON...
WHO CARES ABOUT OTHER PEOPLE?
LOOK, WE'RE THE ONES WHO ARE YOUR FRIENDS!!

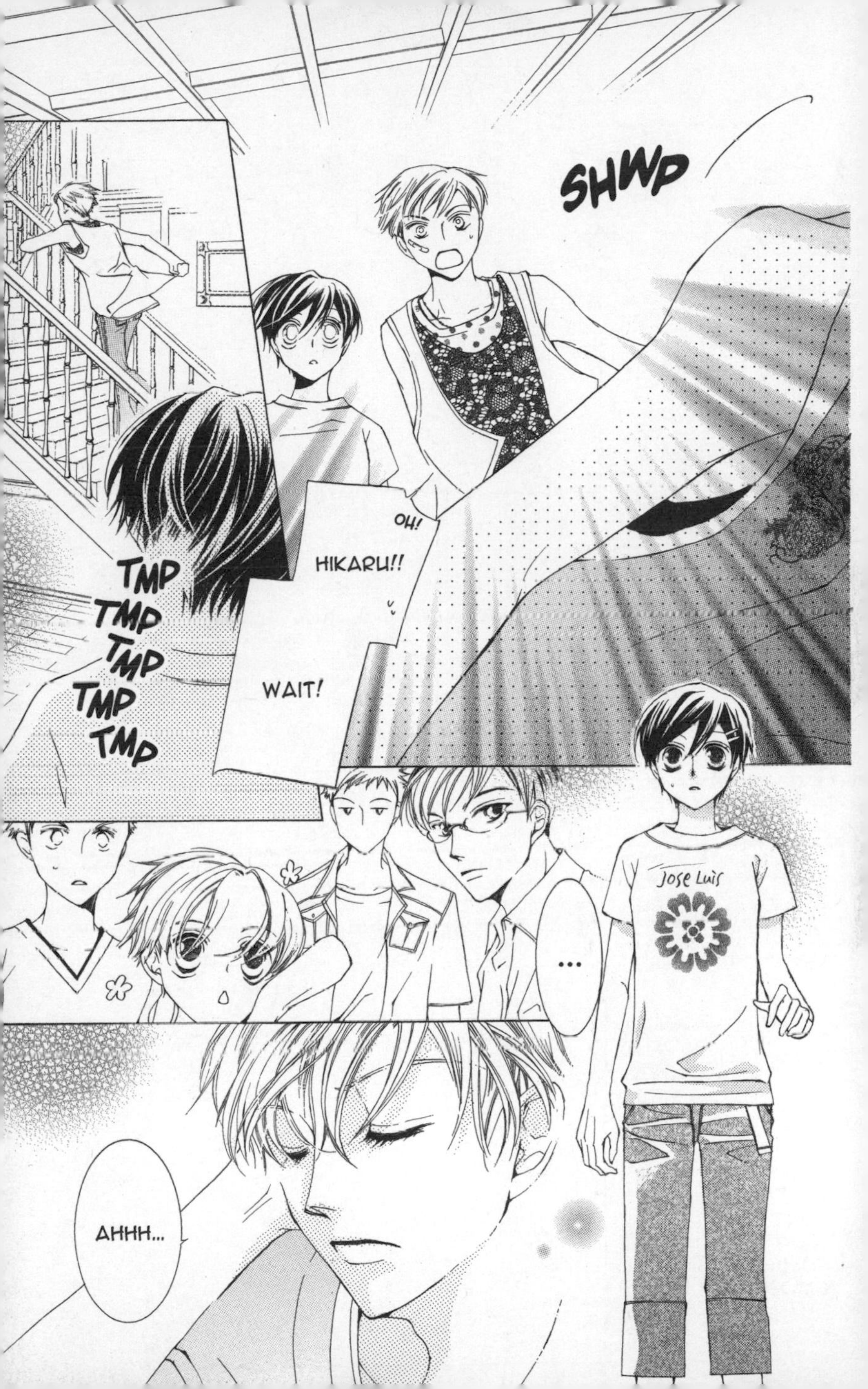
SHWP
OH!
HIKARU!!
WAIT!
TMP TMP TMP TMP TMP
...
AHHH...

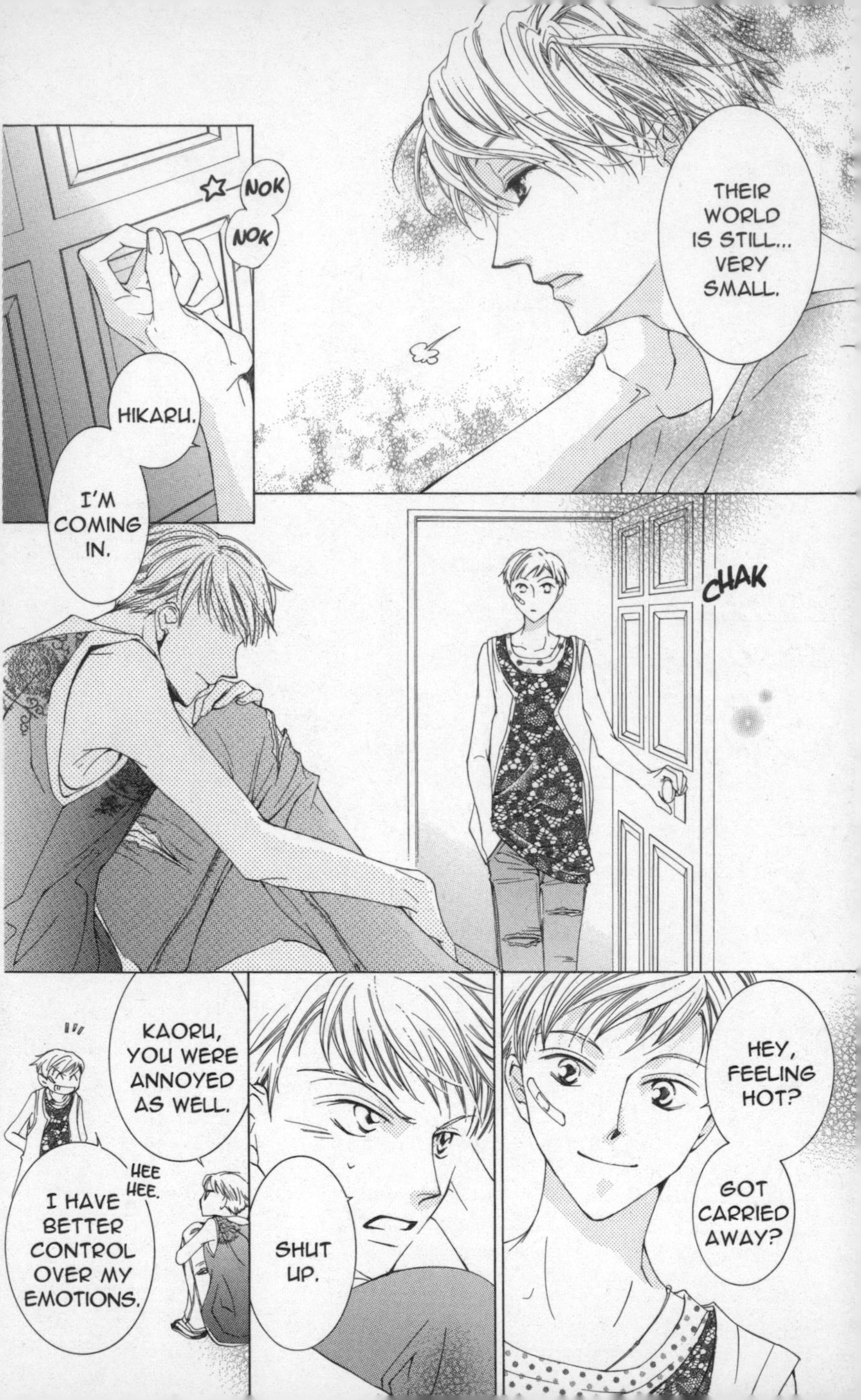
THEIR WORLD IS STILL... VERY SMALL.
NOK
NOK
HIKARU.
I'M COMING IN.
CHAK
HEY, FEELING HOT?
GOT CARRIED AWAY?
SHUT UP.
KAORU, YOU WERE ANNOYED AS WELL.
HEE HEE.
I HAVE BETTER CONTROL OVER MY EMOTIONS.

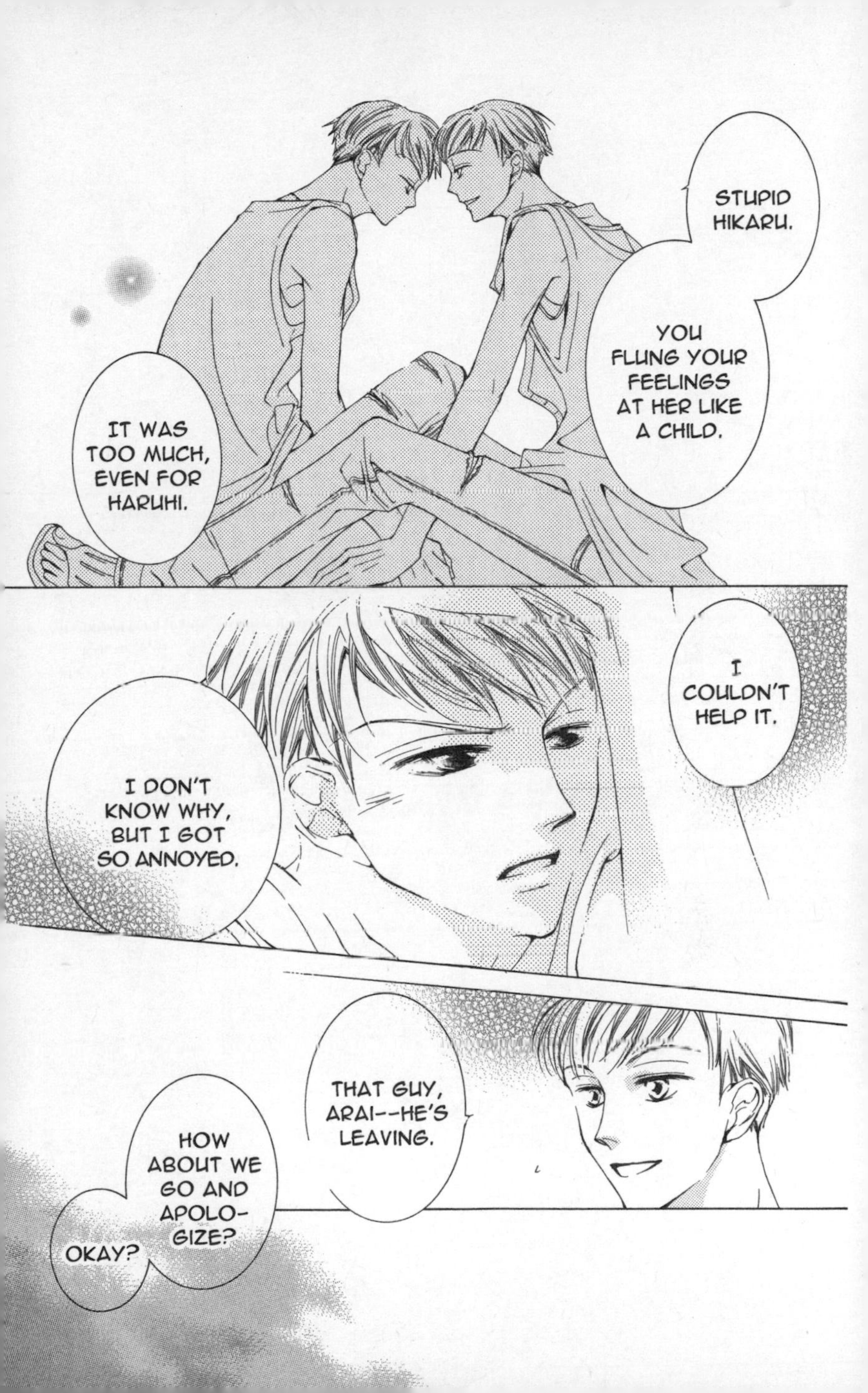
STUPID HIKARU.
YOU FLUNG YOUR FEELINGS AT HER LIKE A CHILD.
IT WAS TOO MUCH, EVEN FOR HARUHI.
I COULDN'T HELP IT.
I DON'T KNOW WHY, BUT I GOT SO ANNOYED.
THAT GUY, ARAI--HE'S LEAVING.
HOW ABOUT WE GO AND APOLO-GIZE?
OKAY?

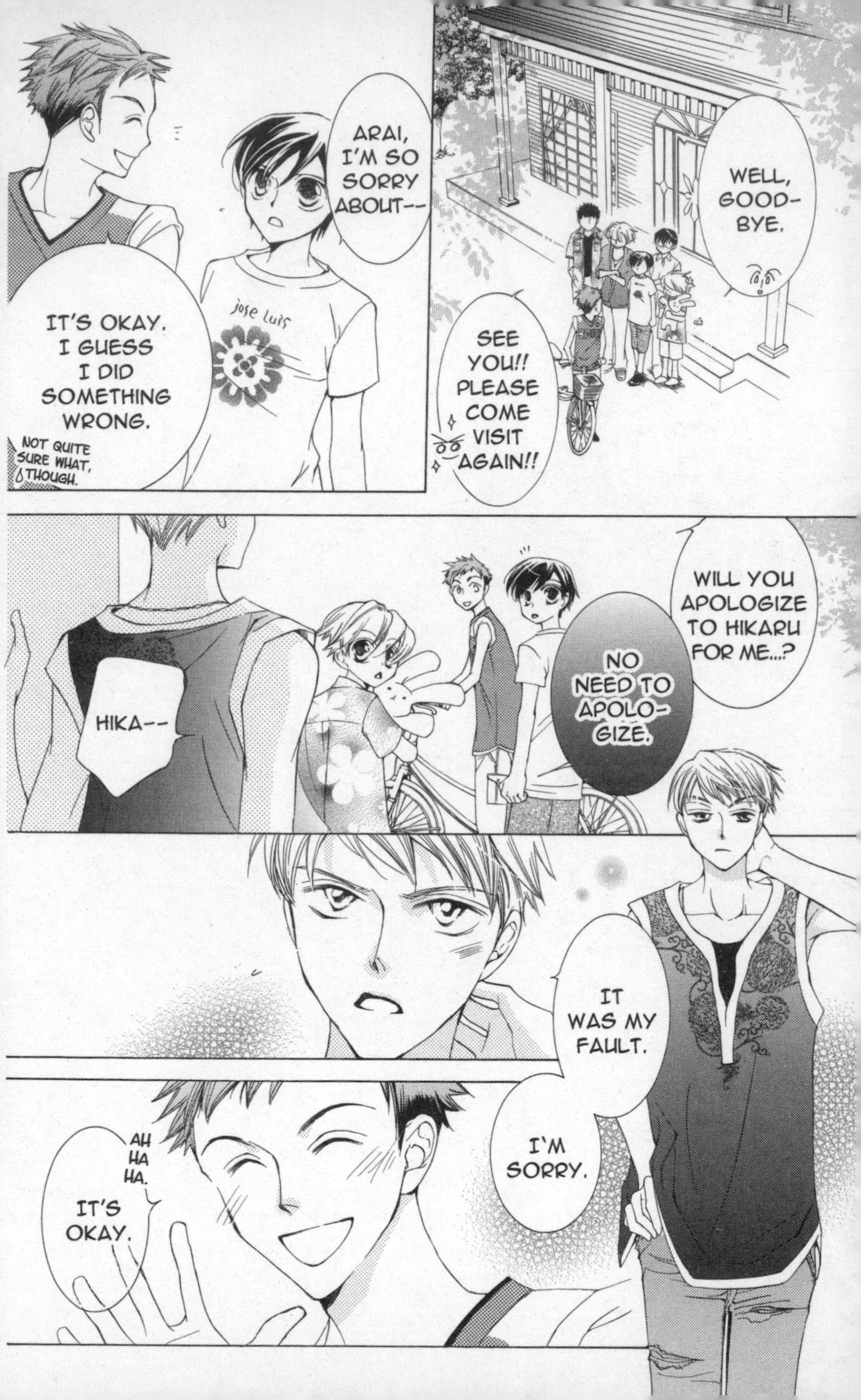
WELL, GOOD-BYE.
SEE YOU!! PLEASE COME VISIT AGAIN!!
ARAI, I'M SO SORRY ABOUT--
jose luis
IT'S OKAY. I GUESS I DID SOMETHING WRONG.
NOT QUITE SURE WHAT, THOUGH.
WILL YOU APOLOGIZE TO HIKARU FOR ME...?
NO NEED TO APOLO-GIZE.
HIKA--
IT WAS MY FAULT.
I'M SORRY.
AH HA HA.
IT'S OKAY.

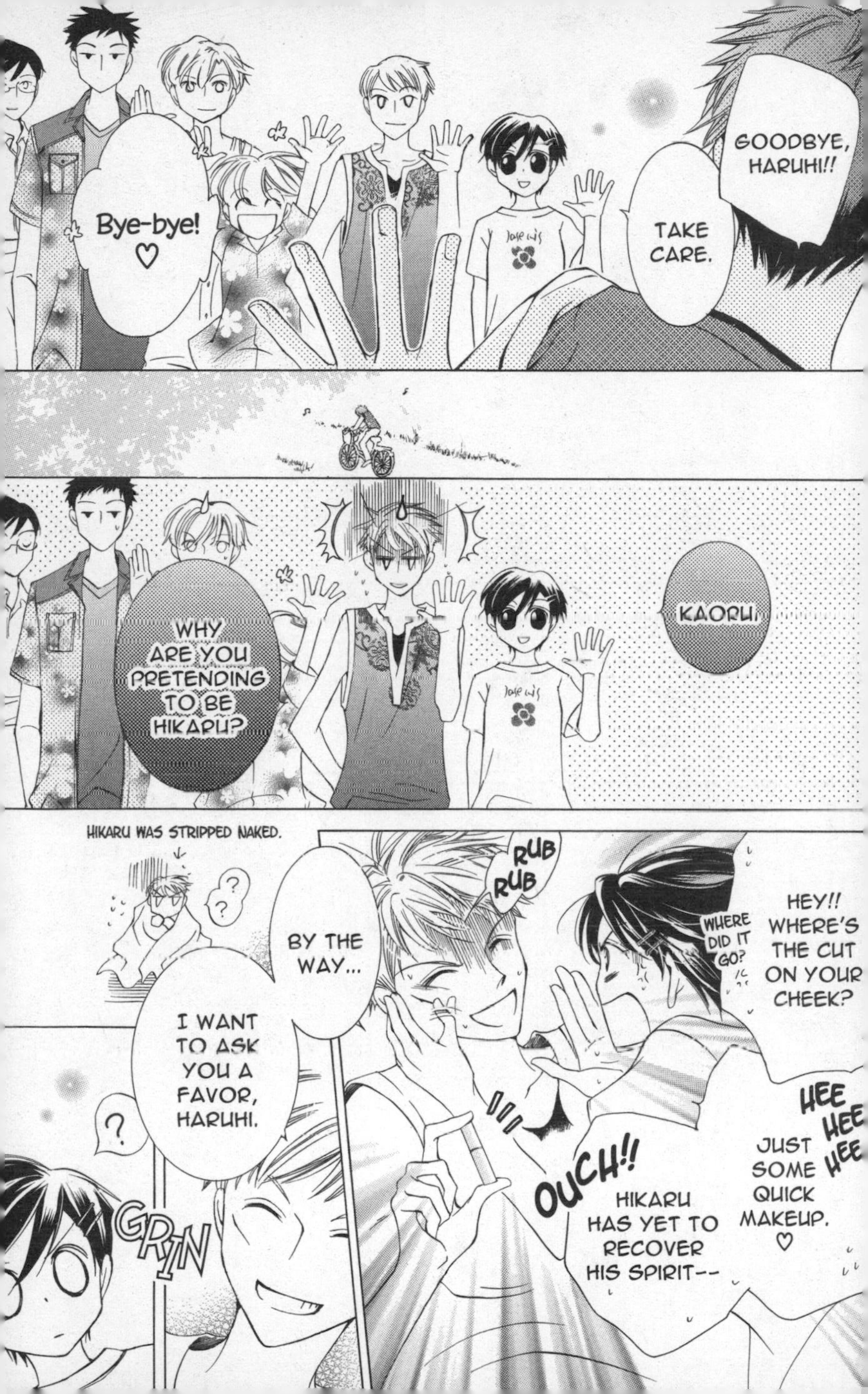
GOODBYE, HARUHI!!
TAKE CARE.
Bye-bye! ♡
KAORU,
WHY ARE YOU PRETENDING TO BE HIKARU?
HEY!! WHERE'S THE CUT ON YOUR CHEEK?
WHERE DID IT GO?
RUB RUB
HEE HEE HEE
JUST SOME QUICK MAKEUP. ♡
OUCH!!
HIKARU HAS YET TO RECOVER HIS SPIRIT--
HIKARU WAS STRIPPED NAKED.
? ?
BY THE WAY...
I WANT TO ASK YOU A FAVOR, HARUHI.
?
GRIN

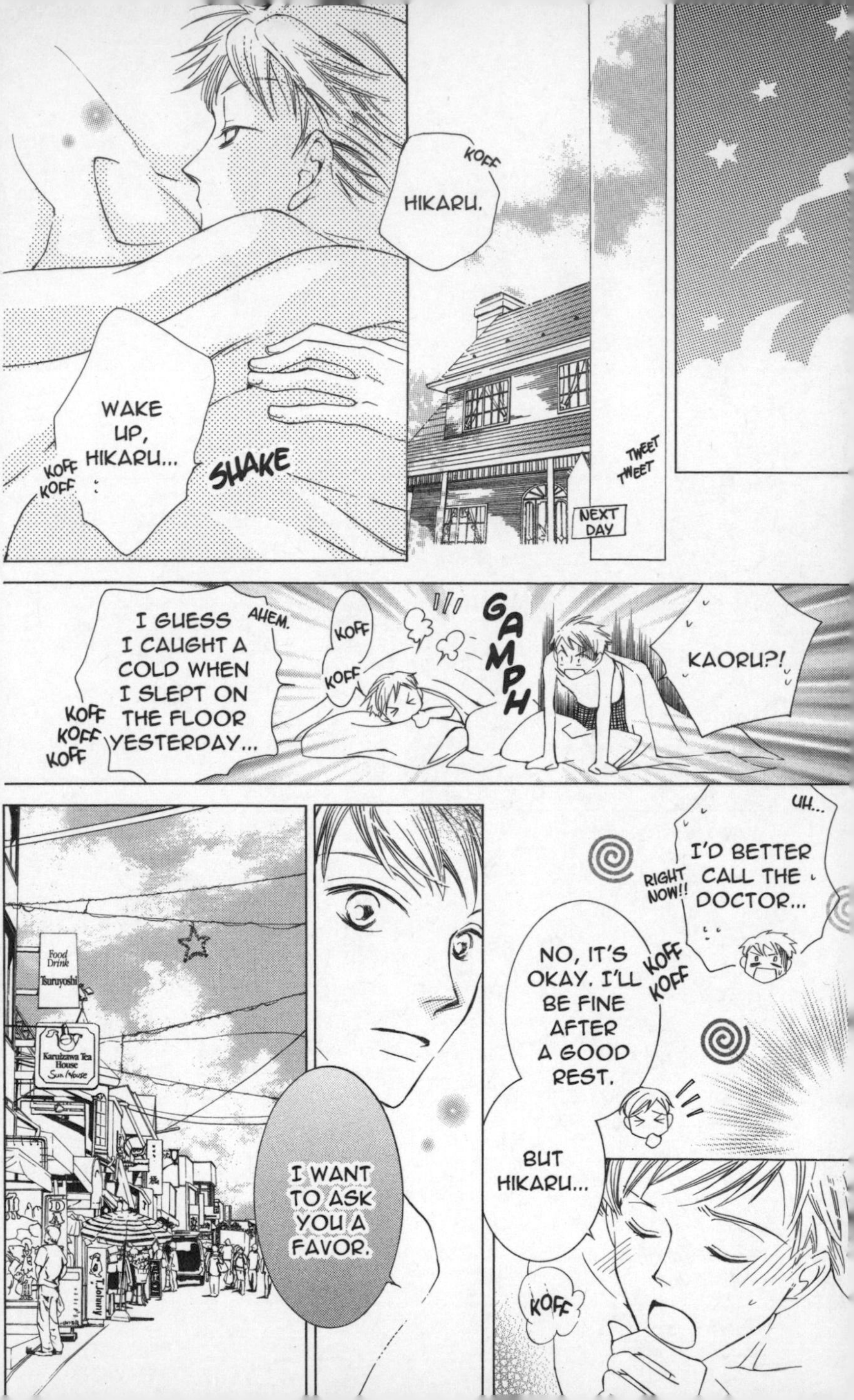
TWEET TWEET
NEXT DAY
KOFF
HIKARU.
WAKE UP, HIKARU...
KOFF KOFF
SHAKE
KAORU?!
GAMPH
KOFF
KOFF
I GUESS I CAUGHT A COLD WHEN I SLEPT ON THE FLOOR YESTERDAY...
AHEM.
KOFF KOFF KOFF
UH...
I'D BETTER CALL THE DOCTOR...
RIGHT NOW!!
NO, IT'S OKAY. I'LL BE FINE AFTER A GOOD REST.
KOFF KOFF
BUT HIKARU...
KOFF
I WANT TO ASK YOU A FAVOR.
Food Drink Tsuruyoshi
Karuizawa Tea House Sun House
T.Johnny

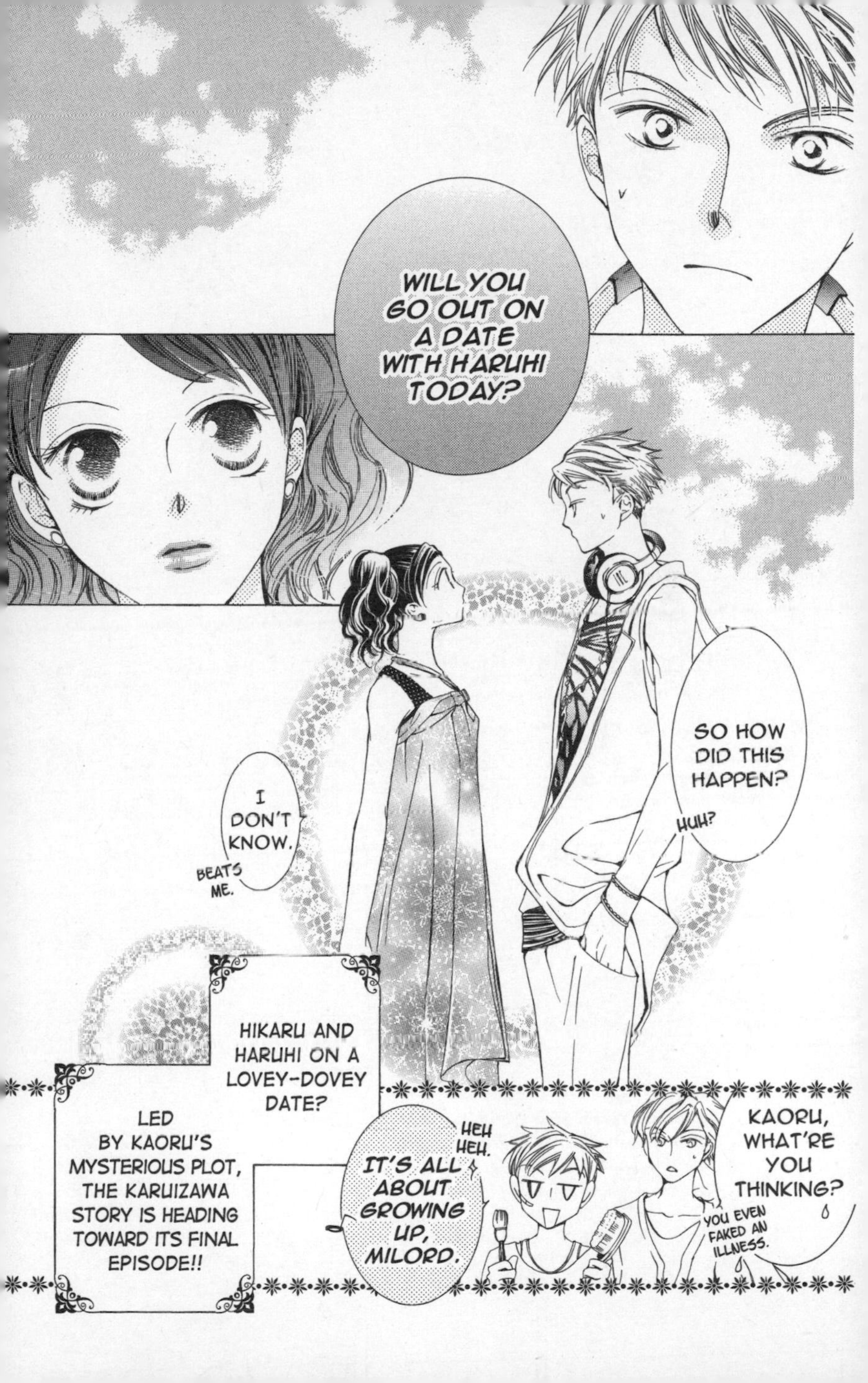
WILL YOU GO OUT ON A DATE WITH HARUHI TODAY?
SO HOW DID THIS HAPPEN?
HUH?
I DON'T KNOW.
BEATS ME.
HIKARU AND HARUHI ON A LOVEY-DOVEY DATE?
KAORU, WHAT'RE YOU THINKING?
YOU EVEN FAKED AN ILLNESS.
HEH HEH.
IT'S ALL ABOUT GROWING UP, MILORD.
LED BY KAORU'S MYSTERIOUS PLOT, THE KARUIZAWA STORY IS HEADING TOWARD ITS FINAL EPISODE!!

GUEST ROOM: FAXES ①

SPECIAL THANKS TO
KANA MASAYA
BY (KANA OF) NIZAKANA!!

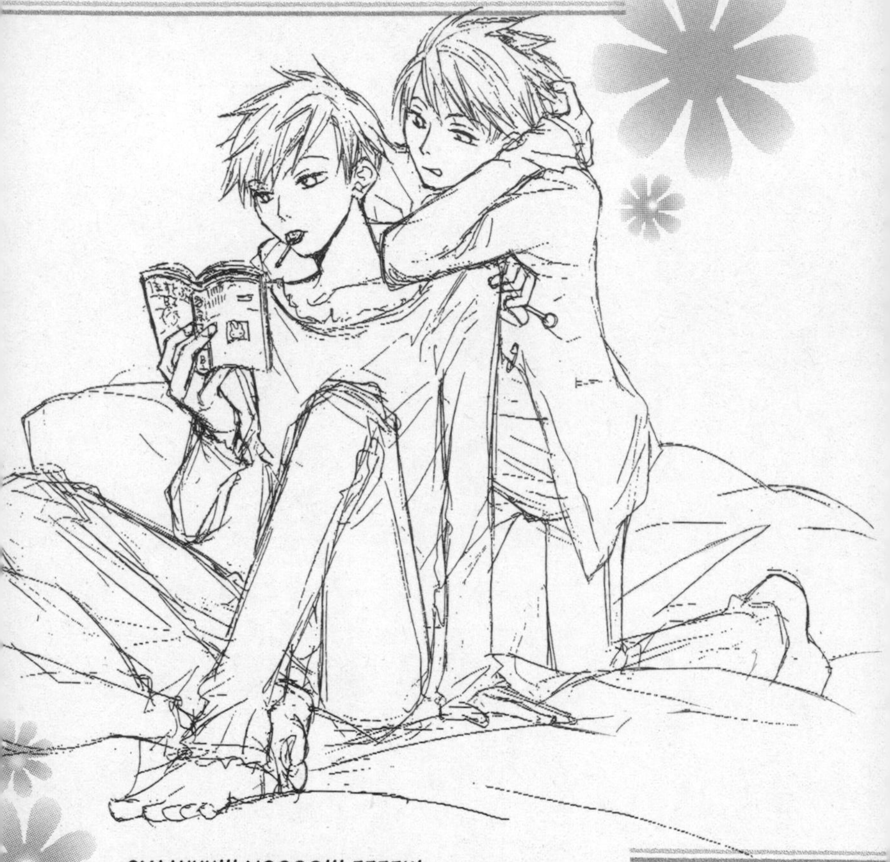

GYAAHHH!!! NOOOO!!! EEEEK!
THE IDEAL TWINS ARE HERE!!! WAAHHH!! THEY'RE SO GREAT!! (TEARS GUSHING OUT!) PLEASE, KANA, COME BACK TO THE WORLD OF MANGA, ASAP! I DO ADMIT IT'S AWESOME THAT SHE'S LENDING HER VOICE TO AN FM STATION IN IWATE! (IF YOU CAN TUNE IN, PLEASE SWITCH OVER TO HEAR HER!!) I ENORMOUSLY RESPECT HER SKILL AS AN ARTIST, AND SHE'S MY SUPER-BEST FRIEND. IF YOU HAVEN'T READ HER MASTERPIECE, *B.B. JOKER* (V.1 THROUGH V. 5.5, PUBLISHED BY HAKUSENSHA), PLEASE DO SO RIGHT AWAY!!

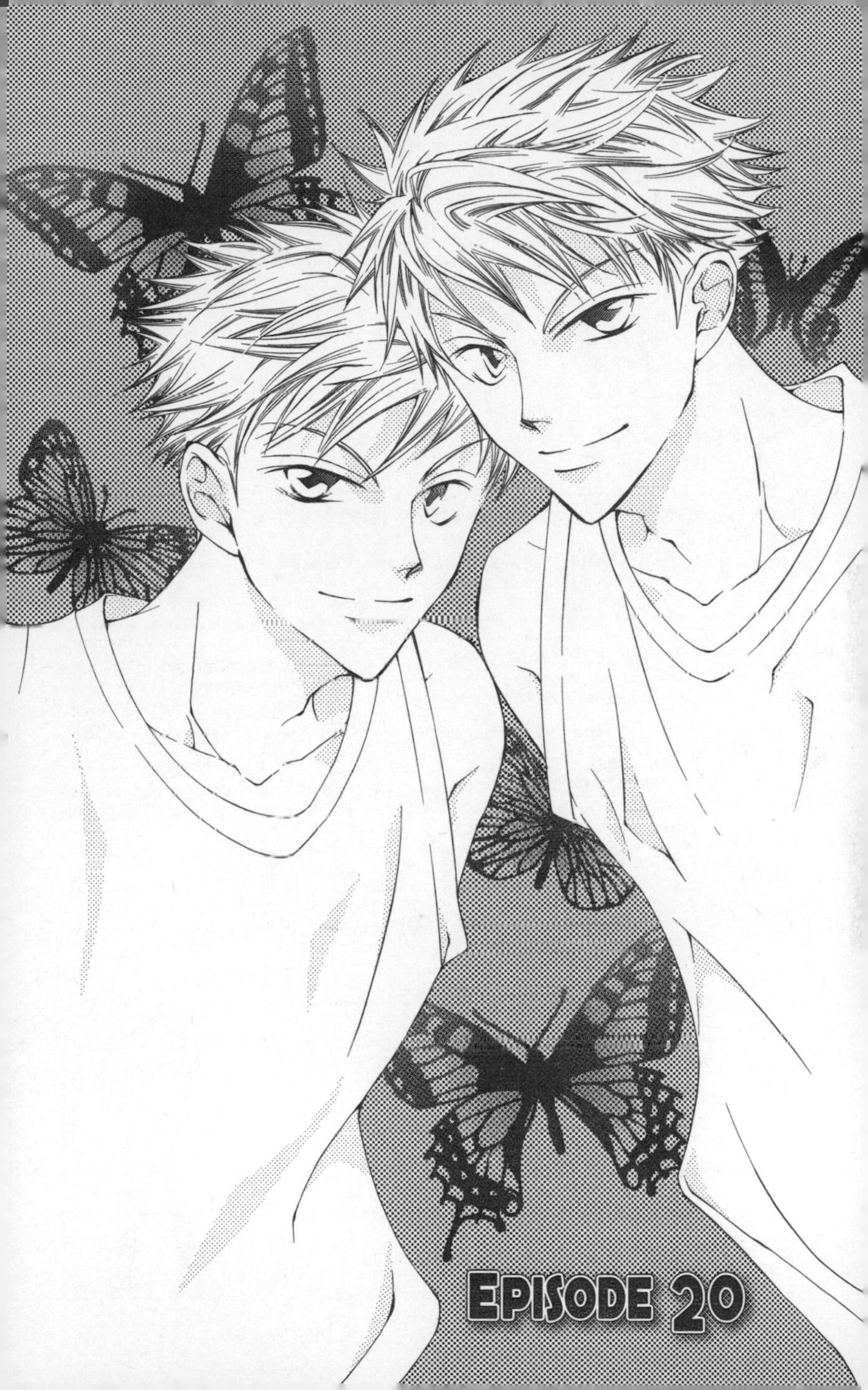
Episode 20

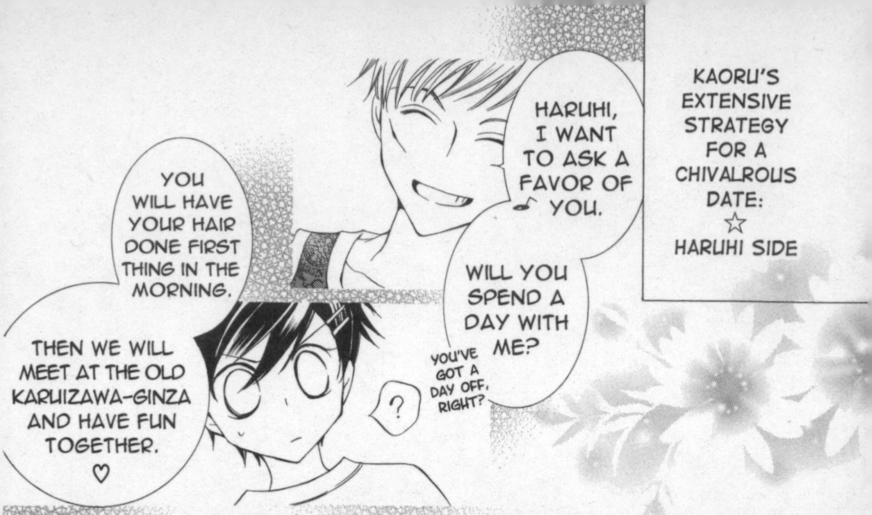
KAORU'S EXTENSIVE STRATEGY FOR A CHIVALROUS DATE: ☆ HARUHI SIDE
HARUHI, I WANT TO ASK A FAVOR OF YOU.
WILL YOU SPEND A DAY WITH ME?
YOU'VE GOT A DAY OFF, RIGHT?
?
YOU WILL HAVE YOUR HAIR DONE FIRST THING IN THE MORNING.
THEN WE WILL MEET AT THE OLD KARUIZAWA-GINZA AND HAVE FUN TOGETHER. ♡

WHY IT WORKED OUT AS IT DID IS A MYSTERY...

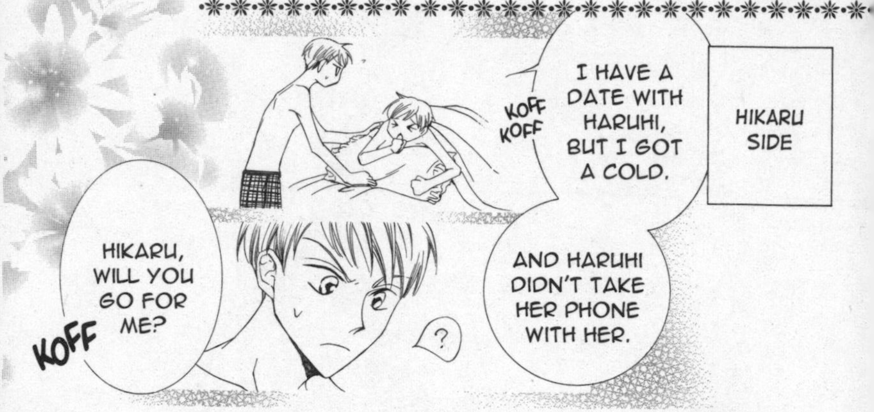
HIKARU SIDE
I HAVE A DATE WITH HARUHI, BUT I GOT A COLD.
KOFF KOFF
AND HARUHI DIDN'T TAKE HER PHONE WITH HER.
?
HIKARU, WILL YOU GO FOR ME?
KOFF

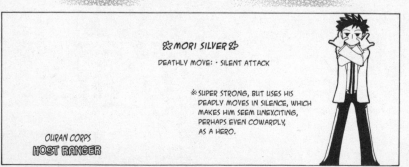

MORI SILVER

DEATHLY MOVE: · SILENT ATTACK

※SUPER STRONG, BUT USES HIS DEADLY MOVES IN SILENCE, WHICH MAKES HIM SEEM UNEXCITING, PERHAPS EVEN COWARDLY, AS A HERO.

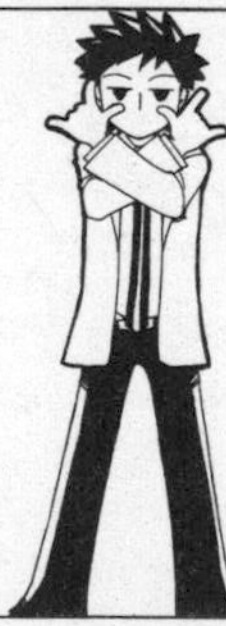

OURAN CORPS
HOST RANGER

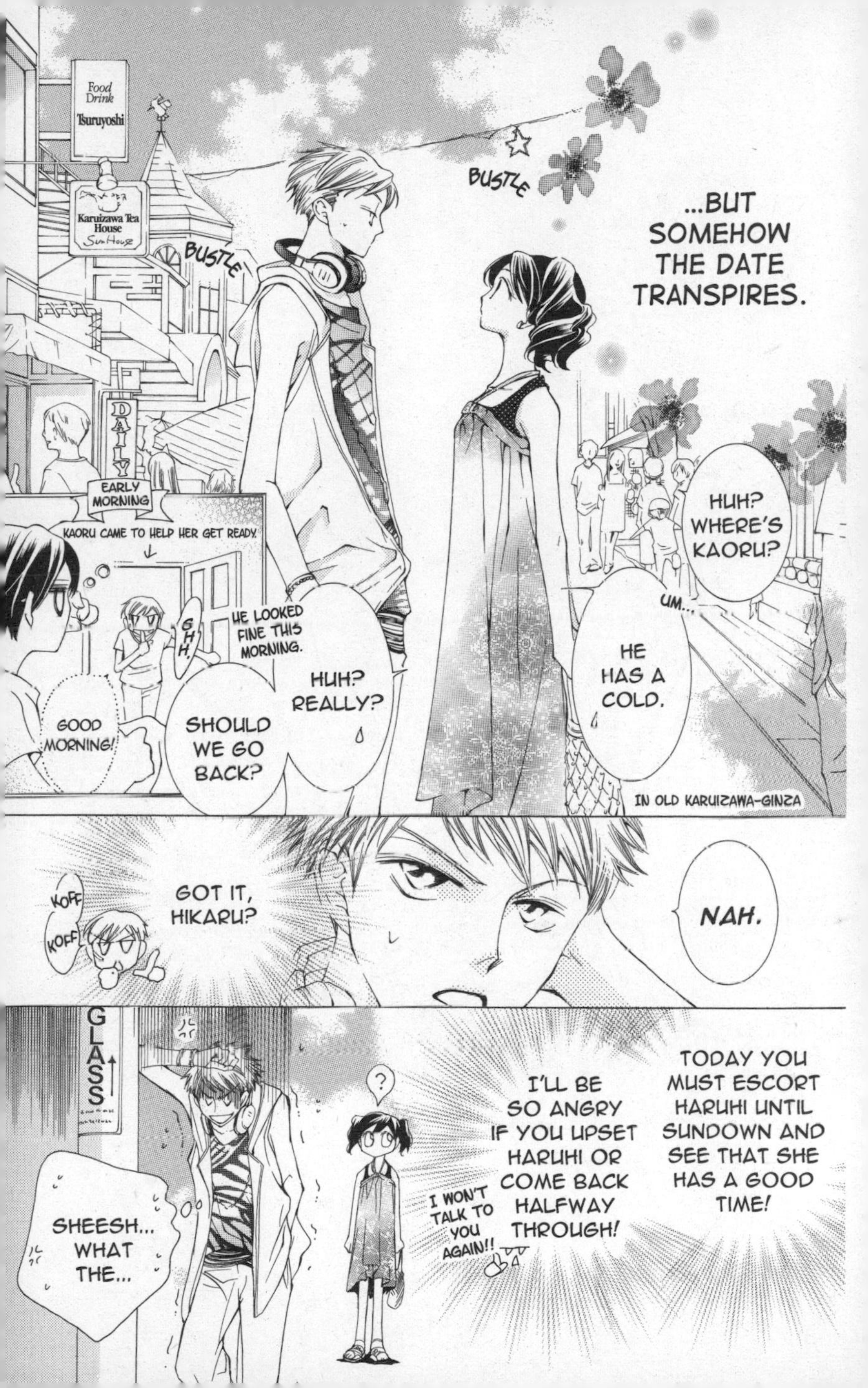
...BUT SOMEHOW THE DATE TRANSPIRES.
BUSTLE
Food Drink Tsuruyoshi
Karuizawa Tea House Sun House
BUSTLE
DAILY
HUH? WHERE'S KAORU?
UM...
HE HAS A COLD.
HUH? REALLY?
SHOULD WE GO BACK?
IN OLD KARUIZAWA-GINZA
EARLY MORNING
KAORU CAME TO HELP HER GET READY.
HE LOOKED FINE THIS MORNING.
GHH,
GOOD MORNING!
NAH.
GOT IT, HIKARU?
KOFF
KOFF
TODAY YOU MUST ESCORT HARUHI UNTIL SUNDOWN AND SEE THAT SHE HAS A GOOD TIME!
I'LL BE SO ANGRY IF YOU UPSET HARUHI OR COME BACK HALFWAY THROUGH!
I WON'T TALK TO YOU AGAIN!!
GLASS
SHEESH... WHAT THE...

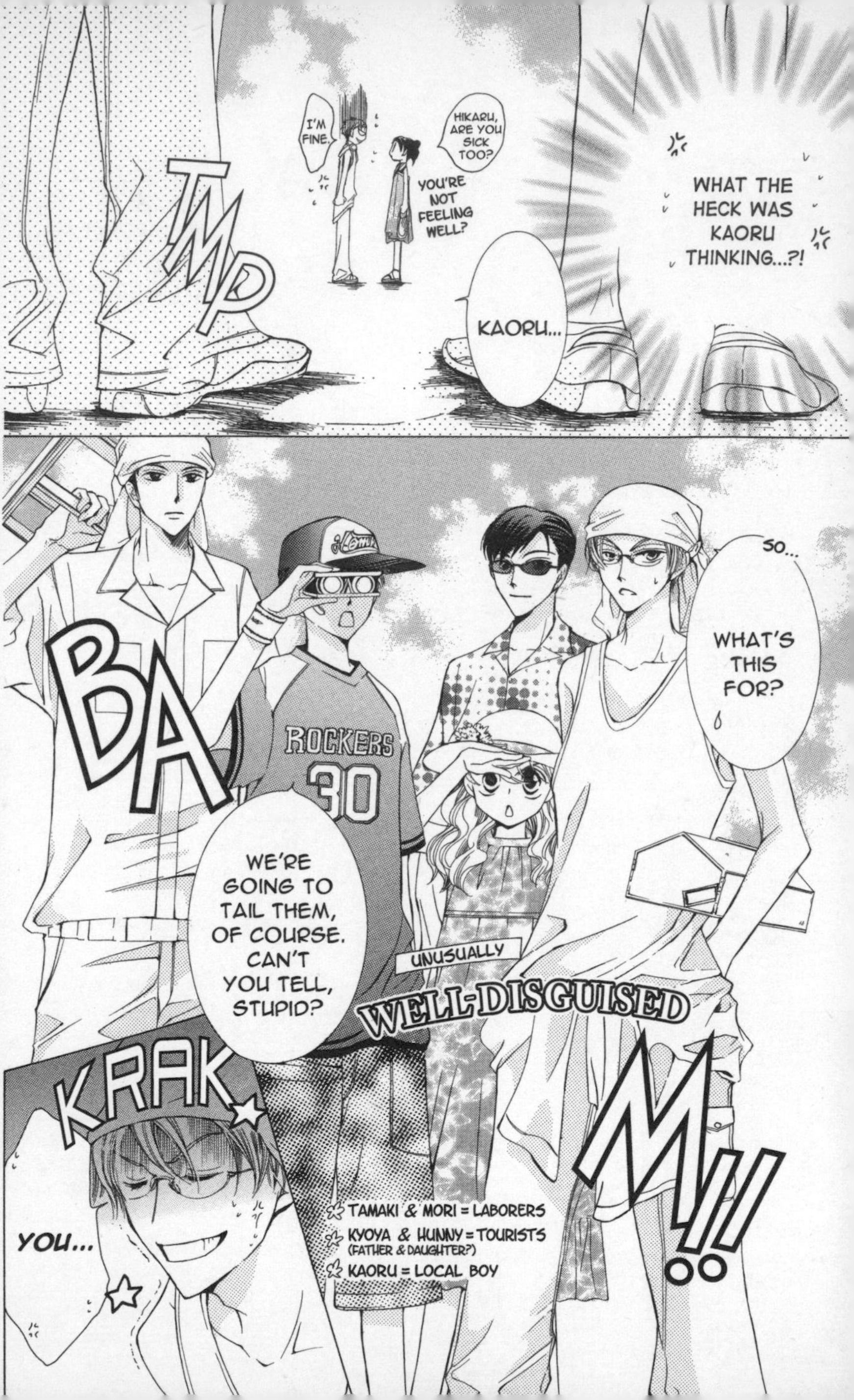
WHAT THE HECK WAS KAORU THINKING...?!
KAORU...
HIKARU, ARE YOU SICK TOO?
YOU'RE NOT FEELING WELL?
I'M FINE.
TMP
SO... WHAT'S THIS FOR?
BA
MI!!
WE'RE GOING TO TAIL THEM, OF COURSE. CAN'T YOU TELL, STUPID?
UNUSUALLY WELL-DISGUISED
TAMAKI & MORI = LABORERS
KYOYA & HUNNY = TOURISTS (FATHER & DAUGHTER?)
KAORU = LOCAL BOY
ROCKERS 30
KRAK
YOU...

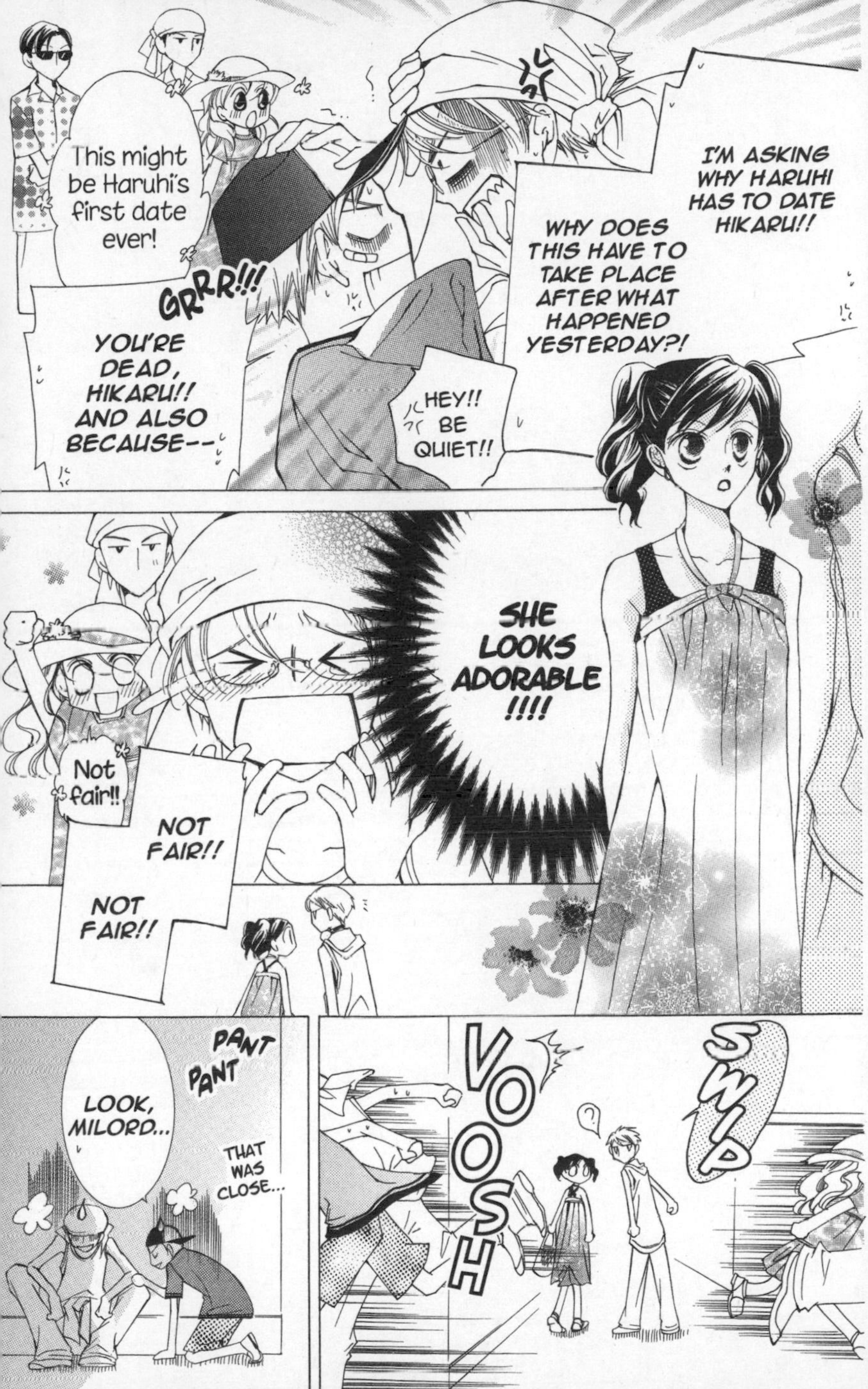
I'M ASKING WHY HARUHI HAS TO DATE HIKARU!!
WHY DOES THIS HAVE TO TAKE PLACE AFTER WHAT HAPPENED YESTERDAY?!
HEY!! BE QUIET!!
This might be Haruhi's first date ever!
GRRR!!!
YOU'RE DEAD, HIKARU!! AND ALSO BECAUSE--
SHE LOOKS ADORABLE!!!!
Not fair!!
NOT FAIR!!
NOT FAIR!!
SWIP
VOOSH
PANT PANT
LOOK, MILORD...
THAT WAS CLOSE...

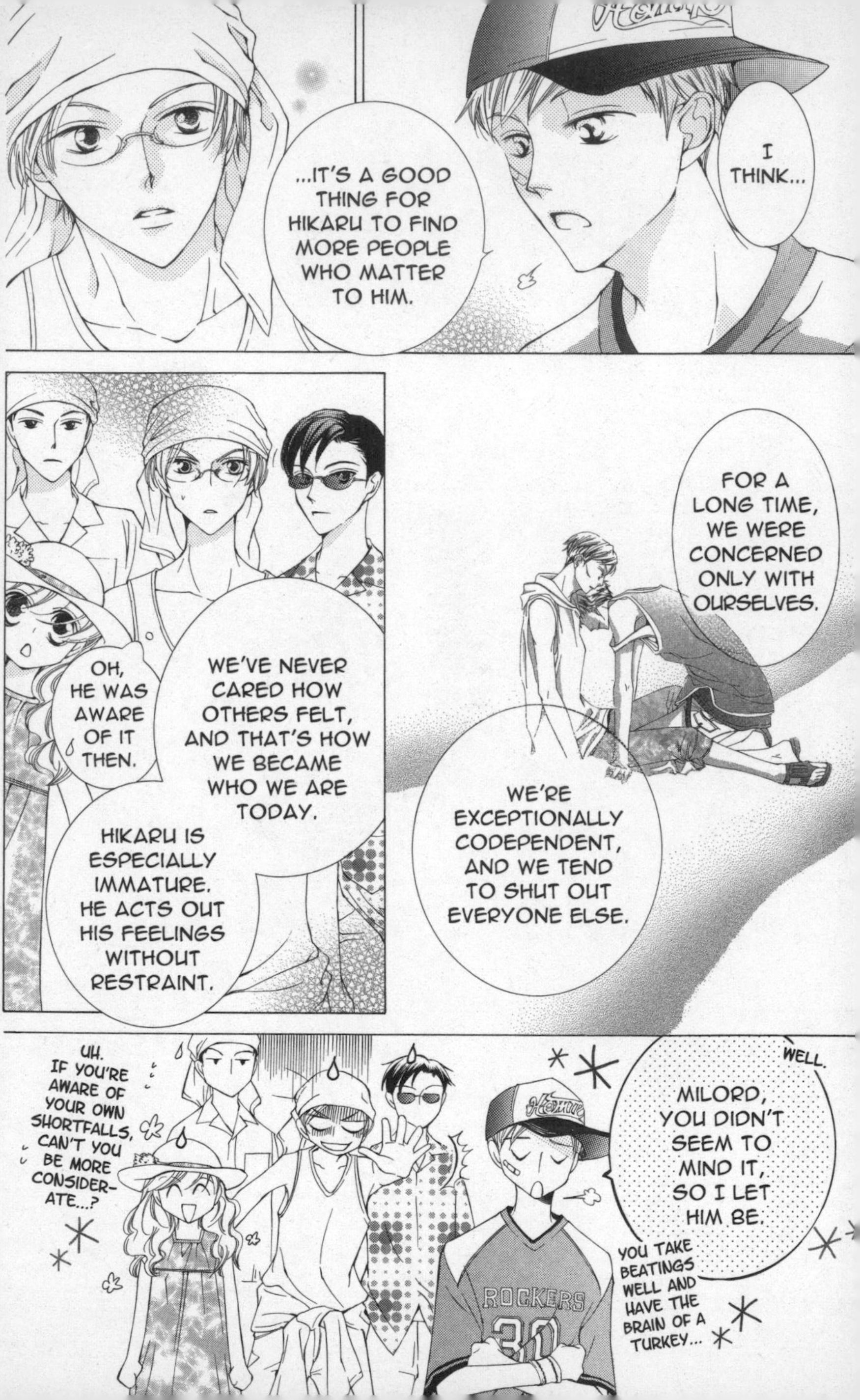
I THINK...
...IT'S A GOOD THING FOR HIKARU TO FIND MORE PEOPLE WHO MATTER TO HIM.
FOR A LONG TIME, WE WERE CONCERNED ONLY WITH OURSELVES.
WE'RE EXCEPTIONALLY CODEPENDENT, AND WE TEND TO SHUT OUT EVERYONE ELSE.
WE'VE NEVER CARED HOW OTHERS FELT, AND THAT'S HOW WE BECAME WHO WE ARE TODAY.
OH, HE WAS AWARE OF IT THEN.
HIKARU IS ESPECIALLY IMMATURE. HE ACTS OUT HIS FEELINGS WITHOUT RESTRAINT.
WELL.
MILORD, YOU DIDN'T SEEM TO MIND IT, SO I LET HIM BE.
YOU TAKE BEATINGS WELL AND HAVE THE BRAIN OF A TURKEY...
ROCKERS
UH. IF YOU'RE AWARE OF YOUR OWN SHORTFALLS, CAN'T YOU BE MORE CONSIDER-ATE...?

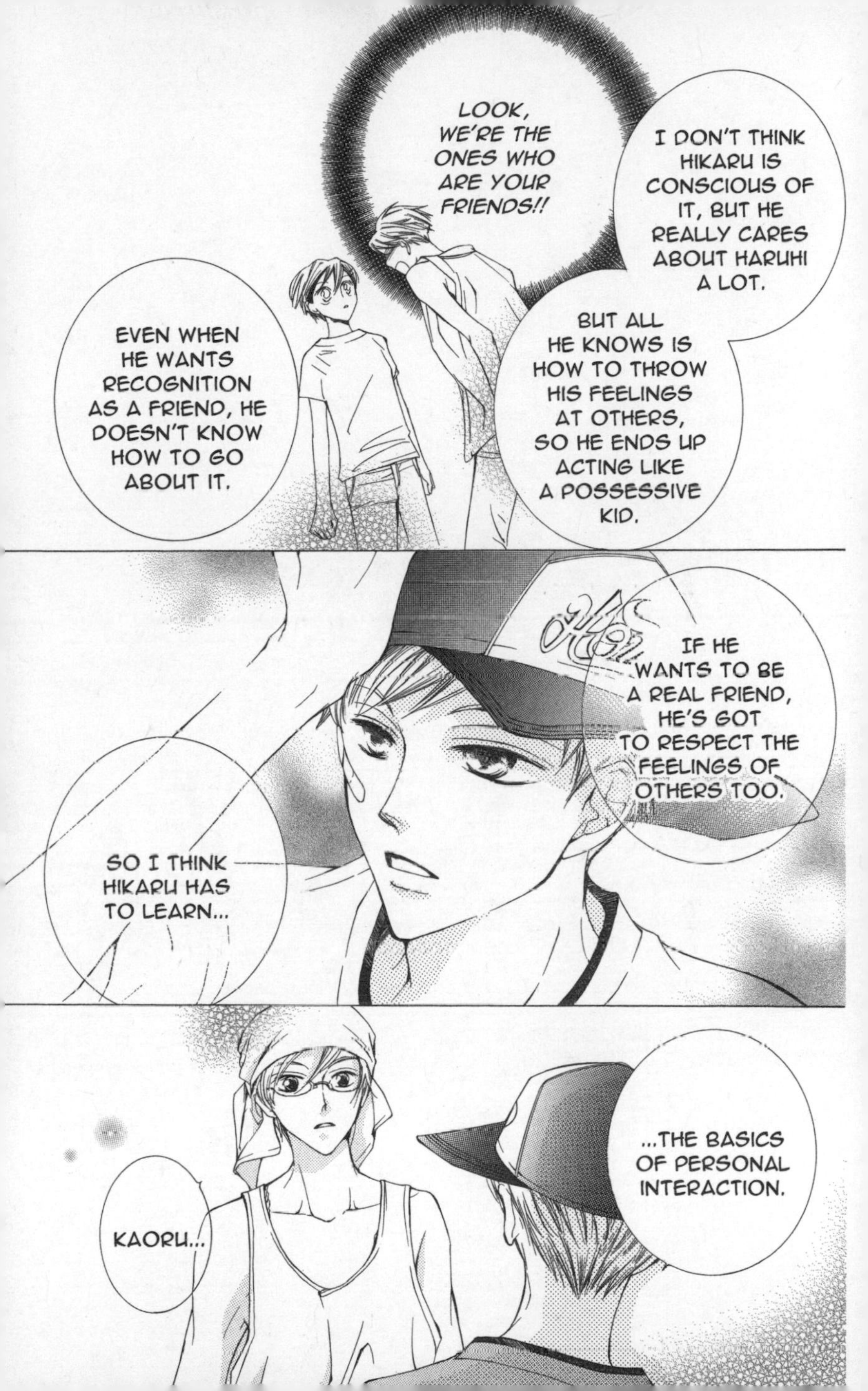
LOOK, WE'RE THE ONES WHO ARE YOUR FRIENDS!!
I DON'T THINK HIKARU IS CONSCIOUS OF IT, BUT HE REALLY CARES ABOUT HARUHI A LOT.
BUT ALL HE KNOWS IS HOW TO THROW HIS FEELINGS AT OTHERS, SO HE ENDS UP ACTING LIKE A POSSESSIVE KID.
EVEN WHEN HE WANTS RECOGNITION AS A FRIEND, HE DOESN'T KNOW HOW TO GO ABOUT IT.
IF HE WANTS TO BE A REAL FRIEND, HE'S GOT TO RESPECT THE FEELINGS OF OTHERS TOO.
SO I THINK HIKARU HAS TO LEARN...
...THE BASICS OF PERSONAL INTERACTION.
KAORU...

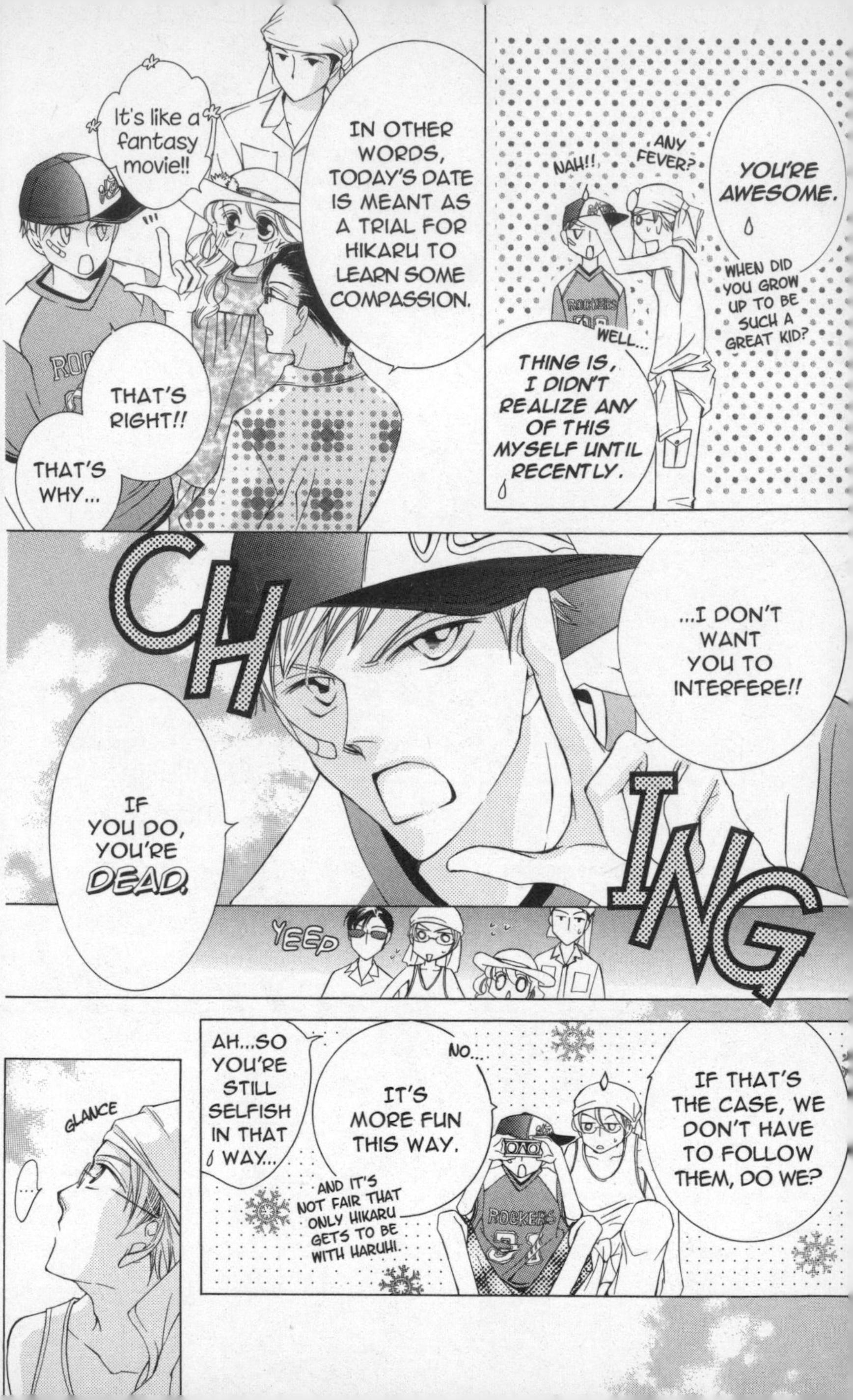
YOU'RE AWESOME.
ANY FEVER?
NAH!!
WHEN DID YOU GROW UP TO BE SUCH A GREAT KID?
WELL...
THING IS, I DIDN'T REALIZE ANY OF THIS MYSELF UNTIL RECENTLY.
IN OTHER WORDS, TODAY'S DATE IS MEANT AS A TRIAL FOR HIKARU TO LEARN SOME COMPASSION.
It's like a fantasy movie!!
THAT'S RIGHT!!
THAT'S WHY...
...I DON'T WANT YOU TO INTERFERE!!
CHING
IF YOU DO, YOU'RE DEAD.
YEEP
IF THAT'S THE CASE, WE DON'T HAVE TO FOLLOW THEM, DO WE?
NO...
IT'S MORE FUN THIS WAY.
AND IT'S NOT FAIR THAT ONLY HIKARU GETS TO BE WITH HARUHI.
AH...SO YOU'RE STILL SELFISH IN THAT WAY...
GLANCE
...

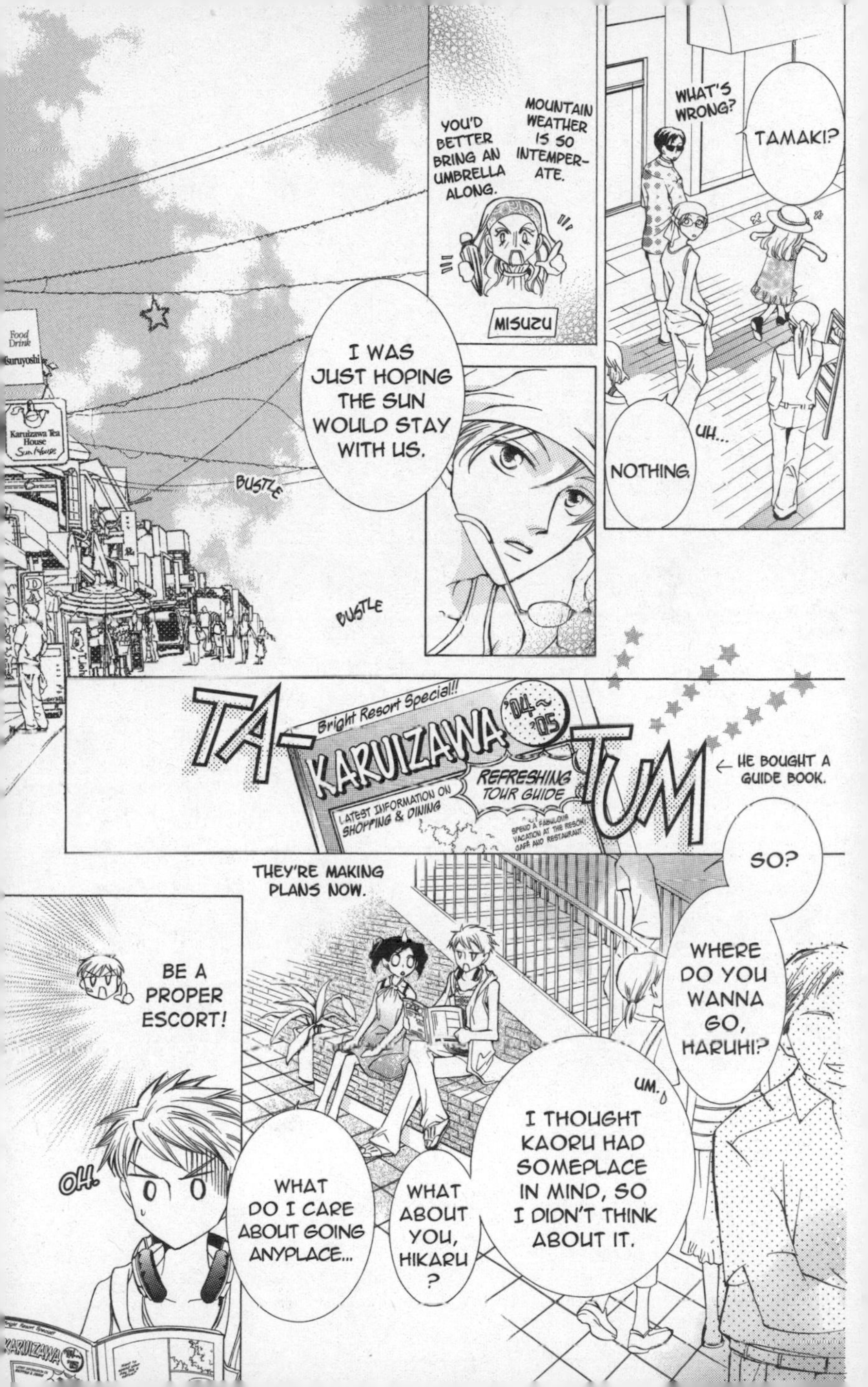

TAMAKI?
WHAT'S WRONG?
UH...
NOTHING.
MOUNTAIN WEATHER IS SO INTEMPERATE.
YOU'D BETTER BRING AN UMBRELLA ALONG.
MISUZU
I WAS JUST HOPING THE SUN WOULD STAY WITH US.
Food Drink
Tsuruyoshi
Karuizawa Tea House
Sun House
BUSTLE
BUSTLE
TA-TUM
Bright Resort Special!!
KARUIZAWA
'04~'05
REFRESHING TOUR GUIDE
LATEST INFORMATION ON SHOPPING & DINING
SPEND A FABULOUS VACATION AT THE RESORT CAFÉ AND RESTAURANT.
← HE BOUGHT A GUIDE BOOK.
SO?
WHERE DO YOU WANNA GO, HARUHI?
THEY'RE MAKING PLANS NOW.
UM..
I THOUGHT KAORU HAD SOMEPLACE IN MIND, SO I DIDN'T THINK ABOUT IT.
WHAT ABOUT YOU, HIKARU?
BE A PROPER ESCORT!
OH.
WHAT DO I CARE ABOUT GOING ANYPLACE...
KARUIZAWA

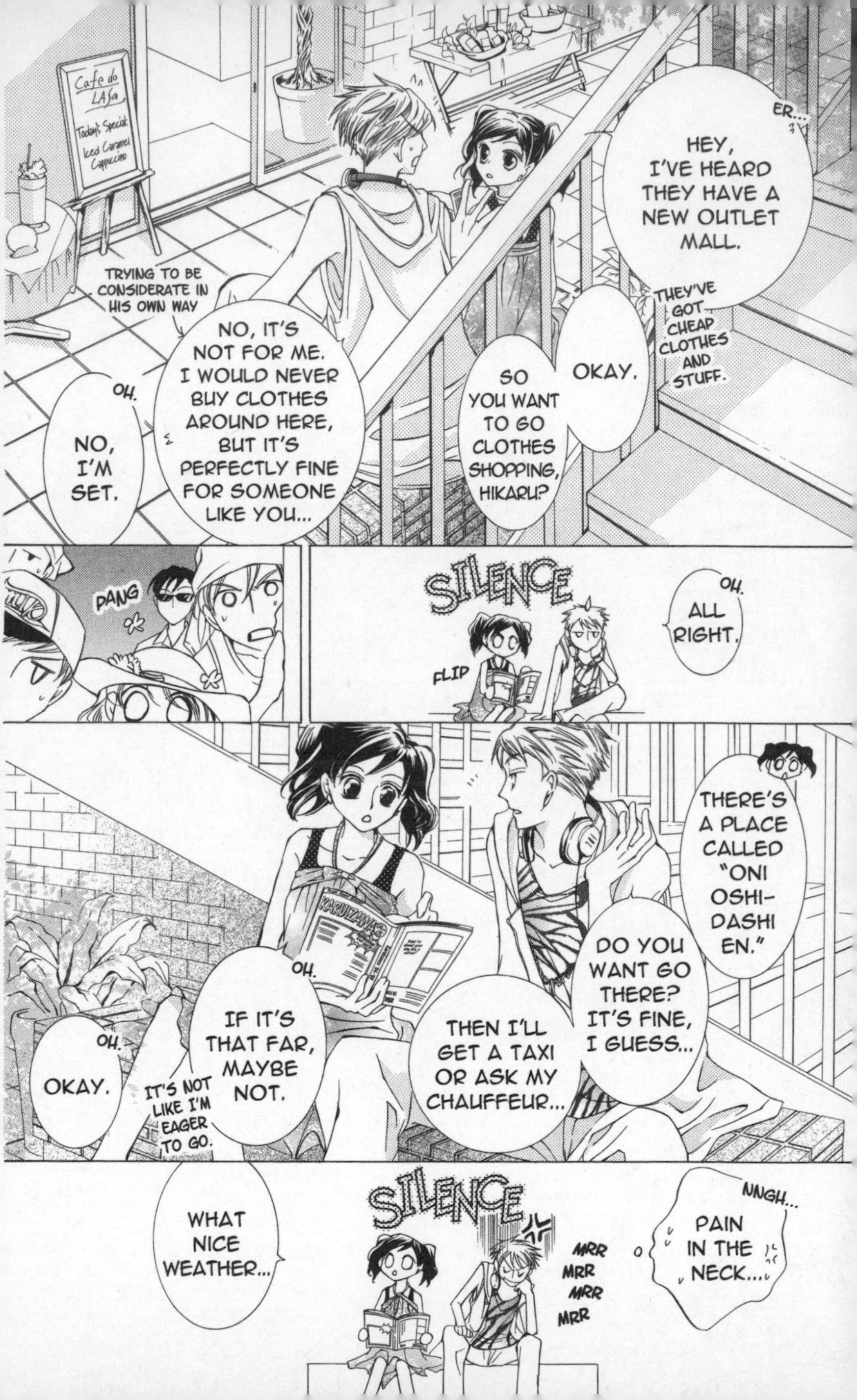

Cafe do LASa
Today's Special Iced Caramel Cappuccino
ER...
HEY, I'VE HEARD THEY HAVE A NEW OUTLET MALL.
THEY'VE GOT CHEAP CLOTHES AND STUFF.
OKAY.
SO YOU WANT TO GO CLOTHES SHOPPING, HIKARU?
NO, IT'S NOT FOR ME. I WOULD NEVER BUY CLOTHES AROUND HERE, BUT IT'S PERFECTLY FINE FOR SOMEONE LIKE YOU...
TRYING TO BE CONSIDERATE IN HIS OWN WAY
OH.
NO, I'M SET.
OH.
ALL RIGHT.
SILENCE
FLIP
PANG
THERE'S A PLACE CALLED "ONI OSHI-DASHI EN."
DO YOU WANT GO THERE? IT'S FINE, I GUESS...
THEN I'LL GET A TAXI OR ASK MY CHAUFFEUR...
KARUIZAWA
OH.
IF IT'S THAT FAR, MAYBE NOT.
IT'S NOT LIKE I'M EAGER TO GO.
OH.
OKAY.
NNGH...
PAIN IN THE NECK...
MRR
MRR
MRR
MRR
SILENCE
WHAT NICE WEATHER...

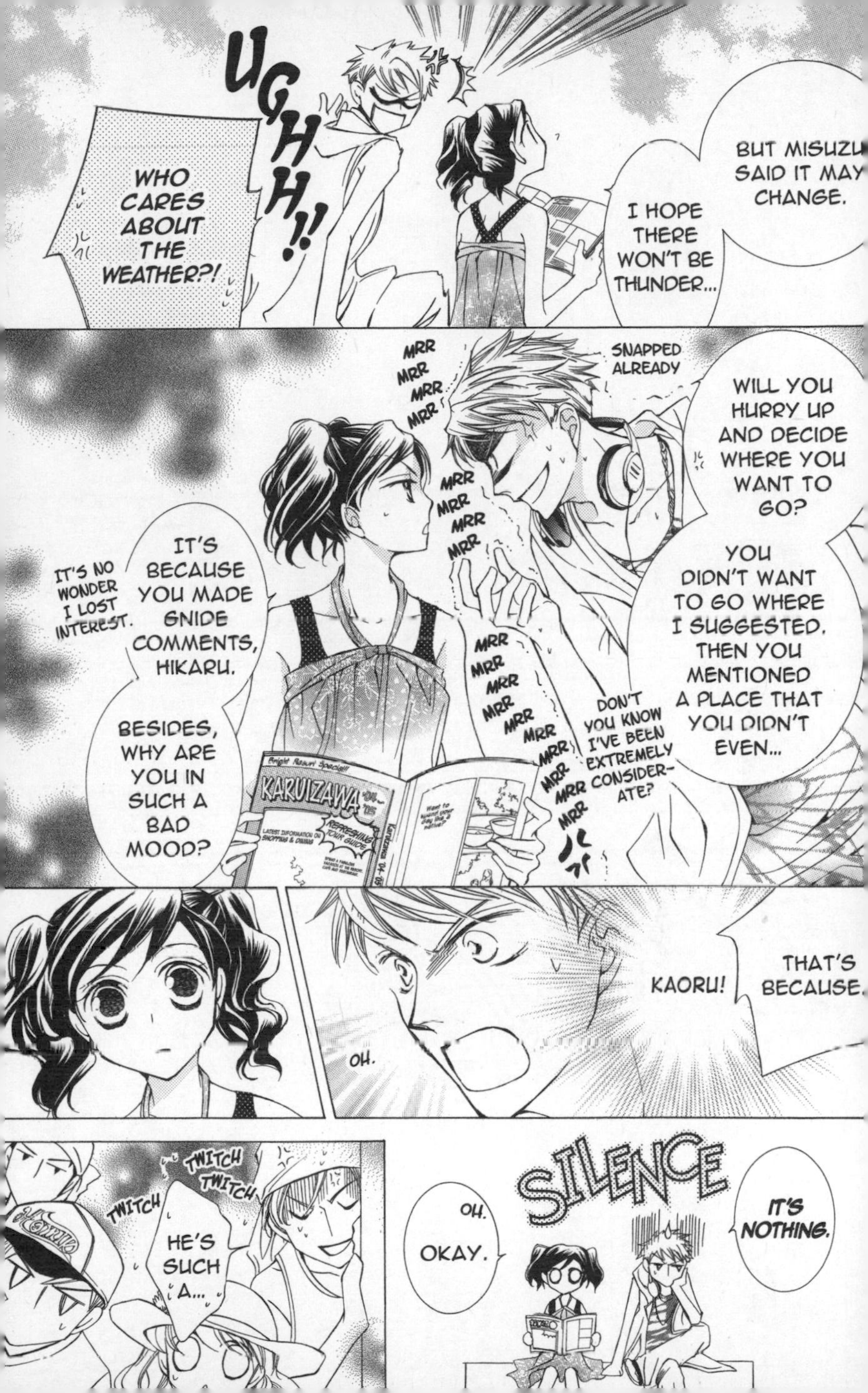
BUT MISUZU SAID IT MAY CHANGE.
I HOPE THERE WON'T BE THUNDER...
UGHH!!
WHO CARES ABOUT THE WEATHER?!
SNAPPED ALREADY
WILL YOU HURRY UP AND DECIDE WHERE YOU WANT TO GO?
YOU DIDN'T WANT TO GO WHERE I SUGGESTED. THEN YOU MENTIONED A PLACE THAT YOU DIDN'T EVEN...
MRR MRR MRR MRR
MRR MRR MRR MRR
DON'T YOU KNOW I'VE BEEN EXTREMELY CONSIDER-ATE?
MRR MRR MRR MRR MRR MRR MRR MRR MRR MRR
IT'S BECAUSE YOU MADE SNIDE COMMENTS, HIKARU.
IT'S NO WONDER I LOST INTEREST.
BESIDES, WHY ARE YOU IN SUCH A BAD MOOD?
Bright Resort Special!!
KARUIZAWA '04-'05
REFRESHING TOUR GUIDE
THAT'S BECAUSE.
KAORU!
OH.
IT'S NOTHING.
SILENCE
OH.
OKAY.
TWITCH TWITCH
TWITCH
HE'S SUCH A...

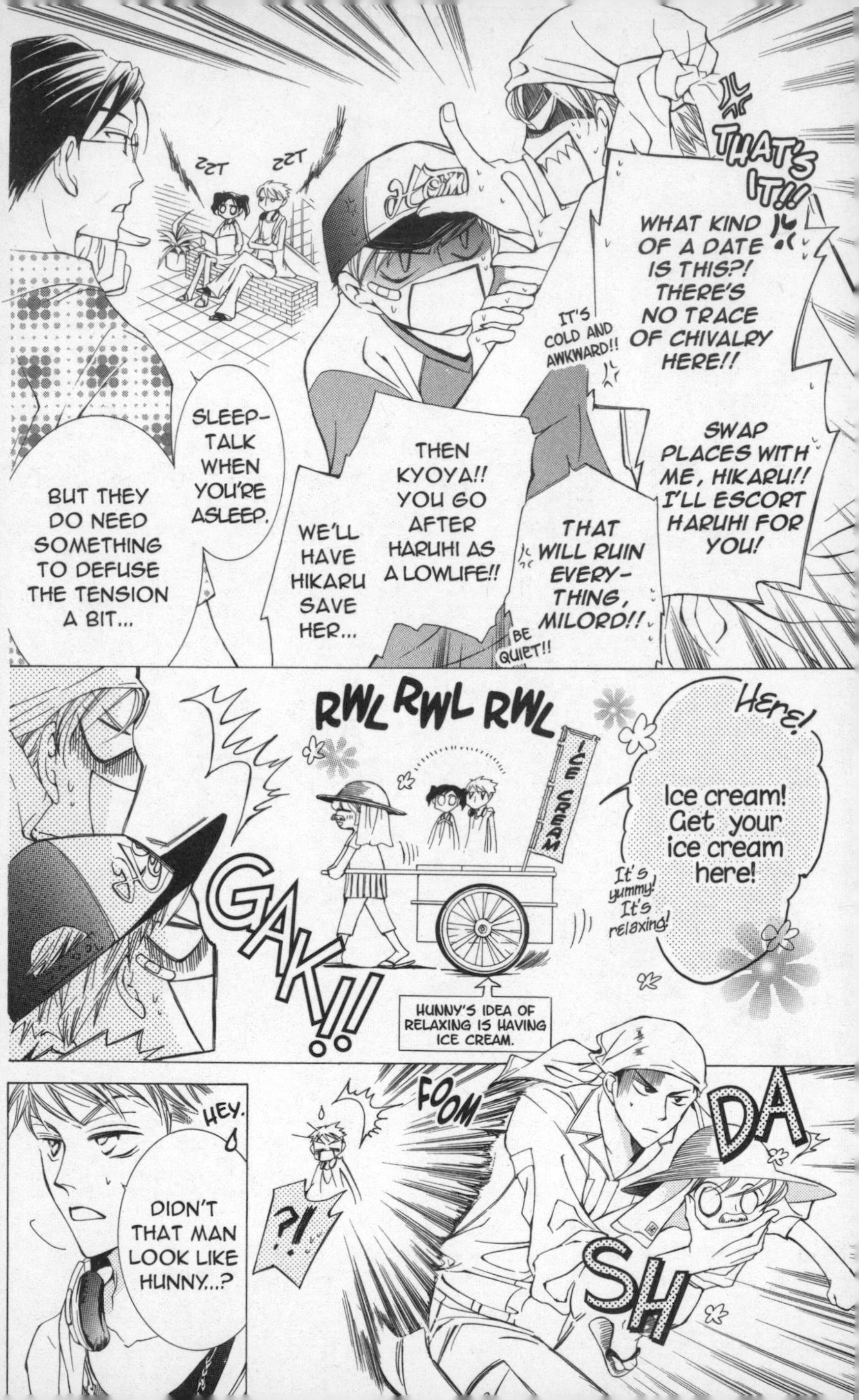
THAT'S IT!!
WHAT KIND OF A DATE IS THIS?! THERE'S NO TRACE OF CHIVALRY HERE!!
IT'S COLD AND AWKWARD!!
SWAP PLACES WITH ME, HIKARU!! I'LL ESCORT HARUHI FOR YOU!
THAT WILL RUIN EVERY-THING, MILORD!!
BE QUIET!!
THEN KYOYA!! YOU GO AFTER HARUHI AS A LOWLIFE!!
WE'LL HAVE HIKARU SAVE HER...
ZZT
ZZT
SLEEP-TALK WHEN YOU'RE ASLEEP.
BUT THEY DO NEED SOMETHING TO DEFUSE THE TENSION A BIT...
HERE!
Ice cream! Get your ice cream here!
It's yummy! It's relaxing!
RWL RWL RWL
ICE CREAM
HUNNY'S IDEA OF RELAXING IS HAVING ICE CREAM.
GAK!!
DA
SH
FOOM
?!
HEY.
DIDN'T THAT MAN LOOK LIKE HUNNY...?

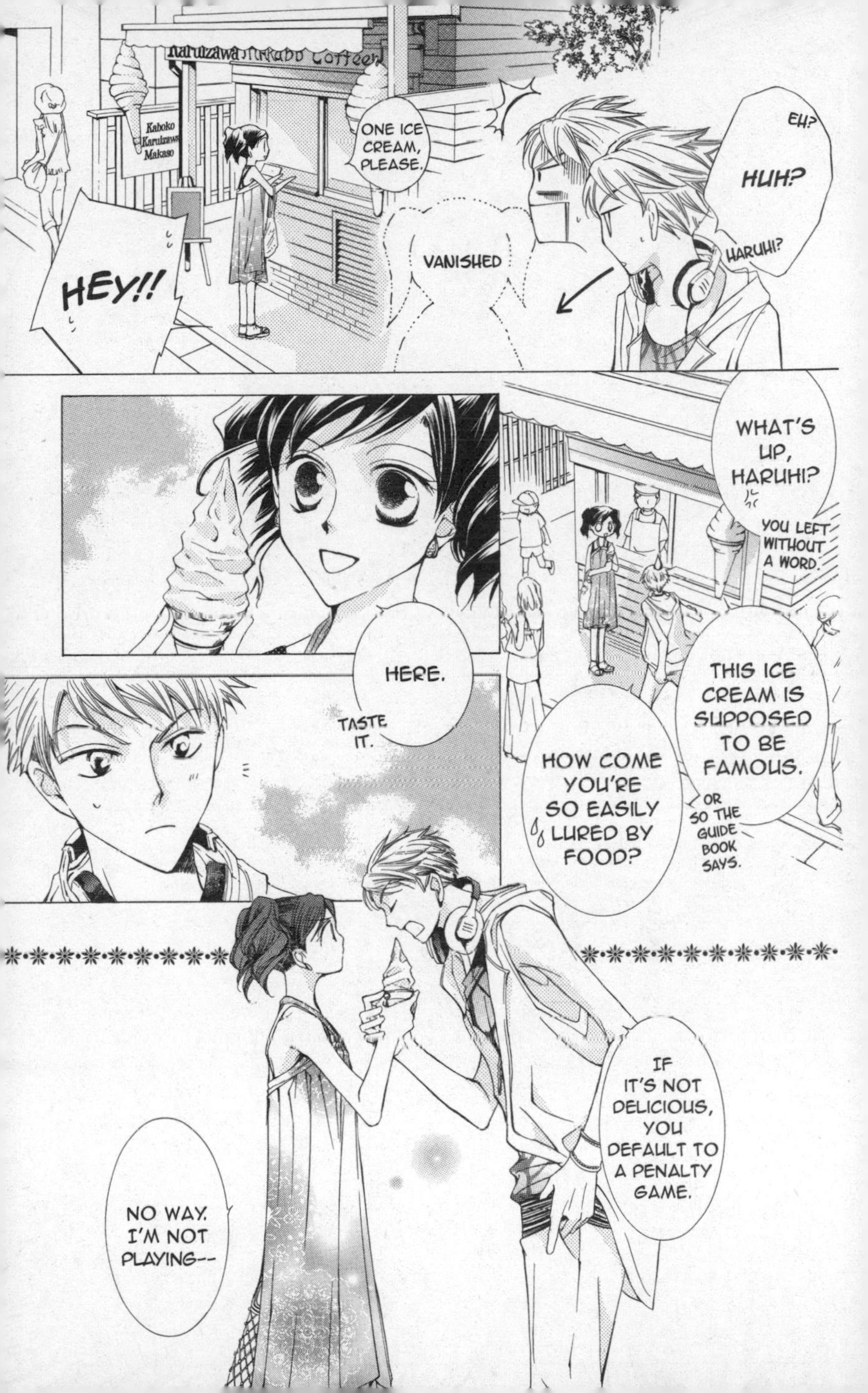
EH?
HUH?
HARUHI?
VANISHED
ONE ICE CREAM, PLEASE.
Kaboko Karuizawa Makaso
HEY!!
WHAT'S UP, HARUHI?
YOU LEFT WITHOUT A WORD.
THIS ICE CREAM IS SUPPOSED TO BE FAMOUS.
OR SO THE GUIDE BOOK SAYS.
HERE.
TASTE IT.
HOW COME YOU'RE SO EASILY LURED BY FOOD?
IF IT'S NOT DELICIOUS, YOU DEFAULT TO A PENALTY GAME.
NO WAY. I'M NOT PLAYING--

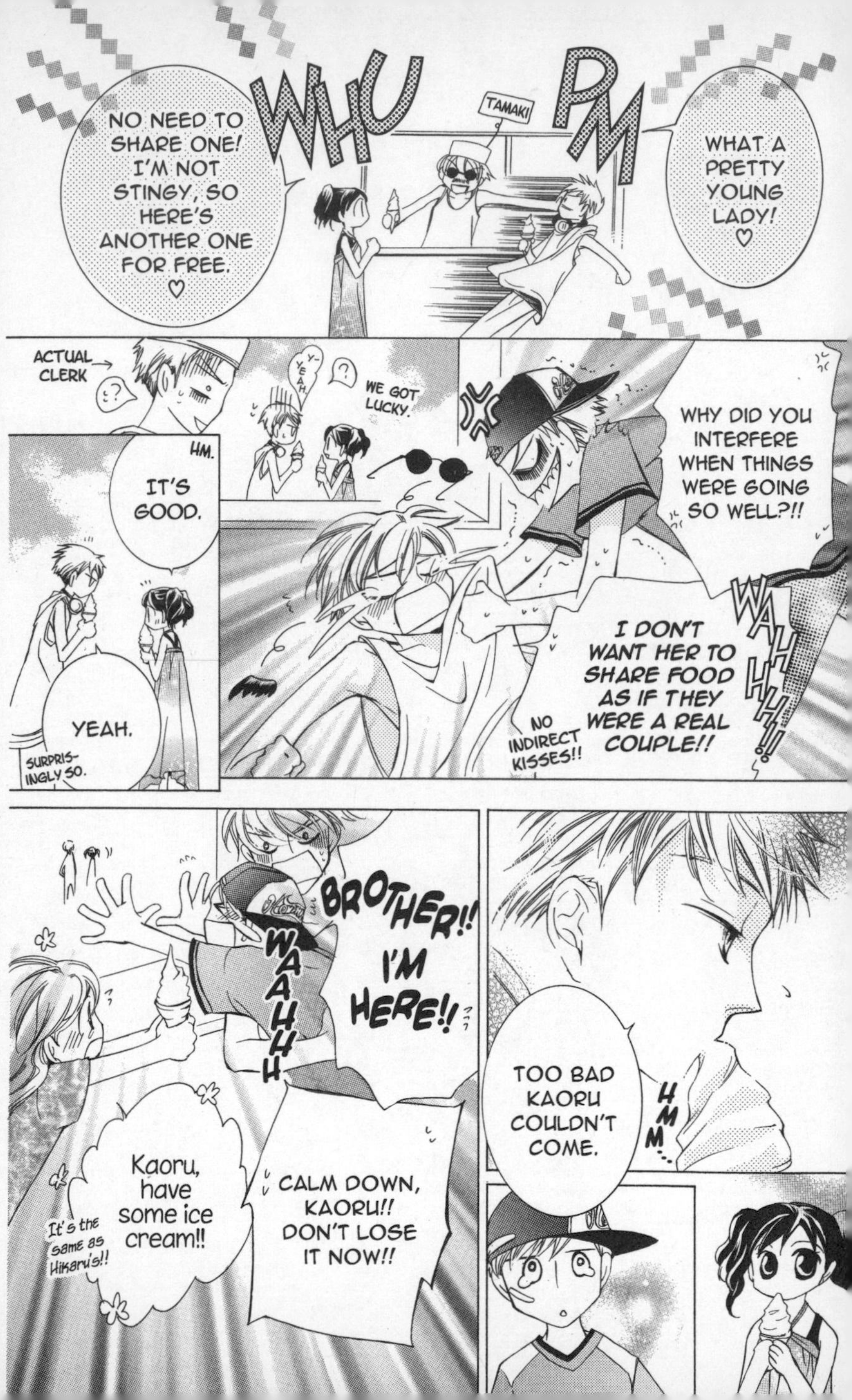
WHAT A PRETTY YOUNG LADY! ♡
TAMAKI
WHUMP
NO NEED TO SHARE ONE! I'M NOT STINGY, SO HERE'S ANOTHER ONE FOR FREE. ♡
WHY DID YOU INTERFERE WHEN THINGS WERE GOING SO WELL?!!
WAHHHH!!
I DON'T WANT HER TO SHARE FOOD AS IF THEY WERE A REAL COUPLE!!
NO INDIRECT KISSES!!
ACTUAL CLERK
?
Y-YEAH.
?
WE GOT LUCKY.
HM.
IT'S GOOD.
YEAH.
SURPRISINGLY SO.
HMM...
TOO BAD KAORU COULDN'T COME.
BROTHER!! I'M HERE!!
WAAHHH
CALM DOWN, KAORU!! DON'T LOSE IT NOW!!
Kaoru, have some ice cream!!
It's the same as Hikaru's!!

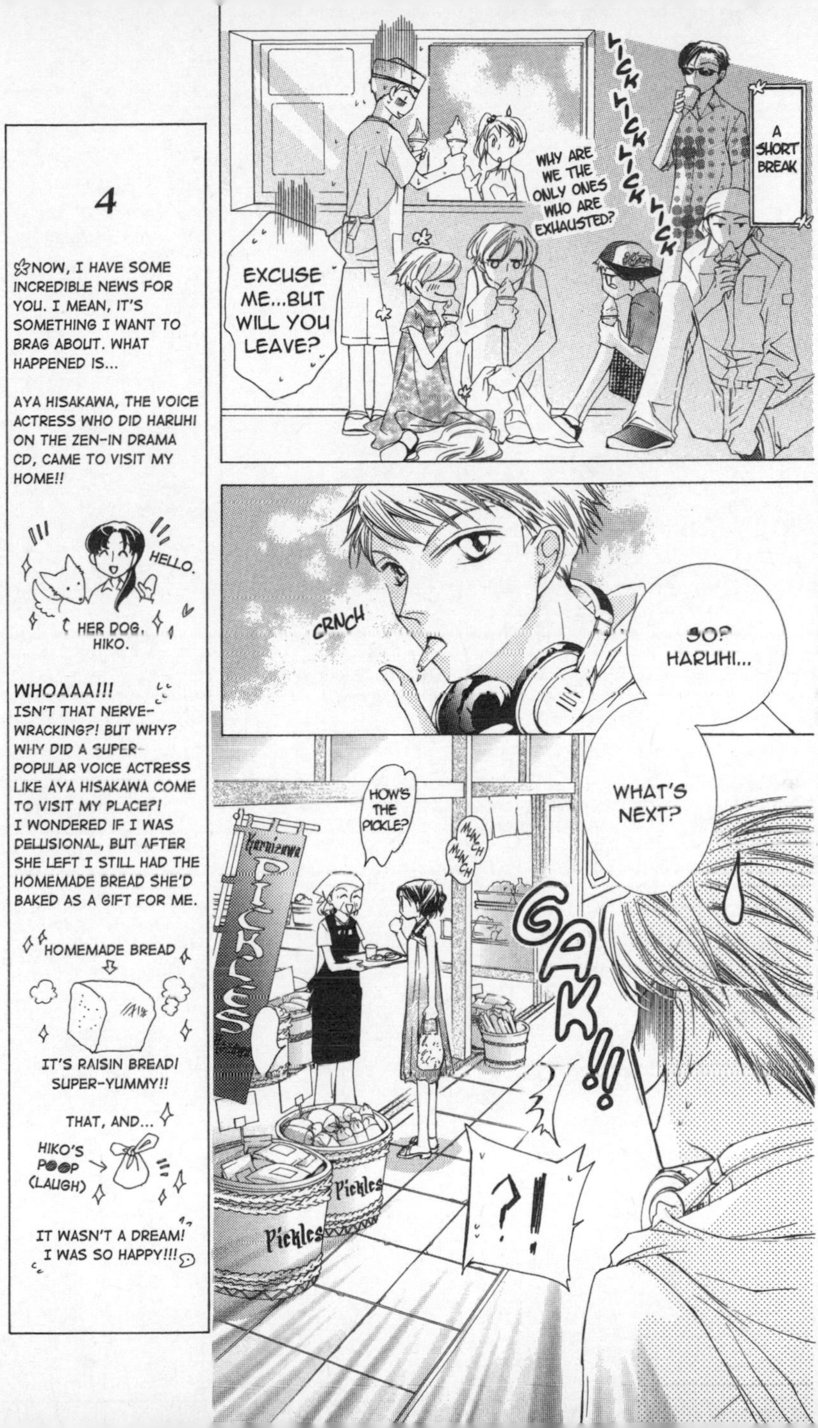
A SHORT BREAK
LICK LICK LICK LICK
WHY ARE WE THE ONLY ONES WHO ARE EXHAUSTED?
EXCUSE ME...BUT WILL YOU LEAVE?
SO? HARUHI...
CRNCH
WHAT'S NEXT?
GAK!!
?!
HOW'S THE PICKLE?
MUNCH MUNCH
PICKLES
Pickles
Pickles

4

✿NOW, I HAVE SOME INCREDIBLE NEWS FOR YOU. I MEAN, IT'S SOMETHING I WANT TO BRAG ABOUT. WHAT HAPPENED IS...

AYA HISAKAWA, THE VOICE ACTRESS WHO DID HARUHI ON THE ZEN-IN DRAMA CD, CAME TO VISIT MY HOME!!

HELLO.

HER DOG, HIKO.

WHOAAA!!!
ISN'T THAT NERVE-WRACKING?! BUT WHY? WHY DID A SUPER-POPULAR VOICE ACTRESS LIKE AYA HISAKAWA COME TO VISIT MY PLACE?! I WONDERED IF I WAS DELUSIONAL, BUT AFTER SHE LEFT I STILL HAD THE HOMEMADE BREAD SHE'D BAKED AS A GIFT FOR ME.

HOMEMADE BREAD

IT'S RAISIN BREAD! SUPER-YUMMY!!

THAT, AND...

HIKO'S POOP (LAUGH)

IT WASN'T A DREAM! I WAS SO HAPPY!!!

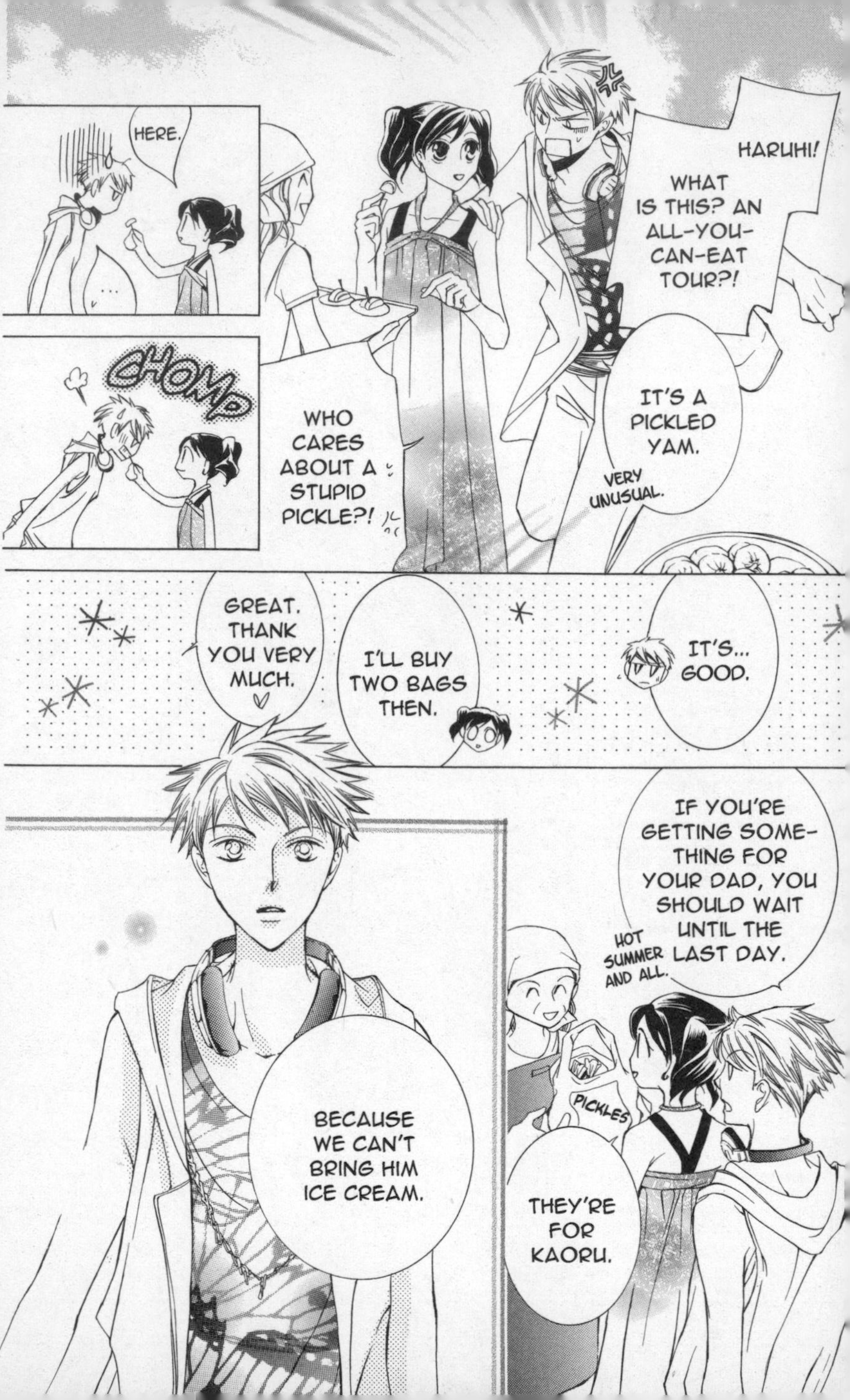
HARUHI!
WHAT IS THIS? AN ALL-YOU-CAN-EAT TOUR?!
IT'S A PICKLED YAM.
VERY UNUSUAL.
WHO CARES ABOUT A STUPID PICKLE?!
HERE.
...
CHOMP
IT'S... GOOD.
I'LL BUY TWO BAGS THEN.
GREAT. THANK YOU VERY MUCH.
IF YOU'RE GETTING SOME-THING FOR YOUR DAD, YOU SHOULD WAIT UNTIL THE LAST DAY.
HOT SUMMER AND ALL.
PICKLES
THEY'RE FOR KAORU.
BECAUSE WE CAN'T BRING HIM ICE CREAM.

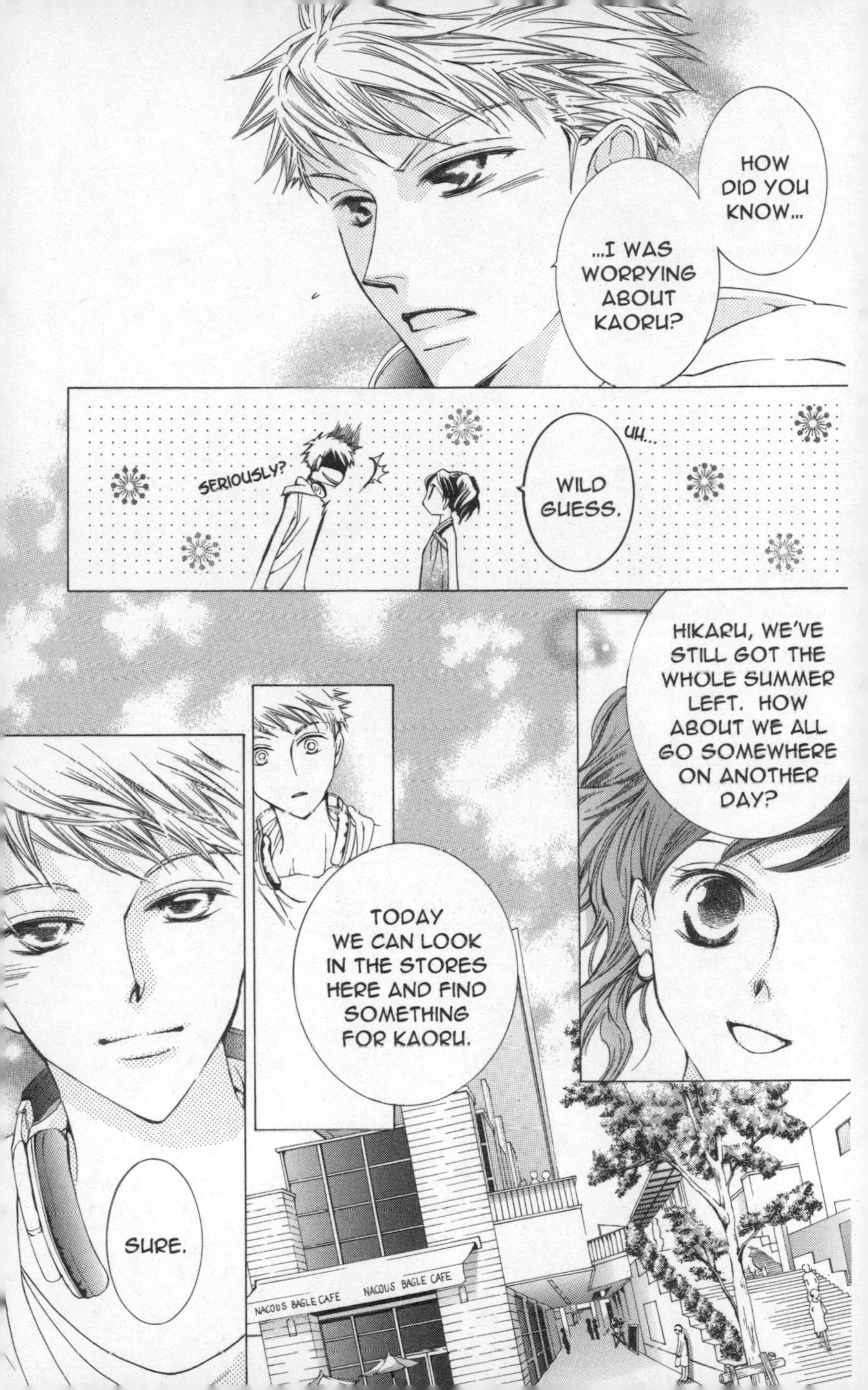
HOW DID YOU KNOW...
...I WAS WORRYING ABOUT KAORU?
UH...
WILD GUESS.
SERIOUSLY?
HIKARU, WE'VE STILL GOT THE WHOLE SUMMER LEFT. HOW ABOUT WE ALL GO SOMEWHERE ON ANOTHER DAY?
TODAY WE CAN LOOK IN THE STORES HERE AND FIND SOMETHING FOR KAORU.
SURE.
NACOUS BAGLE CAFE
NACOUS BAGLE CAFE

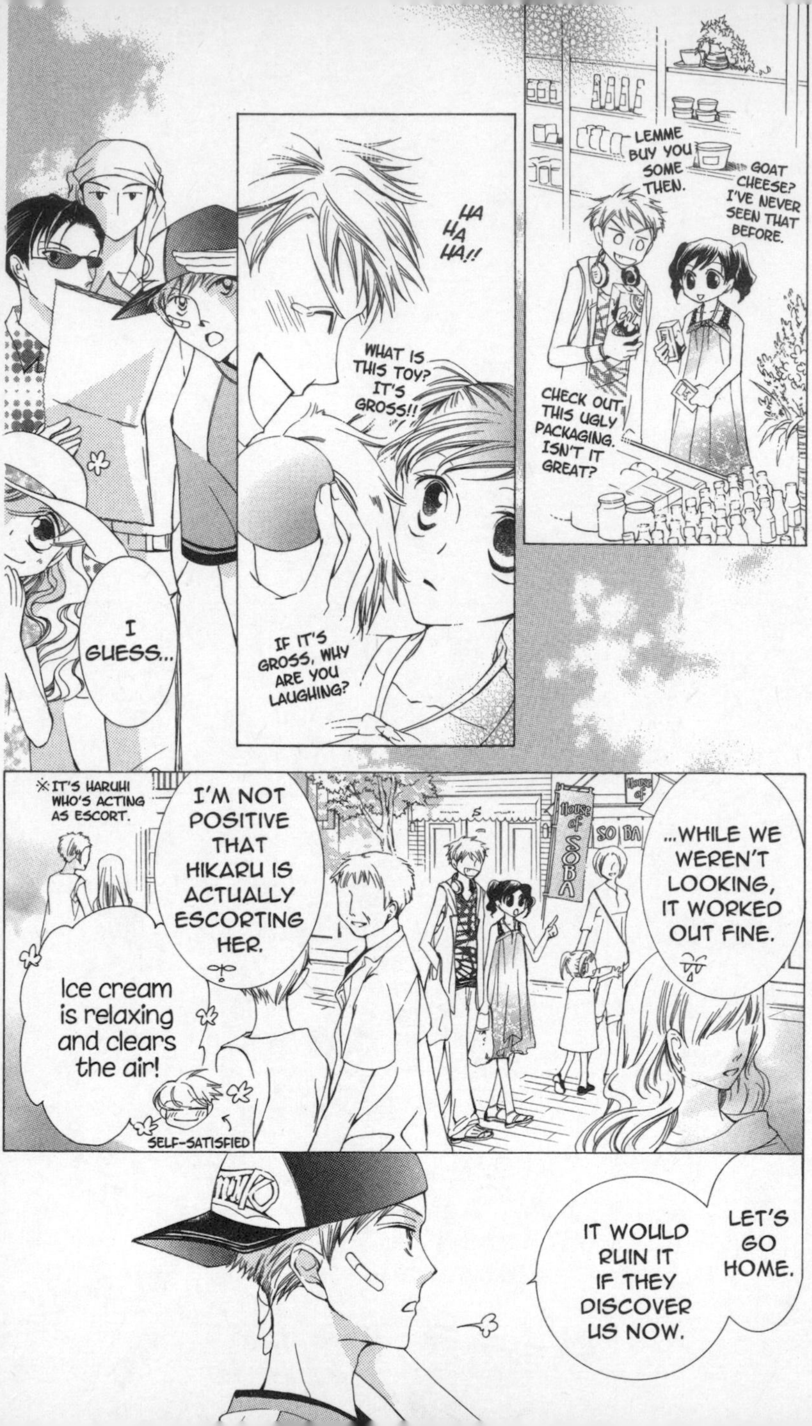
GOAT CHEESE? I'VE NEVER SEEN THAT BEFORE.
LEMME BUY YOU SOME THEN.
CHECK OUT THIS UGLY PACKAGING. ISN'T IT GREAT?
HA HA HA!!
WHAT IS THIS TOY? IT'S GROSS!!
IF IT'S GROSS, WHY ARE YOU LAUGHING?
I GUESS...
...WHILE WE WEREN'T LOOKING, IT WORKED OUT FINE.
House of
House of SOBA
SO BA
I'M NOT POSITIVE THAT HIKARU IS ACTUALLY ESCORTING HER.
※IT'S HARUHI WHO'S ACTING AS ESCORT.
Ice cream is relaxing and clears the air!
SELF-SATISFIED
LET'S GO HOME.
IT WOULD RUIN IT IF THEY DISCOVER US NOW.

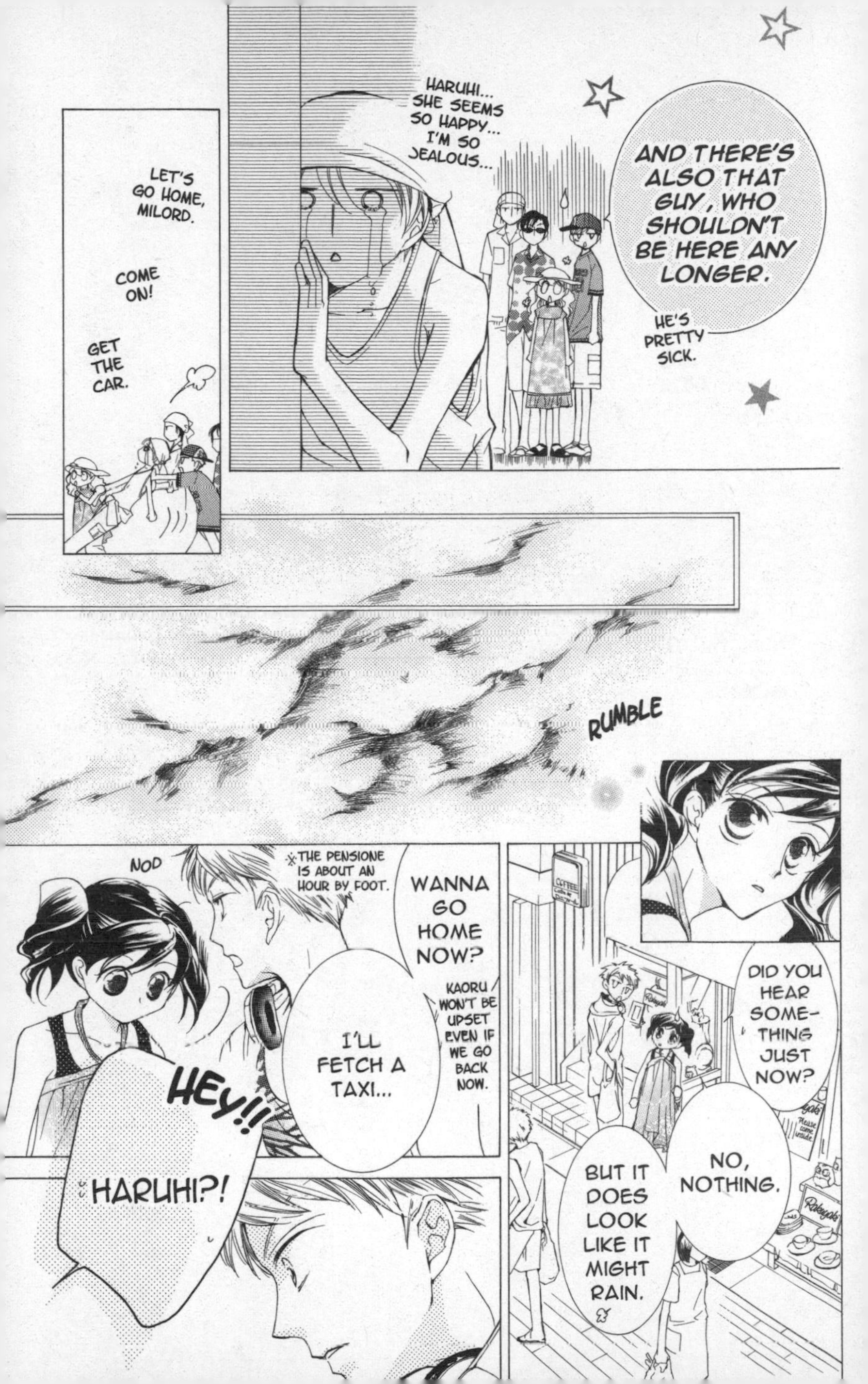
HARUHI... SHE SEEMS SO HAPPY... I'M SO JEALOUS...
AND THERE'S ALSO THAT GUY, WHO SHOULDN'T BE HERE ANY LONGER.
HE'S PRETTY SICK.
LET'S GO HOME, MILORD.
COME ON!
GET THE CAR.
RUMBLE
DID YOU HEAR SOMETHING JUST NOW?
NO, NOTHING.
BUT IT DOES LOOK LIKE IT MIGHT RAIN.
NOD
WANNA GO HOME NOW?
※THE PENSIONE IS ABOUT AN HOUR BY FOOT.
KAORU WON'T BE UPSET EVEN IF WE GO BACK NOW.
I'LL FETCH A TAXI...
HEY!!
HARUHI?!

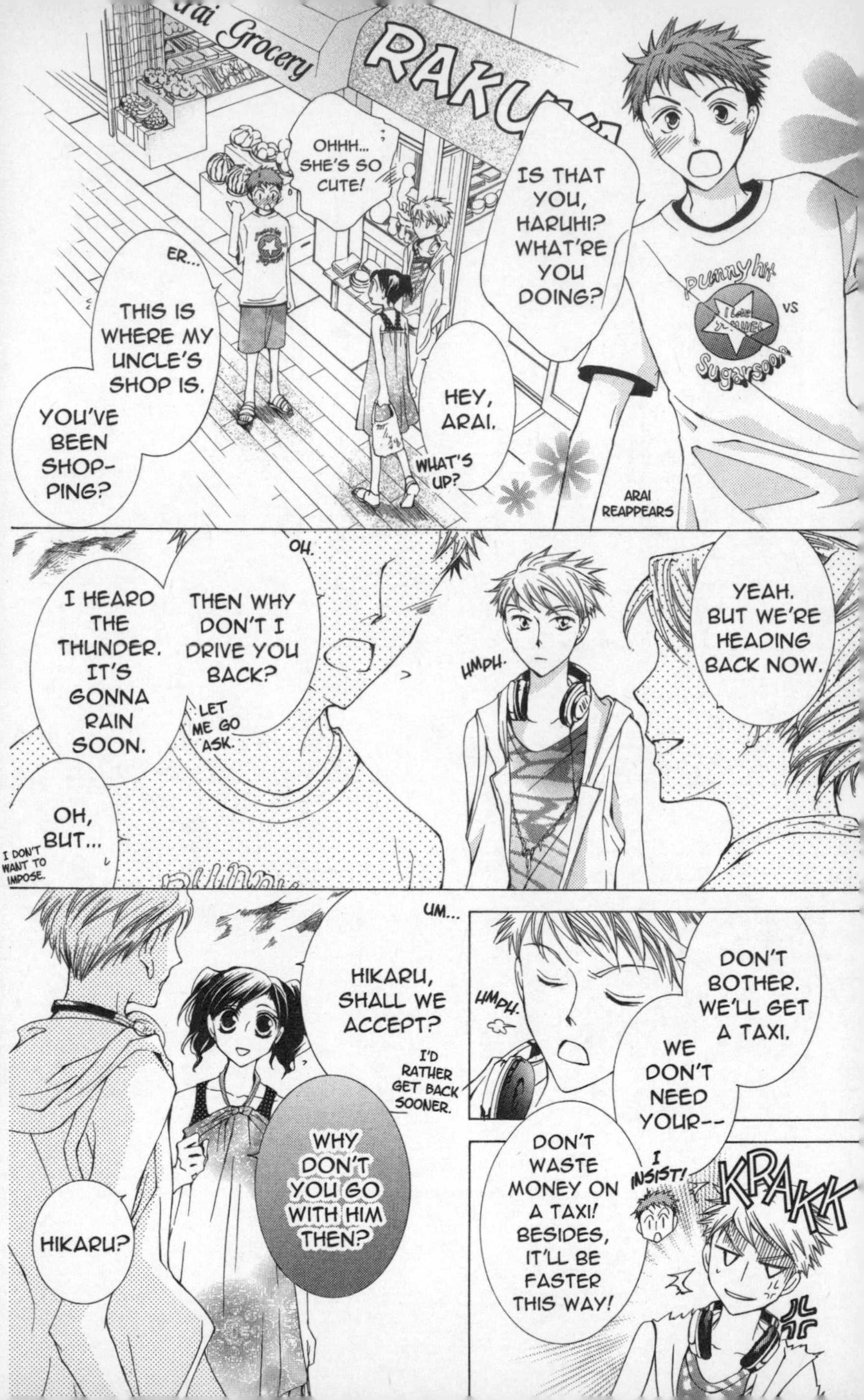
RAKU
rai Grocery
IS THAT YOU, HARUHI? WHAT'RE YOU DOING?
ARAI REAPPEARS
OHHH... SHE'S SO CUTE!
HEY, ARAI.
WHAT'S UP?
ER...
THIS IS WHERE MY UNCLE'S SHOP IS.
YOU'VE BEEN SHOP-PING?
YEAH. BUT WE'RE HEADING BACK NOW.
HMPH.
OH.
THEN WHY DON'T I DRIVE YOU BACK?
LET ME GO ASK.
I HEARD THE THUNDER. IT'S GONNA RAIN SOON.
OH, BUT...
I DON'T WANT TO IMPOSE.
DON'T BOTHER. WE'LL GET A TAXI.
WE DON'T NEED YOUR--
HMPH.
KRAKK
I INSIST!
DON'T WASTE MONEY ON A TAXI! BESIDES, IT'LL BE FASTER THIS WAY!
UM...
HIKARU, SHALL WE ACCEPT?
I'D RATHER GET BACK SOONER.
WHY DON'T YOU GO WITH HIM THEN?
HIKARU?

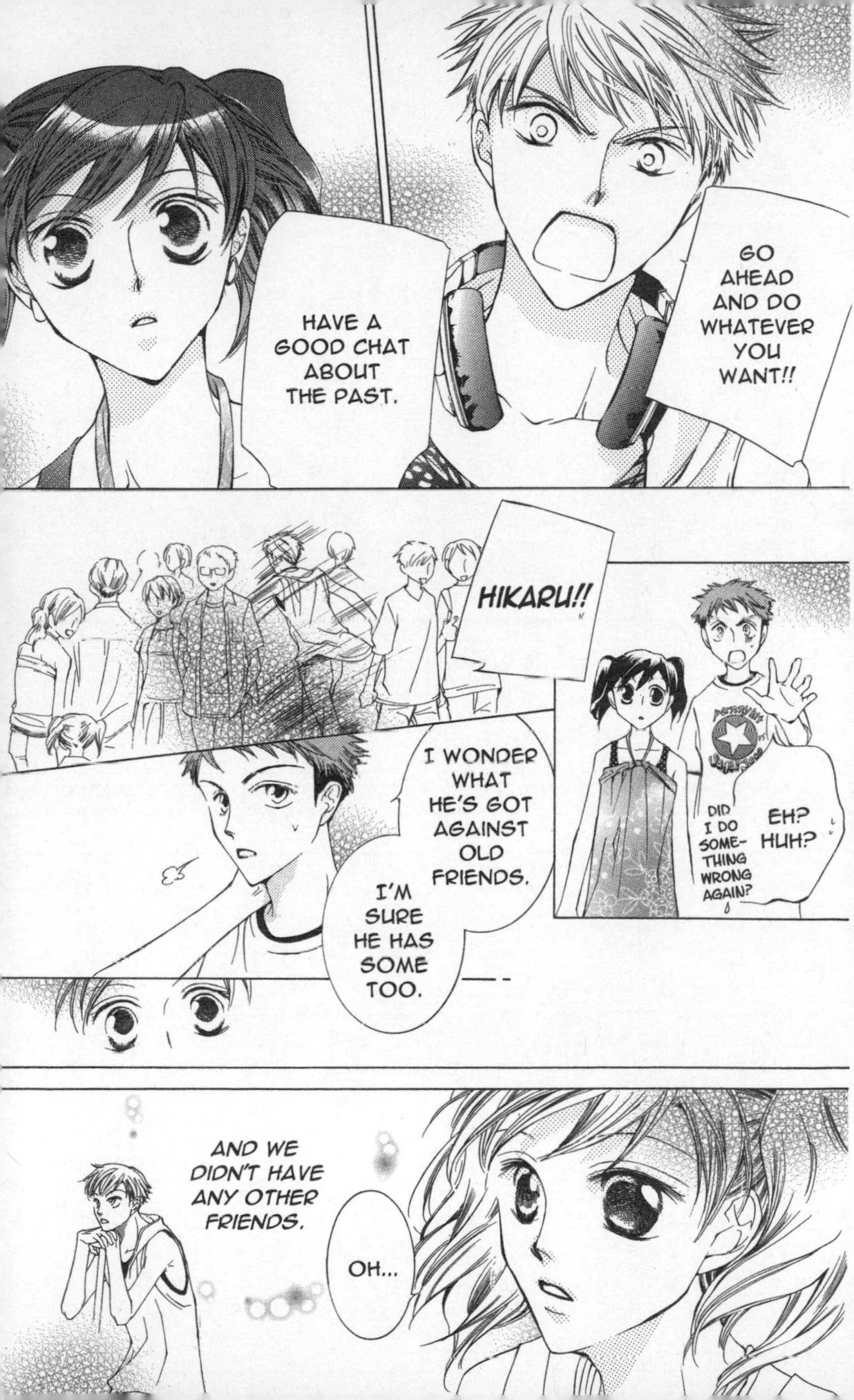
GO AHEAD AND DO WHATEVER YOU WANT!!
HAVE A GOOD CHAT ABOUT THE PAST.
HIKARU!!
EH? HUH?
DID I DO SOMETHING WRONG AGAIN?
I WONDER WHAT HE'S GOT AGAINST OLD FRIENDS.
I'M SURE HE HAS SOME TOO.
AND WE DIDN'T HAVE ANY OTHER FRIENDS.
OH...

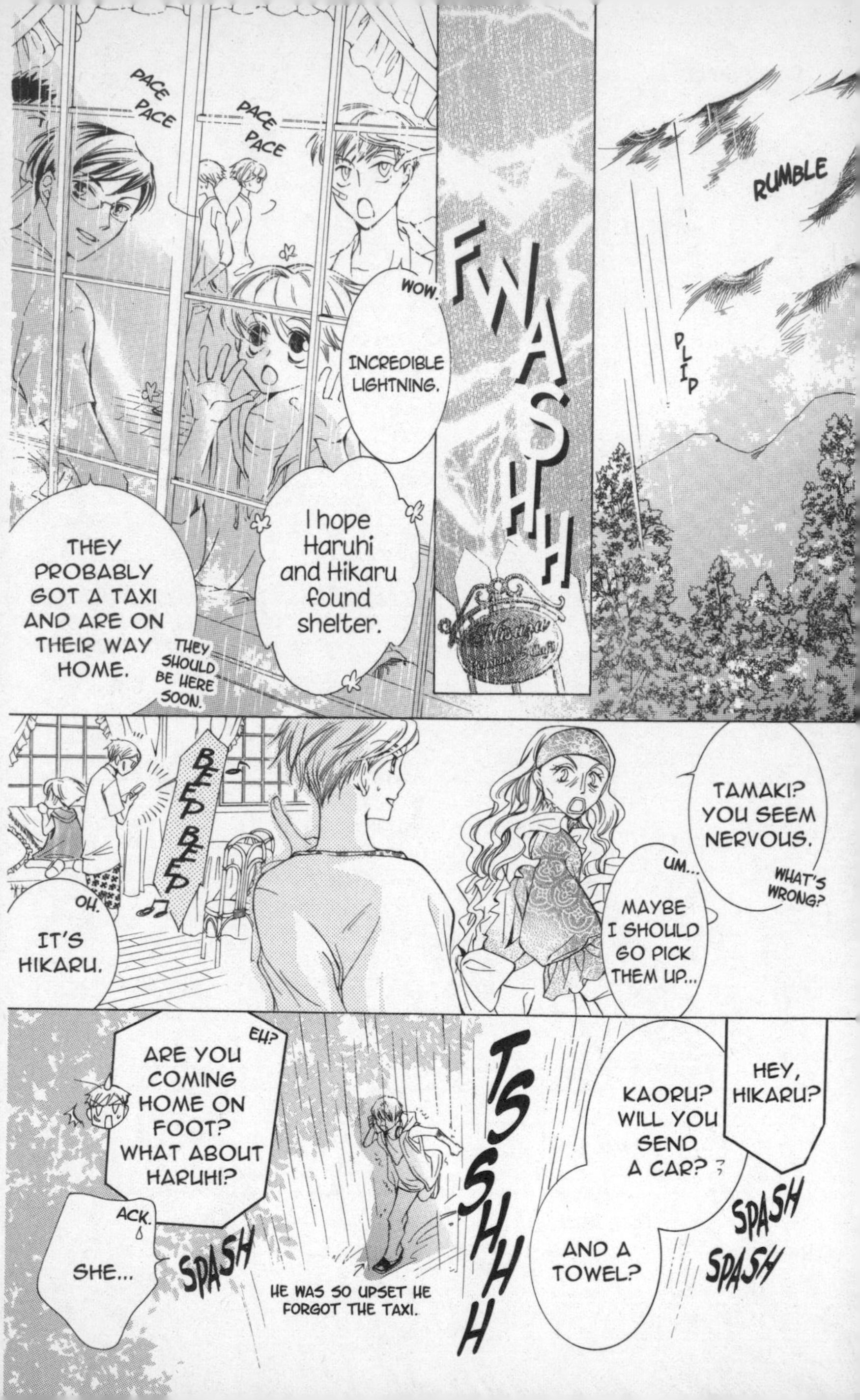
RUMBLE
PLIP
FWASHHH
WOW.
INCREDIBLE LIGHTNING.
PACE PACE
PACE PACE
I hope Haruhi and Hikaru found shelter.
THEY PROBABLY GOT A TAXI AND ARE ON THEIR WAY HOME.
THEY SHOULD BE HERE SOON.
TAMAKI? YOU SEEM NERVOUS.
WHAT'S WRONG?
UM...
MAYBE I SHOULD GO PICK THEM UP...
BEEP BEEP
OH.
IT'S HIKARU.
HEY, HIKARU?
KAORU? WILL YOU SEND A CAR?
AND A TOWEL?
SPASH
SPASH
TSSHHH
EH?
ARE YOU COMING HOME ON FOOT? WHAT ABOUT HARUHI?
ACK.
SHE...
SPASH
HE WAS SO UPSET HE FORGOT THE TAXI.

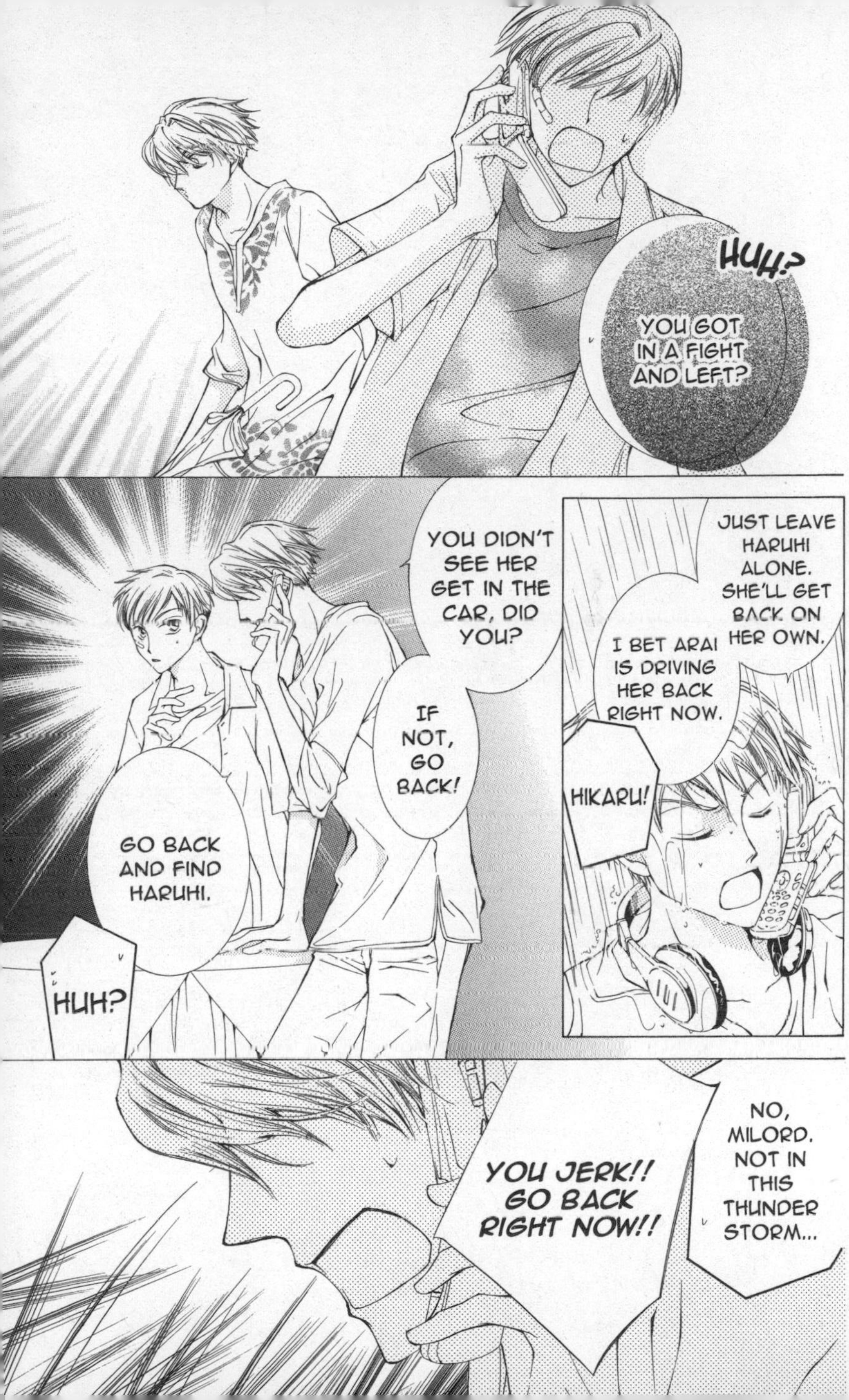
HUH?
YOU GOT IN A FIGHT AND LEFT?
JUST LEAVE HARUHI ALONE. SHE'LL GET BACK ON HER OWN.
I BET ARAI IS DRIVING HER BACK RIGHT NOW.
HIKARU!
YOU DIDN'T SEE HER GET IN THE CAR, DID YOU?
IF NOT, GO BACK!
GO BACK AND FIND HARUHI.
HUH?
NO, MILORD. NOT IN THIS THUNDER STORM...
YOU JERK!! GO BACK RIGHT NOW!!

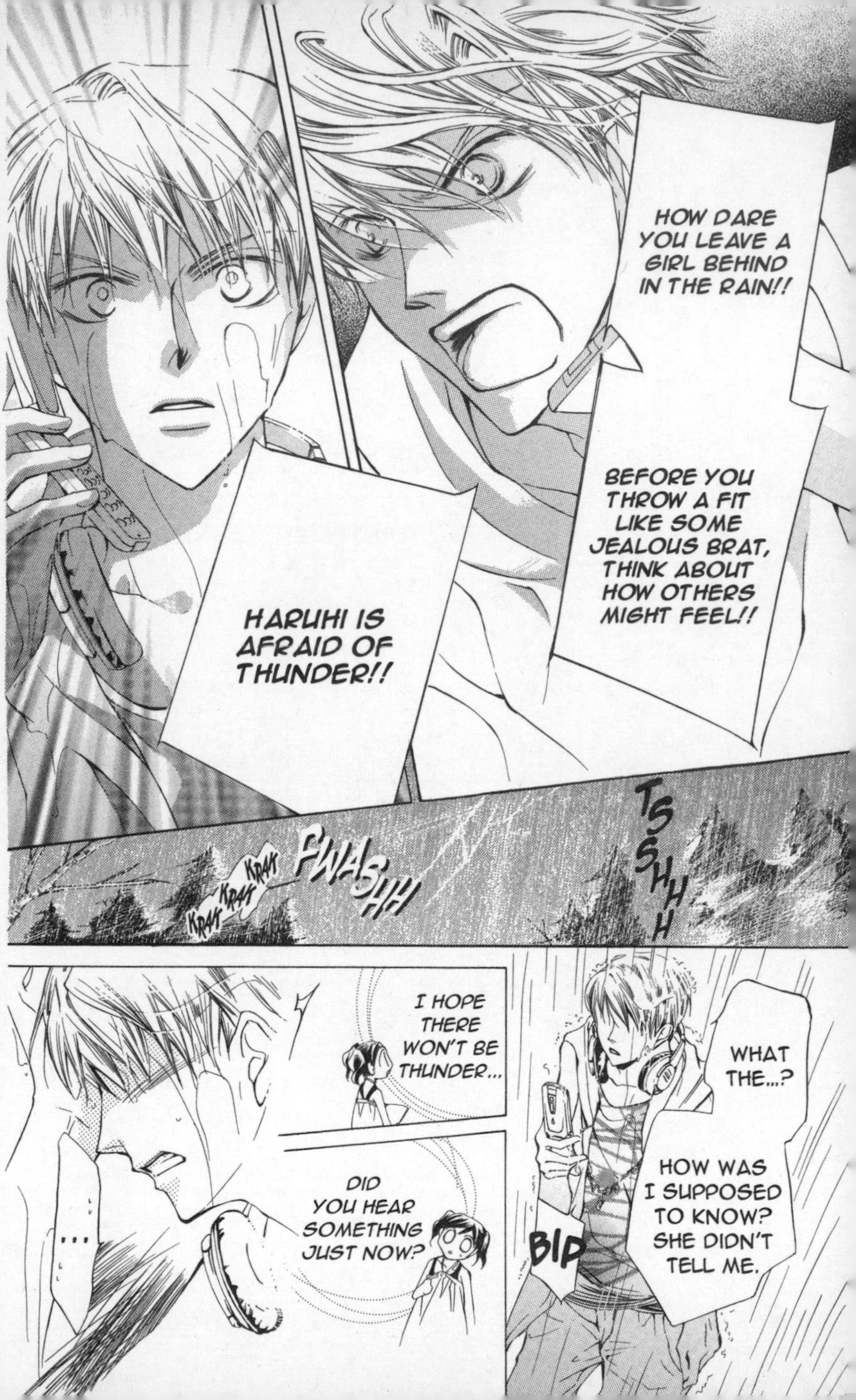
HOW DARE YOU LEAVE A GIRL BEHIND IN THE RAIN!!
BEFORE YOU THROW A FIT LIKE SOME JEALOUS BRAT, THINK ABOUT HOW OTHERS MIGHT FEEL!!
HARUHI IS AFRAID OF THUNDER!!
TSSHHH
FWASHH
KRAK KRAK KRAK
WHAT THE...?
HOW WAS I SUPPOSED TO KNOW? SHE DIDN'T TELL ME.
BIP
I HOPE THERE WON'T BE THUNDER...
DID YOU HEAR SOMETHING JUST NOW?
...

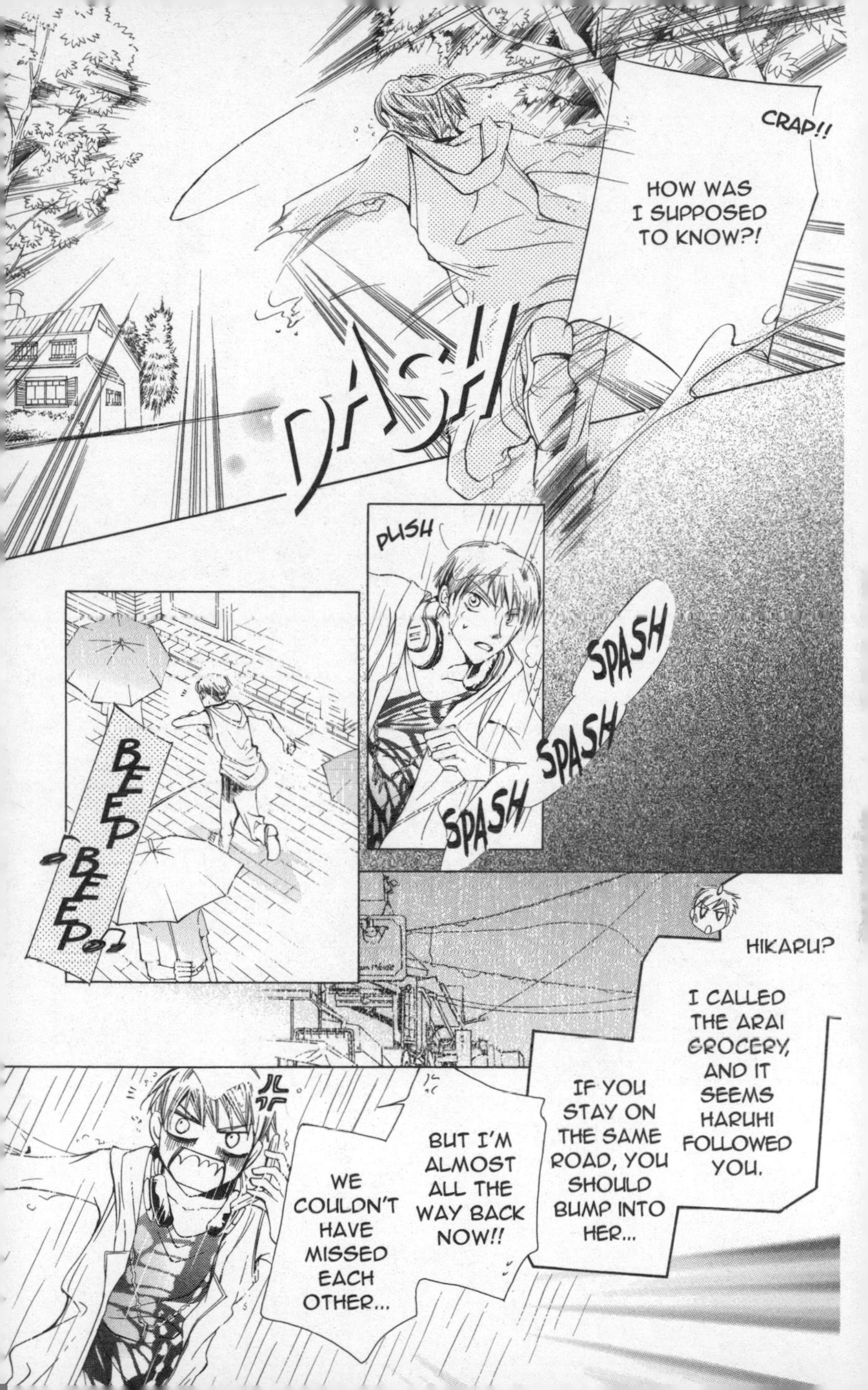
CRAP!!
HOW WAS I SUPPOSED TO KNOW?!
DASH
PUSH
SPASH
SPASH
SPASH
BEEP
BEEP
HIKARU?
I CALLED THE ARAI GROCERY, AND IT SEEMS HARUHI FOLLOWED YOU.
IF YOU STAY ON THE SAME ROAD, YOU SHOULD BUMP INTO HER...
BUT I'M ALMOST ALL THE WAY BACK NOW!!
WE COULDN'T HAVE MISSED EACH OTHER...

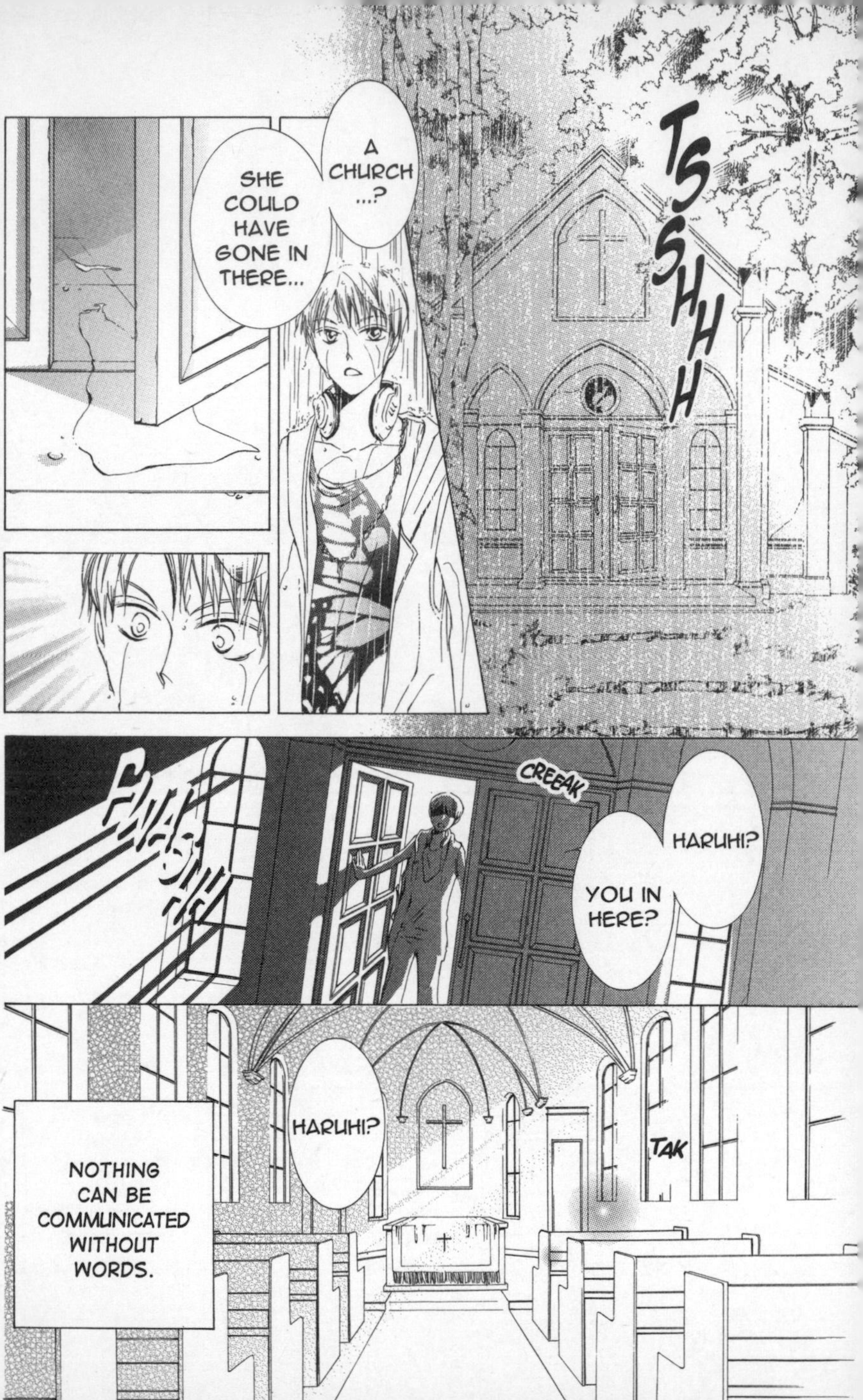
TSHHHH
A CHURCH ...?
SHE COULD HAVE GONE IN THERE...
CREEAK
HARUHI?
YOU IN HERE?
TAK
HARUHI?
NOTHING CAN BE COMMUNICATED WITHOUT WORDS.

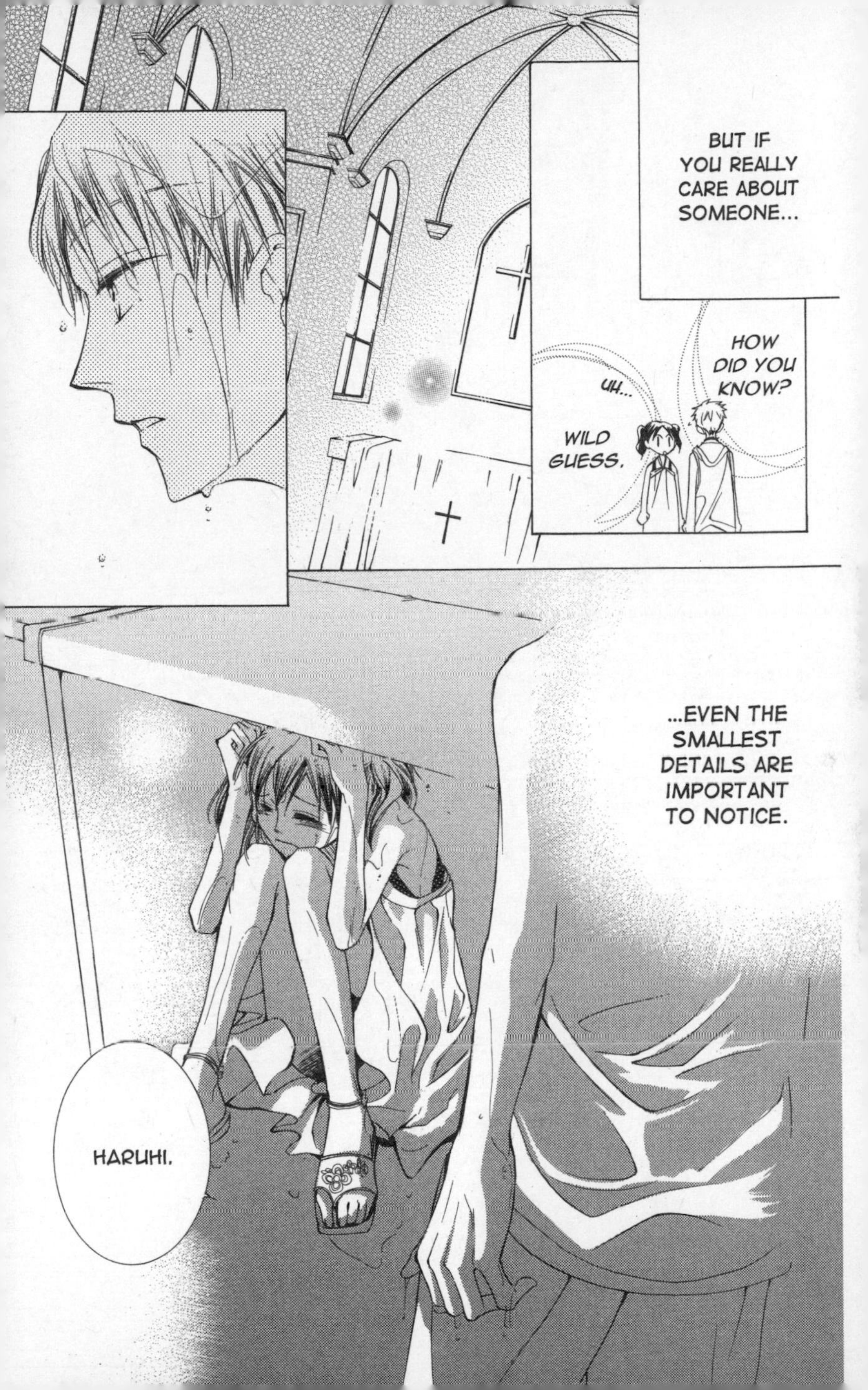
BUT IF YOU REALLY CARE ABOUT SOMEONE...
HOW DID YOU KNOW?
UH...
WILD GUESS.
...EVEN THE SMALLEST DETAILS ARE IMPORTANT TO NOTICE.
HARUHI.

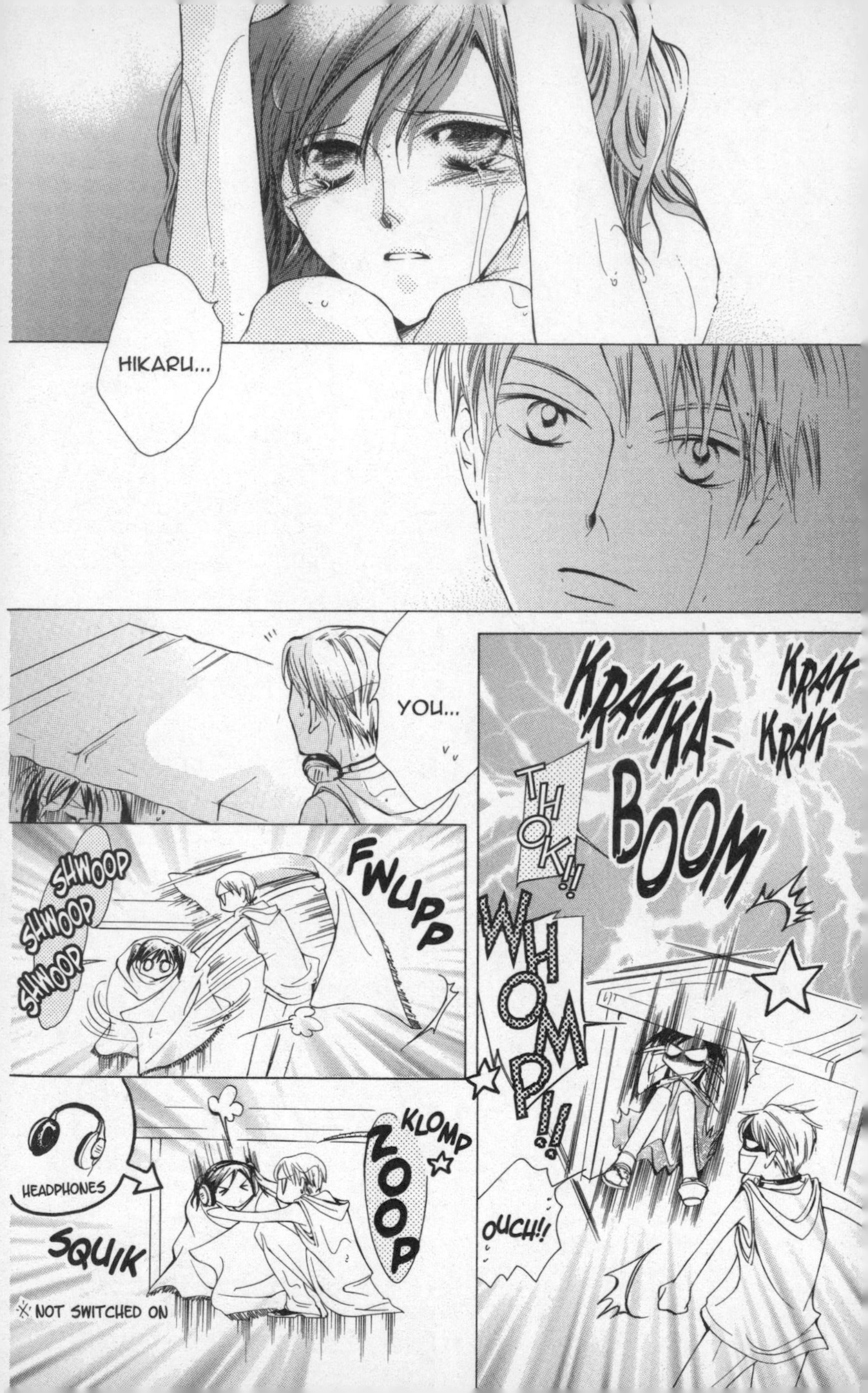
HIKARU...
KRAK KRAK
KRAKKA-BOOM
THOK!!
WHOMP!!
OUCH!!
YOU...
FWUPP
SHWOOP SHWOOP SHWOOP
KLOMP
ZOOOP
HEADPHONES
SQUIK
※ NOT SWITCHED ON

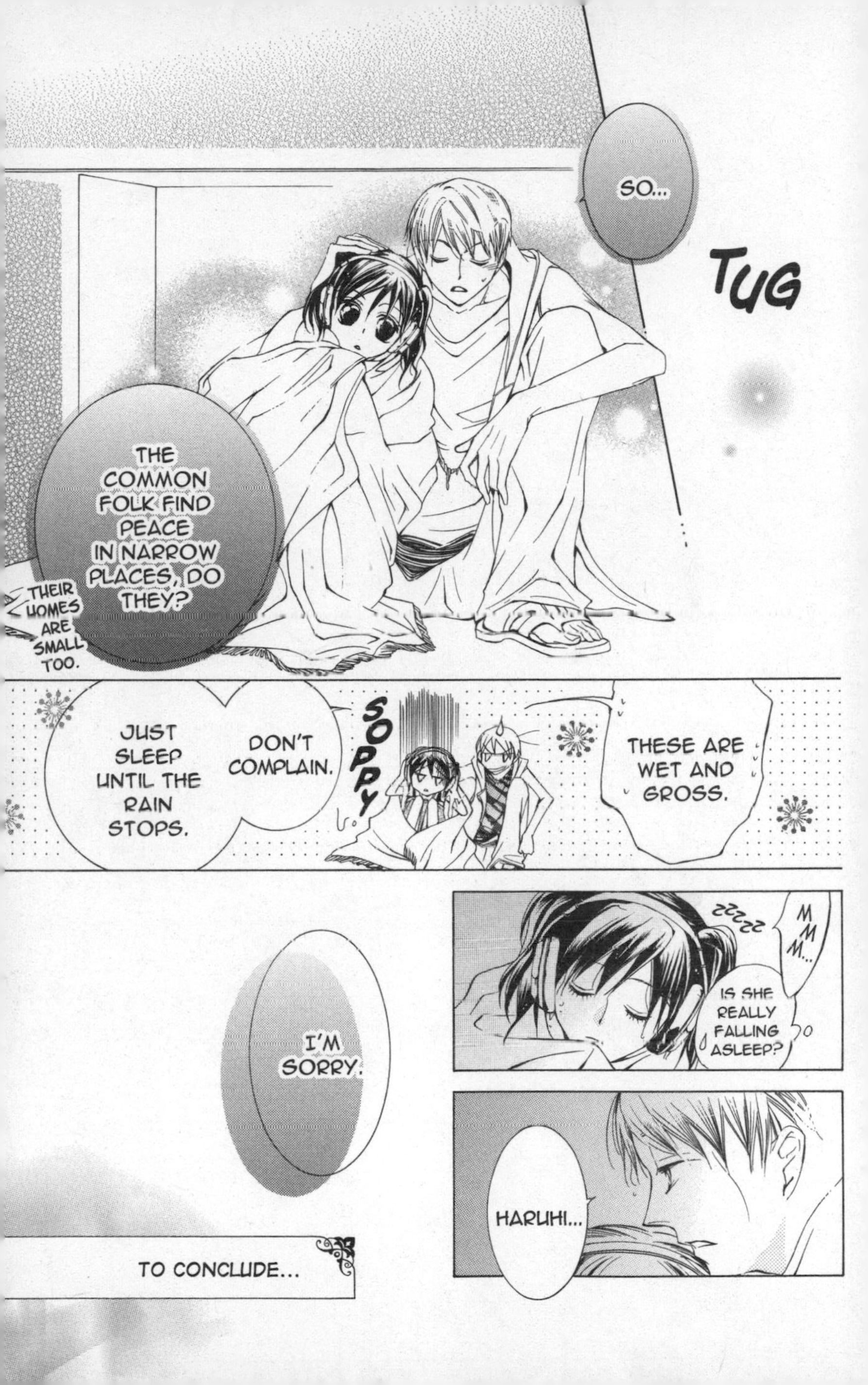
SO...
TUG
THE COMMON FOLK FIND PEACE IN NARROW PLACES, DO THEY?
THEIR HOMES ARE SMALL TOO.
THESE ARE WET AND GROSS.
SOPPY
DON'T COMPLAIN.
JUST SLEEP UNTIL THE RAIN STOPS.
MMM...
ZZZZZ
IS SHE REALLY FALLING ASLEEP?
HARUHI...
I'M SORRY.
TO CONCLUDE...

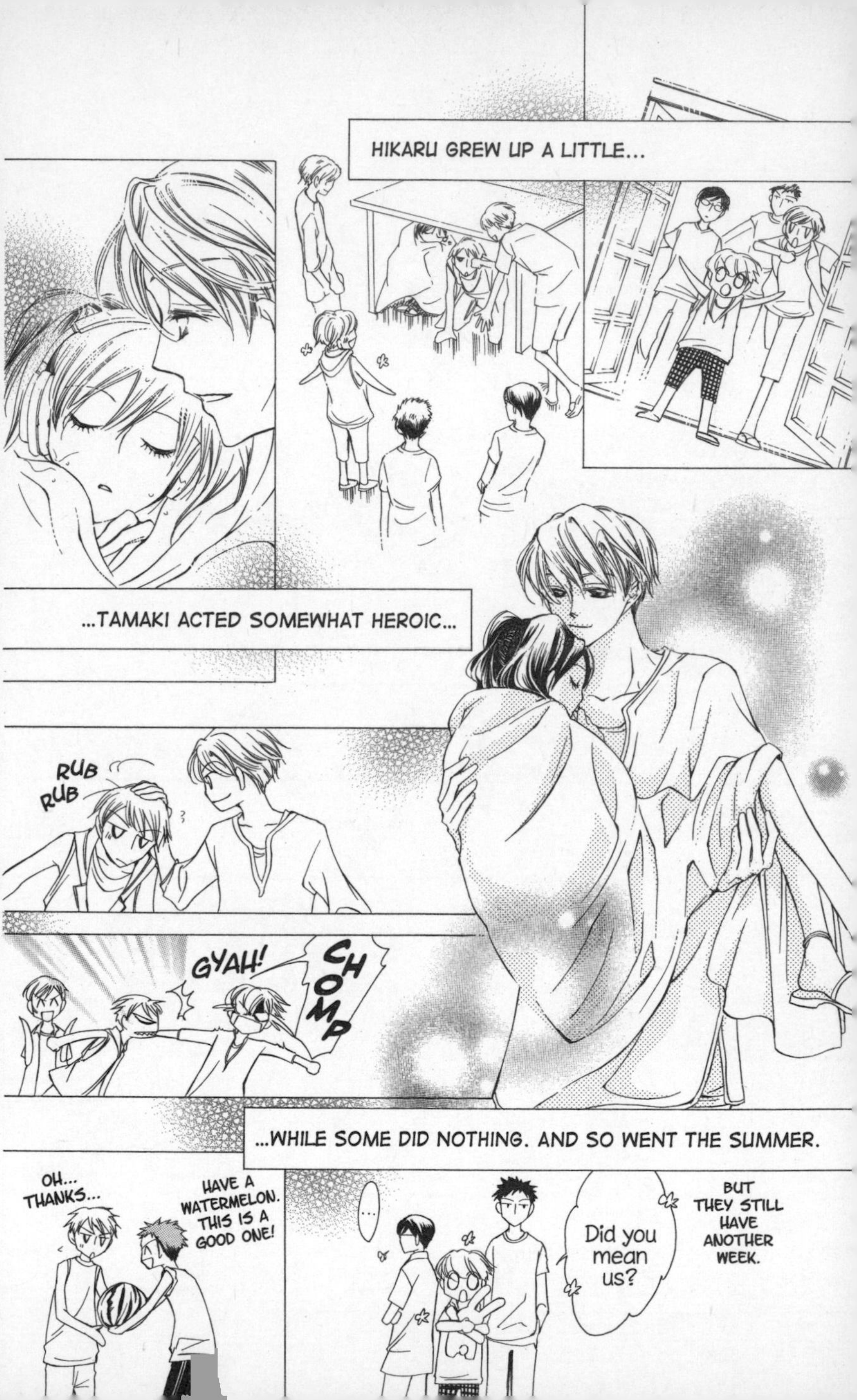
HIKARU GREW UP A LITTLE...
...TAMAKI ACTED SOMEWHAT HEROIC...
RUB RUB
CHOMP
GYAH!
...WHILE SOME DID NOTHING. AND SO WENT THE SUMMER.
BUT THEY STILL HAVE ANOTHER WEEK.
Did you mean us?
...
HAVE A WATERMELON. THIS IS A GOOD ONE!
OH... THANKS...

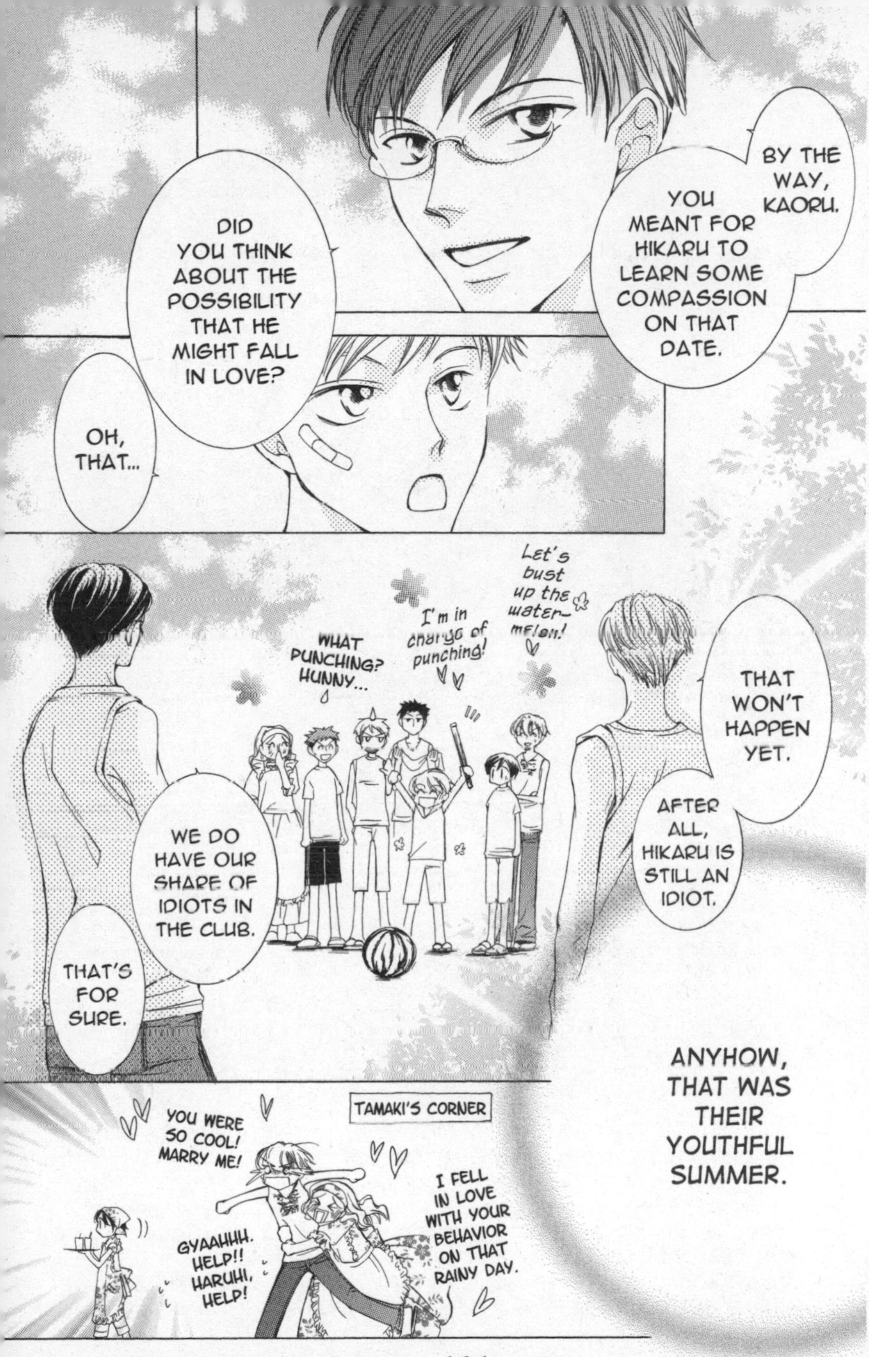
BY THE WAY, KAORU.
YOU MEANT FOR HIKARU TO LEARN SOME COMPASSION ON THAT DATE.
DID YOU THINK ABOUT THE POSSIBILITY THAT HE MIGHT FALL IN LOVE?
OH, THAT...
THAT WON'T HAPPEN YET.
AFTER ALL, HIKARU IS STILL AN IDIOT.
Let's bust up the watermelon!
I'm in charge of punching!
WHAT PUNCHING? HUNNY...
WE DO HAVE OUR SHARE OF IDIOTS IN THE CLUB.
THAT'S FOR SURE.
ANYHOW, THAT WAS THEIR YOUTHFUL SUMMER.
TAMAKI'S CORNER
YOU WERE SO COOL! MARRY ME!
I FELL IN LOVE WITH YOUR BEHAVIOR ON THAT RAINY DAY.
GYAAHHH. HELP!! HARUHI, HELP!

GUEST ROOM: FAXES ②
SPECIAL THANKS TO
MIDORI SHIINO!

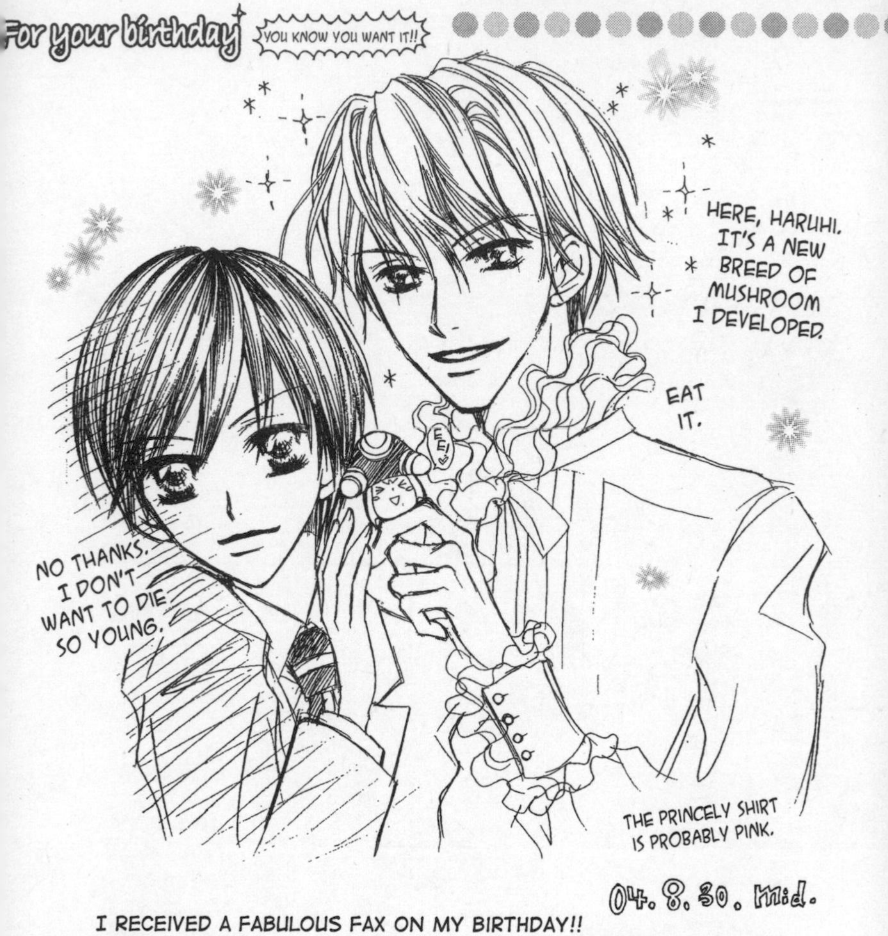
For your birthday
YOU KNOW YOU WANT IT!!
HERE, HARUHI. IT'S A NEW BREED OF MUSHROOM I DEVELOPED.
EAT IT.
NO THANKS. I DON'T WANT TO DIE SO YOUNG.
THE PRINCELY SHIRT IS PROBABLY PINK.
04. 8. 30. mid.

I RECEIVED A FABULOUS FAX ON MY BIRTHDAY!!
THIS IS ONE OF MY *LALA* MANGA-KA FRIENDS. PLEASE READ *LALA DX* TOO.♡
I WAS PLEASED--REALLY PLEASED--BUT IS TAMAKI THIS FOOLISH?
HERE, HARUHI LOOKS AS THOUGH SHE'LL NEVER FALL FOR TAMAKI.
IT'S REALLY WONDERFUL, THOUGH! THANK YOU SO MUCH!
MIDORI'S DRIVING SCARES ME, SO I'D RATHER NOT RIDE WITH HER
AGAIN? BUT PLEASE LET ME.♡ (I'M ONLY BEING POLITE.)

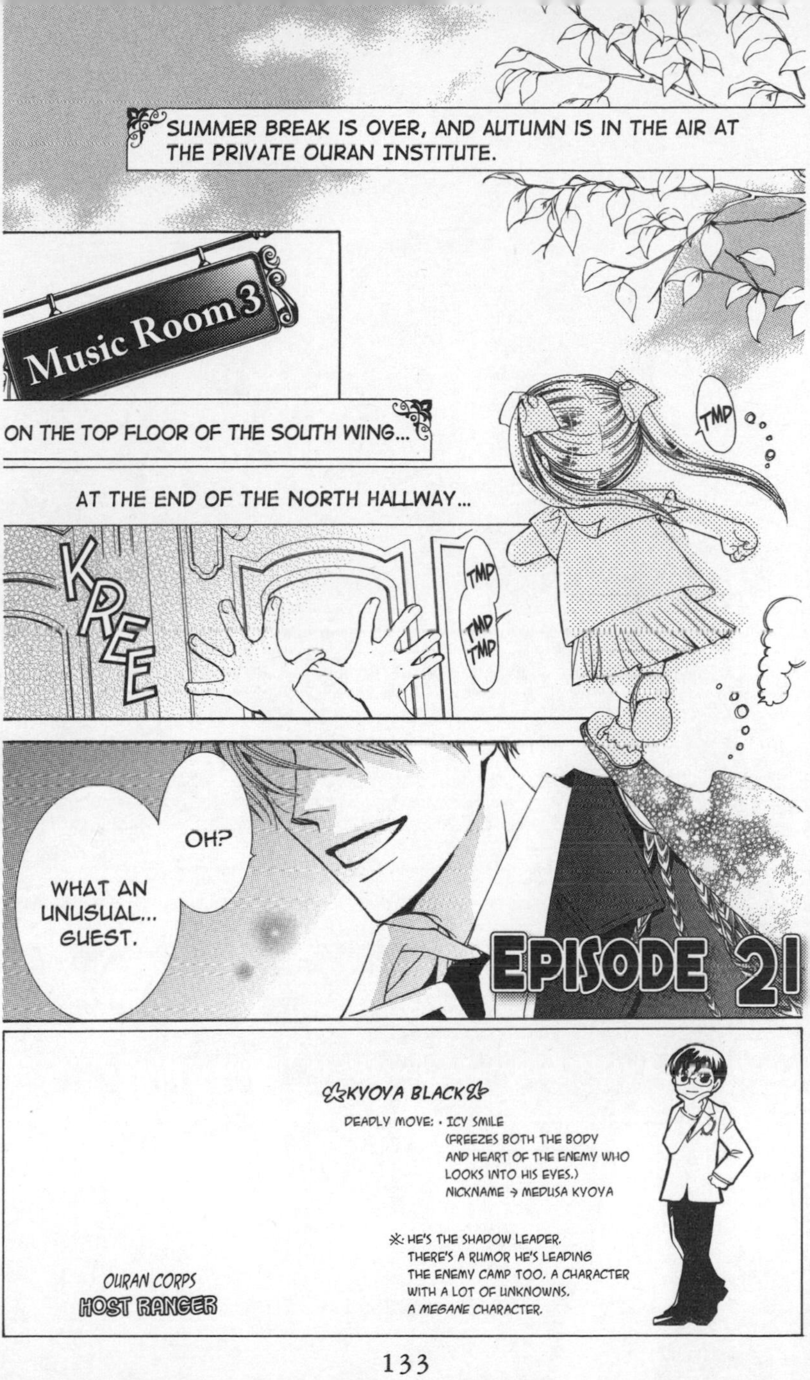

SUMMER BREAK IS OVER, AND AUTUMN IS IN THE AIR AT THE PRIVATE OURAN INSTITUTE.
Music Room 3
ON THE TOP FLOOR OF THE SOUTH WING...
AT THE END OF THE NORTH HALLWAY...
TMP
TMP TMP TMP
KREE
OH?
WHAT AN UNUSUAL... GUEST.
EPISODE 21
KYOYA BLACK
DEADLY MOVE: • ICY SMILE (FREEZES BOTH THE BODY AND HEART OF THE ENEMY WHO LOOKS INTO HIS EYES.)
NICKNAME → MEDUSA KYOYA
※: HE'S THE SHADOW LEADER. THERE'S A RUMOR HE'S LEADING THE ENEMY CAMP TOO. A CHARACTER WITH A LOT OF UNKNOWNS. A MEGANE CHARACTER.
OURAN CORPS
HOST RANGER

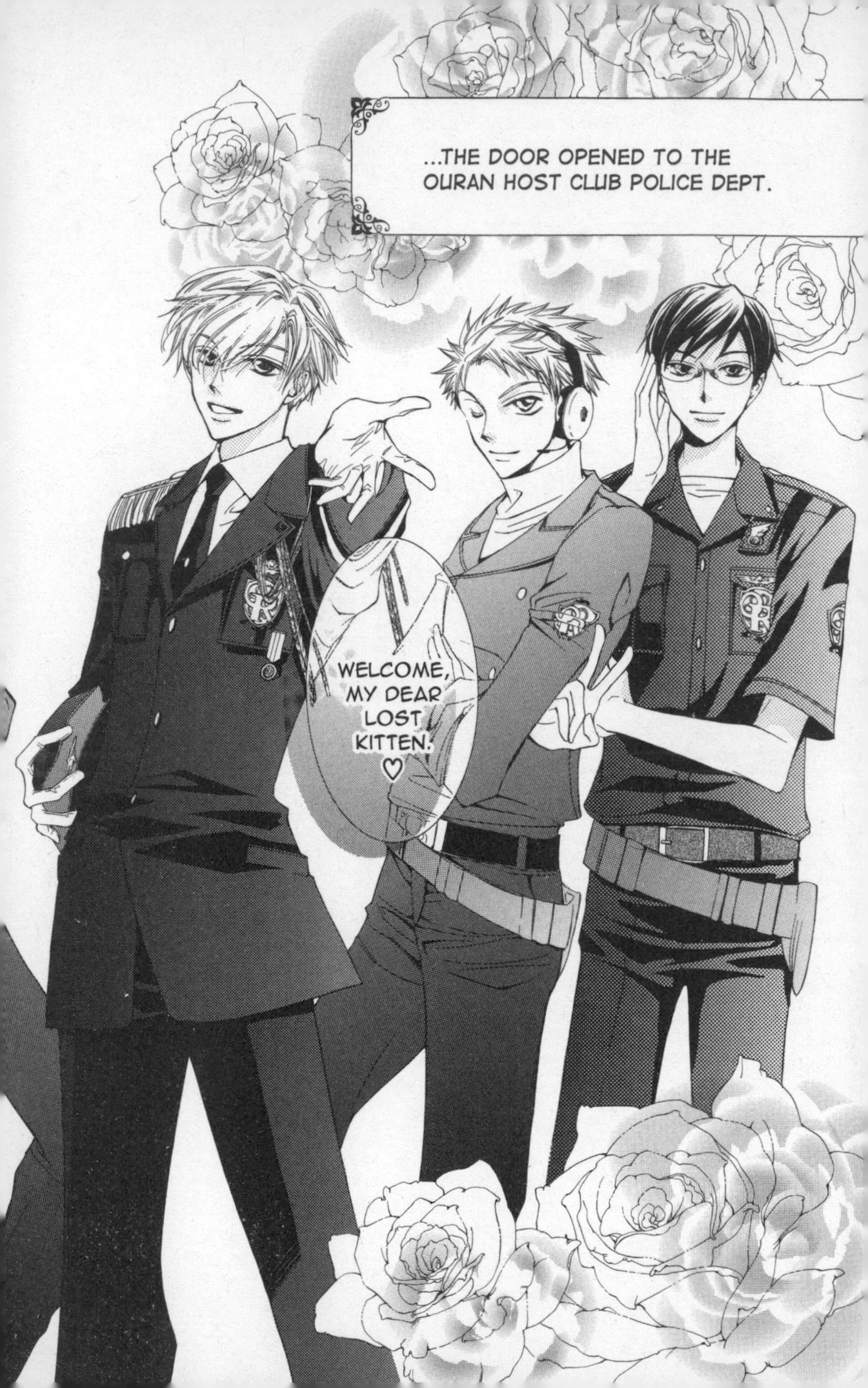
...THE DOOR OPENED TO THE OURAN HOST CLUB POLICE DEPT.
WELCOME, MY DEAR LOST KITTEN. ♡

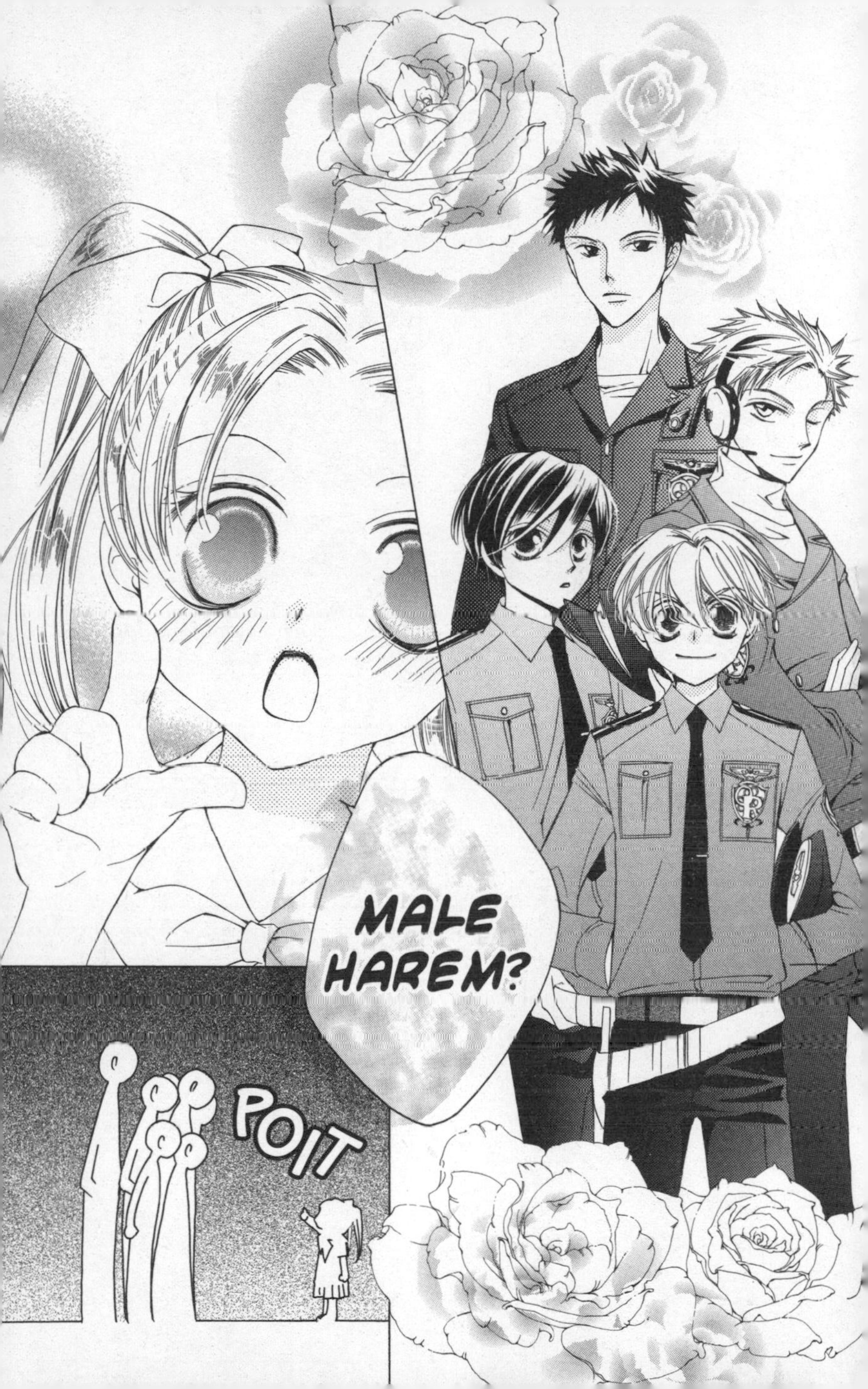
MALE HAREM?
POIT

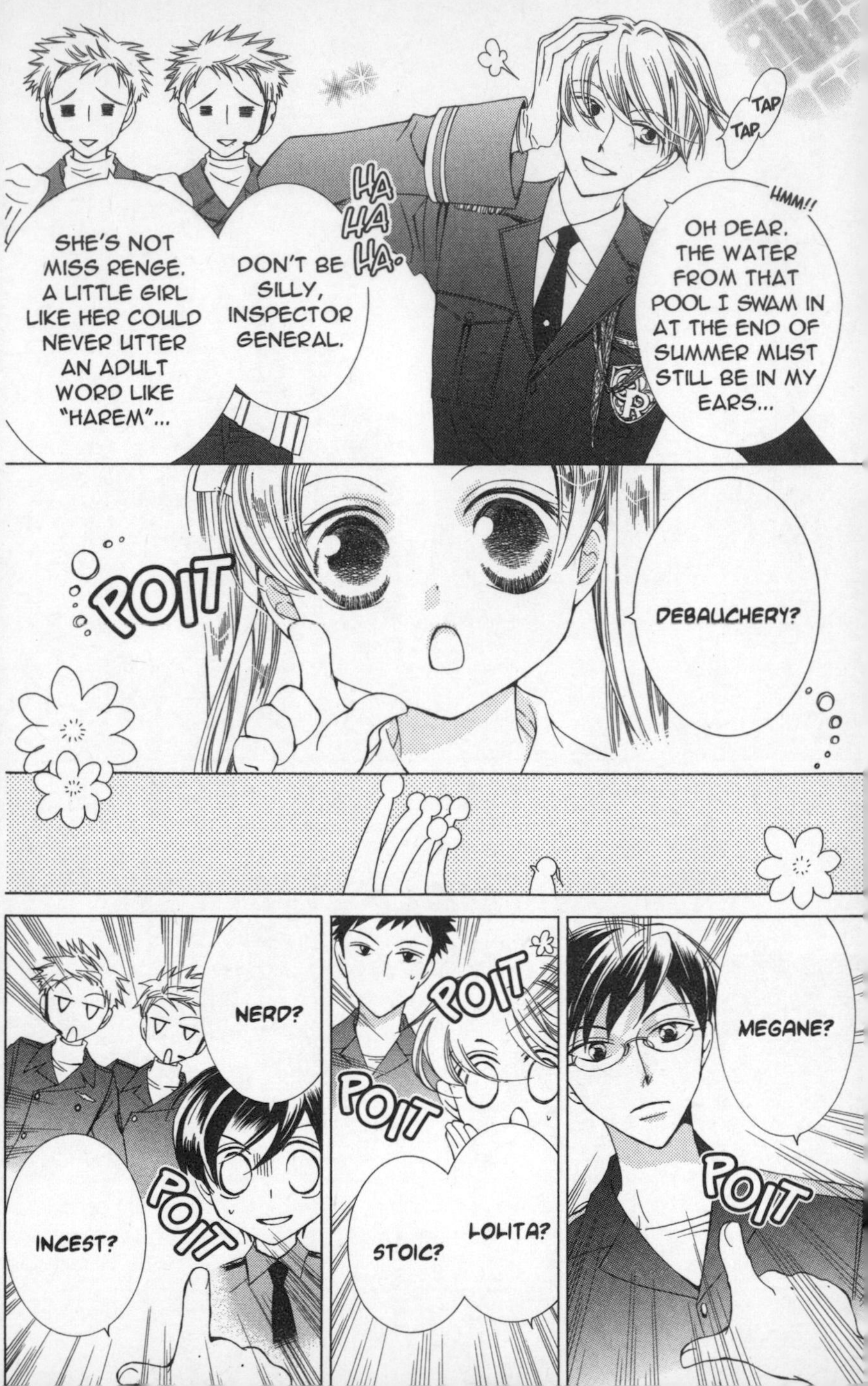
TAP TAP
HMM!!
OH DEAR. THE WATER FROM THAT POOL I SWAM IN AT THE END OF SUMMER MUST STILL BE IN MY EARS...
HA HA HA.
DON'T BE SILLY, INSPECTOR GENERAL.
SHE'S NOT MISS RENGE. A LITTLE GIRL LIKE HER COULD NEVER UTTER AN ADULT WORD LIKE "HAREM"...
DEBAUCHERY?
POIT
MEGANE?
POIT
POIT
POIT
LOLITA?
STOIC?
NERD?
POIT
INCEST?

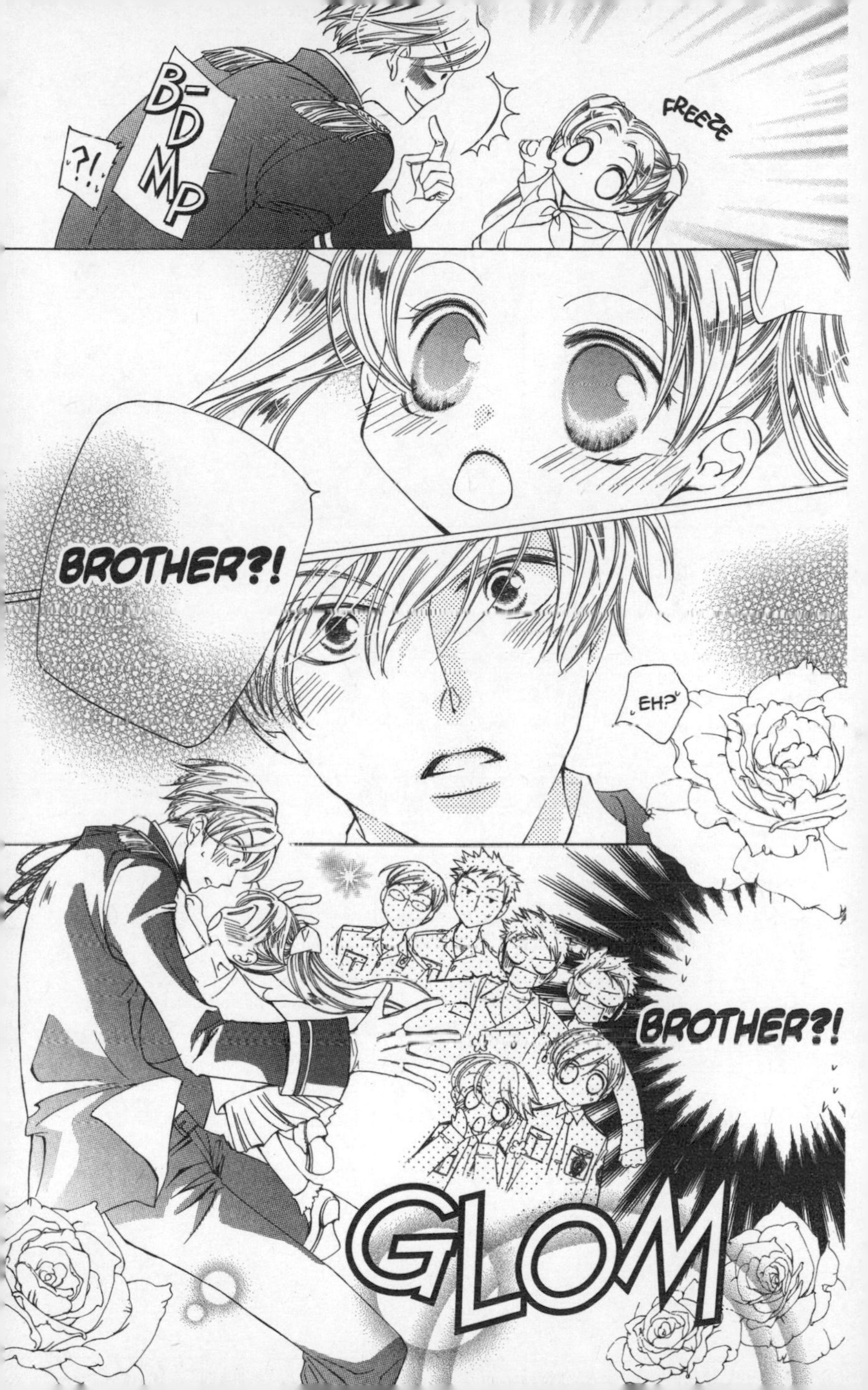
FREEZE
B-DMP
?!
BROTHER?!
EH?
BROTHER?!
GLOM

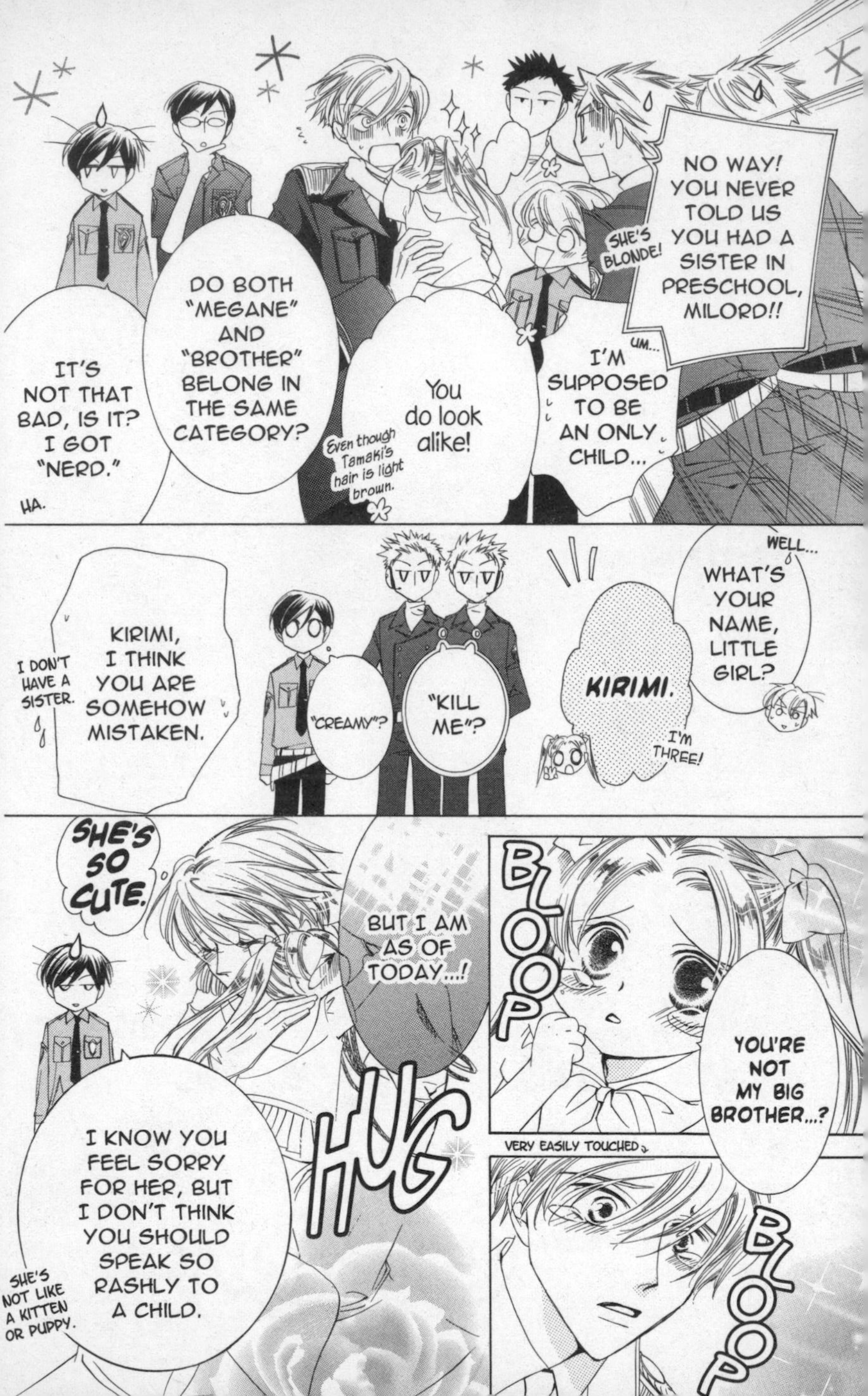
NO WAY! YOU NEVER TOLD US YOU HAD A SISTER IN PRESCHOOL, MILORD!!
SHE'S BLONDE!
UM...
I'M SUPPOSED TO BE AN ONLY CHILD...
You do look alike!
Even though Tamaki's hair is light brown.
DO BOTH "MEGANE" AND "BROTHER" BELONG IN THE SAME CATEGORY?
IT'S NOT THAT BAD, IS IT? I GOT "NERD."
HA.
WELL...
WHAT'S YOUR NAME, LITTLE GIRL?
KIRIMI.
I'M THREE!
"KILL ME"?
"CREAMY"?
KIRIMI, I THINK YOU ARE SOMEHOW MISTAKEN.
I DON'T HAVE A SISTER.
BLOOP
YOU'RE NOT MY BIG BROTHER...?
VERY EASILY TOUCHED
BLOOP
BUT I AM AS OF TODAY...!
HUG
SHE'S SO CUTE.
I KNOW YOU FEEL SORRY FOR HER, BUT I DON'T THINK YOU SHOULD SPEAK SO RASHLY TO A CHILD.
SHE'S NOT LIKE A KITTEN OR PUPPY.

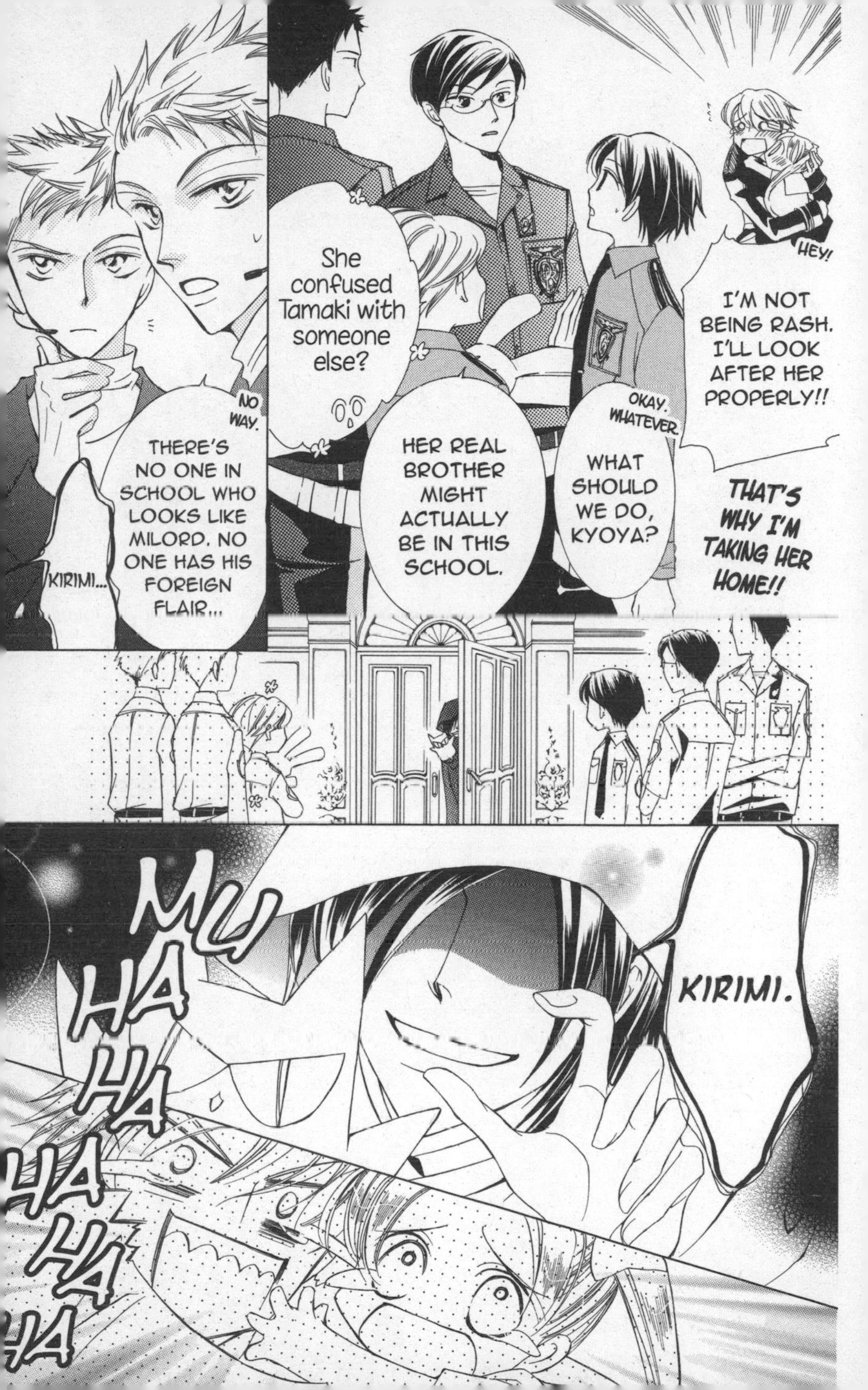
HEY!
I'M NOT BEING RASH. I'LL LOOK AFTER HER PROPERLY!!
THAT'S WHY I'M TAKING HER HOME!!
She confused Tamaki with someone else?
OKAY. WHATEVER.
WHAT SHOULD WE DO, KYOYA?
HER REAL BROTHER MIGHT ACTUALLY BE IN THIS SCHOOL.
NO WAY.
THERE'S NO ONE IN SCHOOL WHO LOOKS LIKE MILORD. NO ONE HAS HIS FOREIGN FLAIR...
KIRIMI...
KIRIMI.
MUHAHAHAHAHAHA

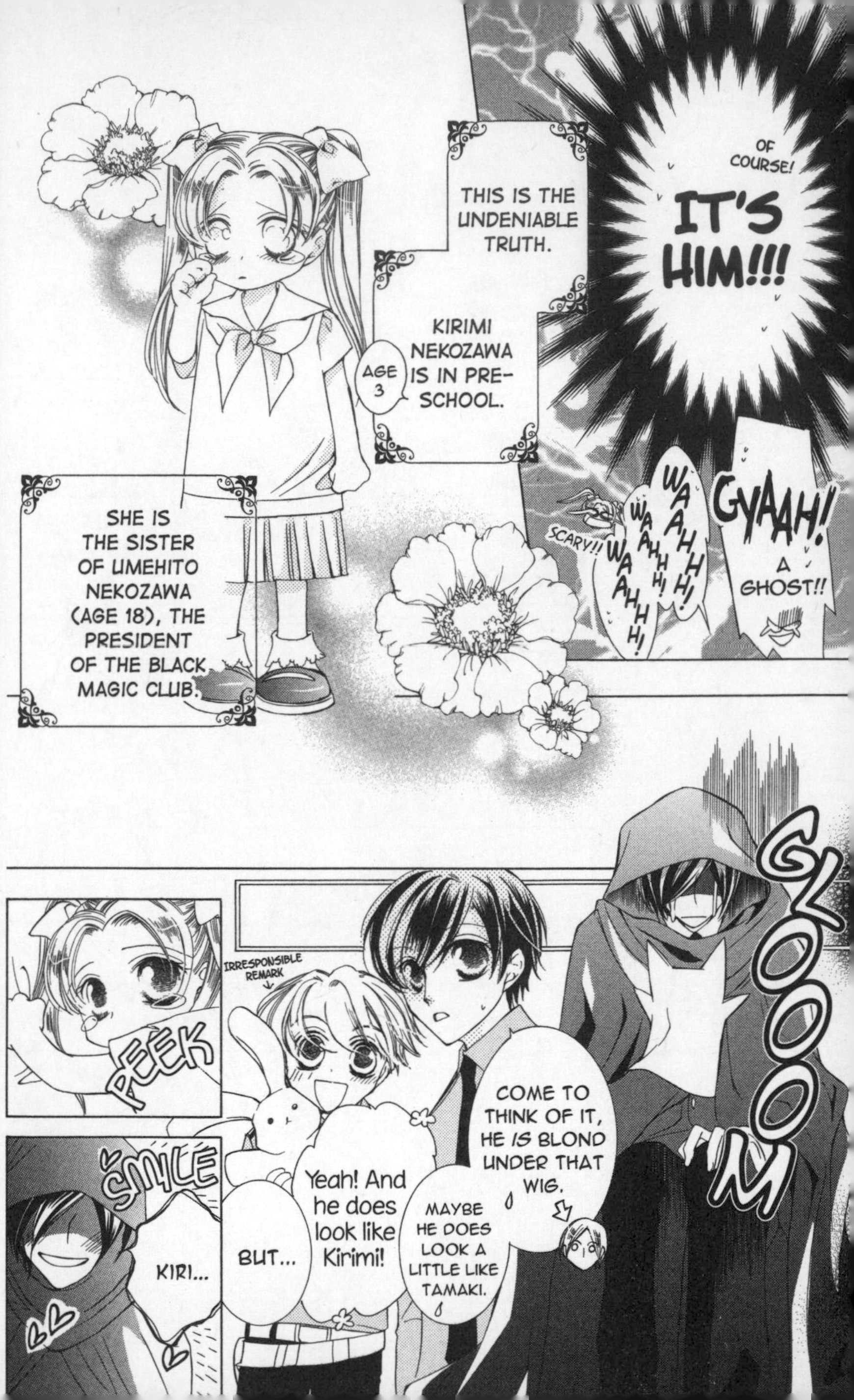

OF COURSE!
IT'S HIM!!!
GYAAH!
A GHOST!!
WAAHHH!
WAAHHH!
WAAHHH!
SCARY!!
THIS IS THE UNDENIABLE TRUTH.
KIRIMI NEKOZAWA IS IN PRE-SCHOOL.
AGE 3
SHE IS THE SISTER OF UMEHITO NEKOZAWA (AGE 18), THE PRESIDENT OF THE BLACK MAGIC CLUB.
GLOOOOM
COME TO THINK OF IT, HE *IS* BLOND UNDER THAT WIG.
MAYBE HE DOES LOOK A LITTLE LIKE TAMAKI.
IRRESPONSIBLE REMARK
Yeah! And he does look like Kirimi!
BUT...
PEEK
SMILE
KIRI...

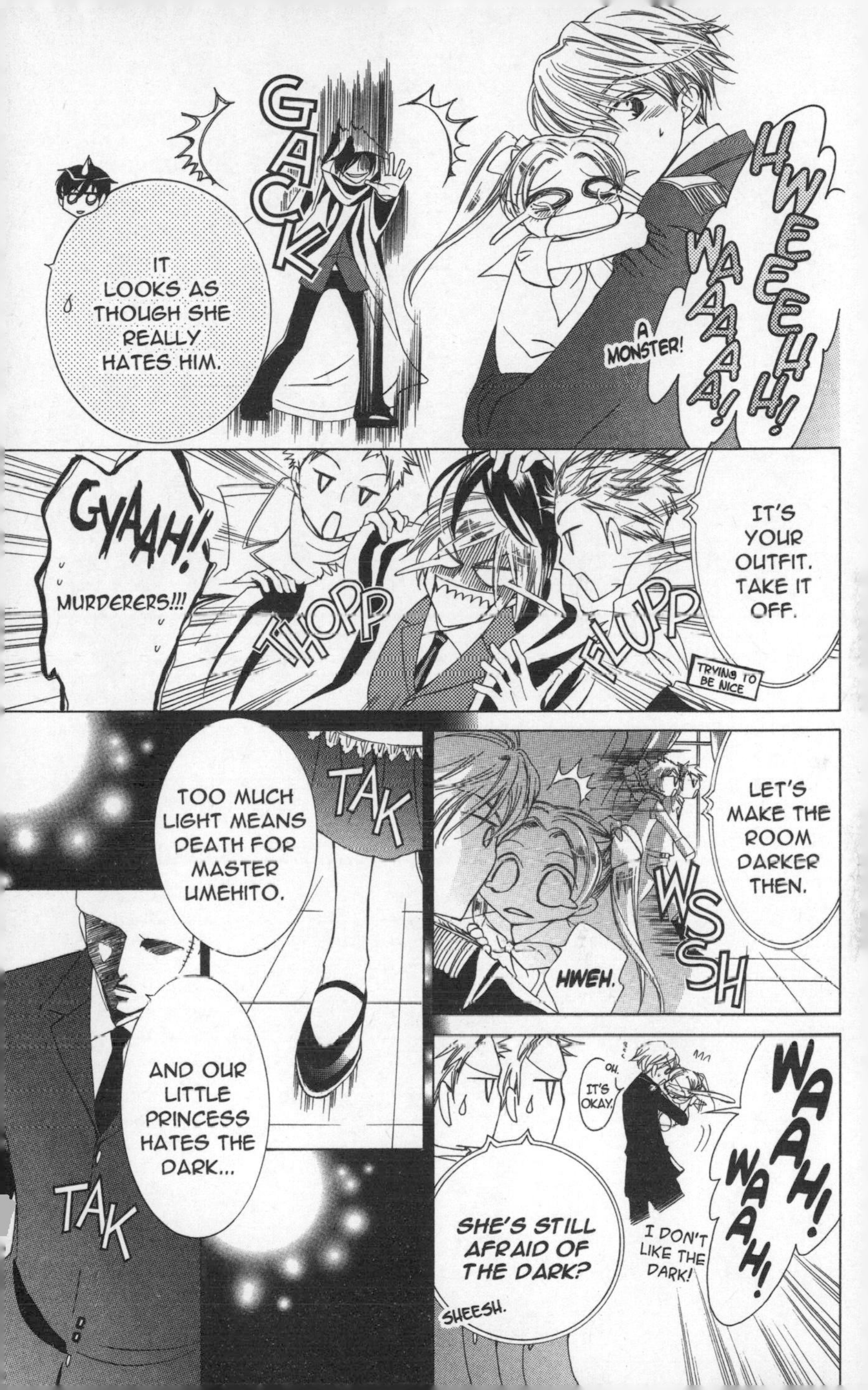
HWEEEEHH!
WAAAAA!
A MONSTER!
GACK
IT LOOKS AS THOUGH SHE REALLY HATES HIM.
IT'S YOUR OUTFIT. TAKE IT OFF.
TRYING TO BE NICE
FLUPP
THOPP
GYAAAH!
MURDERERS!!!
LET'S MAKE THE ROOM DARKER THEN.
WSSH
HWEH.
WAAH! WAAH!
I DON'T LIKE THE DARK!
OH. IT'S OKAY.
SHE'S STILL AFRAID OF THE DARK?
SHEESH.
TAK
TOO MUCH LIGHT MEANS DEATH FOR MASTER UMEHITO.
AND OUR LITTLE PRINCESS HATES THE DARK...
TAK

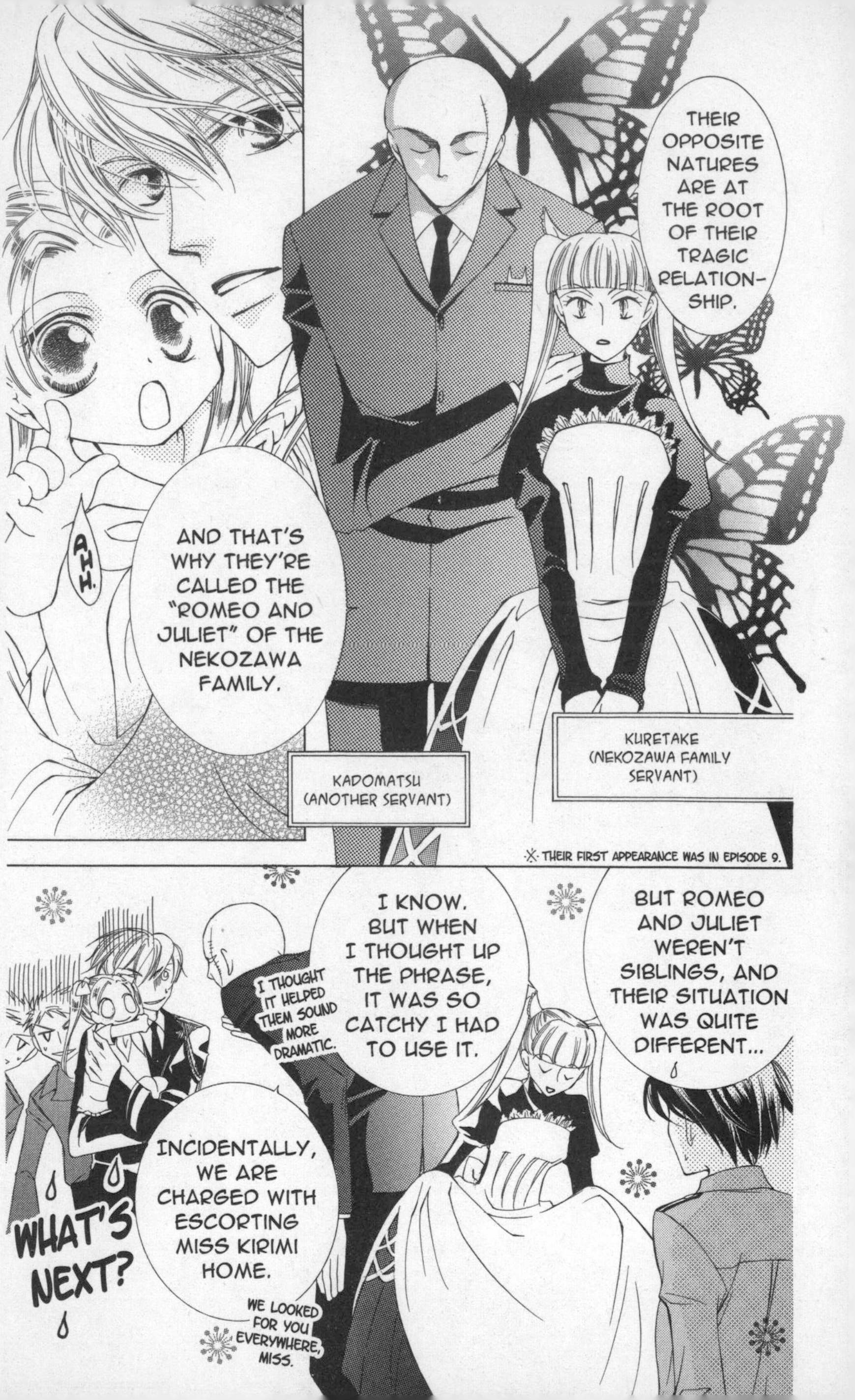
THEIR OPPOSITE NATURES ARE AT THE ROOT OF THEIR TRAGIC RELATION-SHIP.
AND THAT'S WHY THEY'RE CALLED THE "ROMEO AND JULIET" OF THE NEKOZAWA FAMILY.
AHH.
KURETAKE (NEKOZAWA FAMILY SERVANT)
KADOMATSU (ANOTHER SERVANT)
※ THEIR FIRST APPEARANCE WAS IN EPISODE 9.
BUT ROMEO AND JULIET WEREN'T SIBLINGS, AND THEIR SITUATION WAS QUITE DIFFERENT...
I KNOW. BUT WHEN I THOUGHT UP THE PHRASE, IT WAS SO CATCHY I HAD TO USE IT.
I THOUGHT IT HELPED THEM SOUND MORE DRAMATIC.
INCIDENTALLY, WE ARE CHARGED WITH ESCORTING MISS KIRIMI HOME.
WE LOOKED FOR YOU EVERYWHERE, MISS.
WHAT'S NEXT?

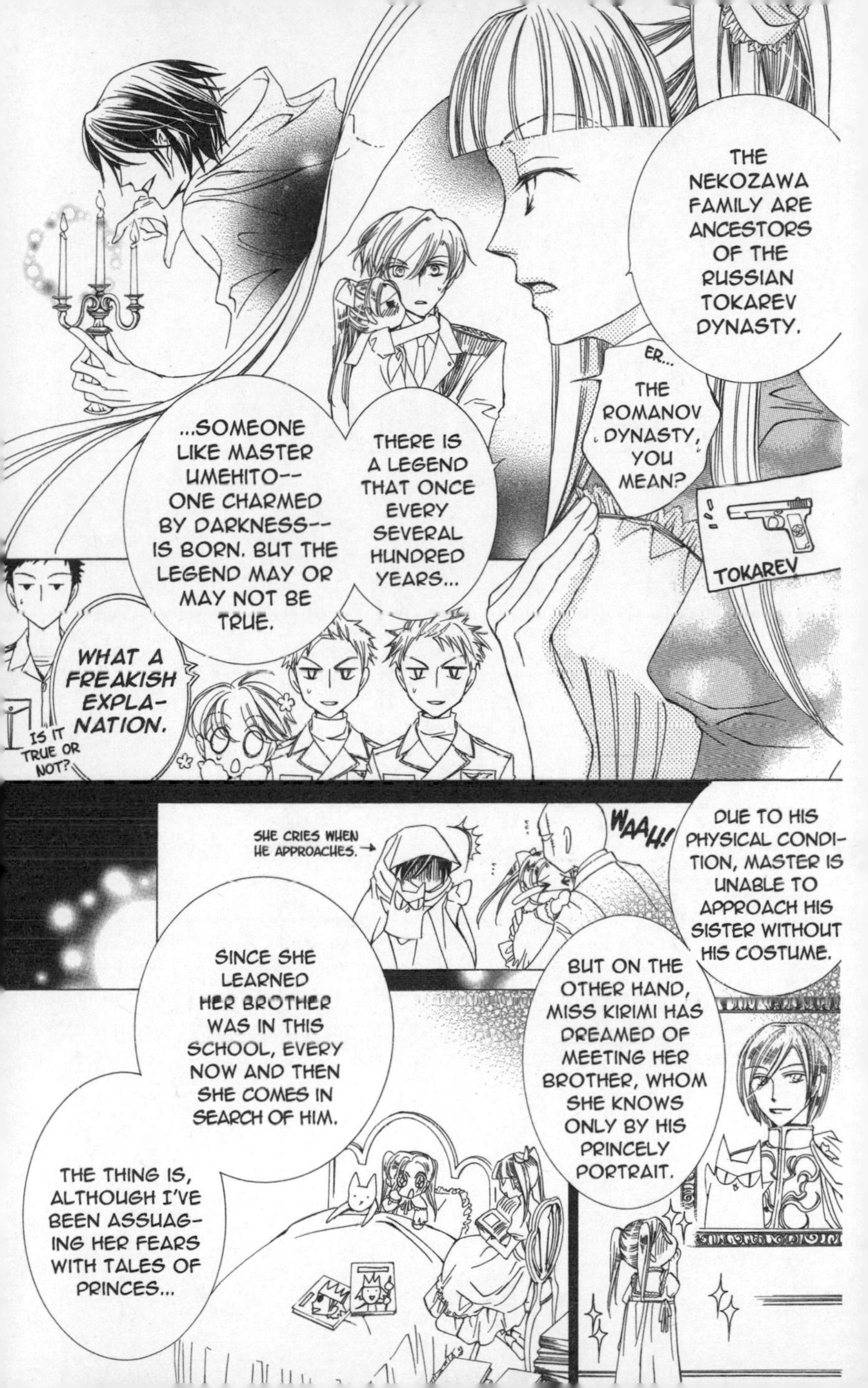
THE NEKOZAWA FAMILY ARE ANCESTORS OF THE RUSSIAN TOKAREV DYNASTY.
ER...
THE ROMANOV DYNASTY, YOU MEAN?
TOKAREV
THERE IS A LEGEND THAT ONCE EVERY SEVERAL HUNDRED YEARS...
...SOMEONE LIKE MASTER UMEHITO--ONE CHARMED BY DARKNESS--IS BORN. BUT THE LEGEND MAY OR MAY NOT BE TRUE.
WHAT A FREAKISH EXPLA-NATION.
IS IT TRUE OR NOT?
DUE TO HIS PHYSICAL CONDI-TION, MASTER IS UNABLE TO APPROACH HIS SISTER WITHOUT HIS COSTUME.
WAAH!
SHE CRIES WHEN HE APPROACHES.
BUT ON THE OTHER HAND, MISS KIRIMI HAS DREAMED OF MEETING HER BROTHER, WHOM SHE KNOWS ONLY BY HIS PRINCELY PORTRAIT.
SINCE SHE LEARNED HER BROTHER WAS IN THIS SCHOOL, EVERY NOW AND THEN SHE COMES IN SEARCH OF HIM.
THE THING IS, ALTHOUGH I'VE BEEN ASSUAG-ING HER FEARS WITH TALES OF PRINCES...

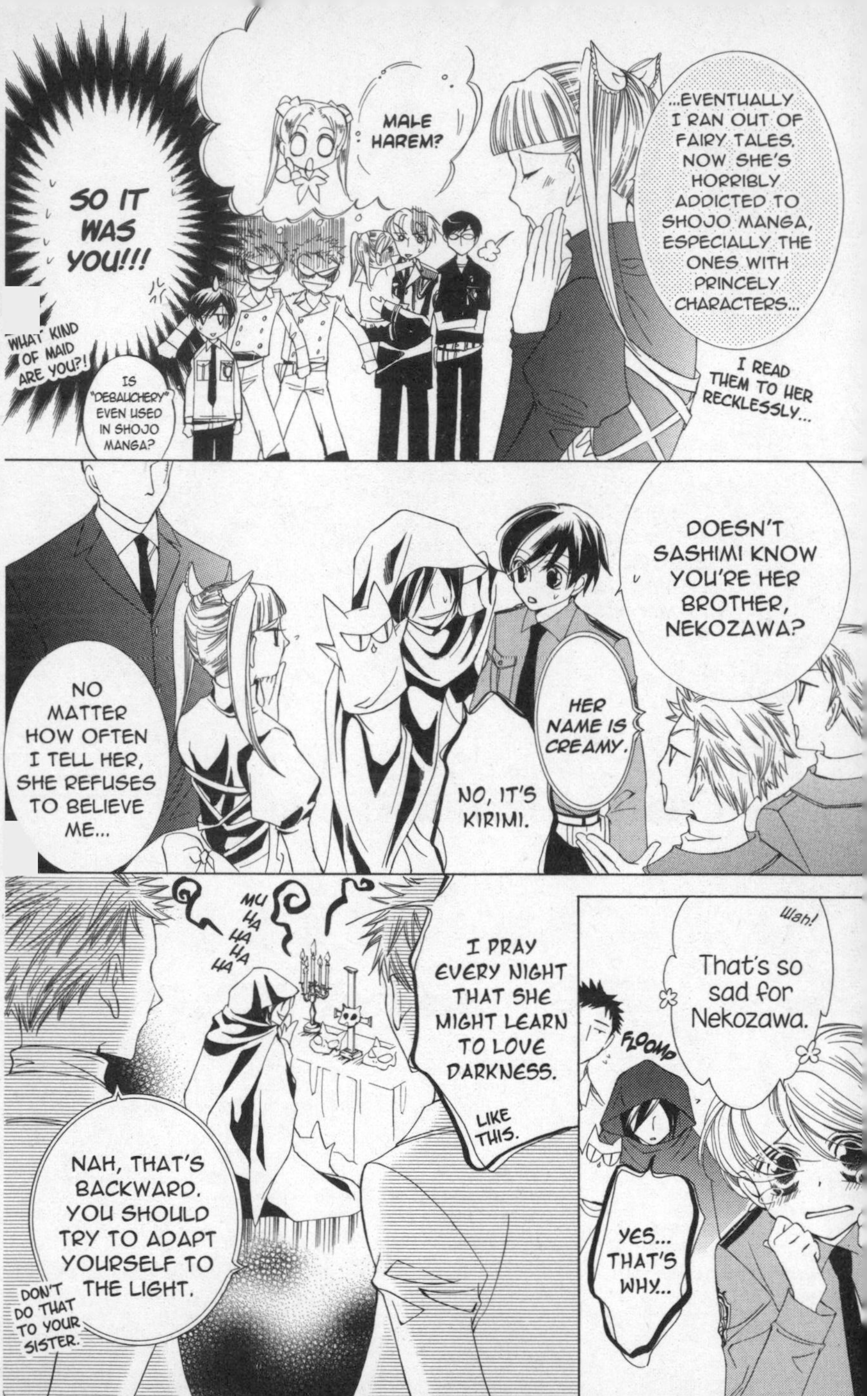
...EVENTUALLY I RAN OUT OF FAIRY TALES. NOW SHE'S HORRIBLY ADDICTED TO SHOJO MANGA, ESPECIALLY THE ONES WITH PRINCELY CHARACTERS...
I READ THEM TO HER RECKLESSLY...
MALE HAREM?
SO IT WAS YOU!!!
WHAT KIND OF MAID ARE YOU?!
IS "DEBAUCHERY" EVEN USED IN SHOJO MANGA?
DOESN'T SASHIMI KNOW YOU'RE HER BROTHER, NEKOZAWA?
HER NAME IS CREAMY.
NO, IT'S KIRIMI.
NO MATTER HOW OFTEN I TELL HER, SHE REFUSES TO BELIEVE ME...
Wah!
That's so sad for Nekozawa.
FLOOMP
YES... THAT'S WHY...
I PRAY EVERY NIGHT THAT SHE MIGHT LEARN TO LOVE DARKNESS.
MU HA HA HA HA HA
LIKE THIS.
NAH, THAT'S BACKWARD. YOU SHOULD TRY TO ADAPT YOURSELF TO THE LIGHT.
DON'T DO THAT TO YOUR SISTER.

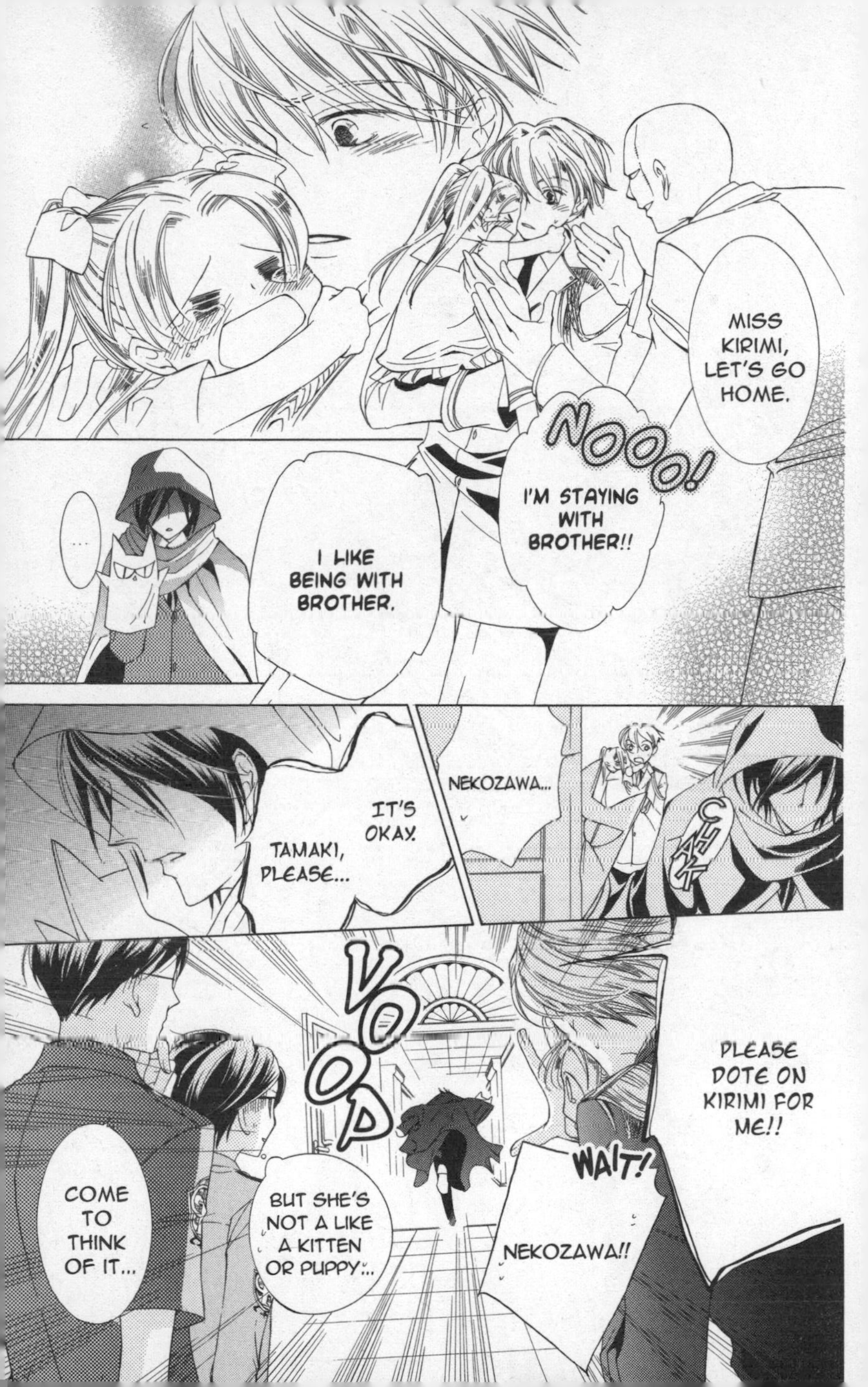
MISS KIRIMI, LET'S GO HOME.
NOOOO!
I'M STAYING WITH BROTHER!!
I LIKE BEING WITH BROTHER.
...
CHAK
NEKOZAWA...
IT'S OKAY.
TAMAKI, PLEASE...
PLEASE DOTE ON KIRIMI FOR ME!!
WAIT!
NEKOZAWA!!
VOOP
BUT SHE'S NOT A LIKE A KITTEN OR PUPPY...
COME TO THINK OF IT...

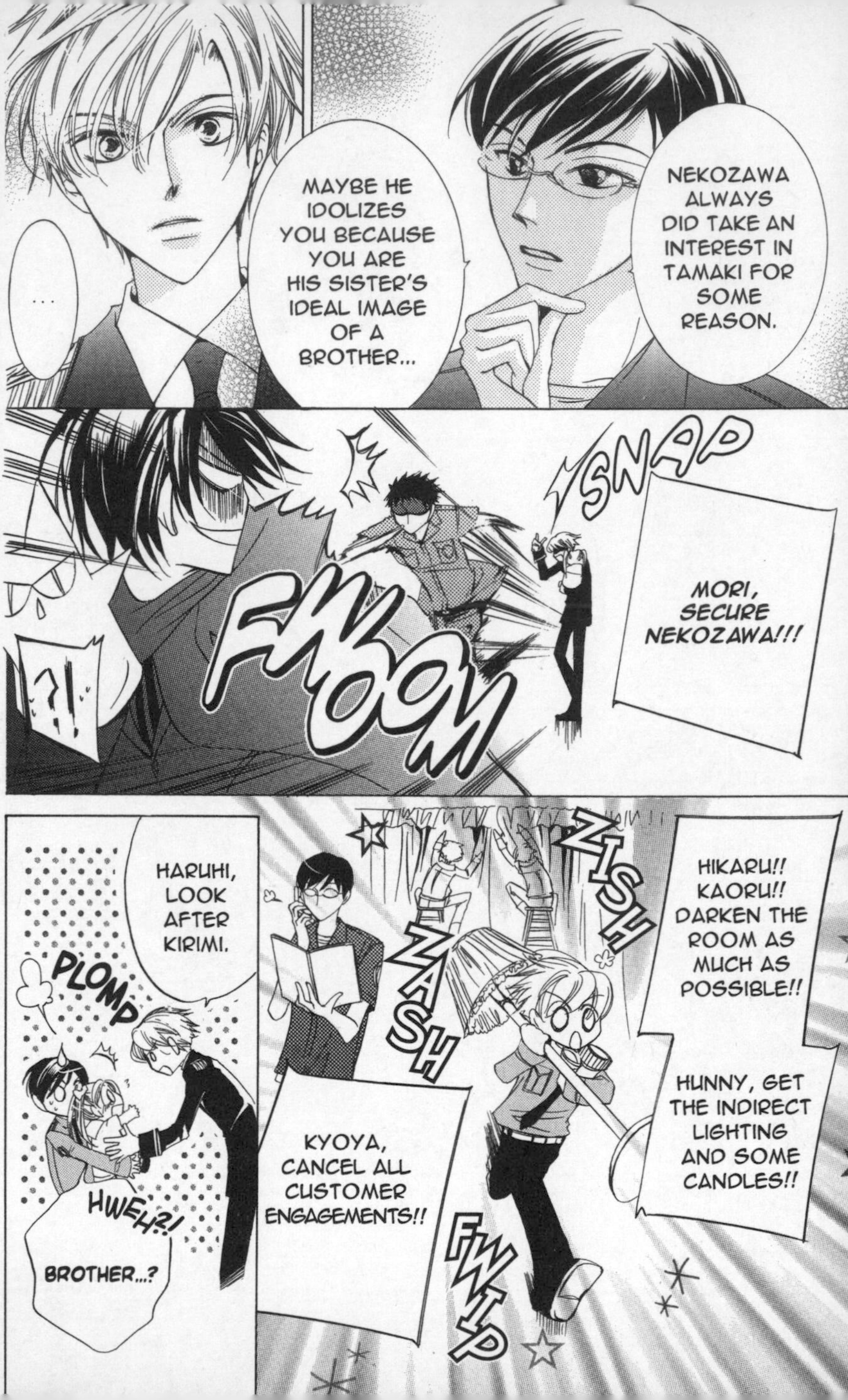
NEKOZAWA ALWAYS DID TAKE AN INTEREST IN TAMAKI FOR SOME REASON.
MAYBE HE IDOLIZES YOU BECAUSE YOU ARE HIS SISTER'S IDEAL IMAGE OF A BROTHER...
...
SNAP
MORI, SECURE NEKOZAWA!!!
FWOOM
?!
ZISH
HIKARU!! KAORU!! DARKEN THE ROOM AS MUCH AS POSSIBLE!!
HUNNY, GET THE INDIRECT LIGHTING AND SOME CANDLES!!
FWIP
ZASH
KYOYA, CANCEL ALL CUSTOMER ENGAGEMENTS!!
HARUHI, LOOK AFTER KIRIMI.
PLOMP
HWEH?!
BROTHER...?

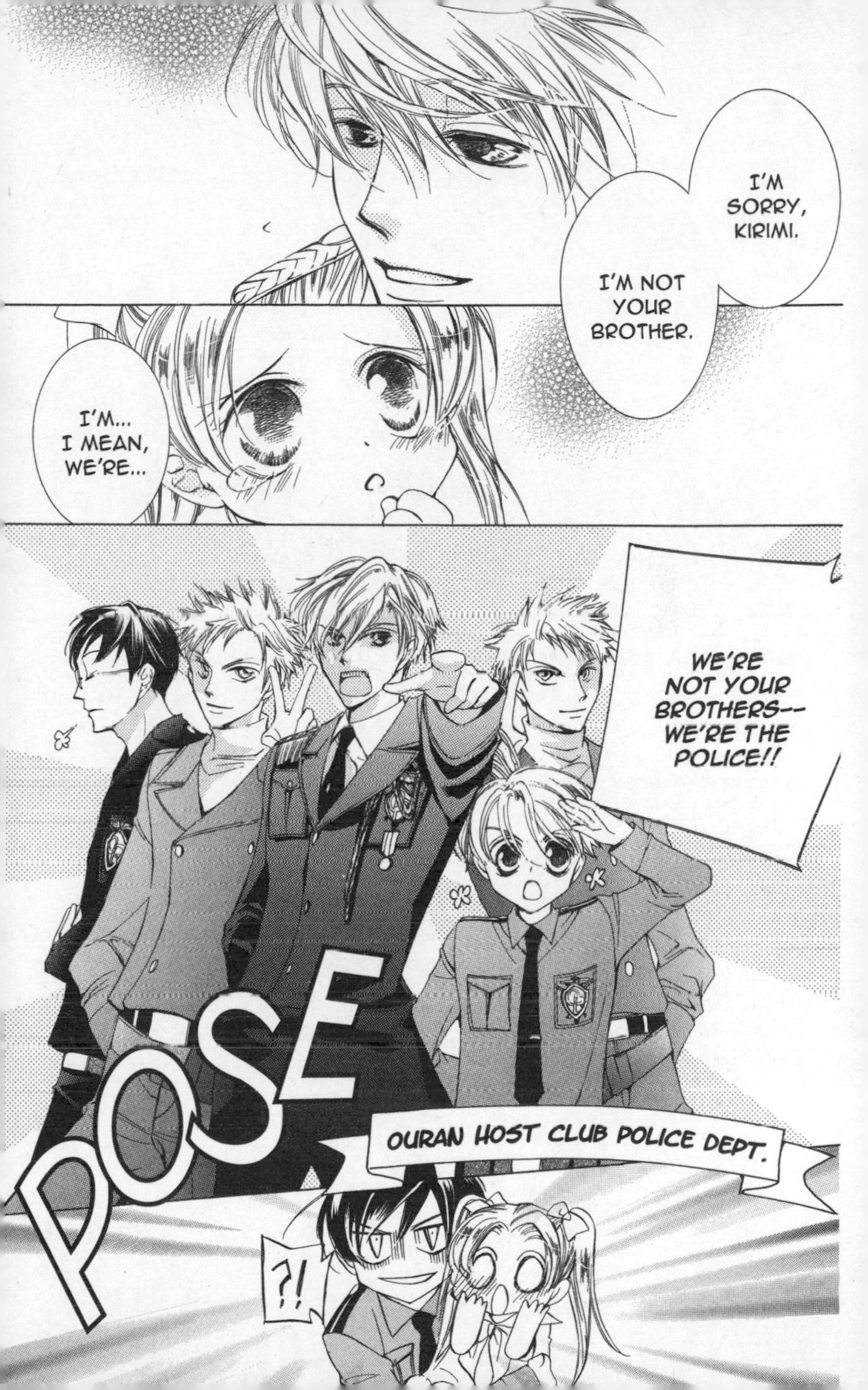
I'M SORRY, KIRIMI.
I'M NOT YOUR BROTHER.
I'M... I MEAN, WE'RE...
WE'RE NOT YOUR BROTHERS-- WE'RE THE POLICE!!
OURAN HOST CLUB POLICE DEPT.
POSE
?!

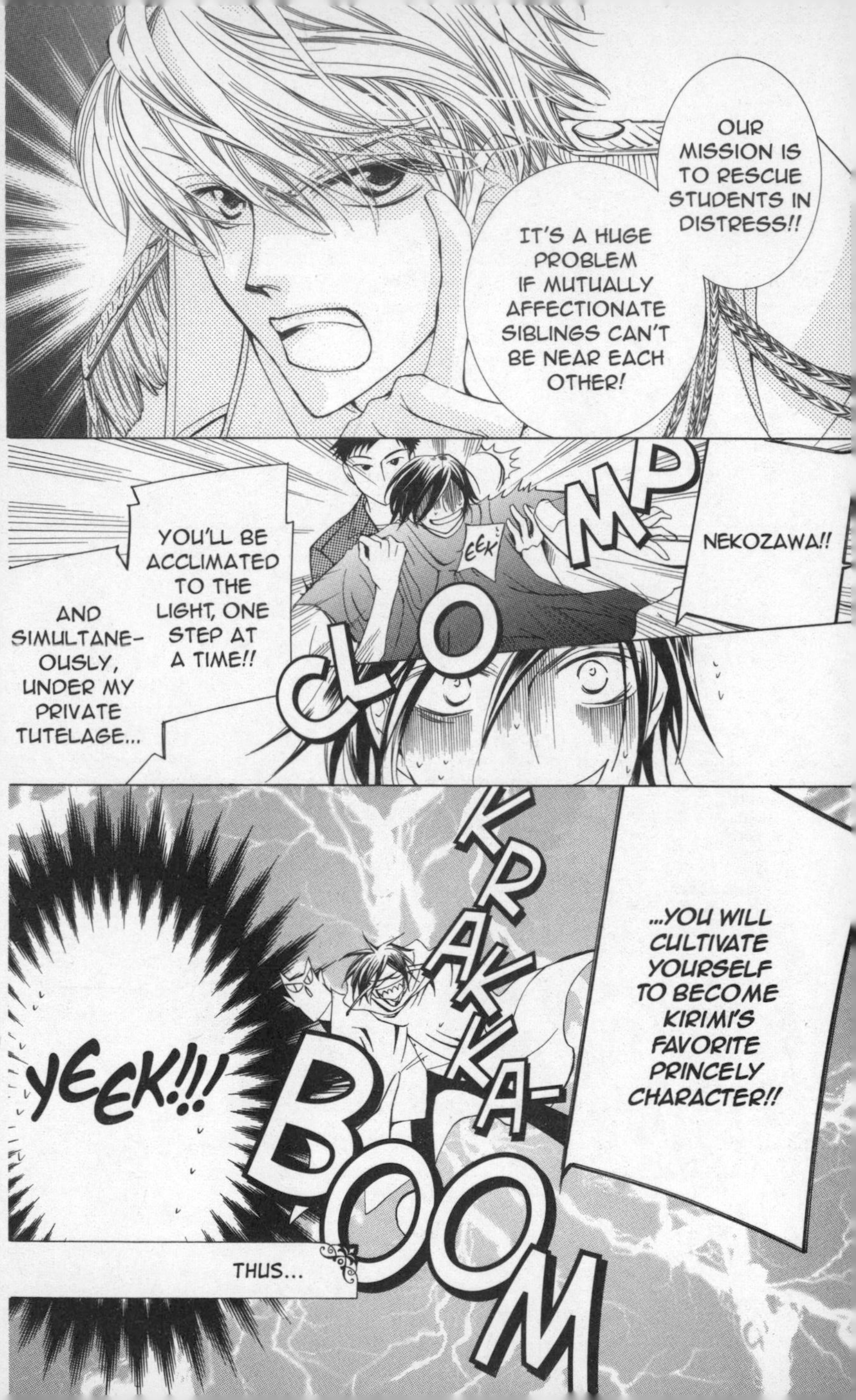
OUR MISSION IS TO RESCUE STUDENTS IN DISTRESS!!
IT'S A HUGE PROBLEM IF MUTUALLY AFFECTIONATE SIBLINGS CAN'T BE NEAR EACH OTHER!
NEKOZAWA!!
CLOMP
EEK
YOU'LL BE ACCLIMATED TO THE LIGHT, ONE STEP AT A TIME!!
AND SIMULTANE-OUSLY, UNDER MY PRIVATE TUTELAGE...
...YOU WILL CULTIVATE YOURSELF TO BECOME KIRIMI'S FAVORITE PRINCELY CHARACTER!!
KRAKA-BOOM
YEEK!!!
THUS...

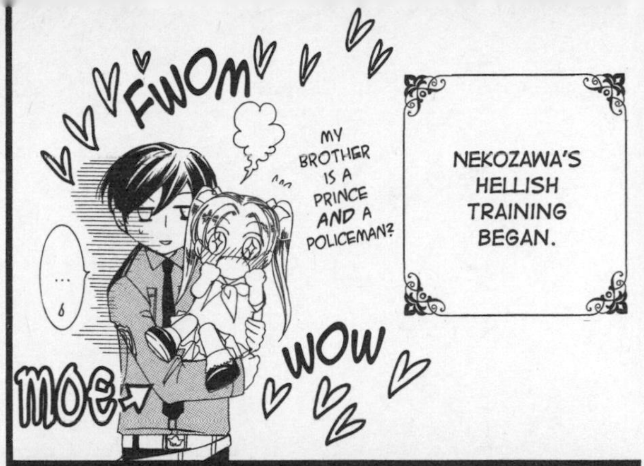
NEKOZAWA'S HELLISH TRAINING BEGAN.
MY BROTHER IS A PRINCE AND A POLICEMAN?
FWOM
...
WOW
MOE

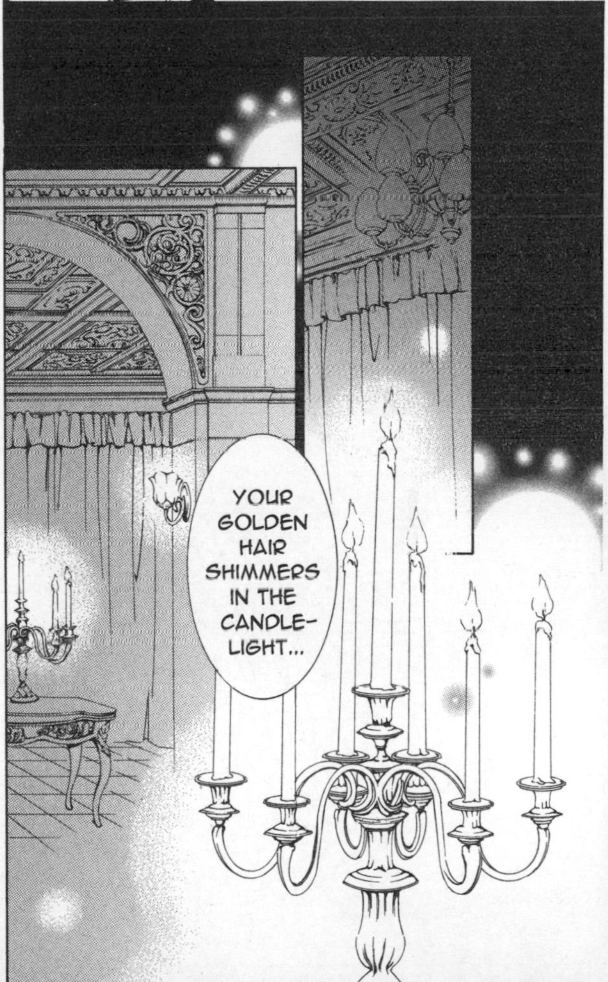
YOUR GOLDEN HAIR SHIMMERS IN THE CANDLE-LIGHT...

5

THE TIMING WAS GREAT. I HAD JUST RECEIVED DRAMA CD #2 THAT DAY, SO OF COURSE WE BOTH LISTENED (WITH THE DOG).

I'M SO SPOILED!

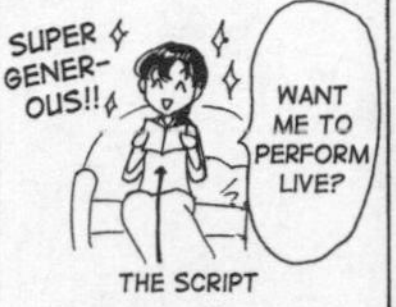
SUPER GENER-OUS!!
WANT ME TO PERFORM LIVE?
THE SCRIPT

AYA WAS SO WILLING TO PLEASE AND HAD SO MANY TOPICS FOR CONVERSATION. AND SHE'S SO KIND, PLEASANT AND HUMBLE THAT I HAD AN INCREDIBLE DAY OF LAUGHTER. IT WAS CHOCK-FULL OF FUN!

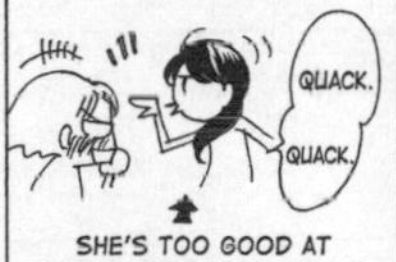
QUACK.
QUACK.

SHE'S TOO GOOD AT MIMICKING DUCKS. WOW!! (IT WAS WHEN SHE TOLD ME ALL ABOUT HER PET DUCK.)

HER DOG, HIKO, IS EXTREMELY CUTE TOO! I'D LOVE TO SEE THEM AGAIN. PLEASE COME VISIT ME AGAIN.

IMPORTANT NOTICE

※ MY EDITOR WAS SAYING THAT WE MIGHT DO A ZEN-IN DRAMA CD #3.* EVERYONE, PLEASE CHECK *LALA* MAGAZINE!

*THE JAPANESE DRAMA CD #3 WAS RELEASED. -ED.

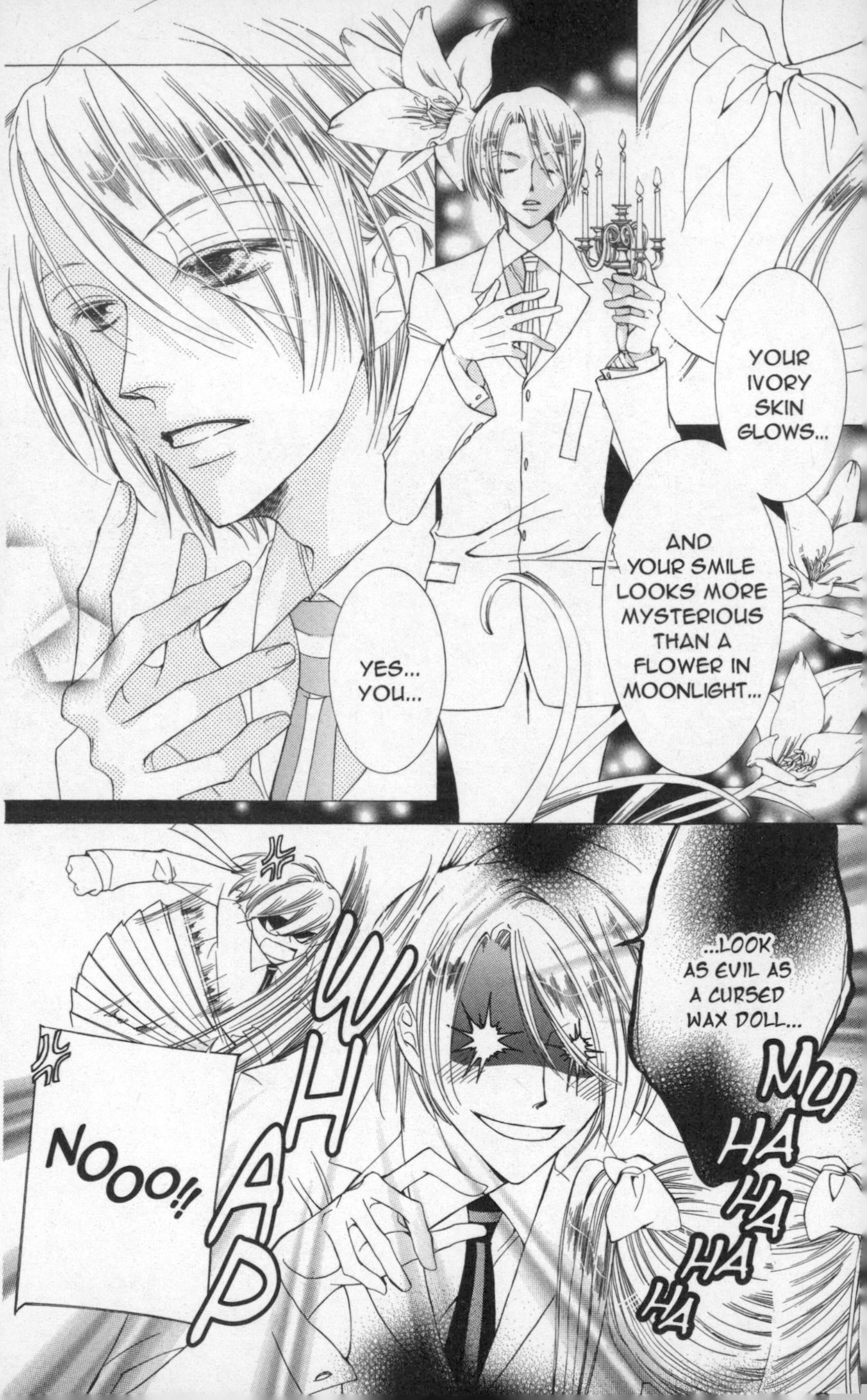
YOUR IVORY SKIN GLOWS...
AND YOUR SMILE LOOKS MORE MYSTERIOUS THAN A FLOWER IN MOONLIGHT...
YES... YOU...
...LOOK AS EVIL AS A CURSED WAX DOLL...
MU HA HA HA HA HA
WHAP
NOOO!!

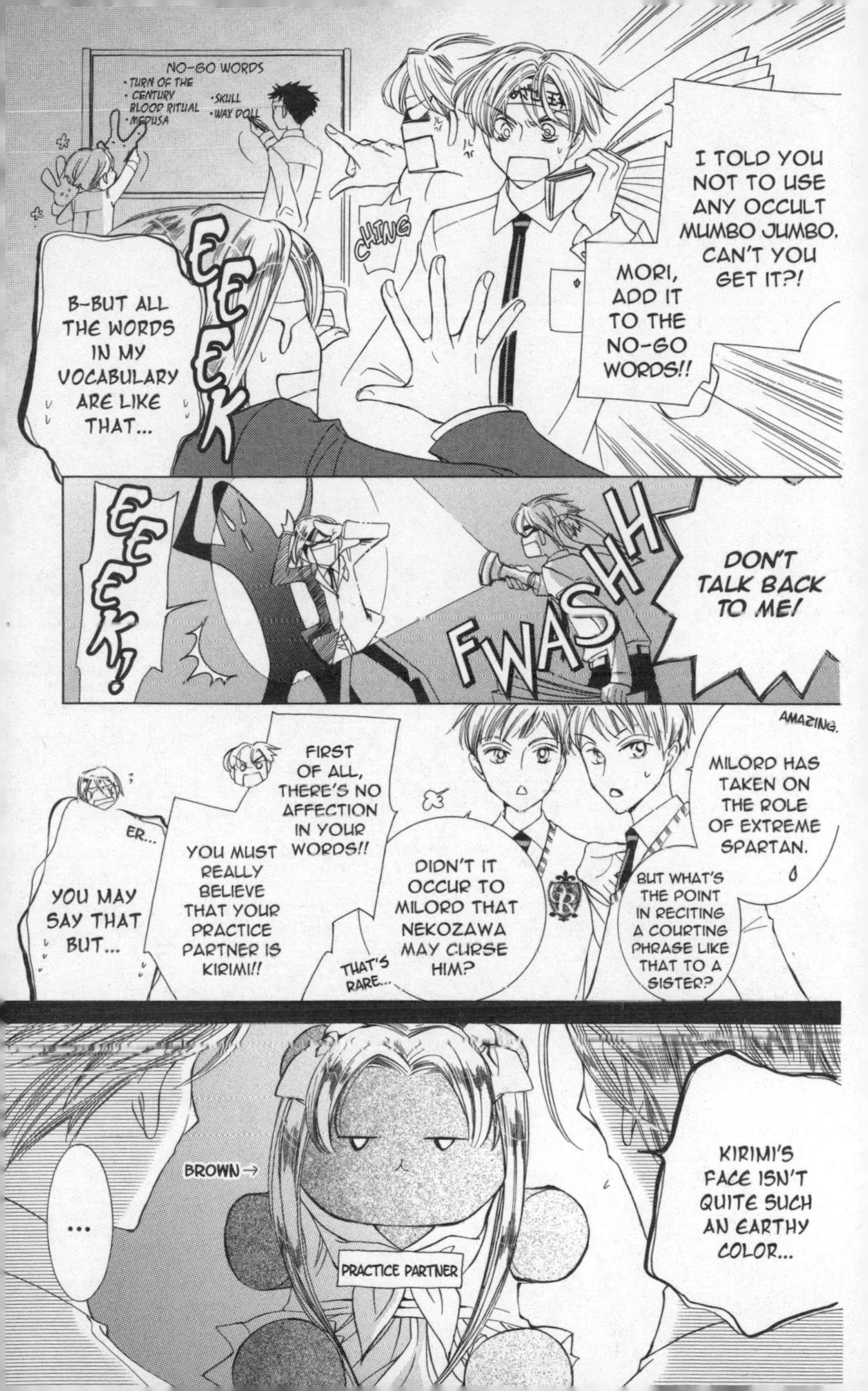
I TOLD YOU NOT TO USE ANY OCCULT MUMBO JUMBO. CAN'T YOU GET IT?!
MORI, ADD IT TO THE NO-GO WORDS!!
CHING
NO-GO WORDS
• TURN OF THE CENTURY BLOOD RITUAL
• MEDUSA
• SKULL
• WAX DOLL
EEEEK
B-BUT ALL THE WORDS IN MY VOCABULARY ARE LIKE THAT...
DON'T TALK BACK TO ME!
FWASHH
EEEEK!
AMAZING.
MILORD HAS TAKEN ON THE ROLE OF EXTREME SPARTAN.
BUT WHAT'S THE POINT IN RECITING A COURTING PHRASE LIKE THAT TO A SISTER?
DIDN'T IT OCCUR TO MILORD THAT NEKOZAWA MAY CURSE HIM?
THAT'S RARE...
FIRST OF ALL, THERE'S NO AFFECTION IN YOUR WORDS!!
YOU MUST REALLY BELIEVE THAT YOUR PRACTICE PARTNER IS KIRIMI!!
ER...
YOU MAY SAY THAT BUT...
KIRIMI'S FACE ISN'T QUITE SUCH AN EARTHY COLOR...
BROWN →
PRACTICE PARTNER
...

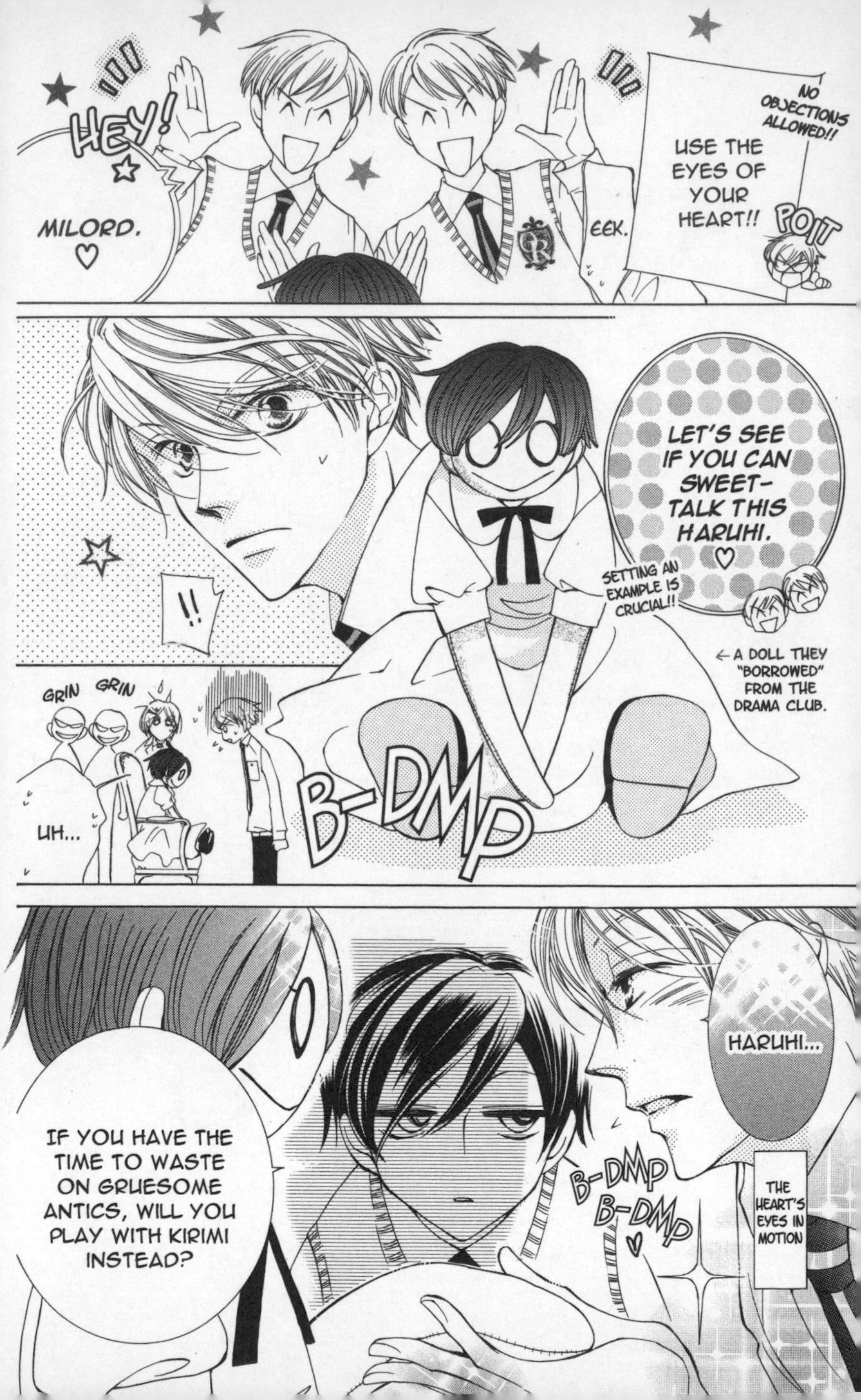
NO OBJECTIONS ALLOWED!!
USE THE EYES OF YOUR HEART!!
POIT
EEK.
HEY!
MILORD. ♡
LET'S SEE IF YOU CAN SWEET-TALK THIS HARUHI. ♡
SETTING AN EXAMPLE IS CRUCIAL!!
!!
← A DOLL THEY "BORROWED" FROM THE DRAMA CLUB.
B-DMP
GRIN GRIN
UH...
HARUHI...
THE HEART'S EYES IN MOTION
B-DMP B-DMP
IF YOU HAVE THE TIME TO WASTE ON GRUESOME ANTICS, WILL YOU PLAY WITH KIRIMI INSTEAD?

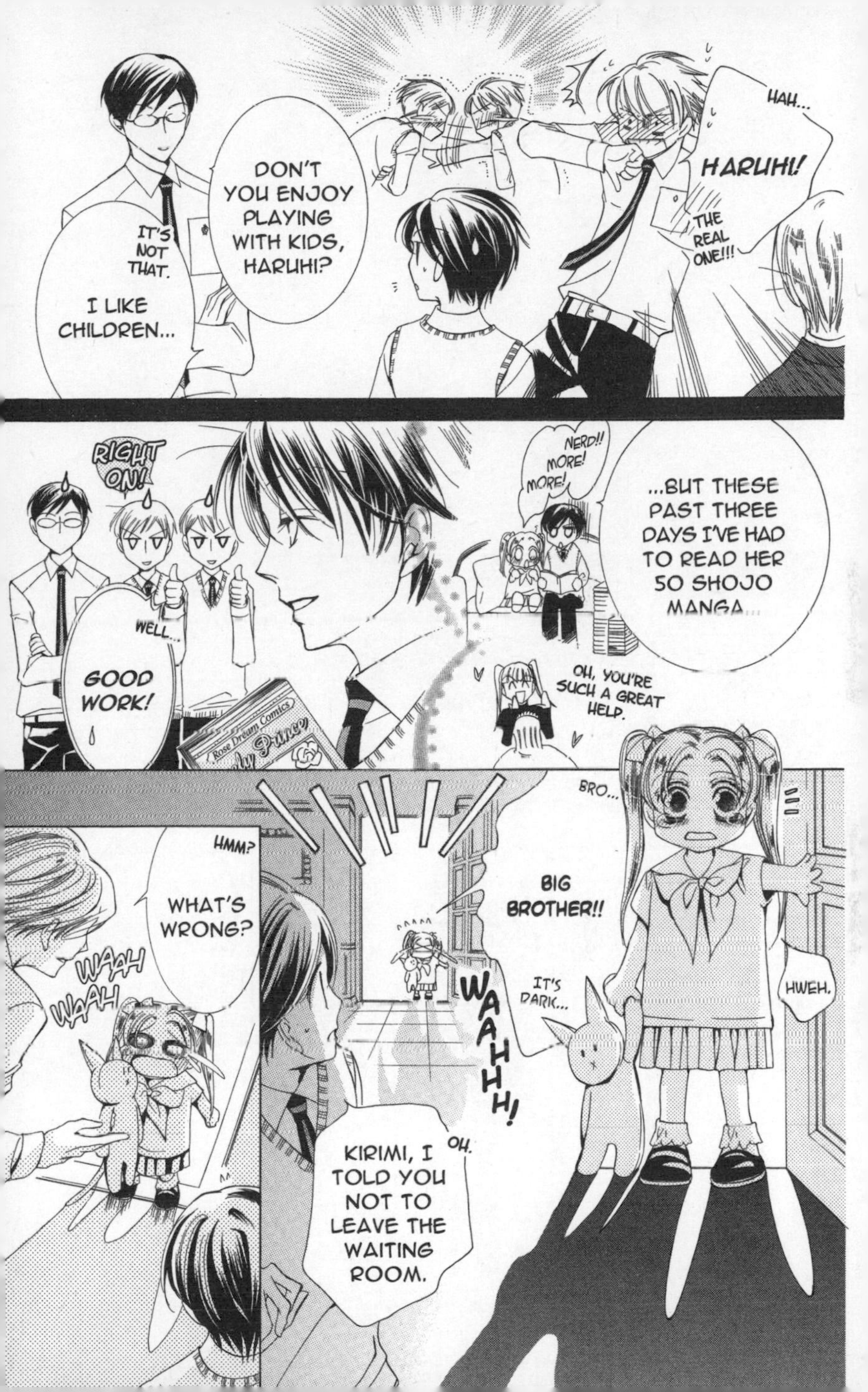
HAH...
HARUHI!
THE REAL ONE!!!
DON'T YOU ENJOY PLAYING WITH KIDS, HARUHI?
IT'S NOT THAT.
I LIKE CHILDREN...
...BUT THESE PAST THREE DAYS I'VE HAD TO READ HER 50 SHOJO MANGA...
NERD!! MORE! MORE!
OH, YOU'RE SUCH A GREAT HELP.
RIGHT ON!
WELL...
GOOD WORK!
Rose Dream Comics
BRO...
BIG BROTHER!!
HWEH.
IT'S DARK...
WAAHHH!
HMM?
WHAT'S WRONG?
OH.
KIRIMI, I TOLD YOU NOT TO LEAVE THE WAITING ROOM.
WAAH WAAH

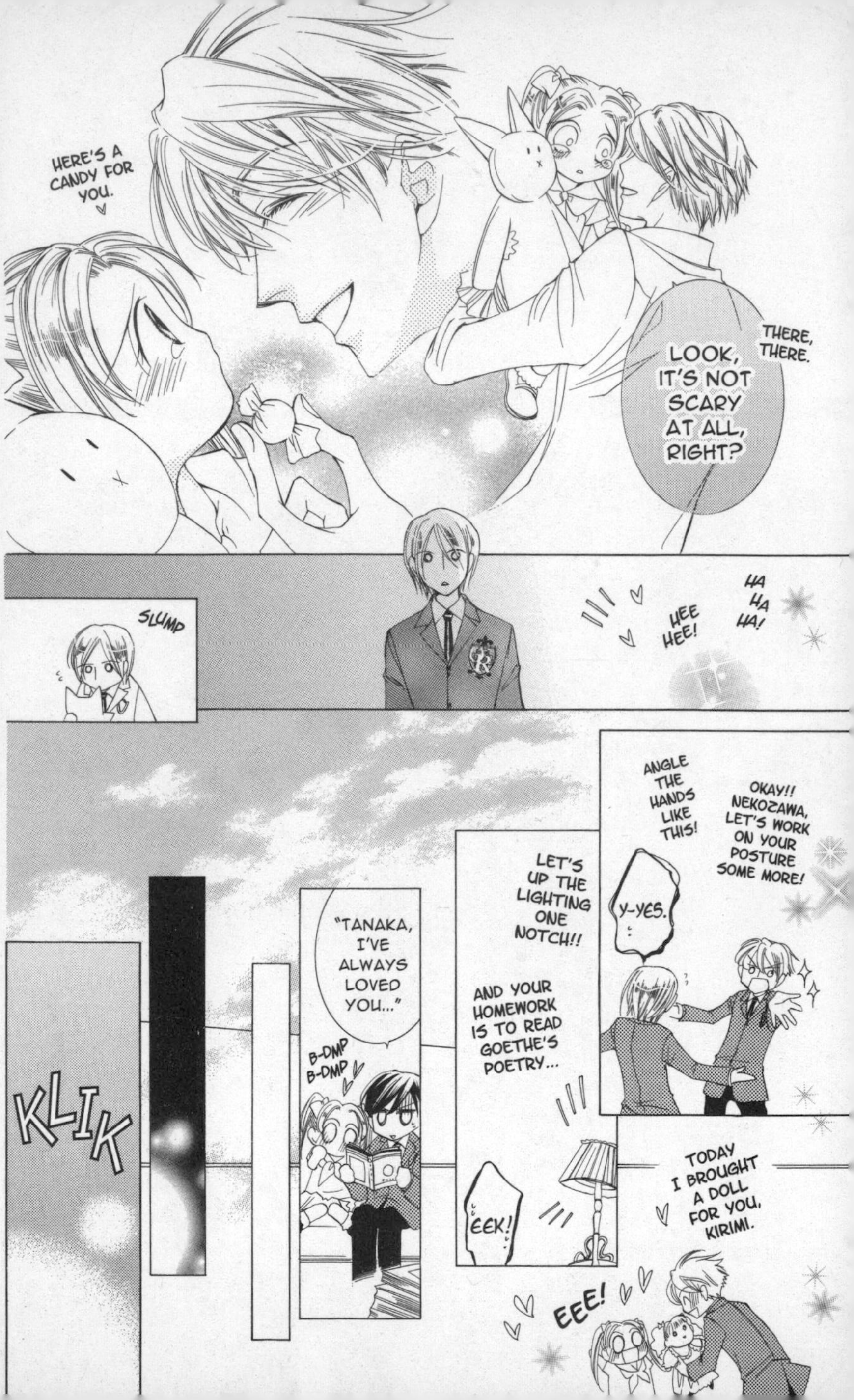
THERE, THERE.
LOOK, IT'S NOT SCARY AT ALL, RIGHT?
HERE'S A CANDY FOR YOU.
HA HA HA!
HEE HEE!
SLUMP
OKAY!! NEKOZAWA, LET'S WORK ON YOUR POSTURE SOME MORE!
ANGLE THE HANDS LIKE THIS!
Y-YES.
TODAY I BROUGHT A DOLL FOR YOU, KIRIMI.
EEE!
LET'S UP THE LIGHTING ONE NOTCH!!
AND YOUR HOMEWORK IS TO READ GOETHE'S POETRY...
EEK!
"TANAKA, I'VE ALWAYS LOVED YOU..."
B-DMP B-DMP
KLIK

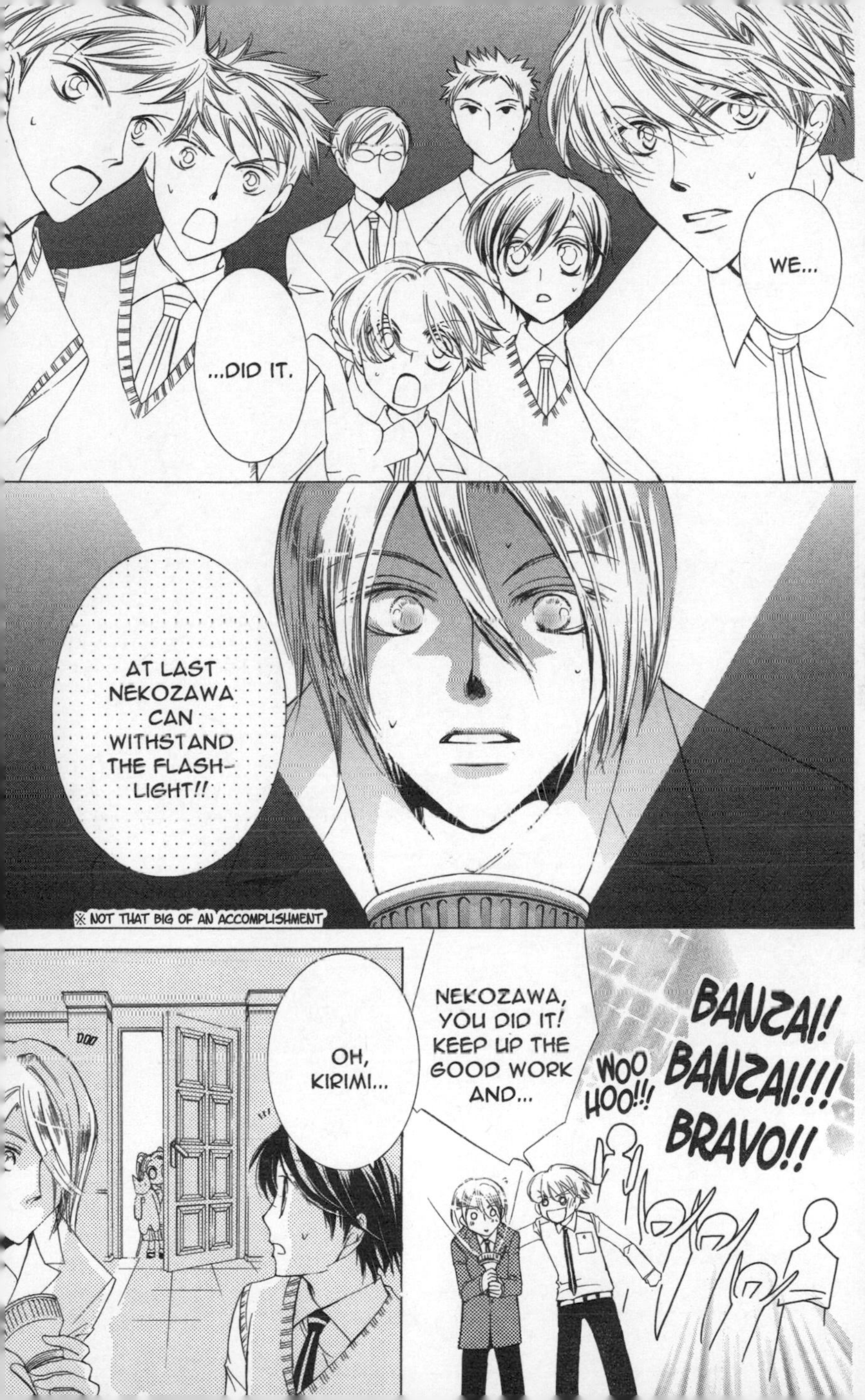
WE...
...DID IT.
AT LAST NEKOZAWA CAN WITHSTAND THE FLASH-LIGHT!!
※ NOT THAT BIG OF AN ACCOMPLISHMENT
BANZAI! BANZAI!!! BRAVO!!
WOO HOO!!!
NEKOZAWA, YOU DID IT! KEEP UP THE GOOD WORK AND...
OH, KIRIMI...

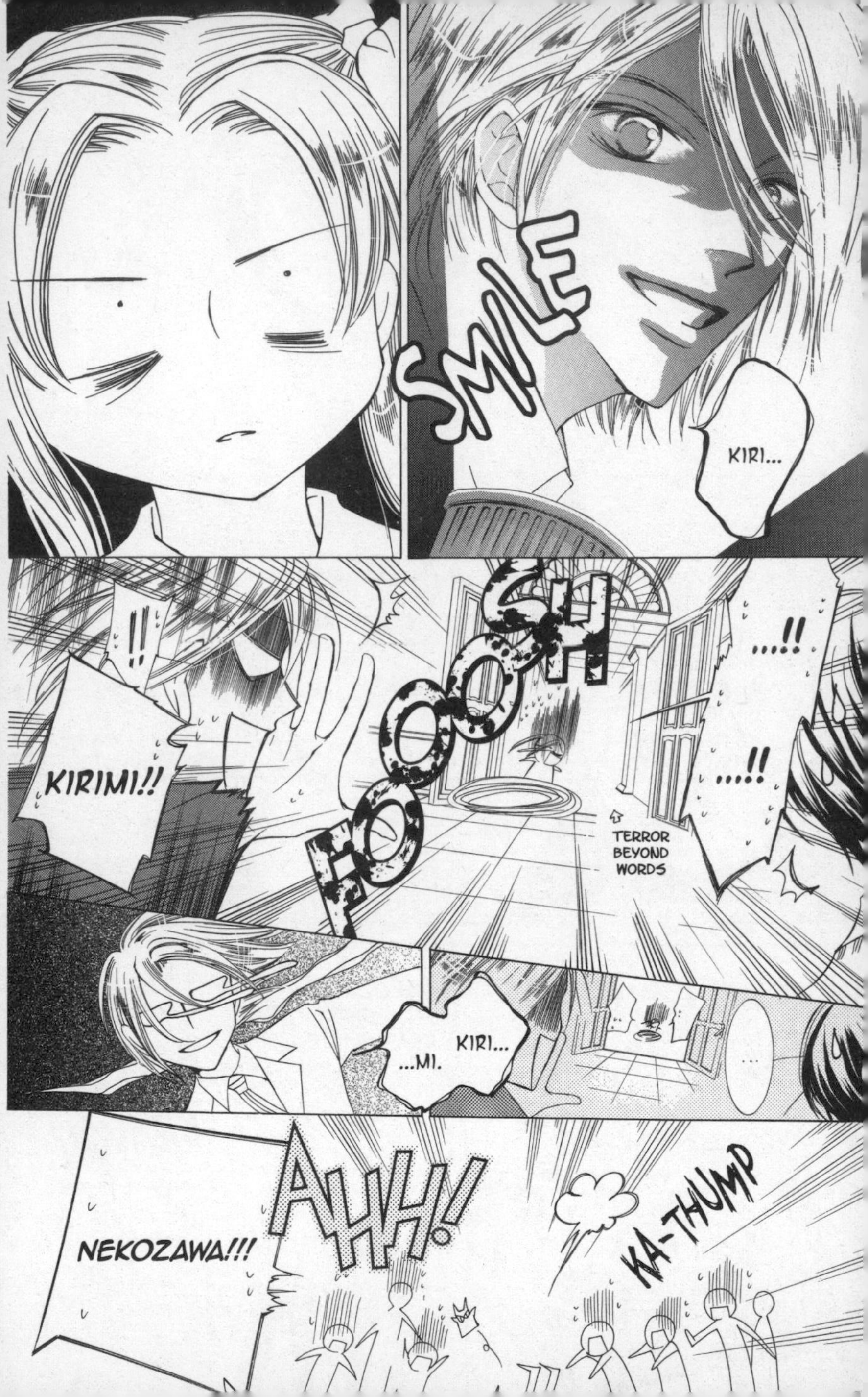
SMILE
KIRI...
...!!
...!!
HOOOOSH
TERROR BEYOND WORDS
!!
KIRIMI!!
...
...
...
KIRI...
...MI.
KA-THUMP
AHH!
NEKOZAWA!!!

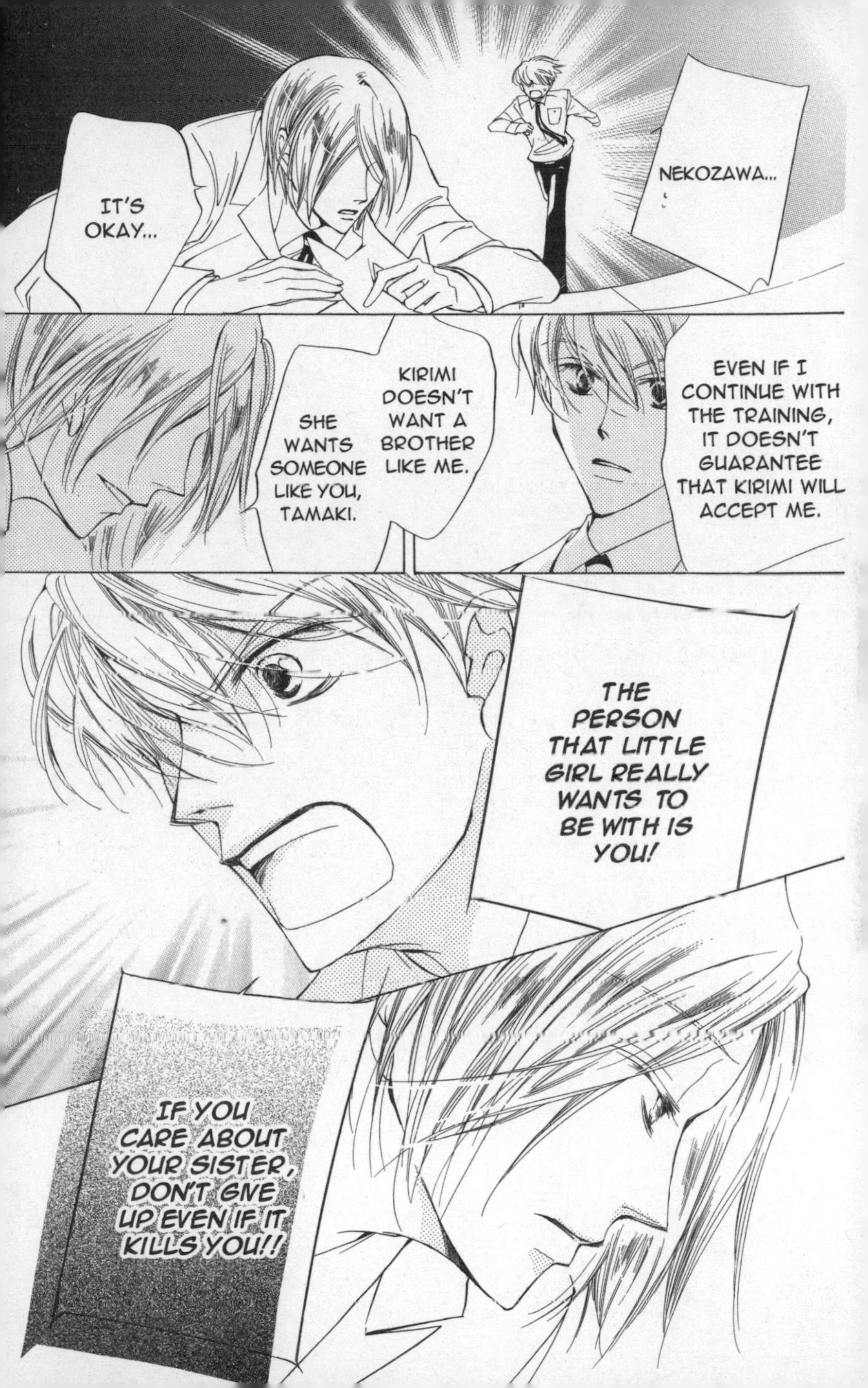
NEKOZAWA...
IT'S OKAY...
EVEN IF I CONTINUE WITH THE TRAINING, IT DOESN'T GUARANTEE THAT KIRIMI WILL ACCEPT ME.
KIRIMI DOESN'T WANT A BROTHER LIKE ME.
SHE WANTS SOMEONE LIKE YOU, TAMAKI.
THE PERSON THAT LITTLE GIRL REALLY WANTS TO BE WITH IS YOU!
IF YOU CARE ABOUT YOUR SISTER, DON'T GIVE UP EVEN IF IT KILLS YOU!!

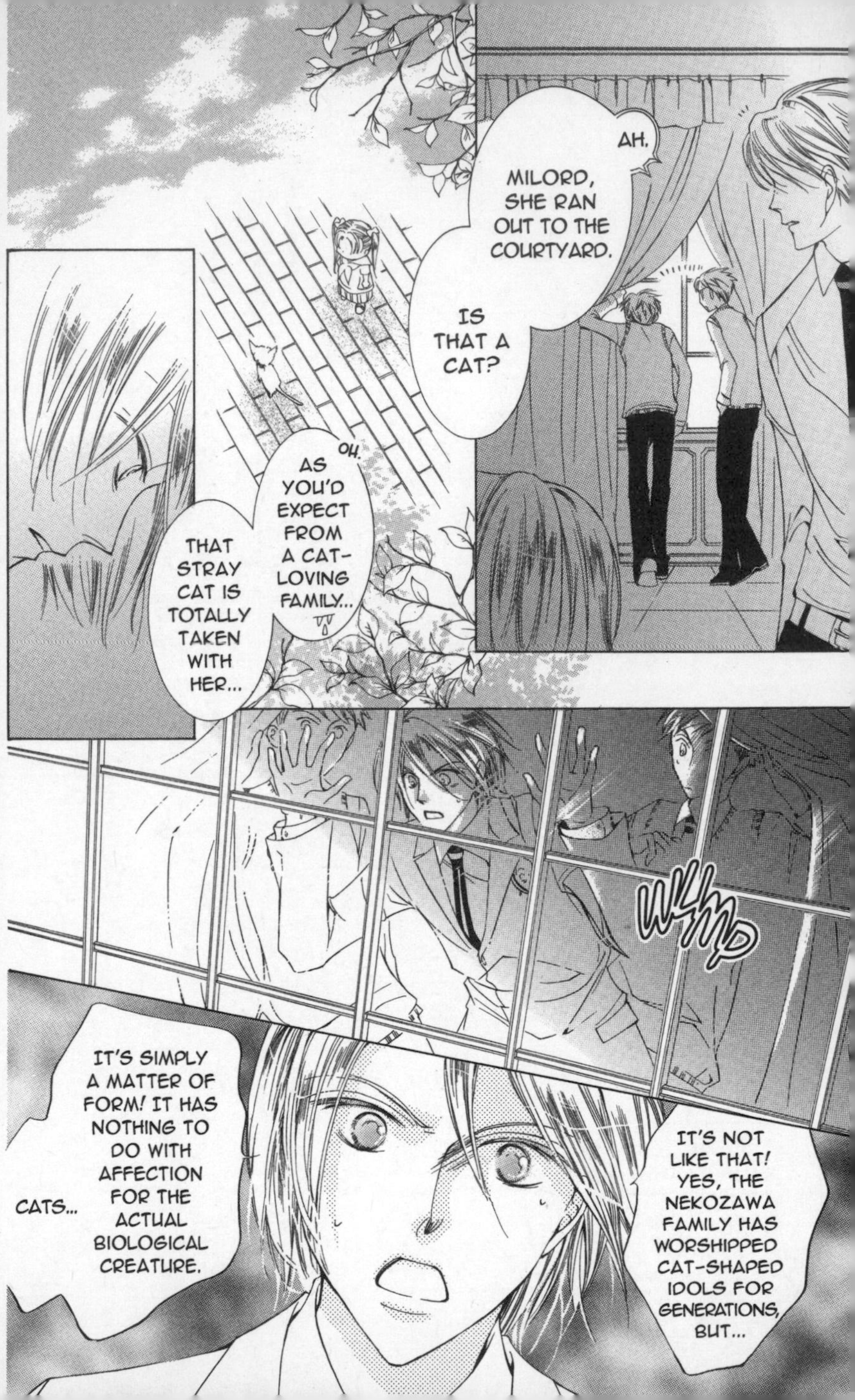
AH.
MILORD, SHE RAN OUT TO THE COURTYARD.
IS THAT A CAT?
OH.
AS YOU'D EXPECT FROM A CAT-LOVING FAMILY...
THAT STRAY CAT IS TOTALLY TAKEN WITH HER...
WHMP
IT'S NOT LIKE THAT! YES, THE NEKOZAWA FAMILY HAS WORSHIPPED CAT-SHAPED IDOLS FOR GENERATIONS, BUT...
CATS...
IT'S SIMPLY A MATTER OF FORM! IT HAS NOTHING TO DO WITH AFFECTION FOR THE ACTUAL BIOLOGICAL CREATURE.

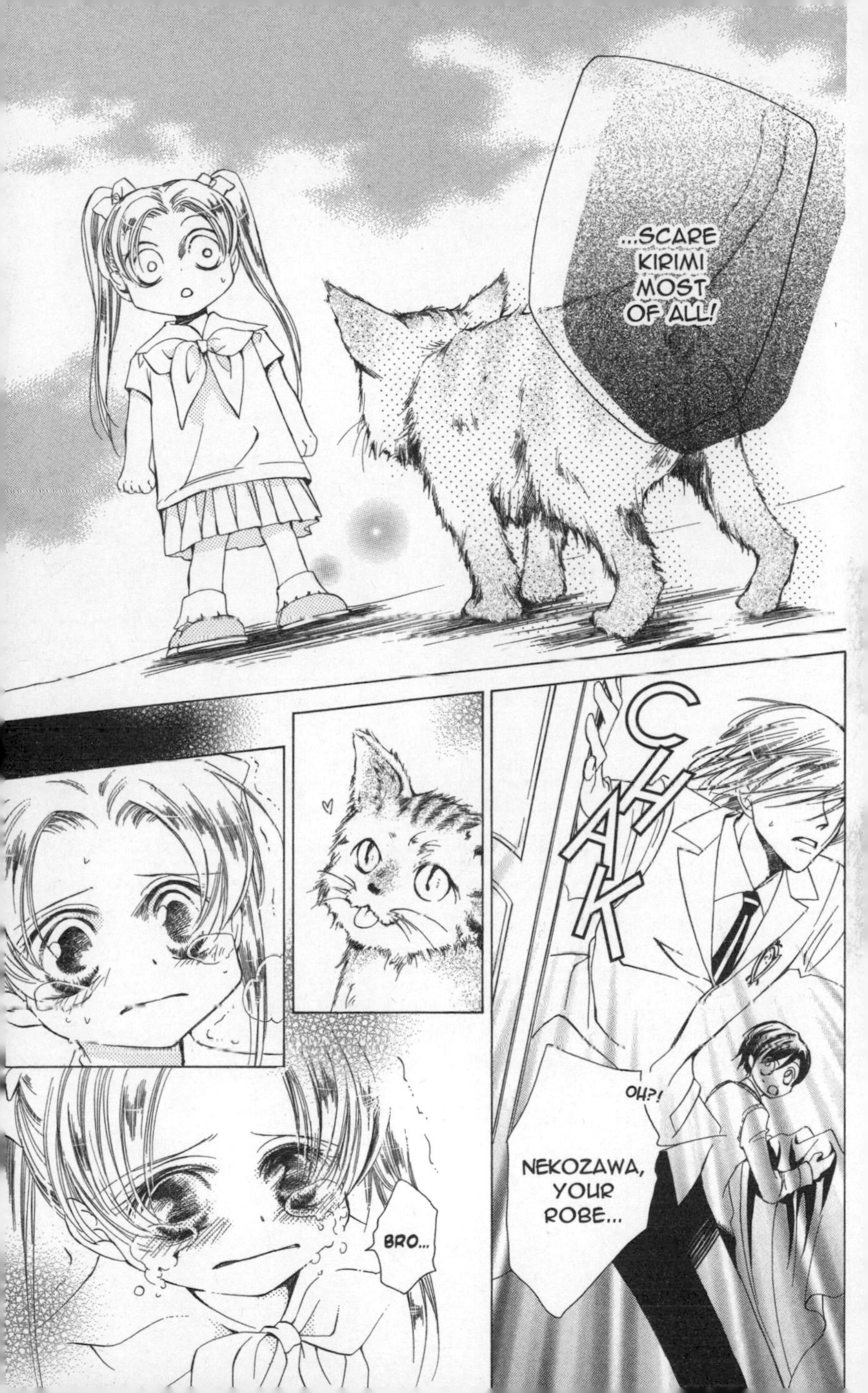
...SCARE KIRIMI MOST OF ALL!
CHAK
OH?!
NEKOZAWA, YOUR ROBE...
BRO...

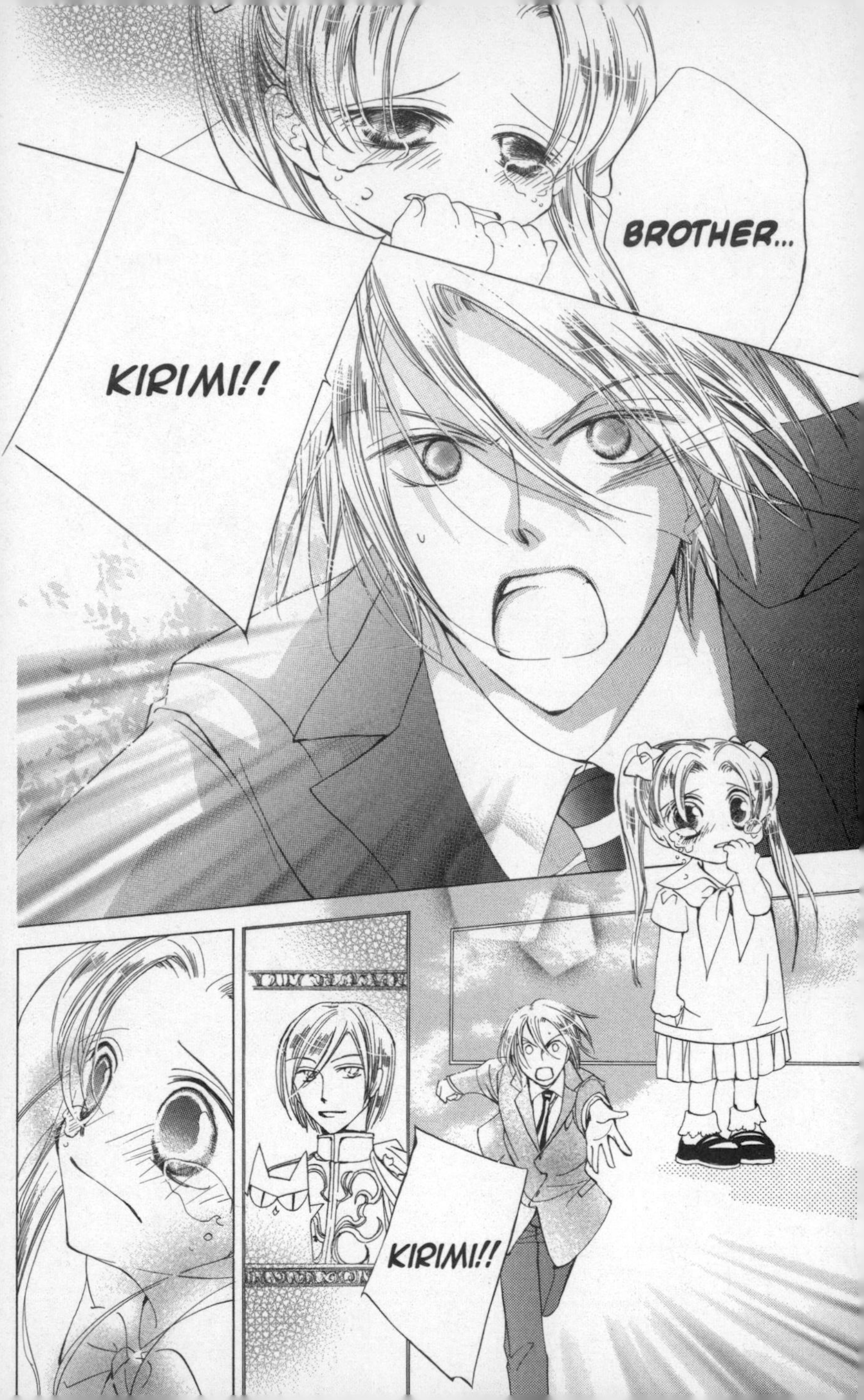
BROTHER...
KIRIMI!!
KIRIMI!!

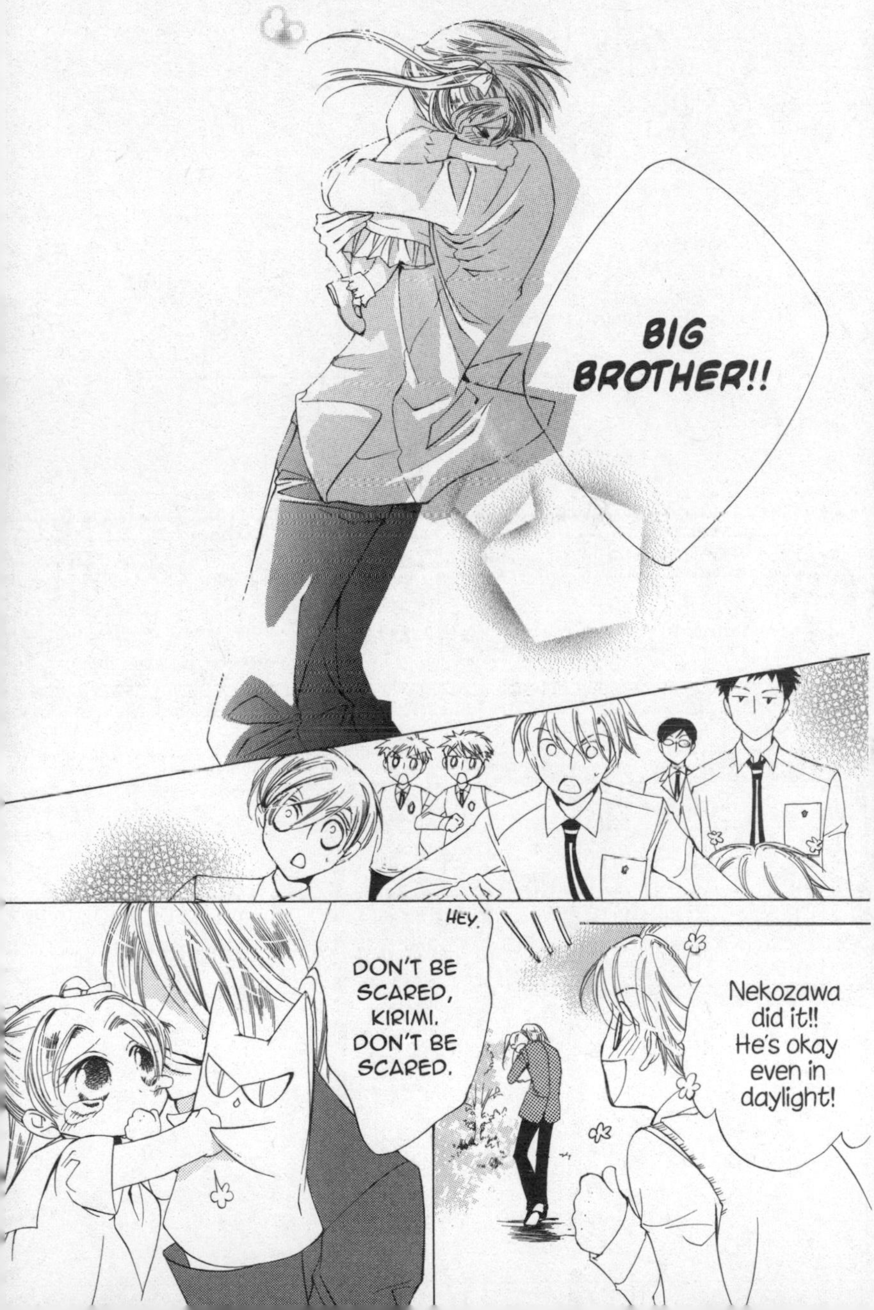
BIG BROTHER!!
Nekozawa did it!! He's okay even in daylight!
HEY.
DON'T BE SCARED, KIRIMI. DON'T BE SCARED.

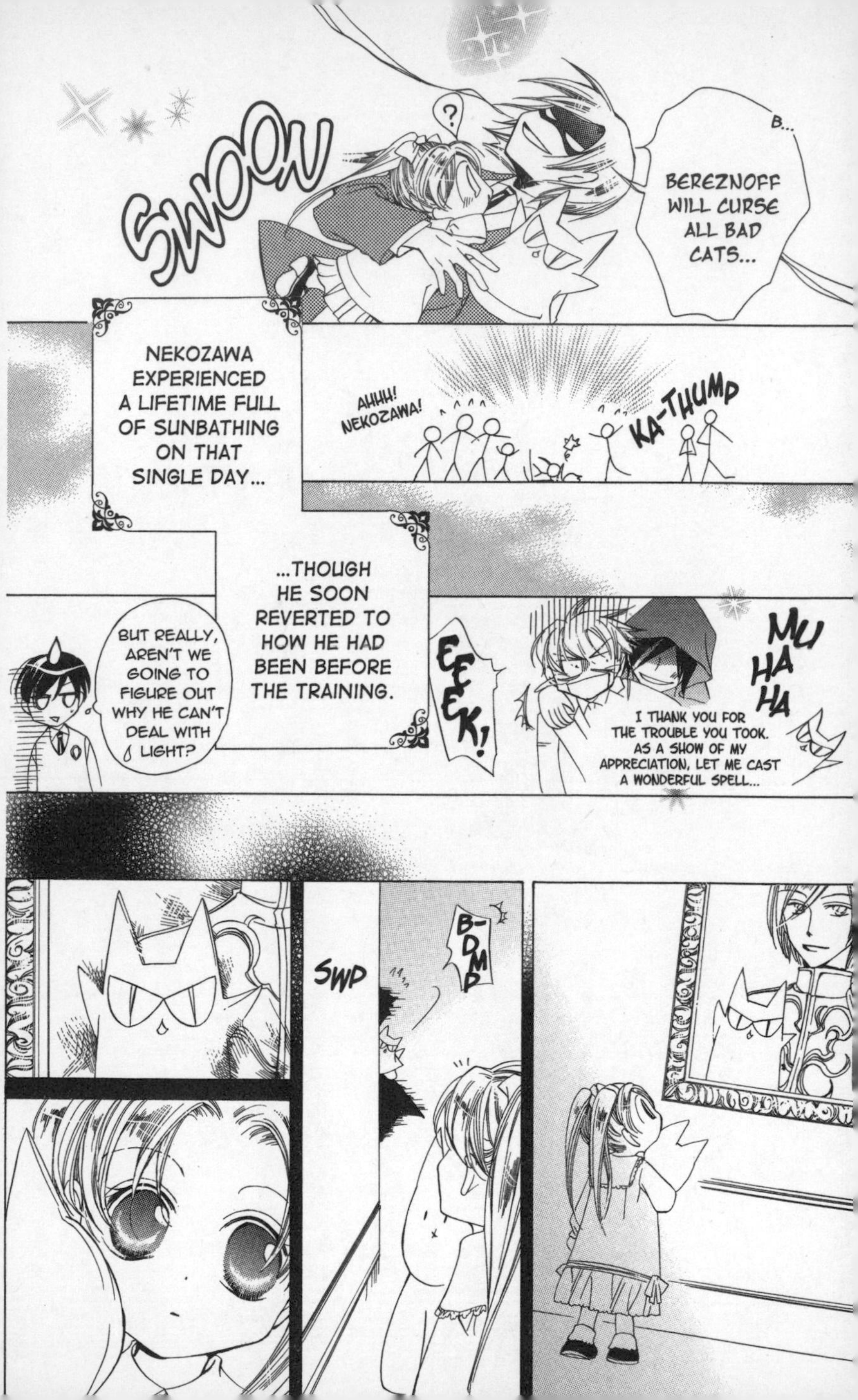
B...
BEREZNOFF WILL CURSE ALL BAD CATS...
SWOON
AHHH! NEKOZAWA!
KA-THUMP
NEKOZAWA EXPERIENCED A LIFETIME FULL OF SUNBATHING ON THAT SINGLE DAY...
MU HA HA
I THANK YOU FOR THE TROUBLE YOU TOOK. AS A SHOW OF MY APPRECIATION, LET ME CAST A WONDERFUL SPELL...
EEEK!
...THOUGH HE SOON REVERTED TO HOW HE HAD BEEN BEFORE THE TRAINING.
BUT REALLY, AREN'T WE GOING TO FIGURE OUT WHY HE CAN'T DEAL WITH LIGHT?
B-DMP
SWP

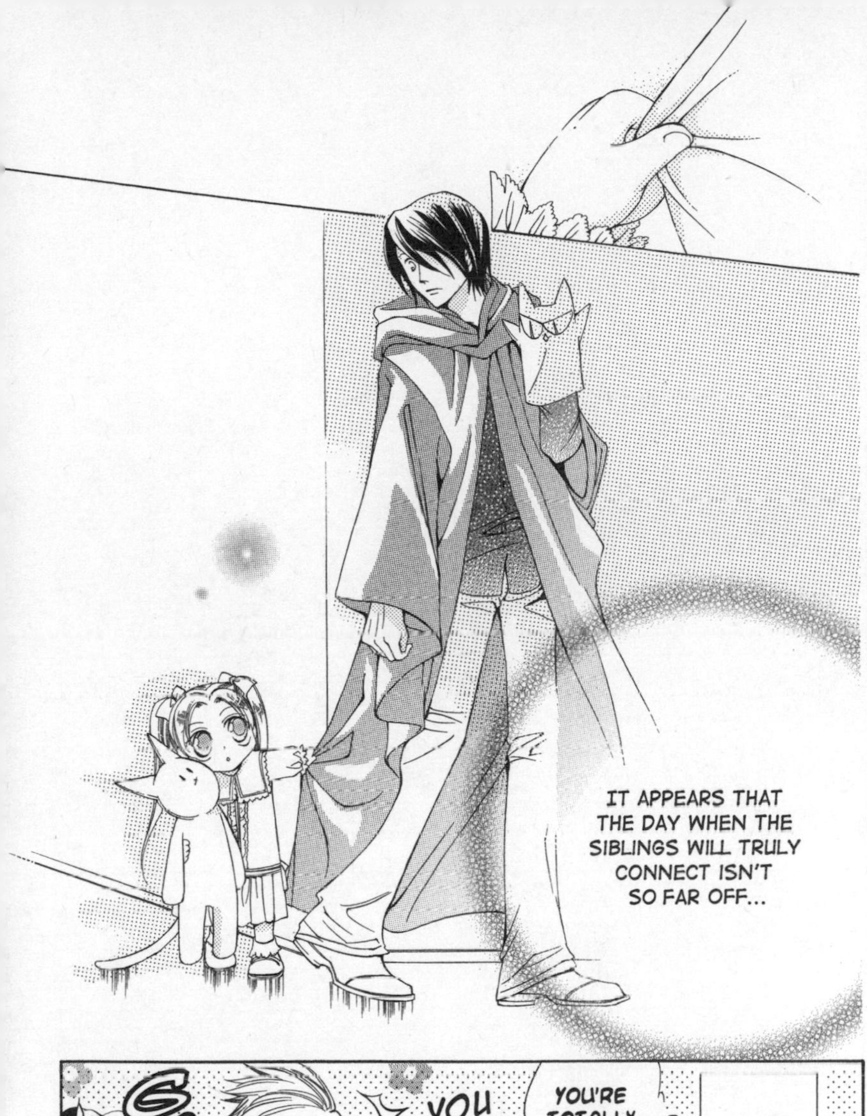
IT APPEARS THAT THE DAY WHEN THE SIBLINGS WILL TRULY CONNECT ISN'T SO FAR OFF...

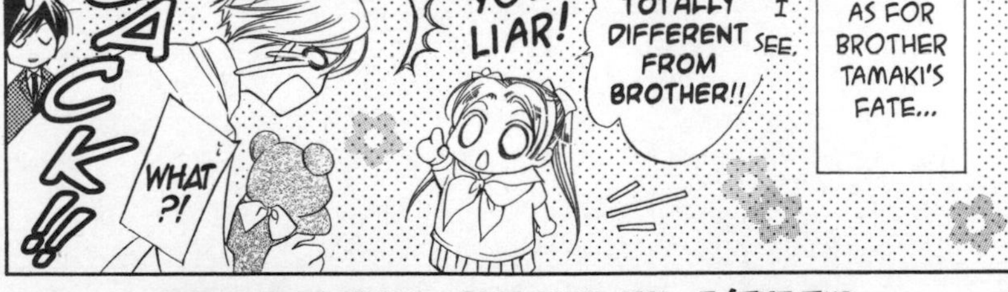
AS FOR BROTHER TAMAKI'S FATE...
I SEE.
YOU'RE TOTALLY DIFFERENT FROM BROTHER!!
YOU LIAR!
WHAT?!
GACK!!

OURAN HIGH SCHOOL HOST CLUB, VOL. 5/THE END

Extra Episode: Mori's Secret

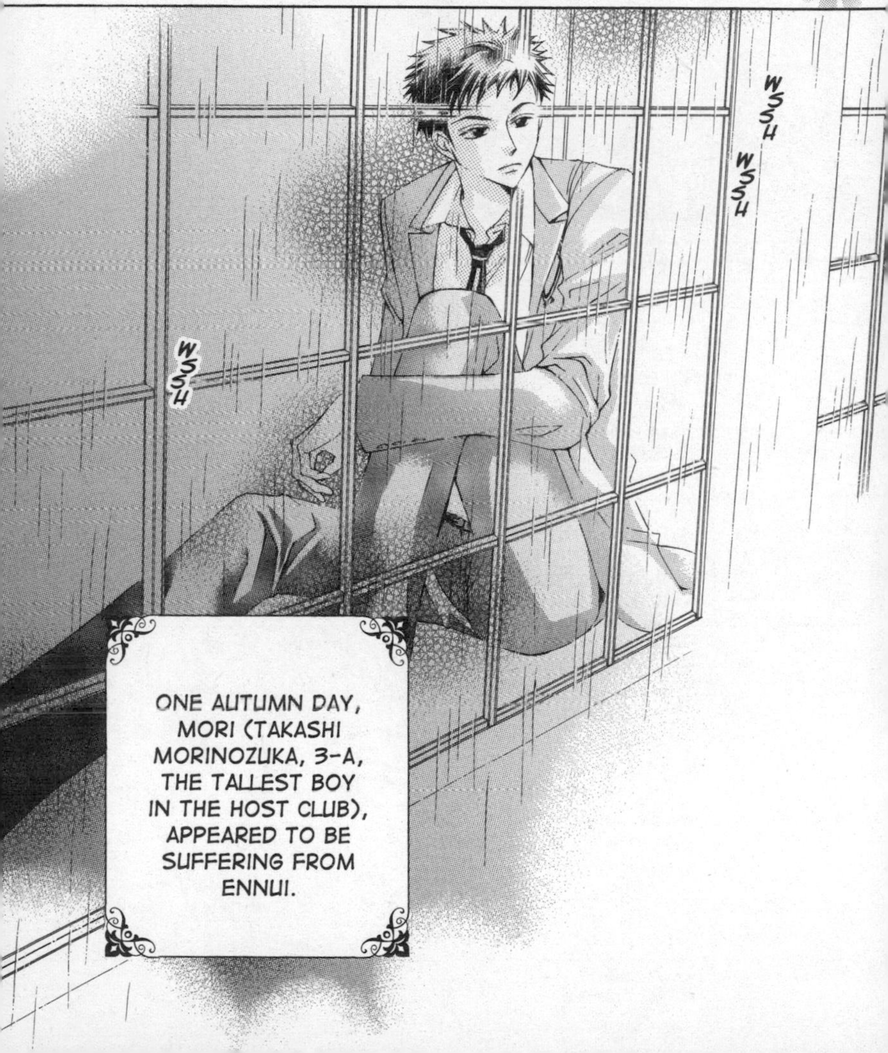
WSSH
WSSH
WSSH
ONE AUTUMN DAY, MORI (TAKASHI MORINOZUKA, 3-A, THE TALLEST BOY IN THE HOST CLUB), APPEARED TO BE SUFFERING FROM ENNUI.

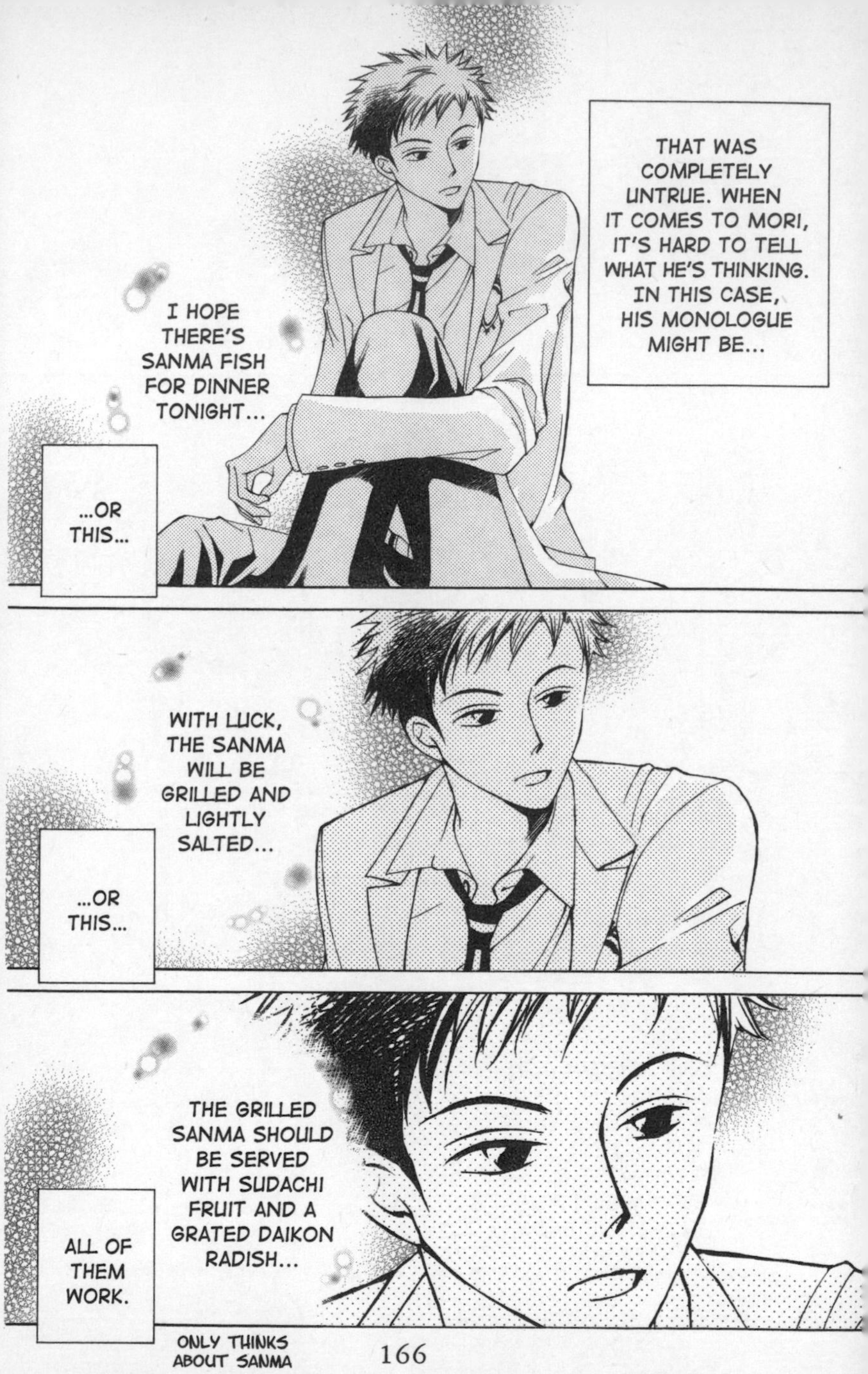
THAT WAS COMPLETELY UNTRUE. WHEN IT COMES TO MORI, IT'S HARD TO TELL WHAT HE'S THINKING. IN THIS CASE, HIS MONOLOGUE MIGHT BE...
I HOPE THERE'S SANMA FISH FOR DINNER TONIGHT...
...OR THIS...
WITH LUCK, THE SANMA WILL BE GRILLED AND LIGHTLY SALTED...
...OR THIS...
THE GRILLED SANMA SHOULD BE SERVED WITH SUDACHI FRUIT AND A GRATED DAIKON RADISH...
ALL OF THEM WORK.

ONLY THINKS ABOUT SANMA

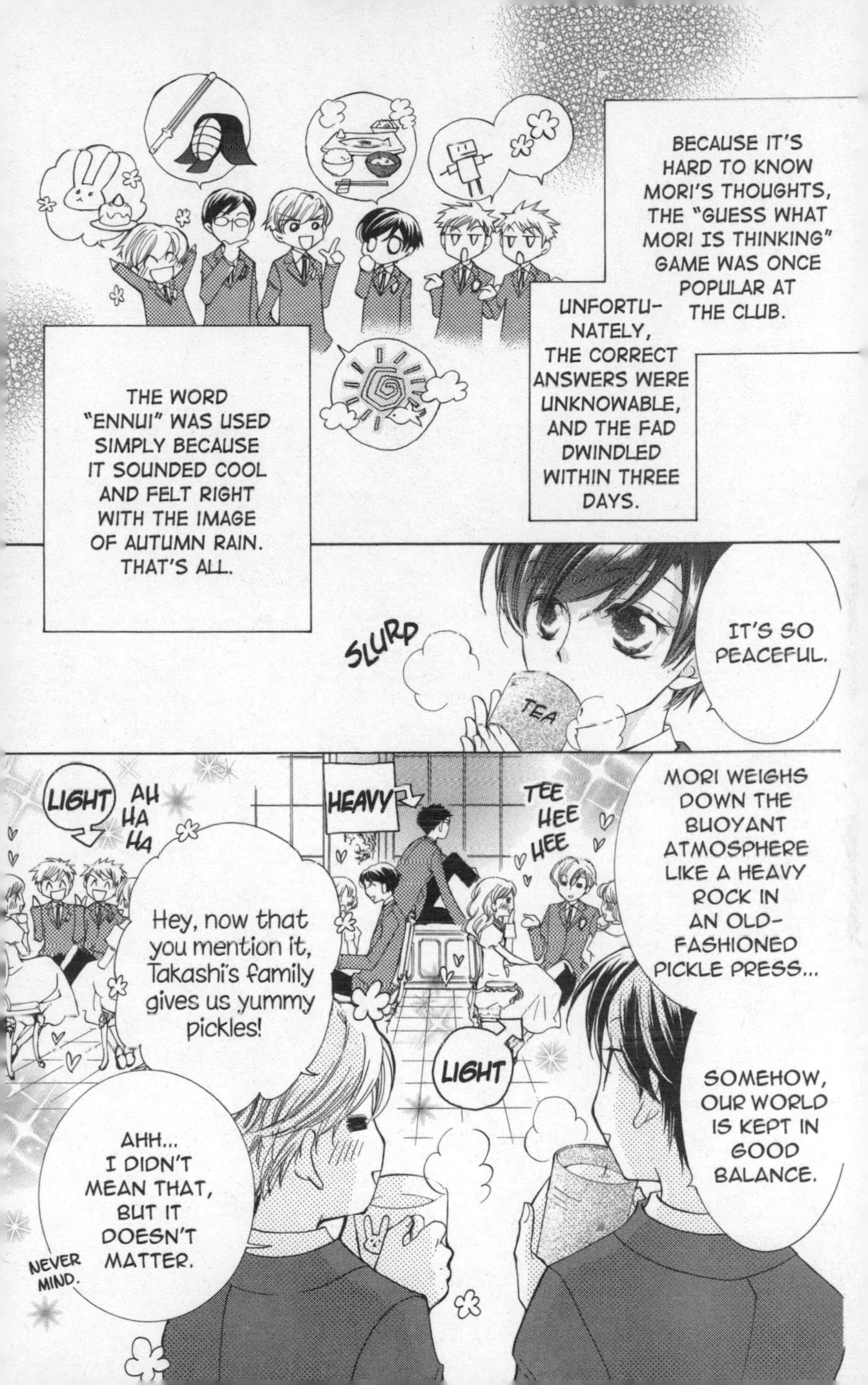

BECAUSE IT'S HARD TO KNOW MORI'S THOUGHTS, THE "GUESS WHAT MORI IS THINKING" GAME WAS ONCE POPULAR AT THE CLUB.
UNFORTUNATELY, THE CORRECT ANSWERS WERE UNKNOWABLE, AND THE FAD DWINDLED WITHIN THREE DAYS.
THE WORD "ENNUI" WAS USED SIMPLY BECAUSE IT SOUNDED COOL AND FELT RIGHT WITH THE IMAGE OF AUTUMN RAIN. THAT'S ALL.
IT'S SO PEACEFUL.
SLURP
TEA
MORI WEIGHS DOWN THE BUOYANT ATMOSPHERE LIKE A HEAVY ROCK IN AN OLD-FASHIONED PICKLE PRESS...
TEE HEE HEE
HEAVY
LIGHT
AH HA HA
Hey, now that you mention it, Takashi's family gives us yummy pickles!
LIGHT
SOMEHOW, OUR WORLD IS KEPT IN GOOD BALANCE.
AHH... I DIDN'T MEAN THAT, BUT IT DOESN'T MATTER.
NEVER MIND.

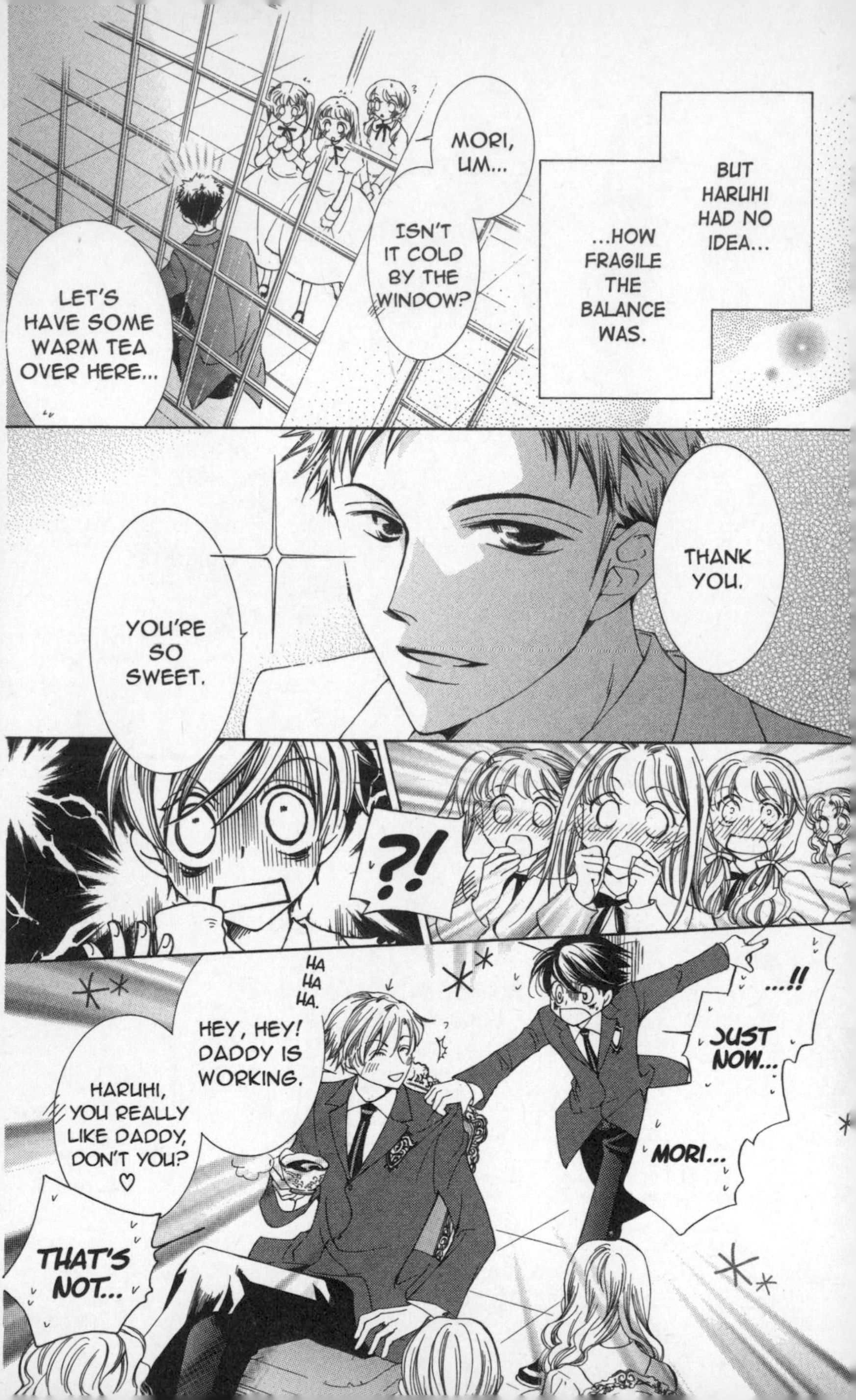
BUT HARUHI HAD NO IDEA...
...HOW FRAGILE THE BALANCE WAS.
MORI, UM...
ISN'T IT COLD BY THE WINDOW?
LET'S HAVE SOME WARM TEA OVER HERE...
THANK YOU.
YOU'RE SO SWEET.
?!
...!!
JUST NOW...
MORI...
HA HA HA.
HEY, HEY! DADDY IS WORKING.
HARUHI, YOU REALLY LIKE DADDY, DON'T YOU? ♡
THAT'S NOT...

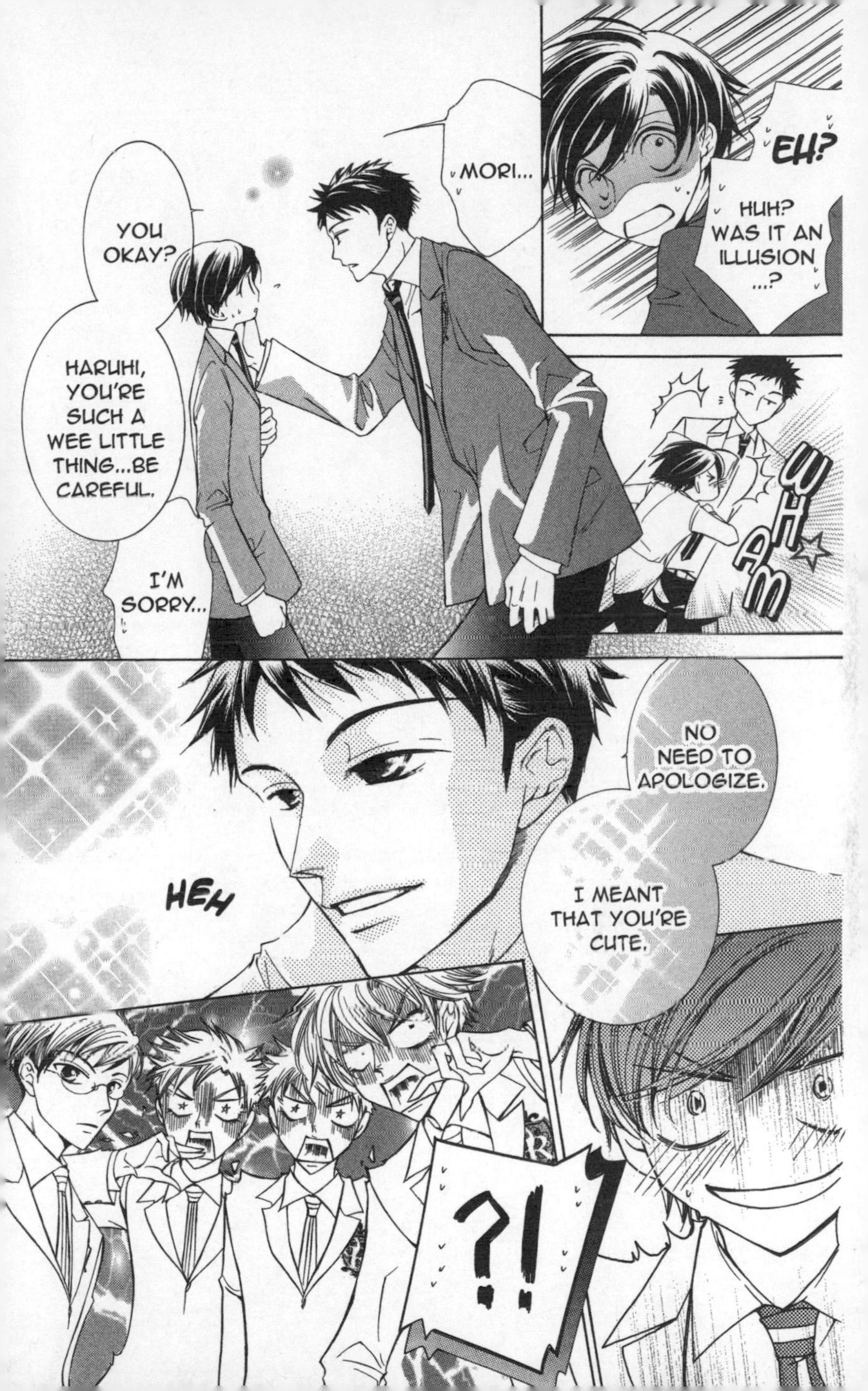
EH?
HUH? WAS IT AN ILLUSION ...?
WHAM
MORI...
YOU OKAY?
HARUHI, YOU'RE SUCH A WEE LITTLE THING...BE CAREFUL.
I'M SORRY...
NO NEED TO APOLOGIZE.
I MEANT THAT YOU'RE CUTE.
HEH
?!

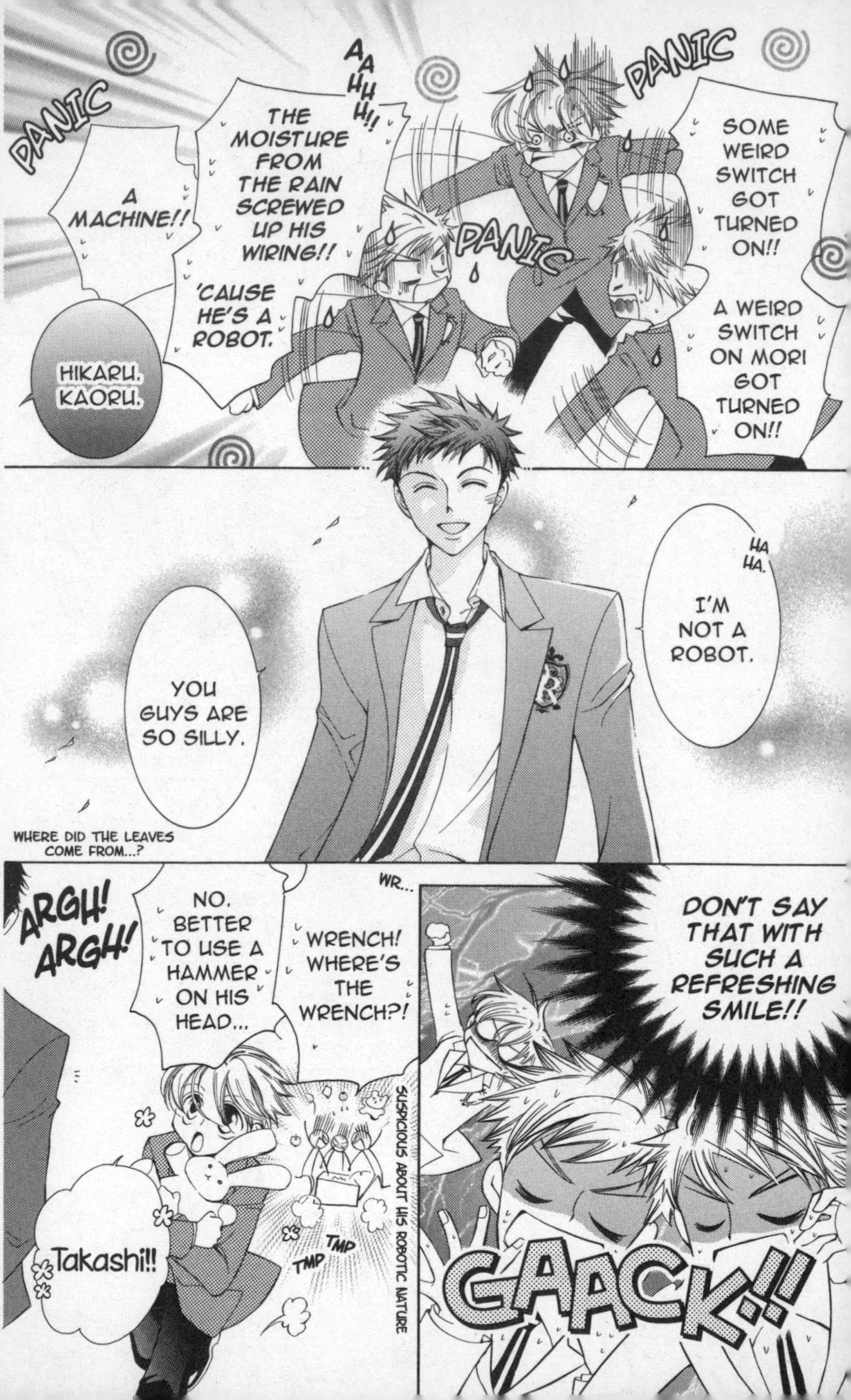
PANIC
SOME WEIRD SWITCH GOT TURNED ON!!
A WEIRD SWITCH ON MORI GOT TURNED ON!!
PANIC
AAHHH!!
THE MOISTURE FROM THE RAIN SCREWED UP HIS WIRING!!
'CAUSE HE'S A ROBOT.
A MACHINE!!
PANIC
HIKARU. KAORU.
HA HA.
I'M NOT A ROBOT.
YOU GUYS ARE SO SILLY.
WHERE DID THE LEAVES COME FROM...?
DON'T SAY THAT WITH SUCH A REFRESHING SMILE!!
GAACK!!
WR...
WRENCH! WHERE'S THE WRENCH?!
NO. BETTER TO USE A HAMMER ON HIS HEAD...
ARGH! ARGH!
SUSPICIOUS ABOUT HIS ROBOTIC NATURE
TMP TMP
Takashi!!

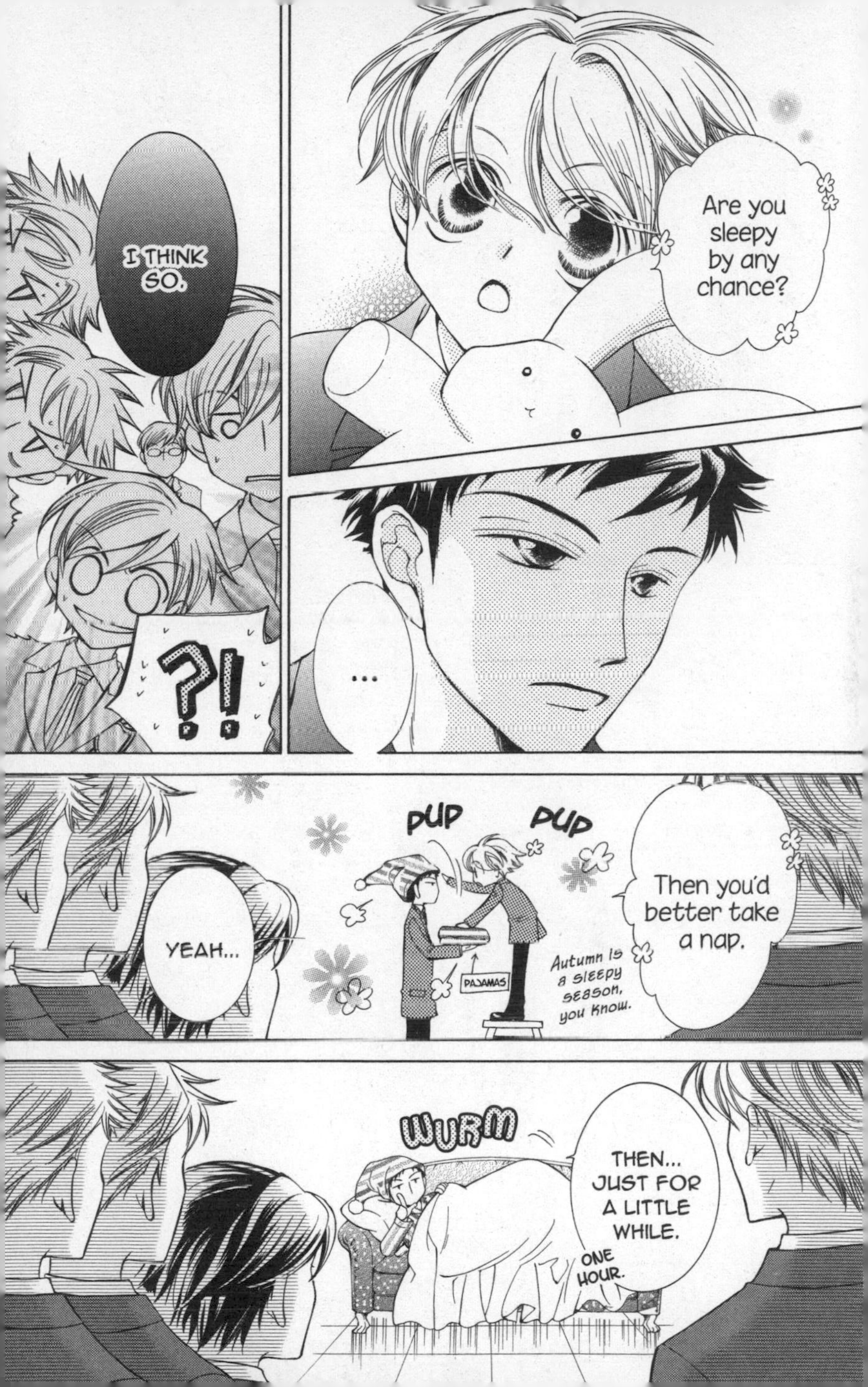
Are you sleepy by any chance?
...
I THINK SO.
?!
Then you'd better take a nap.
PUP PUP
Autumn is a sleepy season, you know.
PAJAMAS
YEAH...
THEN... JUST FOR A LITTLE WHILE.
ONE HOUR.
WURM

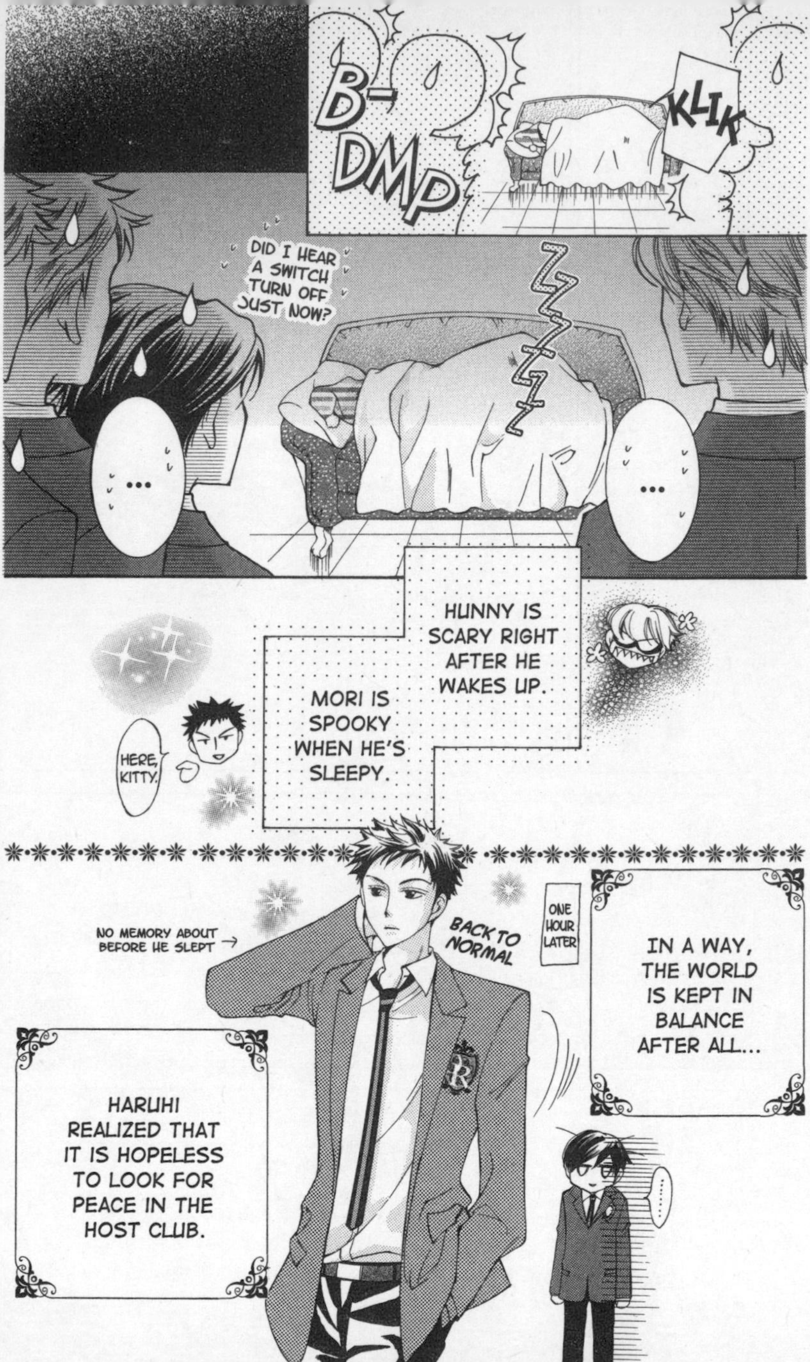
KLIK
B-DMP
...
DID I HEAR A SWITCH TURN OFF JUST NOW?
...
HUNNY IS SCARY RIGHT AFTER HE WAKES UP.
MORI IS SPOOKY WHEN HE'S SLEEPY.
HERE, KITTY.
ONE HOUR LATER
IN A WAY, THE WORLD IS KEPT IN BALANCE AFTER ALL...
BACK TO NORMAL
NO MEMORY ABOUT BEFORE HE SLEPT
HARUHI REALIZED THAT IT IS HOPELESS TO LOOK FOR PEACE IN THE HOST CLUB.

EXTRA EPISODE: MORI'S SECRET / THE END

EGOISTIC CLUB

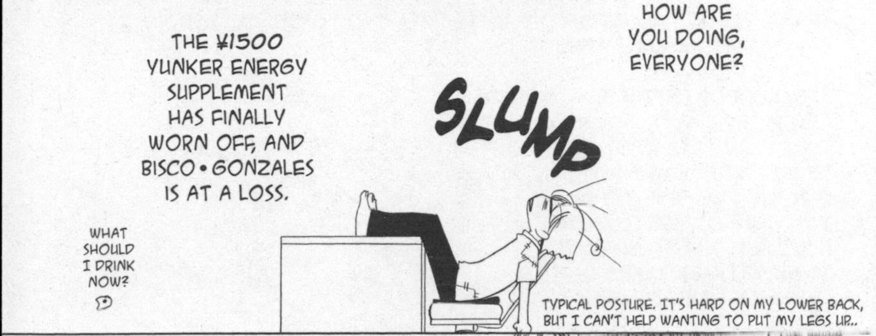
HOW ARE YOU DOING, EVERYONE?
SLUMP
THE ¥1500 YUNKER ENERGY SUPPLEMENT HAS FINALLY WORN OFF, AND BISCO • GONZALES IS AT A LOSS.
WHAT SHOULD I DRINK NOW?
TYPICAL POSTURE. IT'S HARD ON MY LOWER BACK, BUT I CAN'T HELP WANTING TO PUT MY LEGS UP...

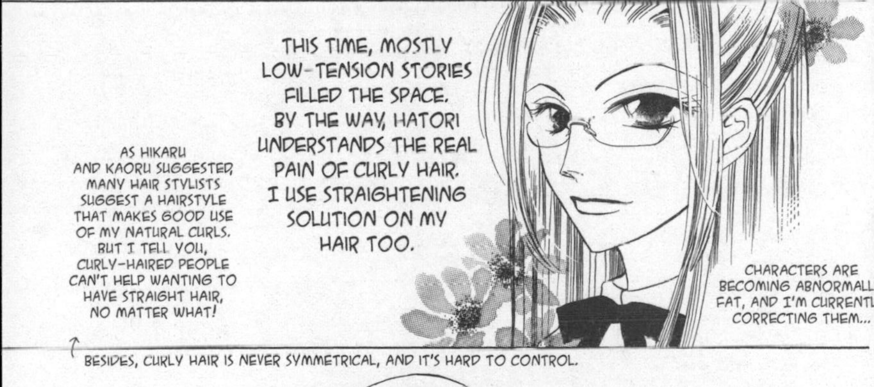
CHARACTERS ARE BECOMING ABNORMALLY FAT, AND I'M CURRENTLY CORRECTING THEM...
THIS TIME, MOSTLY LOW-TENSION STORIES FILLED THE SPACE. BY THE WAY, HATORI UNDERSTANDS THE REAL PAIN OF CURLY HAIR. I USE STRAIGHTENING SOLUTION ON MY HAIR TOO.
AS HIKARU AND KAORU SUGGESTED, MANY HAIR STYLISTS SUGGEST A HAIRSTYLE THAT MAKES GOOD USE OF MY NATURAL CURLS. BUT I TELL YOU, CURLY-HAIRED PEOPLE CAN'T HELP WANTING TO HAVE STRAIGHT HAIR, NO MATTER WHAT!
BESIDES, CURLY HAIR IS NEVER SYMMETRICAL, AND IT'S HARD TO CONTROL.

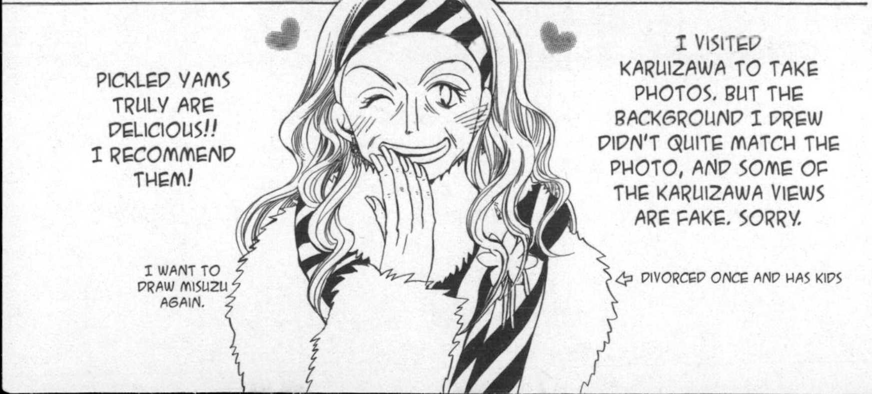
I VISITED KARUIZAWA TO TAKE PHOTOS. BUT THE BACKGROUND I DREW DIDN'T QUITE MATCH THE PHOTO, AND SOME OF THE KARUIZAWA VIEWS ARE FAKE. SORRY.
DIVORCED ONCE AND HAS KIDS
PICKLED YAMS TRULY ARE DELICIOUS!! I RECOMMEND THEM!
I WANT TO DRAW MISUZU AGAIN.

THANKS SO MUCH TO ALL OF YOU WHO CAME TO MY SIGNING EVENT IN OSAKA (SUGO NATSU☆FESTA, SPONSORED BY HAKUSENSHA) ON JULY 31, 2004. I WAS EXTREMELY NERVOUS, BUT I COULD FEEL EVERYONE'S KINDNESS. I GOT SOME GREAT MEMORIES OUT OF IT. IF YOU DIDN'T WIN A PRIZE, PLEASE TRY AGAIN WHEN AND IF YOU GET ANOTHER CHANCE!!

HATORI HAS DONE TWO SIGNING EVENTS SO FAR, AND (FOR SOME REASON) THEY WERE BOTH HELD IN OSAKA. IF THERE'S ANOTHER ONE, I HOPE IT'LL BE EITHER IN KANTO OR TOHOKU...

THANK YOU SO MUCH FOR THE GIFTS RELATING TO OSAKA, AND YOUR OTHER GIFTS AND LETTERS.♡

SPEAKING OF LETTERS, SOMETIME AFTER THE EVENT I OPENED A LETTER THAT READ "I'LL USE ○○○ AS OUR SECRET CODE DURING THE SIGNING EVENT ♡ AND WHEN YOU HEAR IT, YOU'LL KNOW IT'S ME!!" I'M SO SORRY!! IT SOMETIMES TAKES ONE TO THREE MONTHS BEFORE I READ THE LETTERS THAT ARE SENT TO THE EDITORIAL DEPARTMENT.

THE EVENT HALL WAS CROWDED, SO I ASKED SOME PEOPLE TO REPEAT WHAT THEY WERE SAYING SEVERAL TIMES. IF YOU WERE TRYING TO SAY THE SECRET CODE, I APOLOGIZE!!

SEE YOU AGAIN IN VOLUME 6!!

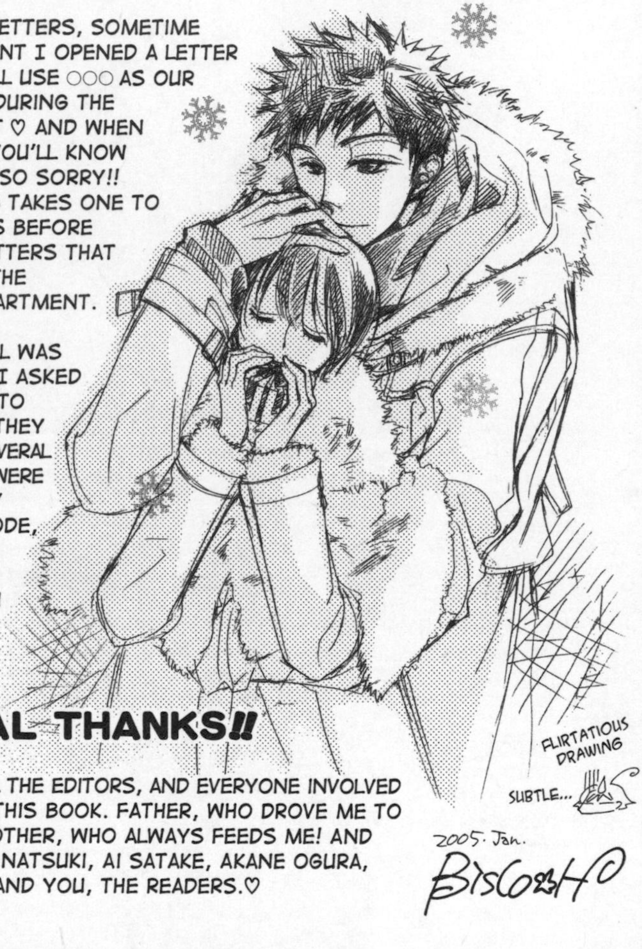
FLIRTATIOUS DRAWING
SUBTLE...
2005. Jan.
Bisco Hatori

SPECIAL THANKS!!

YAMASHITA, ALL THE EDITORS, AND EVERYONE INVOLVED IN PUBLISHING THIS BOOK. FATHER, WHO DROVE ME TO KARUIZAWA. MOTHER, WHO ALWAYS FEEDS ME! AND MY STAFF: YUI NATSUKI, AI SATAKE, AKANE OGURA, AYA AOMURA, AND YOU, THE READERS.♡

EGOISTIC CLUB/THE END

EDITOR'S NOTES

EPISODE 18

Page 38: The ring tone Hikaru set for Tamaki's incoming calls is the theme song from the "Mito Koumon" television series in Japan. "Mito Koumon" is about a lord in Feudal Japan who roams the countryside, helping the plight of the common folk.

Page 49: "Refreshing," or *sawayaka*, is often used to describe youth. It refers to having energy and an open outlook on life.

EPISODE 19

Page 75: *Senpai* is used to respectfully address someone who is your senior—for example, a freshman would address a sophomore as "Senpai."

Page 83: Radio Exercise, or *Rajio Taiso*, is a radio show that has been leading the nation in early-morning calisthenics since 1928. Most listeners tend to be schoolchildren or the elderly.

Page 83: Calpis is a soft drink that contains amino acids.

Page 83: Ochugen is a time when people give gifts to each other. It occurs during the same time as the Oban festival in the summer.

EPISODE 21

Page 133: A *megane kyara* is a character in manga or anime who wears glasses. The term also denotes certain qualities—the male megane character is usually quite intelligent, manipulative, and somewhat indiscernible to others. Kyoya typifies a megane character. Oshitari in *The Prince of Tennis* is another good example.

Page 149: *Moe* is an affection for or attraction to certain types of anime or manga characters. Kirimi has a moe for princely characters.

Page 151: Tamaki is wearing a *hachimaki*, or headband. Students sometimes wear hachimaki with inspirational words written on them when they are taking important exams. Tamaki is wearing a hachimaki that has "Aim for the Prince" written on it.

Author Bio

Bisco Hatori made her manga
debut with *Isshun kan no
Romance* (**A Moment of
Romance**) in *LaLa DX*
magazine. The comedy *Ouran
High School Host Club* is her
breakout hit. When she's stuck
thinking up characters' names,
she gets inspired by loud,
upbeat music (her radio is set
to NACK5 FM). She enjoys
reading all kinds of manga, but
she's especially fond of the sci-fi
drama *Please Save My Earth*
and *Slam Dunk*, a basketball
classic.

OURAN HIGH SCHOOL HOST CLUB
Vol. 5
Shojo Beat Edition

STORY AND ART BY BISCO HATORI

Translation & English Adaptation/Naomi Kokubo & Eric-Jon Rössel Waugh
Touch-up Art & Lettering/George Caltsoudas
Graphic Design/Izumi Evers
Editor/Nancy Thistlethwaite

Published by VIZ Media, LLC
P.O. Box 77010
San Francisco, CA 94107

20
First printing, March 2006
Twentieth printing, May 2022

www.viz.com   www.shojobeat.com

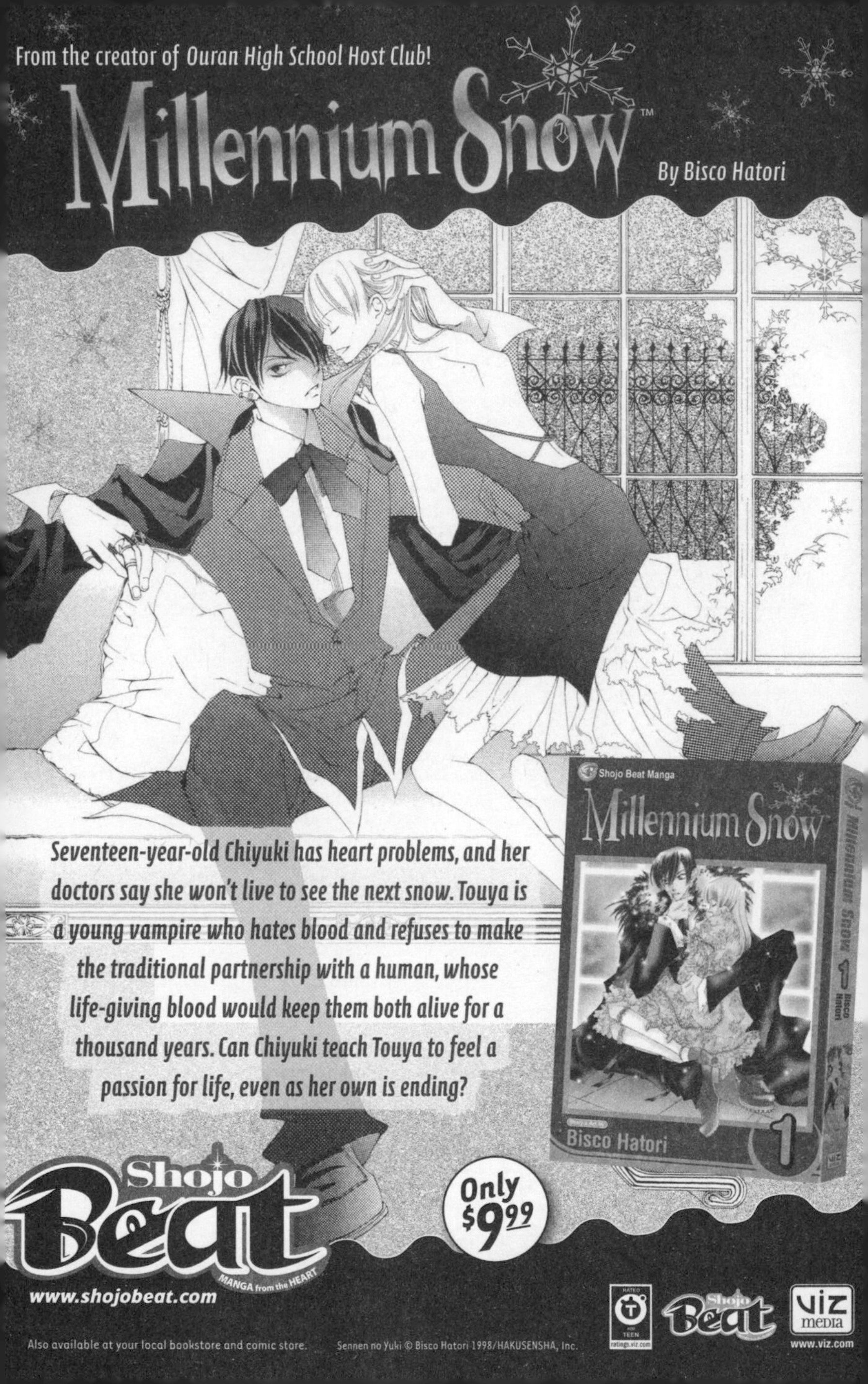
From the creator of Ouran High School Host Club!
Millennium Snow™
By Bisco Hatori
Shojo Beat Manga
Millennium Snow
Bisco Hatori
1
Seventeen-year-old Chiyuki has heart problems, and her doctors say she won't live to see the next snow. Touya is a young vampire who hates blood and refuses to make the traditional partnership with a human, whose life-giving blood would keep them both alive for a thousand years. Can Chiyuki teach Touya to feel a passion for life, even as her own is ending?
Shojo Beat
MANGA from the HEART
Only $9.99
www.shojobeat.com
RATED T FOR TEEN
ratings.viz.com
VIZ media
www.viz.com
Also available at your local bookstore and comic store.
Sennen no Yuki © Bisco Hatori 1998/HAKUSENSHA, Inc.

Behind the Scenes!!

STORY AND ART BY BISCO HATORI

From the creator of Ouran High School Host Club

Ranmaru Kurisu comes from a family of hardy, rough-and-tumble fisherfolk and he sticks out at home like a delicate, artistic sore thumb. It's given him a raging inferiority complex and a permanently pessimistic outlook. Now that he's in college, he's hoping to find a sense of belonging. But after a whole life of being left out, does he even know how to fit in?!

Urakata!! © Bisco Hatori 2015/HAKUSENSHA, Inc.

Don't Hide What's *Inside*

by AYA KANNO

Despite his tough jock exterior, Asuka Masamune harbors a secret love for sewing, shojo manga, and all things girly. But when he finds himself drawn to his domestically inept classmate Ryo, his carefully crafted persona is put to the test. Can Asuka ever show his true self to anyone, much less to the girl he's falling for?

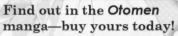

Find out in the *Otomen* manga—buy yours today!

IDOL dreams

STORY & ART BY ARINA TANEMURA

At age 31, office worker Chikage Deguchi feels she missed her chances at love and success. When word gets out that she's a virgin, Chikage is humiliated and wishes she could turn back time to when she was still young and popular. She takes an experimental drug that changes her appearance back to when she was 15. Now Chikage is determined to pursue everything she missed out on all those years ago—including becoming a star!

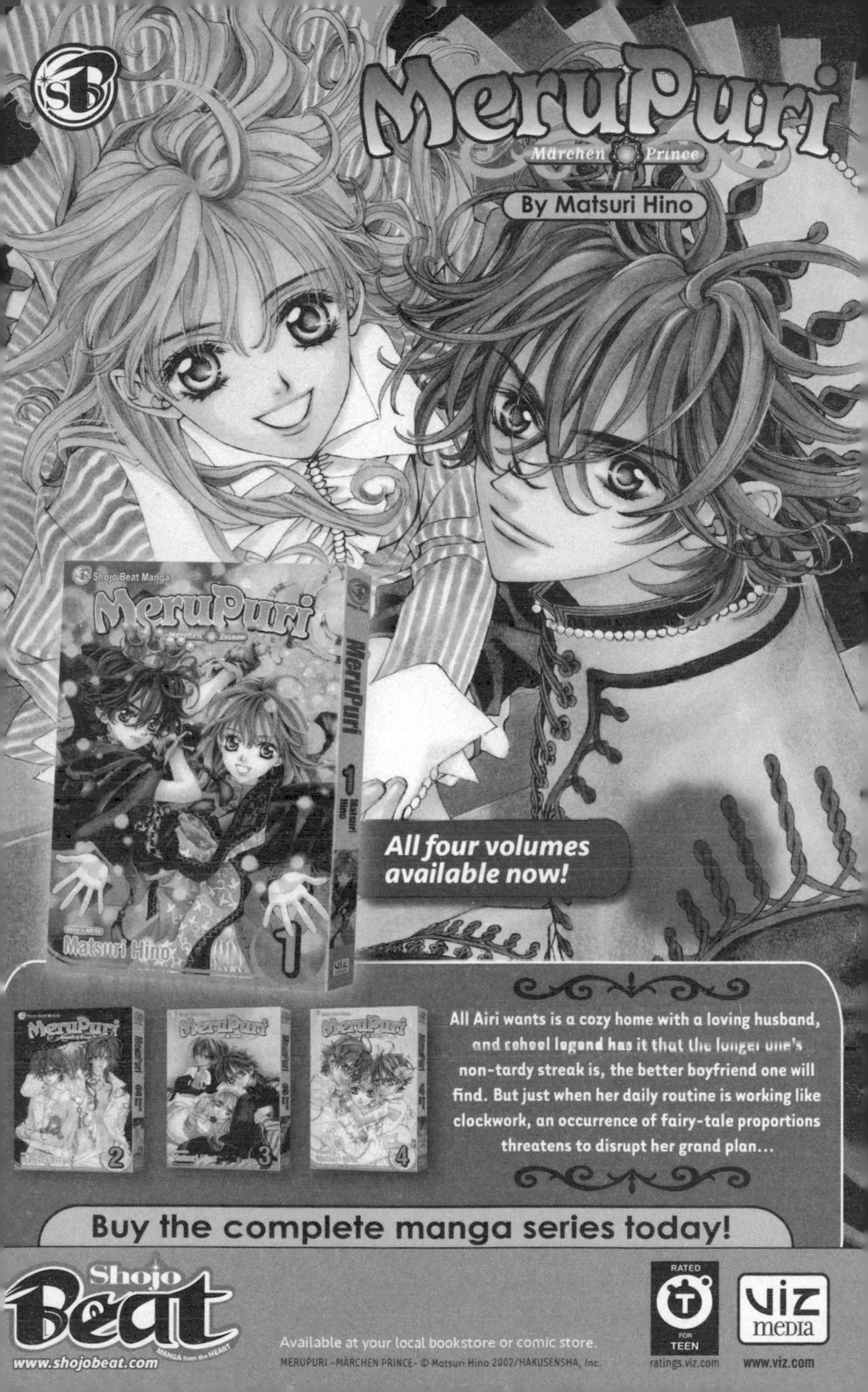
MeruPuri
Märchen Prince
By Matsuri Hino
Shojo Beat Manga
MeruPuri
Matsuri Hino
1
All four volumes available now!
All Airi wants is a cozy home with a loving husband, and school legend has it that the longer one's non-tardy streak is, the better boyfriend one will find. But just when her daily routine is working like clockwork, an occurrence of fairy-tale proportions threatens to disrupt her grand plan...
Buy the complete manga series today!
Shojo Beat
MANGA from the HEART
www.shojobeat.com
Available at your local bookstore or comic store.
MERUPURI -MÄRCHEN PRINCE- © Matsuri Hino 2002/HAKUSENSHA, Inc.
RATED T FOR TEEN
ratings.viz.com
VIZ media
www.viz.com

SURPRISE!

You may be reading the wrong way!

It's true: In keeping with the original Japanese comic format, this book reads from right to left—so action, sound effects, and word balloons are completely reversed. This preserves the orientation of the original artwork—plus, it's fun! Check out the diagram shown here to get the hang of things, and then turn to the other side of the book to get started!

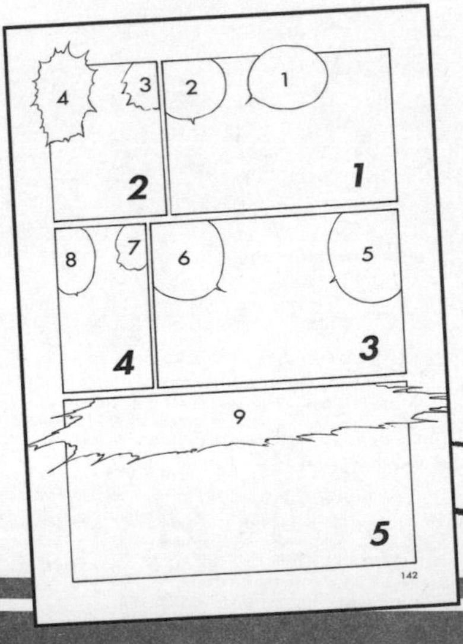
1
2
1
3
4
2
5
6
3
7
8
4
9
5
142

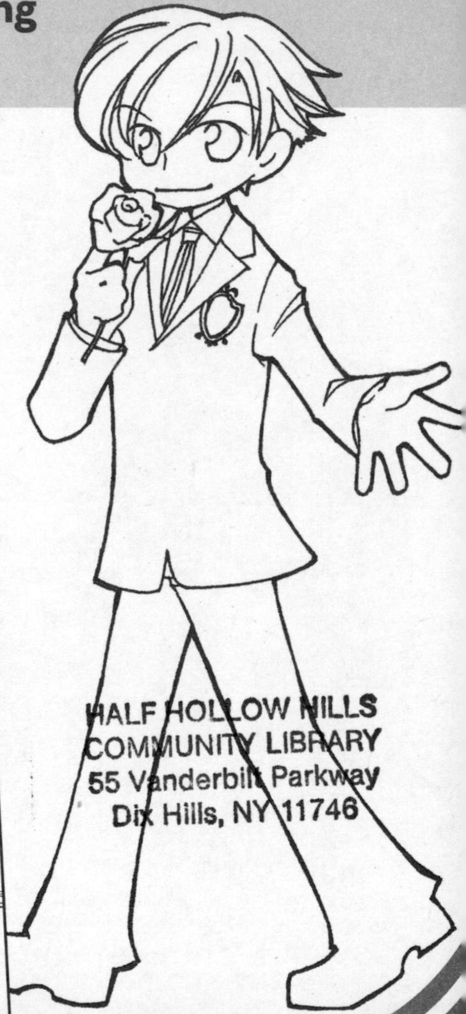